D1585121

THE SCOTTISH MOUNTAINEERING CLUB JOURNAL 2021

Carnmore Crag and the Fionn Loch in late November. Dan Moore on 999 (E1,5c).
Photo: Jack Thompsett.

THE SCOTTISH MOUNTAINEERING CLUB JOURNAL 2021

Edited by Graeme Morrison

Volume 49

No. 212

THE SCOTTISH MOUNTAINEERING CLUB

THE SCOTTISH MOUNTAINEERING CLUB JOURNAL 2021
Volume 49 No 212

Published by the Scottish Mountaineering Club 2021
www.smc.org.uk

ISSN 0080-813X
ISBN 978-1-907233-28-9

Typeset by Noel Williams

Printed and bound by Novoprint S.A., Barcelona, Spain.

Distributed by Cordee Ltd, 11 Jacknell Road, Hinckley, LE10 3BS.

CONTENTS

Lochan Coire nam Miseach and Stob Bàn. Photo: Finlay Wild.

EDITORIAL

It is often remarked how the literature of mountaineering dwarfs that of any other sport, and though the golfer or yachtsman may demur, it surely surpasses the rest in quality of writing as well as quantity. Nevertheless, in an age when the internet can spread information instantaneously and printed newspapers are in decline, a conventional periodical like ours, for all its newest gloss and hardback handsomeness, needs to justify a place on the sagging bookshelf. That the *Journal* is readable, long-established and trustworthy counts for much, but it was also its great variety of content that delighted me 45 years ago on first opening it and is a source of pride today. Always we have embraced the factual as well as the literary, the precision of route descriptions along with the epics of exploration, the casualty statistics besides the heartfelt eulogies. My erudite predecessor, having led a life in the realm of letters, brought to the task a novelist's eye for the tale worth telling and a teacher's skill in nurturing new talent. My own working life has been spent in industry, where language is valued (when valued at all) as a medium for sharing facts unambiguously. In the *Journal* you will continue to discover a miscellany of the objective and the subjective, of obstacles and emotions, of mountains and men.

We could, however, do with yet more diversity. All of us can now take pleasure in the on-line *SMCJ* archive; and on dipping into the early numbers, when the world was young and the Highlands unexplored, we find article after article about freshly discovered ranges and unheard-of routes, described breathlessly by pioneers who needed three issues a year to share their excitement. Room was found for the toothless-tyke retrospective too, but in large part the contributing authors, for all their tweed-clad respectability, were the tigers of their day. I am loath to accept, in this age of protracted education, that our young climbers are less literate or less imaginative than their Victorian counterparts; but like my recent predecessors I despair at their reticence. If they – if you – are 'seeking the bubble reputation' it will be granted, and with greater permanence, in the *Journal* rather than the web. It was said of a very distinguished past Editor, Geoff Dutton, that 'his greatest service to the Club was in dealing intelligently with the next generation of climbers.' What an enviable epitaph! Let us in the 2020s restore some of the vigour of the 1890s, and counterbalance reminiscence and history with next-generation adventure, well recounted.

It may be, of course, that our more active members are too fully occupied on the hills. In this 2021 issue of the *Journal* we record a prodigious number of new routes, both summer and winter. In spite of lockdowns and restricted travel, this section extends to almost 130 pages, or a third of the total, and will strike some readers as disproportionate. New climbs and exploration are, however, a staple of the Club and of the wider climbing community, and a plump volume is surely a sign of health.

No doubt there is some chaff among the grain, but winnowing would be no easy matter and has not been attempted save for the omission of a few short bouldering exercises.

In picking up the editorial pencil I feel the same apprehension as Bill Murray's climber, 'until the rope reminds him that he is tied to men of high heart ... that they, at least, will not falter.' Our previous Editor, Peter Biggar, and his predecessor, Noel Williams, have been generous with their help and expert advice. We are also fortunate that Simon Richardson has continued his peerless work as New Routes Editor, while our Clerk of the List, Alison Coull, has again collated the 'Munro Matters'. As Photos Editor, Ian Taylor has mustered yet another sparkling array of images, and our enthusiastic new Reviews Editor, Geoff Cohen has doubled the number of titles compared with recent years. To these members, and all the other high-hearted stalwarts of the *Journal*, I owe a thousand thanks.

G.D. Morrison

THE BOXER

by George Allan

And he carries the reminders
Of every glove that laid him down
Or cut him 'til he cried out
In his anger and his shame.
— Paul Simon.

HIS HEART WAS PUMPING and he gasped for breath. A sponge was pressed against his brow. There was a voice by his ear: 'Keep that guard up. Keep pressing. You've got a good left hook – use it. Just go for him – you can win.' But the voice lied, he knew damn well it lied. The brightness of the canvas was blinding him with fear. Then the bell rang; it was summoning him to his doom. He rose from the stool.

Keep out of his way. Dance around. Just go for him. He moved in, he jabbed and made contact, try again; then it caught him like a cricket ball on the side of his jaw. He spun sideways and collapsed against the ropes. Blows rained in. The referee pulled them apart. Dodge and run, dodge and run, but there was nowhere left to go. Please let the bell ring, please let it ring. It sounded; he felt a hand grab his wrist and drag him towards the centre of the ring. He looked up; there they were, his parents staring at him. There was clapping, clapping for a raised arm which wasn't his. He burst into tears; God knows he'd tried to stop them welling up, but it's always hard and harder still when you're eleven.

His head was slumped forward. He was sitting in a small room and fingers were untying the knots holding his gloves. 'It's okay son. You did your best; he's good, very good. You'll get another chance.' Such reassurances failed to fill a terrible chasm. He lifted his head; his father passed the door, glanced in and disappeared.

He was walking down the road, his mother by his side. Not a word had been said. He could hear his father's footsteps behind him. Eyes were boring into his very soul. It wasn't the defeat, it wasn't even the manner of the defeat, it was the tears. He had been tried and found wanting; he was a complete disgrace.

Six months later his father died.

***

Two figures left the shelter of the pines. The wind caught them, a westerly but not a cold westerly; it would soon be spring. They stopped when they reached the lip of the corrie.

'What d'you think?'

'Fifty-fifty.'

'Remember what was scrawled on the walls of Jean's Hut before they knocked it down.'

'What was that?'

' "Always set out for the mountain, signed W.H. Murray." '

'Did he say that?'

'I rather doubt it.'

They laughed.

They were the first words that had been spoken since leaving the car. Chatting was for the journey. Once they were on the hill they were like an old, well-oiled machine. Each knew his part. They had been doing this for longer than they cared to remember. Snatched days and odd weekends prised out of busy lives. They had been climbing the same sort of routes for decades, routes that were once described as middle grade but were now viewed as the easy classics – rites of passage for newcomers before they graduated to harder things.

'Is that the ridge, the one to the left of Central Gully?'

'Yeah, looks pretty patchy low down.'

They skirted the half-frozen lochan and climbed to the lowest rocks, where their misgivings were confirmed; the first few hundred feet were soft snow masking unfrozen turf.

'Ah, well, we can always climb the gully and go for a walk.'

As they climbed the wide fault that split the cliff into two sections, the temperature dropped, the soft snow turned to névé and they stopped to put on crampons.

'Is that the route you were talking about in the car?'

On the opposite wall of the gully, a hundred feet up, icicles hung from the lip of a massive overhang above which was an ice sheet. From the top right-hand edge of this, a vertical corner disappeared into the mist.

'Yeah. God, it looks steep.'

'How do you reach it?'

'See that diagonal groove which goes up to the left of the overhang? I think that must be it.'

'Want a go?'

'You must be kidding, it's well beyond me.'

But a niggling ambivalence started to trouble him. Yes, it was beyond what he'd ever done, but not outrageously so. And he'd thought about it, really thought about it when he'd pored over the guide. He wanted to climb it, he could imagine what he would feel like if he succeeded, it was the bit in the middle that now filled him with fear. If the turf was soft, his problem was solved, so he cramponed across the gully. That excuse was removed when he drove his picks into the groove.

'Go on, give it a go.'

The snow in the gully suddenly seemed blindingly white and a siren was luring him towards his fate; flickers of memory told him he had been here long ago. Taking a deep breath, he started to sort the gear. As he did so he repeated the mantra he used to calm himself: 'Divide it into sections; concentrate on the feet; be prepared to retreat.'

He belayed at the top of the first pitch in a niche at the side of the slab, now hidden by a fierce ice bulge. As he pulled in the ropes, a helmet bobbed in and out of sight below him, moving closer and closer up a pitch that had been a pleasure to climb, sustained but well-protected. A screw in the bulge calmed his nerves and, swinging round this, he found himself in a situation that he had never experienced before, space-walking diagonally upwards on steep ice above the huge overhang. Concentrate, concentrate, make sure each point of contact is secure. He paused half-way, relaxed enough to savour the situation. Foot by foot a big ledge below the corner came nearer.

They looked up the corner but said nothing. Above was a small overhang, and further up a large jammed block loomed. He was surprised how easy the first obstacle proved to be. The corner was, indeed, vertical but solid turf on the walls allowed bridging. He found an old but sound peg that gave reassurance for the next section, but after twenty feet the turf ran out to be replaced by blobs of moss. The corner itself was blind. He stopped. The bridging was awkward, his leg began to shake and confidence drained away. Even if he could make the moves to reach the block, he had no clue how to get over it. Carefully, oh so carefully, he edged back down to the peg. He selected a sling for the abseil, then paused and looked up. Somehow it now looked less threatening. Perhaps, just perhaps, if he reached the block he would find something; there must be something, and if he could get some protection … . He stopped again where the turf ran out and tried to hammer a warthog in; it bottomed on rock. Tension ran through him like a current. This was it, the Rubicon and the reckoning. He found a hook, crampons bit into moss and rock and he moved up, the option of retreat now gone. Twisting a pick in a tiny slot in the corner, he leant back and made a wild, bridging move. His helmet banged against the block. The shaking started. 'Just do something. Do something!' Forcing his left points hard into the moss, he reached up and sank his left pick into the snow between the wall and the block; it held. His right foot shot off its edge: 'Oh God, I'm off, I'm off,' but his right pick went into turf. Suddenly he was up. A whoop echoed off the gully walls. He had no memory of those final moves. Above, the angle eased and inviting short corners and walls led upwards.

An hour later, they were walking round the corrie rim towards the cairn. The wind had dropped, the cloud had risen, and rows of snowy hills were painted pink by the setting sun. Something had been laid to rest, he knew that, and two people had been forgiven.

ONE OF THOSE DAYS

by Mike Dixon

A PILE OF MAPS lay on the passenger seat but still no decision was made, as Tore got closer. A wintry experience was sought but with no great expectations – sometimes when the best days occur. With all the recent hysteria, Sutherland was a good choice to get away from it all. Despite being on my own, memories of people and places accompanied me the whole day.

Over the Struie, I can't help smiling when passing the old Aultnamain Inn building, thinking about that once vibrant meeting-place for the stoners and ravers of Easter Ross. Sadly, the characters, the wildness and the music festivals had to find somewhere else. Police enforcement of drink-driving laws killed the Aultnamain, but it's still a grand road to put your foot down.

Then through Bonar Bridge and on to Rosehall. Too early to call on resident minstrel Dave Goulder. Discovered by folklorist Hamish Henderson while sleeping rough in Princes Street Gardens, he went on to run one of the earliest independent hostels, Glen Cottage in Torridon. This was eventually closed by the National Trust on spurious grounds but ostensibly because people were having too much fun there. Bill Brooker, Mike Taylor and Syd Wilkinson once stayed and thanked Dave in his guest book for 'saving us from the squalid horrors of the Ling Hut'. *Plus ça change* ... . It must have been really bad for the Aberdeen-Peterhead contingent to have paid for alternative accommodation when the Ling was free.

Disappointed by the absence of snow in Assynt I turned off at Oykel Bridge, entering a glen I'd not visited for over a decade. Things had changed. A barrier was across the road a mile before Duag Bridge but the bike took me swiftly to Corriemulzie Lodge. The word 'lodge' always seemed an inflated description of the building, but there's nothing underwhelming about the view from just beyond; it's where you get your first proper sighting of Seana Bhràigh. In a winter cloak it was dazzling and made me pedal faster in its direction. This is the finest way to approach the mountain rather than the more popular Inverlael option, which is a long meander and lacks the character of the northern route. Admittedly it's a great moment when you eventually and suddenly arrive at the brink of the corrie crater, but from the north you're with the Luchd corrie the whole day.

There had been a frost, but the snow-level was above the approach track. A week before, skis or snow-shoes would have been the sensible choice. Today all the unavoidable puddles were frozen without being recalcitrant and the cycle from the lodge was pure joy: front tyre ice-breaking, along with crash-and-tinkle acoustics. Ahead, the scene had a simple beauty; the sharp cone of An Sgùrr on the left, the main summit of Seana Bhràigh on the right, their ridges snugly enclosing the Luchd

An Sgùrr (left) and Seana Bhràigh from the north. Photo: Mike Dixon.

corrie, whose back wall is seamed with gullies and buttresses. I had been waiting for a winter day this good on this mountain for some time. But gnawing away was the fact I'd told nobody where I was and there was no phone signal to fire off a text.

Ditching the bike at the main ford over the River Mulzie, I continued on the fine track to the west end of Loch a' Choire Mhòir. The outflow was shallow and I was soon at the base of An Sgùrr. Outflanking the cliff at its base I spiralled up to reach a large platform on the ridge proper. Winter always makes things look more difficult, and that gnawing thought was back. Crampons and axe were now in use, however, and the upward route was straightforward, surmounting the odd step but conscious of the huge plastered slopes to my left, a fall down which would deposit me almost at the loch shore. The superbly situated bothy on the loch's other side was the only sign of civilisation, but nobody was about.

My only other time this way had been one autumn when An Sgùrr cast a giant, triangular witch's hat over the moor to the north. Stepping from the shadow into sun today was a real hallelujah chorus moment, leaving just a short but photogenic arête to the top. The descent was a tad awkward, down small steps and melting snow then a sharp little wall onto Creag an Duine and the plateau. As good and satisfying a Grade ½ or I of its type as you could ask for. From Creag an Duine, An Sgùrr's tooth looks very impressive and is certainly one of the great summits of the Northern Highlands. Sad to say, the conquistadors of the Corbetts have spoilt it by deeming it a Top.

The climbing potential in the corrie can be well appreciated from here. Distance has always deterred casual visits and there are admittedly corries with more impressive features. Most attach the tag 'special' to it, while finding it difficult to succinctly pin down why. Remoteness, the scenery, the reward of finding it in condition, the outlook, the spike of An Sgùrr, the company you're with – it's something greater than the sum of its parts.

Over the years it has attracted some well-known names, beginning with exploration by Philip Tranter and his pals in the Corriemulzie Club. Since the 1960s, Clive Rowland, Roger Webb, Malcolm Bass, Simon Yearsley and inevitably Andy Nisbet have also all made exploratory pilgrimages.

Clive Rowland (belayed above) and Stephanie Rowland on FA of Pineapple Gully, January 1978. Photo: Peter Macdonald.

Near the summit of Seana Bhràigh, *Diamond Edge* looks one of the finest lines. Peter Macdonald told me he had had his eye on this after already climbing two routes on the same buttress. However, the Corriemulzie connection and stranglehold was broken a month after his ascent of *Pineapple Gully* in January 1978 with Clive and Stephanie Rowland (the latter climber uncredited in the FA list). Dougie Dinwoodie climbed two routes then returned from Aberdeen in April with Ronnie Robb and Bob Smith to take the prize. More recent attention has concentrated on harder mixed lines on the Flowerpot, Diamond and Summit Buttresses.

It had been one of those typically Scottish days when every kind of snow was encountered on the way up. Once on the plateau, however, there was consistency, with swathes of *sastrugi* and delicate Mr Whippy swirls on the few exposed rocks. The corrie's lip was fringed with flimsy diving-board cornices and sunken dumpy ones like badly made meringues. Lethal but hypnotic.

By contrast, down on the corrie's floor the southerly part of the lochan was clear, looking like a back-to-front map of Africa – an early memory detail I had of the mountain. To the north-west the fabulous sequence of Coigach and Assynt peaks are arranged like a row of single malts in a bar, each with the stamp of uniqueness and quality.

Some day! But also sobering. A few miles away, Beinn Dearg had been

Luchd Coire of Seana Bhràigh with Coigach hills behind. Photo: Mike Dixon.

the last day for Captain Solo just over a week ago, and another last day had befallen two members a year ago on the country's northern sentinel, Ben Hope. In the Compleators' section of the SMC website there's a picture of Andy Nisbet finishing his first Munro around age 18, reaching out to touch the cairn on this very hill. Of the wide array of mountains and corries I could see, there are next to none that his name is not linked to.

The last time I was here, there was alcohol and a Munro celebration of our own. We're all still around, but today age and injuries are kicking in. I don't take these days for granted now. On that occasion there was an explosion of late sun that gilded the upper mountain, a rare gift from November. Today there was a hint of spring and signs that an indifferent winter was thankfully nearly over.

The descent was easy and relaxed, as I enjoyed the sun seeping into my bones. Crampons were back on for the last huge snowfield of perfect névé. From its end it was a case of linking snow patches as far as I could, to reduce the heather-and-bog-bashing that remained. At the very point they finished I hit an argo-cat trail, which led to the main track just a few metres from the bike. Some days everything just clicks.

There was no signal on the car radio for a while, but when it returned Chuck Berry's *Johnny B Goode* was playing: a glorious piece of classic rock & roll or, as the *Daily Mail* called it, the 'Negroes' revenge'. It sounded so fresh and alive, and for the first time in ages I could drive with the window partly down. Simple pleasures combined with a satisfying tiredness. Just when I thought things couldn't get much better, I was brought back to earth. On the news the worst was confirmed: Snippola was announcing that pubs should close today and the Great Outdoors was to be out of bounds until who-knew-when.

I didn't really care. I could live off today for a very long time.

Thanks to Peter Macdonald, Simon Richardson and Simon Yearsley for providing information.

THE NAMING OF ROUTES

by Sophie-Grace Chappell

THE THING IS, you need something to do with your mind while you're on belay.

There's the mind's own daily internal soundtrack of course. Mine today, ski-touring above the Glen Clova Hotel, was 'West End Girls' by the Pet Shop Boys and 'I Tried to Leave You' by Leonard Cohen – just in case, for some strange reason, you care.

But on belay you need something a bit more, well, cognitive than that. So, thinking up route-names. That's the thing.

In my far-off teenage-anorak days, at school in the early Eighties when we were about 16, the *New Musical Express* used to give the track-listings for all the new albums it reviewed. So my mate Mick and I started off by memorising all the track listings off every Beatles album. And for an encore every post-Beatles album. Forty years later I can still tell you – straight off, and no googling – what is track one, side three on *The White Album*, and which albums 'Crippled Inside' and 'Call Me Back Again' and '1985' are on.

Then Mick and I went freestyle. We moved on to inventing bands, and albums, and writing out the track-listings for those as well. Not being particularly good musicians, we didn't try to write the actual songs or anything, and anyway that wasn't the point. We just wanted to come up with a play-list that looked as good as the lopsided 16 on the back surface of our copies of *Abbey Road*. (Which is, by the way, the greatest album-cover in the history of the world, both back and front. I will hear no argument whatever on this point.)

'Revenge is Sweet', 'Why Won't You Compromise?', 'Double Double Bed', 'Praying Like a Mantis', 'Eriskay', 'Down at Central Station in a State of Desperation', 'Poisoned Sugar', 'Hot Gospel, Cold Heart', 'Together but Alone' – those were some of mine. No question, the standards have been set high in this department, and none of these is anywhere near as good a song-name as 'Ticket to Ride', or 'Highway 61', or 'Darkness on the Edge of Town', or 'Famous Blue Raincoat', or 'Everybody's Got Something to Hide Except Me and My Monkey'. But I still wonder sometimes what the songs might have been to go with those names.

It was something to do with our minds, and in the stark bleak inhumanity of school something was needed.

Some kinds of stark bleak inhumanity are thrust upon us; some we're born to; others we achieve. And others again, for whatever reason, we actively seek out. Every Scottish winter climber knows how hard it is to leave the warm and sleepy partner in the feathered fragrant nest of the 3am bed, to gulp down reheated porridge and coffee in a cold silent empty-stage kitchen, to scrape the ice off a frozen car, leap into it, and drive alone, as fast as you can in the conditions, for 90 miles to a pre-dawn rendezvous on a glistening, crackling, moonlit roadside.

And that's the *comfortable* bit. What comes next is the breath-taking spindrift down the neck, the teetering up icy rock-filled crampon-sparking paths, the perishing wind and the plunging posthole breakthroughs into unfrozen but freezing burns. What comes next is the hours of harsh panting, wading uphill with half the rack and one of the ropes on your back, always into the fangs of the gale, always with a partner who seems twice as fit as you are, always on a torch battery that you don't entirely trust, always wishing you'd slept better and longer and drunk more water before you started on this, always with all the cares you thought you'd left at home snapping at the heels of your psyche.

And then you look, pretty much, for the harshest and bleakest place on the whole bloody mountain, the dark, moon-shadowed, snow-devil-bedevilled foot of some overhanging horror-show of a bitter north-face cliff – and that's your belay. This stance here, or another one rather like it only much more exposed, 40 or 80 metres up there: this is your home for the next hour or so, until a muffled shout from above is borne down to you on the murderous clobbering wind, and the ropes pull tight and tight again. And you hurriedly snatch a sip, a bite, and a pee if the wind will let you (or if you're past caring). You strip the belay, check your crampons, grip your tools, re-aim your still-needed head-torch. And you move on up to tackle whatever sunk-head warthog horrors need fumblingly unhammered from their ice-welded fissures without being dropped into the blackness, banging your heels and wrists together to restore circulation, praying for all you're worth that you won't get hot aches today, and that at some point you will actually escape the black ice-breathed shadow of the cliff, actually feel the sunlight on your face.

Bleak stark inhumanity. It's no sunny grove of turtle-dove-filled peach-trees in a fragrant Andalusian cicada spring. We look down our noses at the 18th-century authors who were openly horrified by the Scottish mountains in winter. We think they were overdoing it, but they really weren't. The Scottish mountains in winter *are* horrifying. They're other things too, for sure, but they are definitely horrifying. I once hung off an improvised ice-ledge at the top of pitch one of Zero Gully in a gathering snow-storm for five hours, waiting (praying) for a helicopter, with a broken right hip, a fractured left ankle, torn cartilages in my left knee, one crampon, one axe, no glasses, and no gloves. That was horror all right. But there is at least a faint touch of horror about being half-way up an ice cliff even when things are completely under control.

So as I say, you need something to think about while you're up there. And – in line with the curious parallelism between thumbing through track-listings from albums you haven't heard, and thumbing through climbing guides that list routes you haven't climbed – what I think about is route-names.

This is part of the amazing privilege of climbing a new route, that you get to name it. But there are high standards in this department too.[1] At least some route-names are not entirely discretionary, of course: if you climb a frozen waterfall, then the route-name is just the name of the waterfall, at least as long as there's only one route there. So Steall Falls is just *Steall Falls*; and Easan Feidh, the magnificent near-vertical 90-metre high waterfall just south of Ben Klibreck that Steve Perry and I bagged in March 2018, is just *Easan Feidh* – at least until someone goes back and adds *Easan Feidh Left-Hand* or maybe even *Easan Feidh Central*. (If it really gets cold. But it was a torrent in the middle when Steve and I were there. I don't actually think it's ever been repeated.[2])

So in general what I do is, during the walk-in I quiz my partner about the crag, about what route-names there already are up there, what the Gaelic name of the crag means if I don't know already, what outstanding features it has, and what the history is. (When it's the New Routes Editor of the *Journal* you're climbing with, he tends to have good answers to your questions.) With any luck his responses will give me something to go on during a long day's thinking.

On this matter, one law or superstition is pretty well absolute: until the route is in the bag, you must never let on what you'd like to call it. And no route-name is decided without both partners agreeing to it. (Because we were both there to restore our morale, because I was bumbling with gear-lifts, and because we'd been discussing transgender, I wanted to call a route on Perseverance Buttress *Lost Nuts*; unfortunately this was vetoed.)

The best route-names that aren't just toponyms have a thrilling simplicity to them, and they say something about the route, and/or the story of its first ascent. *Indicator Wall* because it's the wall below the indicator. *Orion* for the skewed-H constellation-shape of the face it's on, with a whisper of the thrillingly mad idea of climbing it by starlight. *Vanishing Gully* because it peters out, and because, very often, you can't see it for the spindrift. *Scorpion* for the sting in the tale. *Royal Pardon* because Roger Webb and Simon Richardson had already climbed *King's Ransom* nearby, and because one of Roger's axes snapped on the first ascent, but they got up it anyway: a kind of reprieve. *Jenga Buttress* because you really shouldn't go there without a good freeze to hold the blocks together.

Good route-names also, very often, fit in with larger themes that are going on across the whole crag.[3] The Pinnacle Buttress of Tower Ridge

---

[1] Geoff Dutton when Editor deplored 'the polyglot drivel that disfigures our New Climbs section' and pleaded: 'Let us respect these places among which we are able to climb … . Besides conveying something to others, the name should be a worthy one.' (*SMCJ*, 27/151(1960), 45–7.) – Hon. Ed.

[2] No repeats recorded on UKC as of 1 February 2021. In Steve's words on UKC: 'A truly memorable experience on such a rarely appearing route. The climbing was a combination of fear and awe, as good as it gets.' Yes. That.

[3] For Sheila Young's scholarly and exhaustive analysis of the route-names on

already had *Goodfellas* and *Stringfellow* on it when Simon Richardson and I got there in March 2018; so what we added was another nightclub name, *Moulin Rouge*. And Lurcher's has *Deerhound Ridge*, *Pug Face*, *Rottweiler*, *K9*, *Canis Major*, *Collie's Ridge* (rather neat, that one). The dog theme is rightly central to the crag, and it has spawned sub-themes: for example there's a move via *Hound of the Baskervilles* and *Werewolves* to the Perry-Rennard-Nisbet route *Shapeshifter*. When Steve and I were there on 30 January 2019 we tried a line next to *Shapeshifter*, and Steve backed off it because, in the conditions, there wasn't any gear. I had a name in mind for it, and so did he; but we never heard either name, because we never finished the line. (Dave Almond and Jamie Skelton later finished it, though, and they called it *Berserker*. Clearly they found more gear than we did, as they graded it VI,8. For what it's worth, my route-name plan had been this: I was going to reference Lou Reed, and myself a little, and call it *Transformer*.)

You can play the name game in summer too, and the naming standards are high there too, whether mystically psychedelic like *Dream of White Horses*, pleasingly ridiculous like *With A View to a Shag*, or just plain menacing like *Grey Panther* and *Indian Face*. Sometimes, winter or summer, the names are obvious from the situation. The 'beanstalk' theme was already there on that sector of Red Craigs in Glen Clova, when Simon Richardson and I named a new HVS route *For a Handful of Beans*. And I once spent a remarkably uncomfortable August afternoon somewhere above Loch Earn, watching Stephen Venables wriggle up the vegetable-garden rock face in front of me wearing a midge net. I didn't have a midge net, and as a good belayer both my hands were on the rope, so all I could do to defend myself was shake my head and huff air sideways through my lips. I was sneezing black. When I looked in the mirror later, I had black eyeliner on, entirely composed of tiny insect corpses. *If You Want Blood*, *A Million Famished Mouths*, *The Edinburgh Tattoo*, *Love Bites*, *Blood Brothers*, *Nonconsensual Transfusion*, *Hunger in The Air*, *Wee Basturts* and *The Scottish Air Force* were all possible route-names that came to mind, though in the end I think the only thing we actually climbed before we ran away was *Midgy Ridge*.

Sometimes it's dead easy. A quick route in Corrie Clova that you snatch in a hurry, at last light just before Christmas, is *Carpe Diem*. If it's New Year's Day and you're climbing above Loch Brandy, *First Footing* works for your first route of the day – and the year – and so do *VSOP* ('very slow old-style pioneers'?) and *Napoleon* (a stiff and haughty and in-your-face kind of a route). If you climb a route exactly on the centenary of Gallipoli, it's only right to call it *Anzac Day* or, if it weaves about a bit, *Waltzing Matilda*. When Andy Nisbet, Sarah Sigley and I climbed *Maundy Buttress* and *Maundy Gully* on Sròn nan Forsair behind Clach Leathad, it was indeed Maundy Thursday in 2018. If you climb a pinnacle on Cairn Broadlands that looks like a king enthroned and it's Holy

Lochnagar, see *SMCJ*, 41/201 (2010), pp 76–85. – Hon. Ed.

Innocents' Day 2015 – the day of the alleged massacre in Matthew ii – then *King Herod* makes perfect sense.

Or a route-name can fit in with a private joke. Jamie Bankhead told Mike Lates and me that we had no chance of new-routing in the Cuillin in mid-November: 'But sure, give it a try if blunting your axe-points on hoar-flecked scree-rubble is your thing.' So after a sensational day of snow-showers in the rainbowed sunlight, when we tracked fox-prints in the snow all the way up Coire Lagan to the foot of a bow-curved groove on Sgùrr MhicChoinnich with a spectacular outlook over Soay and Rum and Barra and the infinite North Atlantic – after that magical experience, Mike quite rightly dubbed our new route *The Silver Fox*.

The first route I ever named was *Silver Threads Among The Gold*, in the Corrie of Farchal of Glen Clova, which I climbed in March 2013 with Henning Wackerhage and Simon Richardson. They'd already established an old-age theme in the corrie, and I kept it going. It's a soppy old song, and it means 'Your hair's going grey' (or silver, like Jamie's), but it says it indirectly and poetically. And we were threading together the pure-white ice-runs around the sun-yellowed rocks.

We climbed three routes that day. I can't remember who named *Age before Beauty*, the next route we did: Henning, I think. But the last route of the day was *Pearls before Swine*, which was me, in honour of Dorothy Parker's famous riposte to that phrase. One later visit there yielded a stroke of route-naming genius from Ben Richardson, a name that fitted perfectly with the fact that the top of the route is one of those situations where there's a bare plateau with no belays, so you just keep walking backwards away from the climb – *Over the Hill*. Later on, in 2016, we put up *Too Old to Rock and Roll* and *Too Young to Die* in the same corrie; though perhaps my favourite name there is *Coffin Dodger*.

Simon and I also named at least three routes in Corrie Sharroch of Glen Clova. We started with a gambling theme, which gave us *One-Armed Bandit* for a brilliant crack-route that starts by passing a dodgy-looking block the size of a fruit-machine, and where one of us, and never mind who, ended up climbing with a single axe. Also *Turf Accountant* for a route that was, well, a bit on the grassy side.

And near *One-Armed Bandit* there is another route that Simon and I climbed on 5 February 2019. I can't now remember what our first name for it was. That was the day when our phones started going mad as we drove back down Glen Clova to our rendezvous at the Camera Obscura in Kirrie. Truth to tell, on 30 January, our Lurcher's Crag day, Steve had invited me to Ben Hope for 4 February, to climb a long new route with him and Andy Nisbet; but Steve withdrew the invitation when he realised that his project with Andy was too long for a three-person approach. I believe there had been a separate mix-up, and Andy had said the same to Sandy Allan. I don't know what Sandy did instead that day, but I went to Clova with Simon.[4]

---

[4]Andy Nisbet & Steve Perry died on Ben Hope on 5 February 2019. – HON. ED.

These days when I am on belay, 5 February 2019 is one thing that I think about. Because whatever our first name for that route was, we ended up naming it in memory of Steve and Andy. We called it *Brothers in Arms*. It's an excellent five-pitch route. If VI,6 is your kind of grade, then some day when all this pandemic is over, go to Corrie Sharroch and climb it, and think of them.

HARRIS

An island off an island,
Sleeping, rocked
Amidst enormous seas.
Sheep crop the delicate
Grass behind the blowing sand.

The peat stack is deserted
Beside the narrow road,
But the wind and the gannets
Do not observe the Sabbath;

Voices are hushed in the bar.
  'Two whiskies, please.'
  'Water?'
  'Oh yes.'
It's everywhere.

P.J. Biggar

FRONTIERSMEN

by Finlay Wild

EVENING'S GOLDEN LIGHT reflects off my ski tips, shouldered on my pack as we descend a wind-scoured section of Na Gruagaichean. I fall slightly behind Es Tresidder to put an extra layer on: safe travel requires more concentration now; twilight is coming, we are tired but persisting. This is peak 17 of 24 and, as the sun sets magically beyond the remaining Mamores, we are – affirmingly – still going. Sunset hues take our minds back through thirteen hours of movement to the excitement of first light as we ascended Stob Coire Easain after a night of moonless ski mountaineering across the Grey Corries from Ben Nevis. The snow is getting firmer now as the blues darken to black, the wind strengthening. As we lumber on up Stob Coire a' Chàirn we switch on head torches again, the full allotment of mid-March daylight spent. Off to the right, corniced drops gleam brightly in the torch-beams then fade into the void.

The way here is wide, but Ramsay's Round doesn't particularly lend itself to ski mountaineering, the many sharp edges and rough peaks a tougher objective than the rolling Cairngorms tundra which is a more obvious venue for long ski days. We'd made good time up the Ben, chatted our way along the Càrn Mòr Dearg arête at midnight as the lights of Fort William glimmered below, and found the only entry point without a huge cornice from which to drop from Stob Coire Bhealaich to the Grey Corries beyond. Breakfast at Fersit in the sun had been well received, and had fuelled the sustained ascent to Stob Coire Sgriodain and the far side of the round, which proved agreeably amenable to skis. The 10km jog from Corrour back west along the Abhainn Rath carrying skis and boots had been less so, but had then led us on to Sgùrr Eilde Mòr, to marvel at the closeness of Ben Nevis standing out in the sun across the deep glen. Somewhere in those hours, time had taken on a different meaning. There was now no rush nor rest, only a relentless continuing beyond questioning, a flow state.

We cache the skis, then descend steeply in crampons to a col before tackling the out-and-back to An Gearanach. This blocky exposed crest is one of the more involved sections of the famous Ring of Steall route; a brilliant summer romp but several degrees more serious in winter, in the dark, and with 21 hours elapsed. The wind is getting up, it's harder to stay warm and Es seems tense on the ridge. 'I'm not happy with this exposure,' he says suddenly. 'I'm going back.' For him, the delicate balance of fatigue, risk and reward has shifted. My ego flares in frustration: I've been feeling relatively decent. My legs are tired, but they were tired after the first six hours and haven't got any worse. I feel galvanised by the goal: only a handful more summits, I have enough food and water – what now? We confer briefly as spindrift swirls around our two points of light. Es starts to return along the ridge to easier ground and our skis; I will

Sunrise in the Easains, with Es Tresidder on ski.   Photo: Finlay Wild

continue the short distance to An Gearanach and then catch him up to make our next decision.

Moving faster now I feel a burst of unexpected energy. There is base defiance in this – the stubborn child who refuses to go to bed though exhausted – but also something loftier, something special. This is our longest day; for endless hours we have been committed to the present; we are bound to the landscape through deep immersion. I glimpse new depths, a time-worn impetus that has been propelling humans onwards against bodily languor for millennia; the psyche over the flesh. I feel solid on this terrain, with an axe and a ski-pole and a good knowledge of these mountains in all conditions. But how many hours have we spent on ski-edges near precipices? How many exposed traverses on firm névé above killer drops? Between us Es has more hard alpinism to his name, but recently I have spent more time moving on this sort of winter terrain, especially on skis. Though our communication has long since receded to the monosyllables of necessity we have been a well-matched team. How long will my own drained body and concentration remain trustworthy against accumulating fatigue? Jeopardy is tiring: our fortitude has been slowly depleted over almost a full day now. How close to a dangerous edge – metaphorical or real – are we?

By the time I catch up with Es the right choice is obvious – the only choice. Some would have realised this immediately, and maybe I did too, but selfish denial had – for a moment – hijacked me. We will go down. Certitude is calming. Splitting up now would be anathema, an asinine egotism. We are both strung-out, tired, atop a winter Munro in the dark; even taking the easiest bail-out route is not straightforward. Our objective is not complete, but our reasons for being here are more than an oval on a map. We are probing ambition, exploring our reach. Though no rope connects us we are a mountaineering team; our combined efforts have brought us here. Each man's peaks of euphoric ease and tired troughs have been managed collectively. Success is a shared concept.

We get out a lightweight bothy-bag shelter on the summit of Stob Coire a' Chàirn and sit down for a bite. The wind is still strong so we don't rest long, just enough time to confirm our route of retreat – to Kinlochleven. Wind buffets the walls, and the fabric imparts a red hue to everything inside: we are a tiny red bubble of light in the indifferent darkness. With a clarity that will stick with me for a long time I realise that this isn't failure. This is the objective. This is the joy of doing. We have found what we seek.

HAROLD RAEBURN – HIS PILGRIMAGES ABROAD

by Robin N. Campbell

HAROLD RAEBURN (1865–1926) will be well known to most readers as a prodigious Scottish pioneering climber,[1] and many will also know of his unfortunate end of life.[2] He succumbed to illness shortly after the 1921 Everest Reconnaissance (on which he was very ill with dysentery), and never recovered his health, before dying in Edinburgh at the end of 1926. But as well as his exploits on Scottish crags, he also climbed abroad throughout his life, and it is his efforts outside Scotland that I want to describe here. He made his mark in England, in Norway, in the Caucasus, in the Himalaya, and most particularly in the Alps. Nowadays, it is not unusual to find climbers who spread their wings in a similarly extravagant manner. Among contemporary members, Dave Broadhead, Geoff Cohen and the late Des Rubens come to mind. But 'wings' is an appropriate word here. There were no wings in Raeburn's day, and only iron wheels: he made his way about the world by ship, train, carriage and horse. He did not start serious climbing until 1896. He lost two years (1911–12) to what I presume was injury, and four years to war, but used the remaining 18 years to achieve real mountaineering mastery.

This is also the story of William Ling, who was Raeburn's second on most of his climbs abroad. We know a great deal about Raeburn's climbing thanks to the diligence of his rope-mate of 15 years, Ling, who kept a continuous climbing diary from 1893 to September 1953, in 21 notebook volumes.[3] This is a record of early 20th century climbing without parallel, and is particularly valuable as Ling recorded full dates, and the full names of his companions. Thanks to Ling's diary, and Raeburn's own archives[4] and *Journal* contributions, we know about some 340 climbing days of Raeburn's career. Ling and Raeburn met on the 1897 Yacht Meet and climbed together for the first time at Easter 1900 on the Northern Pinnacles of Liathach. At that time Ling was a close friend of Henry Lawson, an Edinburgh actuary who lived at 34 George Square[5] and soon became SMC Librarian. They had met in the Lake District in 1897, and Lawson recruited Ling to the Club. The pair had several busy seasons

---

[1] See Ken Crocket's *Mountaineering in Scotland: The Early Years* (SMT, 2015) for details.

[2] Mike Jacob: 'Harold Raeburn – The Final Journey', *SMCJ*, 40/199 (2008), 41–51.

[3] Referred to here as *LD*. In Alpine Club Archives, but I can supply any wanted excerpts.

[4] NLS Acc. 11538, Items 121–35.

[5] Later named Cowan House, now part of the space occupied by the University Library.

in the Alps together, climbing with guides, before Lawson's death from typhoid, age 35, in 1902.

My topic here is Raeburn's activities abroad between 1900 and his final reported climbing expedition to Kangchenjunga in 1920, and my claim is that no other British mountaineer demonstrated such all-round mastery during this period. His 15 seasons were as follows: 1900–01 Alps (with guides); 1902–03 Norway; 1904–10 Alps; 1913–14 Central Caucasus; 1919 solo E–W traverse of La Meije; and 1920 Kangchenjunga reconnaissances.

In addition, I will say a little about his activities in the English Lake District, and it may be as well to begin with these. Ling had made some innovations of his own on both sides of Great Gable with George Glover, but when together Raeburn and Ling were always just a little off the pace in the Lakes, perhaps because they didn't use Wasdale as a base but preferred to stay in the farmhouse at Seathwaite. Despite this awkward base, they climbed almost every route on Scafell, Gable and Pillar. They climbed there mostly in the late spring and early autumn. Raeburn and Ling's climbing year was therefore usually configured as follows: Scotland until Easter, Lakes until late June, Europe until end of August, and Lakes until November. Perhaps the highlight of their efforts in the Lakes was to make very early ascents of the novelties on Pillar, notably the *North-West Climb* and *North-East Climb* on Pillar Low Man. *North-West Climb* is still graded Very Severe, and Raeburn and Ling's ascent – a desperate affair over 'greasy and slippery rocks' – involved a new variation finish.

After a climb on Pillar in 1912 the pair separated, Ling returning to Carlisle while Raeburn carried on to Wasdale. His notebook has the following interesting entry.

> Down to Wasdale. Large party arrived from Skafell. Hereford [Herford], Gibson, Brunskill, etc, etc; had been working out Girdle Traverse of Skafell and almost completed it. G- climbs slabs in bare feet. As I foresaw chimney work has gone out and it is now open work and very much more scientific and delicate slab climbing on faces that attracts the elite. The boys try all kinds of games for practice. Trying how long they can stand being hung up on the rope, holding on by hands to ledge, to rope-climbing up rope, etc. Very keen and very strong but inclined to overstep the edge of the permissible. They all have rather more than a respect for the N.W. however. Had heard of my descent alone and seemed to think it a bit risky. It was not of course as I did it.

If this refers to a solo descent of the *North-West Climb*, it is little wonder that they showed him a bit of respect.[6]

---

[6] For the North-West Climb see *LD* **7**, 37–9; for Wasdale comments see *Raeburn's 1910–12 Diary*, 29. NLS Acc. 11538, Item 122.

Alps 1900–01

In 1900 Raeburn enjoyed a short holiday with William Douglas in the Dolomites, where they climbed the Fünffingerspitze, the Marmolada and other peaks. In 1901 he visited the main chain for the first time, climbing Monte Rosa, the Matterhorn and the Weisshorn with Douglas, William Garden and guides before moving to Chamonix to meet William and Jane Inglis Clark. The weather was bad and little was achieved there beyond an ascent of the Dent du Géant.[7]

Norway 1902–03

The mountains of Norway were a popular alternative to the Alps at this time, thanks to the explorations by Cecil Slingsby with his wool-trade friends, by Norman Collie and by Charles Patchell (a teacher at Glenalmond School). There was strong British and indeed SMC involvement there before the First World War, particularly in the Horungertinde (now known as the Hurrungane), a group of spectacular gabbro mountains situated south-west of the Galdhøpiggen-Glittertind group at the head of Lyster Fjord. In August 1902, Raeburn enjoyed a holiday there with Howard Priestman, staying in the hotel at Turtagrø along with several other climbers. Despite a poor spell of weather, he managed to climb with various partners the South Dyrhaugstind from Bandet (second ascent) – a new variation that is now the route usually taken; made the first ascent of the season of Store Skagastølstind; traversed all five peaks of the Skagastølstinder; and made a new route on Soleitind from the glacier on the east side.

In 1903 he returned with Ling and Priestman. Their first targets were some unclimbed peaks in West Sunnmøre, the three Sætretinder and three Grötdalstinder, which they accomplished before moving east to the Hotel Union at Øye, the usual base for exploring Sunnmøre. From there Raeburn and Ling made an amazing new ascent of the neighbouring mountain Slogen, climbing the fjord face, which involved 4000 feet of difficult rock-climbing, in a day. They concluded their visit to Sunnmøre with a new traverse of the Brekketind and Gjeithorn peaks before making a long southwards traverse over land, mountain and sea to Turtagrø. In the Hurrungane, where they again found poor weather, they climbed with Erik Ullén and the famous lady climber Therese Bertheau.[8] Their most interesting day was perhaps a failed attempt to traverse Kjerringa and Mannen, two difficult rock peaks at the south end of the range.[9]

---

[7] 1900 – *SMCJ*, 6/34 (Jan 1901), 127; 1901 – *SMCJ*, 7/37 (Jan 1902), 40.

[8] Erik Ullén was a well-known Swedish mountaineer. He attended our 1905 Easter Meet in Skye, where he participated in a new climb in Harta Corrie and a wintry traverse from Garsbheinn to Sgùrr Alasdair, and our 1906 Easter Meet in Glencoe. Despite his strong supporters, Ling and Raeburn, his application to join the SMC was unaccountably rejected. Therese Bertheau was Norway's foremost lady climber for many years. She scandalized the bourgeoisie by wearing trousers on the crags.

Turtagrø Hotel, Norway, 1903. Raeburn is fifth from left of standing group; Ling is rightmost standing man; Erik Ullén is on left of front row; Therese Bertheau is in centre of second seated row. Photo: SMC Image Archive.

It is something of a mystery why the mountains of Norway are not more popular amongst British climbers today, apart from the frozen waterfalls of Rjukan – a venue possibly slightly more interesting than the Kinlochleven indoor ice wall. Amongst our recent members, only David Ritchie, Neil McGougan and Martin Moran seem to have grasped their enormous potential for winter climbing.

Alps 1904–05

Raeburn's visits in these two years were devoted to guideless ascents of *grandes courses*. Ling was ill with a complicated 'flu throughout 1904, so Raeburn's guideless Alpine career began with Charles W. Walker, one of the Walker cousins of Dundee who managed Harry Walker & Company's jute business.

In 1904 they visited Dauphiné and Vanoise. Climbing highlights were La Meije from the newly-opened Promontoire Hut, and the North Face of the Grande Casse. Moving to Courmayeur, they then climbed the Aiguille Noire. In 1905, Ling was added to the party. In the Dauphiné they traversed Les Écrins before moving to Chamonix where they all

---

[9] 1902 – *SMCJ*, 7/40 (Jan 1903), 237; 1903 – *SMCJ*, 8/43 (Jan 1904), 79–80; *LD* **4**, 46–83; *LD* **5**, 1–8; *AJ*, 22/163 (Feb 1904), 72–3; *AJ*, 22/167 (Feb 1905), 394. A full account of the climb on Slogen is given by Raeburn in 'Slogen. A day on the Seaward Face', *The Yorkshire Ramblers' Club Journal*, 2/6 (1904–5), 134–40.

became seriously ill after eating bad fish at the Montenvers Hotel. Walker was so ill that he left for home, but Raeburn and Ling struggled on, attempting the Petit Dru from the Charpoua. Eventually Ling succumbed to pains and cramps, but Raeburn persevered solo to the summit and the pair endured a cold bivouac high on the Dru.[10]

Alps 1906–08

In one of his notebooks, Raeburn lists 'Proposed peaks to try – all traverses if possible', and this was to be his agenda for these three seasons.[11] 1906 began differently, however. Raeburn climbed Green Gully on Ben Nevis earlier in 1906, along with Eberhard Phildius, a Swiss student of theology at Edinburgh. Phildius was a climbing friend of the great Alpine authority Marcel Kurz, then only 18, and Kurz passed on tips – possibly filched from his father's project book – to Raeburn.[12] One of the tips was an unclimbed peak of the Petites Aiguilles Rouges du Dolent, which they climbed in early July from Val Ferret and named 'La Mouche', and then from the Saleinaz Hut they traversed the Aiguille d'Argentière by the North-east Face and the Flèche Rousse (another first ascent) then over the west peak and down to the Chardonnet glacier.[13]

They then travelled to the Concordia Hut in the Oberland, making a planned rendezvous with Eric Greenwood en route, then on to the Finsteraarhorn Hut. From there they traversed the Finsteraarhorn, ascending by the South-East Ridge and descending the North-West Ridge to the Finsteraar glacier, from where they crossed the Finsteraarjoch and descended to the Schwarzegg Hut. After two off-days around Grindelwald, they went back to the Schwarzegg Hut and traversed the Schreckhorn, ascending by the North-West Ridge and descending by the South-West Ridge, the first traverse in this direction.[14]

The trio then embarked on a complicated journey through Central Switzerland, finally reaching the Rhône Valley, where Greenwood left for home and Ling and Raeburn continued to Zermatt. On 30 July they embarked on a traverse of the Matterhorn via the Zmutt and Italian ridges. It was early in the season for this, and they had to cope with difficult icy conditions throughout, taking eleven hours from their gîte at the base of the Zmutt ridge to the summit, and a further five hours to descend the Italian Ridge. Ling remarked that 'Raeburn's route[-finding] and leading

[10] 1904 – *SMCJ*, 8/46 (Jan 1905), 218; *AJ*, 23/177 (Aug 1907), 574–5; 1905 – *SMCJ*, 9/49 (Jan 1906), 51–2; *LD* **5**, 20–41.

[11] Research Notebook, p. 4 (numbering back from end of book). NLS Acc. 11538, Item 131.

[12] See *SMCJ*, 9/52 (Jan 1907), 220 for Raeburn's acknowledgement of Kurz' assistance, passed on by Monsieur E. Phildius.

[13] *SMCJ*, 9/52 (Jan 1907), 220; *AJ*, 23/174 (Nov 1906), 327; 'Some Traverses in 1906', *AJ*, 23/176 (May 1907), 425–43; *LD* **5**, 67–76.

[14] *SMCJ*, 9/52 (Jan 1907), 220–21; *LD* **5**, 81–3; *LD* **6**, 2–4.

up the snow-covered slabs were beyond praise.'[15] It was the end of a very successful season in which four major mountains were traversed in novel ways, in all cases involving first British guideless ascents or traverses – thanks to the excellence of Raeburn's research and route-finding, his determined leading, and Ling's steadfast support.[16]

1907 was a season of stormy weather. Ling and Raeburn began at the Meije, where they reconnoitred the unclimbed West Ridge from the Promontoire Hut but were defeated by bad conditions. Out of food, they crossed the Brèche and descended to La Grave before attempting an east-west traverse of La Meije from there. Once again the weather stopped them, a blizzard catching them *en bivouac* not far short of the Pic Central, and they endured a difficult descent. They then gave the Dauphiné up and transferred to 'the picturesque village of Val d'Isère with its church spire and quaint houses'. From there they traversed the Dôme de la Sache and Mont Pourri, a very long and high ridge route, before embarking on a complicated journey to Italy. They first climbed Tsanteleina, then continued on the frontier ridge south over three other peaks before traversing the Col de la Galise to the Orco Valley and Ceresole, a twenty-hour day. After much bad weather, they climbed the Gran Paradiso by the so-called Circular Traverse, encountering a severe thunderstorm at the summit. Both were struck by lightning, Raeburn more severely, and they raced down the normal route with everything hissing and their hair standing on end. Next day they traversed the Col d'Entrelor to Val di Rhêmes, suffering a further storm and lightning strikes, before traversing the Bec de l'Invergnan to Valgrisenche and thence to Courmayeur on the day following. They ended this most adventurous tour of impressive expeditions plucked from the eye of storms by traversing Mont Blanc from the Sella Hut to Chamonix. Caught on the summit by another severe storm they made their way down to Chamonix by the ordinary Grands Mulets route through mist and driving snow in just over four hours.[17]

In 1908 the Alpine season was spoiled by very poor weather. Ling and Raeburn began their season on 31 July by traversing the Zinal Rothorn from the Trift Hotel to the Cabane du Mountet along with W.A. Brigg and Eric Greenwood. The latter two went off to Ferpècle the following morning; Ling and Raeburn spent the day reconnoitring the approach to the Col de Zinal before returning to the Mountet via a traverse of the Roc Noir, a sharp *rognon* dividing the Durand and Grand Cornier glaciers. On the following day they set out on one of Raeburn's projects, a traverse of the Dent Blanche commencing with a second ascent of the South-East Ridge.

[15] *SMCJ*, 9/52 (Jan 1907), 221; *AJ*, 23/174 (Nov 1906), 341; *LD* **6**, 8–13.

[16] H. Raeburn, 'Some Traverses in 1906', *AJ*, 23/176 (May 1907), 425–43.

[17] *SMCJ*, 10/55 (Jan 1908), 44–5; *LD* **6**, 46–82; Ling: 'Traverse of the Dôme de la Sache and Mont Pourri', *AJ*, 24/184 (May 1909), 482–7; Raeburn: 'The Gran Paradiso by the South Face', *AJ*, 23/178 (Nov 1907), 592–98 & 'The Bec de l'Invergnan by the E. Ridge', *AJ*, 24/182 (Nov 1908), 321–7.

The configuration of the Dent Blanche is complex. Going clockwise from the normal South Ridge, or Wandfluh, there is next the steep West or Ferpècle Ridge, where Owen Jones met his death in 1899, then the steeper North Ridge, not climbed until 1928, and finally the East 'Viereselsgrat' or Four Asses Ridge climbed by Ulrich Almer in 1882. But the East Ridge, after falling gently from the summit for 300m, bifurcates into a North-East Ridge (used by the Four Asses) and a steep South-East Ridge climbed by two Swiss amateurs in 1900 and not since then. Ling and Raeburn made good progress on the steep South-East Ridge, but when they arrived at the junction they discovered that the bad weather and contrary winds of June had decorated the kilometre of easy ridge to the summit with double cornices throughout. It took six hours to negotiate this, traversing the slopes below the cornices and crossing the ridge several times. A bivouac on the Wandfluh was inevitable, but it was not unduly cold. A tremendous alpenglow and electric storms around the Matterhorn helped to pass the time.

After a week of bad weather at the Montenvers, they gave up and transferred to the Cabane d'Orny. From there they made an extraordinarily complicated double traverse of the Chardonnet, first crossing to the Glacier du Tour, dropping their rucksacks, then traversing below the Chardonnet to reach the normal route by the North Face and West Ridge. They then descended the East Ridge over the Aiguille Forbes to recover their rucksacks, then ground back up to the Fenêtre du Tour and across the head of the Glacier de Saleina to yet another grind up to the Col du Chardonnet before descending from there to the Argentière Glacier and Hut – an absolutely brutal day, but accomplished in 13 hours.

After walking round the Verte back to the Montenvers, they went up to the Charpoua Hut, back down in a snowstorm in the morning, up again in the evening, and on the day following they traversed the Grand and Petit Drus, a project left over from the 'bad fish' season of 1905. This went well until the descent, when another snowstorm developed through the afternoon, and as darkness and thicker snow fell they were unable to proceed and endured a standing bivouac for nine hours of rain and snowfall.

After recovering from this dire experience, they went round to the Swiss side again and up to Champex where they met Erik Ullén, Maria and Persida Yovitchitch, and Miss M. Johnston for a 'tea-party, dancing and concert'. The plan was for all six to move on to the Cabane d'Orny the following day, but Persida had to turn back with illness. From there they had a day of misty but manageable weather in which all climbed the Aiguille du Tour in the morning, and the men climbed the Purtscheller in the afternoon. Their holiday ended on the following day with another night of wine, women and song in the Champex Hotel.[18]

---

[18] *SMCJ*, 10/58 (Jan 1909), 219–20; *LD* **7**, 45–48; Raeburn: 'The Dent Blanche by the East Ridge (Col de Zinal)', *AJ*, 24/186 (Nov 1909), 627–45.

Alps 1909–10

1909 provided Ling and Raeburn with a third season of poor weather in succession. Their first outing, at the end of July, was a simple ascent of the Aiguille du Midi by the laborious old route of the Géant Icefall and the Vallée Blanche to reach the hut at the Col du Midi, before traversing below the peak to reach the East Ridge. They had Hugh Munro for company and two porters, but Munro found the going hard. The hut was half-full of snow and ice, and only after a major effort by the porters and a German party of three was it possible to gain entrance, clear the floor, and thaw out the blankets. In the morning Munro walked only to the start of the East Ridge, while Ling and Raeburn found reaching the ice-plastered summit of the Aiguille quite awkward. This was a foretaste of what to expect in August. After some days of bad weather the Grépon was tried, but they were battered by a storm on the Nantillons Glacier and obliged to retreat to Montenvers. With new snow well down the Aiguilles, they settled for traversing the Petit Charmoz and l'M, led throughout by a Miss C.M. Campbell. A pleasant day was then ruined by witnessing and dealing with a fatal accident to Herbert F.W. Tatham[19] who fell on the descent path. On the day following they went to the Charpoua with the object of climbing the Aiguille Verte by the Moine Ridge. Although conditions were very icy, the weather was good, but they had the misfortune to be followed by a solitary German who eventually had to be put on their rope. He had no gloves and little food, and Raeburn called off the effort 800 feet from the summit; none too soon, since the German was 'out of gas' and required careful shepherding on the descent. Next they tried the Grépon traverse again, and encountered much ice below the Mummery Crack. It took Raeburn over an hour 'to beat this into subjection'. But the crack itself was ice-free, and their progress around the traverse more or less straightforward. On the summit, they were treated to the spectacle of Captain Spelterini in his giant yellow balloon attempting to sail over Mont Blanc.[20] Unfortunately the wind changed, and he ended up in the Oberland instead.

After more bad weather they gave up on Mont Blanc and transferred to Macugnaga via Brig and a hired carriage from Domodossola, arriving there on 11 August. The following day they went up to the Marinelli Hut in good weather and inspected the crossing of 'the murderous funnel' in the great Couloir. They set out for the East Face just after midnight, and crossed the Couloir without incident. The rocks of the Imseng Rücken went easily, as did the seracs and bergschrund above, but when they reached the lowest rocks of the Grenz Gipfel these were very badly iced, and they found it difficult to find a way on to the buttress, and once on it they had to keep to the steepest rocks to avoid ice. They reached the

---

[19] A master at Eton. See *Croydon's Weekly Standard*, 14 August 1909, for details.

[20] See Wikipedia page on Eduard Spelterini. His amazing aerial photographs of the Alps, taken from a balloon, are unequalled.
<https://en.wikipedia.org/wiki/Eduard_Spelterini> retrieved 4 September 2021.

*The East Face of Monte Rosa, with its peaks Signalkuppe, Zumsteinspitze, Dufourspitze &
Nordend mere pimples at the top. The Rifugio Marinelli lies on the spur to the right of the
'murderous funnel' at half height. Photo: SMC Image Archive.*

summit at 3 p.m., however, and made their way down the normal route to
reach the Riffelhaus shortly after 8 p.m.[21]

At the Monte Rosa Hotel they met Edith Gray, Ruth Raeburn and
Natalia Yovitchitch. A combined expedition to the Rimpfischhorn from
the Fluh Alp followed. Then Raeburn and Ling finished their season off
with a traverse of the Wellenkuppe and Ober Gabelhorn, the Grand
Gendarme providing a long pitch of very steep ice.[22]

---

[21] *SMCJ*, 11/61 (Feb 1910), 51; *LD* **8**, 22–49; Ling, 'A Traverse of Monte Rosa
and Other Expeditions', *AJ*, 25/188 (May 1910), 97–107.

[22] Equipped with a fixed rope after 1918.

In February 1910 Raeburn suffered a serious accident (see 'Accidents' below) but recovered sufficiently to set off to the Alps with Ling, arriving in the Arolla valley for a rendezvous with Ruth Raeburn and Natalia Yovitchitch. After climbing the Dent de Satarma on 27 July, the party moved to the Bertol Hut to climb the Bouquetins on the 29th before traversing to Zermatt on the 30th. Following a day with the ladies on the Unter Gabelhorn, the pair attempted to cross to Italy via the Lyskamm but were beaten back to Zermatt by storms.[23]

After a complicated journey through the Simplon to Lake Maggiore, and then north by ferryboats and trains to Sondrio and by carriage to Chiesa in the Val Malenco, they set out for the Disgrazia via Chiareggio on 7 August, inspired by a photograph of its North Face taken some years before by Arthur Russell and hoping to achieve its first ascent. They approached the North Face by scrambling up rocks under the Pizzo Ventina to reach the glacier.[24] Direct ascent of the North Face is prevented by a huge barrier of seracs, so all routes are forced to detour to the western side of this obstacle. Two couloirs reach towards the summit ridge. Ling and Raeburn chose the more westerly one, but were forced on to the buttress on its eastern side by impassable cornices. The transfer to the rocks was very awkward but after several failures they found a route and reached the summit ridge just west of the forepeak Syber-Gysi at 3 p.m., over eight hours since crossing the bergschrund. Descending to the Capanna Cecilia (now the Rifugio Cesare Ponti), they then made their way through the Bregaglia to Maloja.[25]

Moving to the north side of the main Bernina Group, they endured a good deal of bad weather, before managing to traverse the Crast' Agüzza in difficult icy conditions to the Marinelli Hut on 15 August. From there they attempted a traverse of the Scersen and Bernina, but had to abandon it after completing the Scersen – the first traverse of the season – because of a snowstorm, retreating down the couloir on the south side to return to the Marinelli. This was an exhausting day of 20 hours, and the ridge of the Scersen had been encumbered with ice and 'obnoxious cornices'. At one point Ling noted that Raeburn, having left his axe with Ling at the stance below an awkward pitch, had to resort to excavating ice from rock-holds with his penknife. Raeburn remarked in his 1910 Notebook that the Scersen traverse 'was about as hard a climb as I have ever had'.

On the 17th they made a late start, after 8 a.m., meaning only to cross the col to the Boval Hut, but were seduced into detouring to the Piz Bernina by its East Ridge, reaching its summit at 4 p.m., whence they

---

[23] *SMCJ*, 11/64 (Feb 1911), 238; *LD* **8**, 78–82.

[24] Nowadays, the glacier is reached by a descent from the Bivacco Oggioni.

[25] *SMCJ*, 11/64 (Feb 1911), 238; *LD* **8**, 84; *LD* **9**, 1–5; Raeburn, 'The Disgrazia by the N. Face', *AJ*, 25/194 (Nov 1911), 691–9; Ling: 'The North Face of the Monte Disgrazia and Other Climbs', *AJ*, 35/226 (May 1923), 36–41.

returned down the ridge and carried on to the Boval for a pot of coffee, and on down to Pontresina at 10 p.m.[26]

Clearly they had had a very good season in what were universally adverse conditions, with frequent storms and every high ridge corniced. Raeburn remarked that he had stopped losing weight at 9 stone 12 pounds and regained strength as the weeks went by. The line taken on the Disgrazia North Face is worth further investigation with the *AJ* articles and Raeburn's 1910 Notebook as guides, but I have been prevented from doing this thoroughly because of library closures. His Notebook ended with the observation that 'The Engadine is hardly worth a second visit. We got the best of it.' but he then went on to praise the Bregaglia.

Caucasus

Raeburn made expeditions to the Central Caucasus in 1913, and again in 1914. I have described the 1913 expedition in detail in an earlier number of the Journal,[27] so I note here only its principal achievements: the ascent of several new peaks, including the formidable Chanchakhi (4462m) at the head of the Tsaya/Zea Glacier, and – after a horseback traverse of the southern flanks of the range from Mamison to Mestia – a determined but unsuccessful attempt on the East Face of Ushba North from the Chalaat Glacier.

The 1914 expedition was a more compact affair, exploring solely on the North side of the Central range, but they climbed four new peaks before the outbreak of war cut the expedition short. Raeburn was this time without Ling, who could not join the expedition for unknown reasons, but recruited H. Scott Tucker and R.C. Richards along with Rembert Martinson, a young Russian cadet of Danish origin, who had been a stalwart member of the 1913 party. Ling went to the Alps instead with Harry MacRobert, Arnold Brown and George Sang. They had a mere week in the Gran Paradiso group before the War sent them back home.

The expedition began on 12 July at the Tsaya valley base-camp used in 1913. From there attempts were made to find an easy pass leading south-west to the Karagom Névé, but nothing particularly feasible was found. Then Raeburn took his party onto the North Tsaya Glacier using a 'side-door' couloir discovered by Vittorio Ronchetti that avoids the very troublesome ice-fall, and they made the first ascent of the southern of the twin Bubis peaks, at 4516m the second highest summit after Uilpata (4649m) in the Tsaya/Karagom region. Ronchetti had used this route to climb Uilpata in 1913, but suffered a high benightment and subsequent loss of part of a foot. There is now a Russian Hut at the foot of the 'side-door' couloir.

---

[26] *SMCJ*, 11/64 (Feb 1911), 239; *LD* **9**, 6–15; H. Raeburn: The Alps in 1910 (NLS Acc. 11538, Item 122).

[27] R.N. Campbell, 'The Caucasus Expedition of 1913', *SMCJ*, 42/204 (2013), 353–61. Raeburn's companions were W.G. Johns, Ling, R. Martinson & James R. Young.

Raeburn's Map: detail of the Karagom–Tsaya (Zea) peaks in the East Central Caucasus. The 1914 expedition made first ascents of Bubis, Vologata, East Karagom and Laboda (further west, not shown). Geog. J. 45/3, March 1915.

The party then moved with some difficulty west into the Urukh valley and south to Dsinago, the starting point for the Karagom Glaciers. A base camp was then established on the glacier's right moraine. Leaving this on 27 July, they moved up the right moraine of the North Karagom Glacier to a high camp at 2800m. On the 28th, keeping to the moraine, they attained the watershed ridge, where they climbed a rock-peak –Vologata (4180m) – by its south-west ridge. Retracing, they moved down to the col below the East Ridge of East Karagom peak (4513m). Although now rather late, they pressed on, and reached the peak without great difficulty, where they enjoyed a storm sunset over the great Bezingi peaks. 'I have seen nothing in my life to equal it,' wrote Raeburn. It was a formidable day's work, and they were out for just under 24 hours.[28]

---

[28] *SMCJ*, 13/76 (Feb 1915), 227; Raeburn, 'In the Caucasus—1914', *AJ*, 29/208 (May 1915), 142–58; Raeburn, 'The Adai-Khokh Group, Central Caucasus', *Geographical Journal*, 45/3 (Mar 1915), 181–99. Both articles are illustrated by

The huge Karagom Icefall, with the peaks of East and West Karagom to its left. Photo: Vittorio Sella, 1890 (detail), SMC Image Archive.

The final objective of the expedition was Laboda (4313m). Clinton Dent had visited Laboda in 1895 but reached only a subsidiary peak, Ziteli (4250m). Laboda lies at the head of the Stir-Digor valley, the most western tributary of the Urukh. The party made their way up the valley, camped on the Tana Glacier at 2500m, and on the following day, 1 August, found a way up to the upper glacier and followed the rocky East Buttress of Laboda to its summit. On the descent of the Stir-Digor and Urukh valleys they encountered rumours of war, and these were confirmed at Elchatova station. The party endured a long and complex journey through the Black Sea and Mediterranean, taking almost a month to return to England. Once safely in Italy, Raeburn travelled slowly home, stopping off in Venice, Milan (where he visited his friend and Caucasus explorer Vittorio Ronchetti), Zermatt (where he might have climbed had the weather been less atrocious), and Geneva.[29]

It was Raeburn's intention, and Freshfield's wish, that the Central Caucasus would become a second 'Playground of Europe', and his efforts in its eastern ranges would seem to have brought its Golden Age to a conclusion. The War and the Russian Revolution intervened, however, and that goal was never realised.

La Meije, 1919
The unclimbed West Ridge of the Meije had been a target of Raeburn's

---

Raeburn's excellent map of the district – an updated and annotated version of the Russian map.

[29] *SMCJ*, 13/76 (Feb 1915), 228.

since his first visit to the Dauphiné in 1904. He travelled out alone to attempt it in late August 1919, but discovered on arrival that the ridge had just received its first ascent by two young Grenoble climbers, Albert Plossu and Claudius Main. (Plossu, who had led throughout, was not yet 17.) So instead he planned a solo east–west traverse of the Meije, culminating in a descent of the new West Ridge route. Raeburn set off from La Grave for the Aigle hut on 12 September, but the night was stormy and he could not get away until 7 a.m. He traversed the Meije, arriving at the Pas de Chat at 3 p.m., and began to descend the West Ridge in deteriorating weather. As he put it, 'prudence and the hour now counselled' and he climbed back to the Pas de Chat and descended the normal route to the Promontoire Hut, reaching it at 5.50 p.m.[30]

Kangchenjunga Reconnaissances, 1920

Raeburn spent the period from mid-July until 9 October making two separate reconnaissances of approaches to Kangchenjunga. In the first of these his object was to descend to the Talung glacier from the Guicha La, investigate the south-east side of Kangchen and explore the Talung glacier. Delayed by rain in Darjeeling until 22 July, he set off accompanied by Col. H.W. Tobin, a Sherpa sirdar called Gyaljen, a cook and 21 porters; a camp was established at Alukthang in the Praig Chu valley on 1 August, and eight of the porters sent home. The party then moved over the Guicha La to camp on the meadows on the south side of the Talung glacier. After inspecting Kangchen from there, they went no further, but trekked down the Talung to Sakyong, arriving on the 9th, the last date of Tobin's leave. It is not clear whether they had planned to attempt any peak, but clearly they had not enough time to do so.

On 2 September Raeburn left Darjeeling again, with Colin G. Crawford. A support party of Gyaljen and 30 porters had gone ahead, with rendezvous planned for Yampung, which was reached on 6 September. On 10 September they reached Tseram, a former village above the snout of the Yalung glacier on its west side, now reduced to one deserted yak-hut at about 4000m, and half of the porters were sent home. Bad weather now kept them in camp for six days, and Crawford became unwell. The party then split, Gyaljen remaining at Tseram, while Crawford was taken down to Yengutang (about 2200m) to recuperate. By the 20th the weather and Crawford had both improved, and the party was once more united at Tseram on the 22nd. The Yalung glacier is long and twisting, and several camps were needed to reach its upper reaches. On the 30th, however, with Gyaljen and three booted porters, they camped on the upper glacier at about 6100m, approaching from its eastern flank, and sent the porters back. On 1 October Raeburn, Crawford and Gyaljen prospected up Kangchen for a further 300m, but 'were compelled to recognise that our European, coolie and food strength was inadequate to allow of any serious

[30] H. Raeburn, 'The Western Arête of the Meije', *AJ*, 33/221 (Nov 1920), 215–24.

attack'. The high point cannot have been far from the Crowley–
Guillarmod high point reached in 1905, and in a similar position.

The party then dropped down the Yalung to the point where an obvious
col on the eastern side, south of Little Kabru, appeared to offer a passage
over to the Rathong glacier. At 3.30 a.m. on the 4th Raeburn, Crawford
and three booted porters crossed the Yalung and set off up the central
moraine of the glacier leading to the Rathong col. An ice-fall was
successfully negotiated and the col (5200m) reached at 11.15. The
Rathong glacier was easily descended, and after a night near Dzongri they
marched to Pemionchi (Pemayangtse) on the 7th, arriving just ahead of
Gyaljen and the remaining porters, and the expedition returned to
Darjeeling on the 9th.[31]

Although Crawford and Raeburn achieved no better result than the 1905
expedition, they might have done so had they employed 230 porters, as
Guillarmod did. It is disgraceful that this expedition is consistently
overlooked in published histories of Kangchenjunga.[32] Raeburn's crossing
of the Rathong La was the first recorded, but he thought that it might well
have been an old route between Nepal and Sikkim. He suggested that
Little Kabru of the Garwood map should be renamed Rathong Peak
(6679m), and this name is used today. Crawford went on to enjoy a long
career in mountaineering, being on Everest in 1922 and 1933, and he died
aged 70 after hitting a six on the Rosemarkie cricket ground.[33] At any rate,
Raeburn's energy and drive in Sikkim in 1920 amply rebut the slanders
levelled at him at the time of the 1921 Everest Reconnaissance, and
thereafter, that he was too old to have been the climbing leader of that
expedition.

Accidents

On 27 February 1910, while Raeburn was belaying three people on the
North Face of Stùc a' Chroin, one fell off, pulled the others off, and then
pulled Raeburn off his stance. The others were uninjured but Raeburn,
who suffered the worst fall, was badly affected. Until I came across it in
Ling's diary, there was no current knowledge of his Stùc a' Chroin
accident. This accident seemed to be rather superficial at first (concussion,
broken ribs), but there were later abdominal complications. He wrote to
Geoffrey Young (13 May 1910):

> My accident though bad enough for me was less so thro' the actual
> injury than to the digestive troubles ensuing. It kept me six weeks on
> my back however and of course I am still very weak and not able to
> get about much. The place was not a definite climb was not difficult

---

[31] Raeburn, 'The Southerly Walls of Kangchenjunga and the Rathong Pass', *AJ*,
34/223 (Nov 1921), 33–50.

[32] A notable exception is Douglas Side's thoroughly researched history 'Towards
Kangchenjunga', *AJ*, 60/290 (May 1955), 83–95.

[33] Obituary by Noel Odell, *AJ*, 64/298 (1959), 280–82.

and only about 25 feet high. My injuries were caused more by the fearful jerk of 30 stones weight on the rope round my waist than by the fall.[34]

Despite this severe accident he then enjoyed a very productive Alpine season. But his obituarists, Ling and George Sang suggest that there were one or two other accidents.[35] He was more or less out of climbing for 21 months between January 1911 and September 1912, his only recorded expedition being his *Easy Route* on Ben Nevis (28 September 1911). The excellent *Scotsman* obituary (23 December 1926) is quite categorical about a second accident during this period, and it may be that there were more than one of them. Raeburn's absence from the fray in the Alpine season of 1911 is doubly regrettable, as it was a far better season for weather than any of those he had enjoyed with Ling or Walker.

On the 1921 Everest Reconnaissance he almost died from dysentery and sustained several falls from his horse on the way to rejoining the expedition, then stranded in the dead-end Kartha Valley. I think it likely that by the end of 1921 his body had been so battered about that his gut was more or less done for, and his psychiatric symptoms of suicidal depression may have distracted his doctors from dealing with his general physical condition.

Relations with Women: The Yovitchitch Sisters

Raeburn was certainly interested in women. He made many visits to Ladies Scottish Climbing Club meets, and frequently climbed with leading lights of that club, such as Mabel Inglis Clark (later Mabel Jeffrey), Lucy Smith, and of course his sister Ruth. For instance, in October 1904 he led 'a large and merry party' of three men and two ladies up Recess Route on the Cobbler, a route later credited to Jock Nimlin. And at Easter 1909 he organised a 13-strong mixed assault on Beinn an Dòthaidh. Two overlooked new routes were made that day – later credited to others as *Taxus* and *Stairway to Heaven*.[36]

In the Alps, Raeburn and Ling also climbed with women frequently, sometimes picking up hapless strangers for an off-day on the Petit Charmoz. For example, in 1905 they enjoyed an outing there with Hilda Hechle, a gifted artist, and in 1909 the Petit Charmoz and Aiguille de l'M were traversed with a Miss C.M. Campbell.[37]

His principal involvement, however, was with Natalia Yovitchitch, one of the four pretty daughters of Alexander Z. Yovitchitch, a Serbian

---

[34] *LD* **8**, 54–55; letter from Raeburn to Young, *Alpine Club Archives*.

[35] Obituary by Ling in *SMCJ*, 18/103 (Apr 1927), 26–31; Obituary by Sang in *F&RCCJ*, 7/2 (1926), 300–02.

[36] Cobbler – *SMCJ*, 9/49 (Jan 1906), 54–5; Beinn an Dòthaidh – *SMCJ*, 10/59 (May 1909), 271 & *SMCJ*, 10/60 (Sep 1909), 336–7; *LD* **7**, 80–3.

[37] with Miss Hechle – *SMCJ*, 9/49 (Jan 1906), 51–2; *LD* **5**, 38–9; with Miss Campbell – *SMCJ*, 11/61 (Feb 1910), 51–2; *LD* **8**, 23–4.

Happy faces at the Hotel Mont-Collon, Arolla, July 1910: Natalia Yovitchitch, Raeburn, Ruth Raeburn and Ling. Photo: SMC Image Archive.

diplomat. Despite their exotic names and appearance, they had a Scottish mother, descended from an Edinburgh boot-maker, and Natalia became an LSCC member after the War. She became ill in 1921, the same year as Raeburn's nemesis, and never recovered her health, dying in 1937. She is buried, or at least memorialized, in the Dean Cemetery.[38] Raeburn and Ling climbed in the Alps, Scotland and England with Natalia and the other sisters on numerous occasions between 1907 and 1910, and of course Raeburn may have had other dealings with her, not reported by Ling, and vice-versa. In 1910 Ling, Raeburn, Natalia and Ruth Raeburn were together for a week, climbing from Arolla, from the Bertol Hut and from Zermatt.[39]

It is certainly strange that Raeburn and Ling – both good-looking, rich men – went through life 'in want of a wife'.

---

[38] Ruth Raeburn supplied an obituary for Natalia in LSCC's *Annual Record* for 1937.

[39] *SMCJ*, 11/64 (Feb 1911), 238; *LD* **8**, 78–81.

Assessment

It goes without saying that Raeburn, so far as Scotland is concerned, was the greatest mountaineer of his age, perhaps of any age. But his determined efforts in Norway, the Alps, the Caucasus, and the Himalaya show him to have been a master of all forms of mountaineering. Among his close contemporaries, one might pick out Valentine Ryan and Geoffrey Young as achieving more in the Alps than Raeburn did. But they did it with guides – the Lochmatters and Josef Knubel – and did not stray much beyond the Mont Blanc ranges and the great peaks of the Pennine Alps, whereas Raeburn employed no guide after 1902, climbed in every major Alpine range except the Mischabel, and of course moved on to the Greater Ranges. Ryan and Young were perhaps too sybaritic to put up with the hardships of camp and expedition. Ryan led no pitch, and had his rucksack and ice-axe carried by his guides.[40] Young's enthusiasm was also dampened by the death of so many close friends in the mountains, and his career was cut short by his injury in the War. Lastly, Alexander Kellas should be considered. His record in the Himalaya in the Edwardian years, especially in Sikkim, was extraordinary, far surpassing that of any other European. He did not seek out difficulty, however, and his Alpine experience was limited. It seems to me that Raeburn's record stands up well to comparison with any of these.

---

[40] See the excellent biography of Ryan by Frank Nugent in his *In Search of Peaks, Passes & Glaciers: Irish Alpine Pioneers* (Cork: Collins Press, 2013), Chapter 11, 228–44.

ALMOST LOST AT SEA

by Tim Pettifer

THE MOST USEFUL TWO HOURS of religious education I ever received were from a *rinpoche*[1] from Lhasa. Buddhism never came into it, nor did Christianity nor any other worthwhile faiths. He simply explained that the world spun on the human need to treat everyone as you would like to be treated yourself. I maybe took this blurring of religions too deeply, and in following the demands of life I can easily swing between being a Christian or an atheist with Buddhism thrown in, and even being a pagan when I am working in the woods.

Wherever I am on the swingometer I always feel there is an afterlife. I say this with some confidence as I believe I have been as close as you can get and still be able to say I went there and came back. Others say they went further and that it is like a sudden, bright dazzling light just before being run over on an unlit, single-track road, walking home from the pub.

The concept of hell as being downward, where you permanently wear a midge hood, contrasts with the conventional, popular concept of heaven being up in the sun, where the good guys such as Martin Luther King, Lennon, Mother Teresa and Gandhi float about in fleecy cumulus against a perpetually blue sky. When my judgement day arrives I will need a packed lunch while it is decided if my life was spent on the right side of wrong or the wrong side of right.

I believe in the concepts of heaven and hell for good reason, but being adventurous I will take what comes, whereas some of my older friends as they reach late maturity have taken to studying a particular book with very small type at great length, especially on Sundays.

Drowning is a good way of glimpsing the afterlife. If you fall a long way, head-first from the top of a rock pinnacle, you only have a short time to think of the possibilities before *smack*! and you're dead. If you go in feet-first you might survive your body collapsing in on itself with lots of broken bones. There will be plenty of tears, pain and apologies for all the inconvenience you have caused. All your friends will rally round with lots of embellishments to the tale, whether they saw what happened or not. When it reaches that point you might think you will wish you were dead and not care if you go up or down. It doesn't work like that. Nature has provided all living things with the desire to fight on with whatever is left and for everything they can get, and it's called '**the survival instinct**'.

Drowning is different. Unless you have fallen a long way before hitting the water you will be pleased you learnt to swim at an early age, and as no one has yet learnt to fly you can see the difference from climbing. So there you are, shooting down a rapid with your life-jacket holding you up, or having just been swept off your feet crossing a swollen river or just

---

[1] *Rinpoche* is an honorific used for important teachers in the Tibetan tradition. It literally means 'precious jewel'.

gone over the rail of sinking boat. You have time to think and time to hope you can change the outcome. Which is when prayer comes in.

I have tried prayer four times. Twice I got the opposite to what I hoped for, and unreasonably reckoned there was not much future in the practice. Twice I was saved and twice I became seriously but only temporarily religious. This is known as '**battlefield syndrome**'.

In these situations emergency survival gear is a great bonus as it provides extra time to think it through, while you discover it's not performing as well you imagined it would. This is more to do with your expectations as such gear is only capable of delaying the inevitable, but even so you won't regret the effect on your overdraft, which went into emergency mode when you bought it all.

Hanging on to the bows of an upturned canoe halfway across the lower reaches of the Firth of Clyde was a good time to calculate the worth of my investment in a state-of-the-art life-jacket that was struggling to stop my head passing through the nearly vertical crests of waves big enough for it to appear calm in the troughs. But being afloat all was not lost, and hope sprang eternal in my heart and the bells rang, because coming from the south was a ferry appearing and disappearing as the life-jacket and its cargo went up and down the waves.

I was not expecting it to stop for a lone canoe, but the investment had included three flares and given such a unique opportunity could not be wasted. The first produced nil response; the second flare looked like it was ignored; and the third flare looked to be a direct hit, with all passengers and crew joining me in the sea; but luckily it missed and unluckily was missed by all on board, it being a mini-flare and more like a flying spark.

Then I noticed how beautiful the skies were. The sun was just coming from behind the perfect cumulo-nimbus clouds and I sensed there was something called God up there in the heavens. Not beneath my feet where I must admit were many fathoms of water but very definitely up there.

I asked for help, promising all sorts of pledges to my young family and a one-week-old baby daughter. But God helps those who help themselves, which accurately describes the scramble for school dinners during the long and hungry coalminers' strikes. So the message was clear and loud: leave the canoe and swim.

And two hours later I dragged myself onto the shore. Standing clear of the seas the wind froze the marrow in my bones, but Allah's providence arrived just when it was most needed. At the back of the beach a small fire, lit to clear the gorse, was coming to its smoky end, and it was a heaven-sent opportunity to beat the hypothermia. Lying in the warm ashes I was restored to life all too quickly when my top-of-the-range cagoule went up in flames.

The English have never been fully understood anywhere in the world, least of all in Scotland, and you must appreciate the patience of the farmer, who on responding to a knock on his door on a quiet, sunny Sabbath was

'I asked for help...'   Sketch: Finlay Morrison

looking at a nearly drowned man in a melted jacket covered in ashes. However, he was an understanding fellow and I eventually got the use of a phone and I could proudly report to the world a deliverance from the other side.

'My God, I am lucky to be alive!' Now this is a very common exaggeration. It can be used to describe a heavy night's drinking with your worst friends, and the withering comments of your partner the next morning and of the staff when you arrive 30 minutes late with the office keys on a wet morning. It takes on a different meaning after the NHS have very professionally saved your life and repaired many of your most important bones. You then realise just what a wonderful caring organization it is, and that you do actually have a future. Your heart and thanks go out to your lifesavers and you know there is so much more to life than chasing money, or chasing just enough money to be able to enjoy yourself doing something very silly and ending up where you are.

You might think you are a waster and your time going forward will be better spent helping others. You might also want to actually thank God and seek a suitable religion. Some have done this with great success but for most it's soon back to business as usual, though with significantly more caution because they now realise that believing 'it won't happen to me' means that it more certainly will.

The young can be very good at ignoring the experience of their elders. But the best of the young watch and learn, and they reach the highest levels of their own achievement by applying the highest levels of personal skill and fitness, so they come back with the experience to go one step further and possibly go where none have gone before.

Going there runs considerable risk. Which brings us to a most interesting state of mind, '**the superhero**'. You can go to the ends of the earth or the bottom of the sea and reach the skies and beyond, and the achievement will be more remembered if you arrive home as damaged goods or don't come back at all, even if you haven't achieved much. This is all about the media and the public, who believe it must be hard if the outcome is a disaster. How the hero struggled back from not achieving the impossible dream has always more media appeal than a perfectly planned and executed success.

If the outcome was a disaster and the objective was worthless then it was very stupid and all such things should be banned. Going over Niagara Falls in a barrel is banned, but the media will love you for it and will ask anyone who has met you in the last ten years for a comment. Anyone running the London Marathon in a furry Paddington Bear suit should be banned if it brings on a heart attack but given a gong if they raise £100k for charity. Pushing a piano up Ben Nevis should not be banned if students or nurses do the pushing but definitely banned for over 65s because they should know their station and be at home watching the grandkids watching Bear Grylls, who is living proof it does not pay to be modest if you want to be believed.

How fast, how far, how high does not always equate to fame. Eddie the Eagle, the ski-jumper, finished last in the 70m and 90m 1988 World Championship events, and landed himself worldwide media coverage and more column inches than the gold, silver and bronze medal winners combined could ever hope to jump. This was a definite 'no-no' so the sport introduced the 'Eddie The Eagle Rule,' which changed the course of Olympic history and did everything needed to preserve his name in the hall of fame for all time.

Before giving up the day-job remember that stereotyping and public image are important, and you will get more press coverage if you are young and good-looking and speak well. Joe Brown, the charismatic, climbing plumber, was well known but never really cut the ice because of his north of England accent until he had achieved twice as much as anyone else. The Brits want their heroes ideally to come from public schools and preferably be in uniform. The Royals are aware of this and quickly become colonels, generals and commanders-in-chief with a chestful of medals.

Your PR machine needs to know the important of appearance if you want to be remembered. Climbing down the drain-pipe of a blazing building with an old lady over your shoulder will make the back page if you're in pyjamas but the front page if wearing breathing apparatus and a fireman's uniform. Similarly, no matter how many lone sorties he had flown in the Battle of Britain, no one would have become a superhero climbing out of a Spitfire looking like Jimi Hendrix.

If you are not quite at the top of your media game, don't dismiss the idea of becoming a superhero as a profession. The careers of many superheroes prospered greatly after their latest plan was derailed, even though the plan did not include the holy grails of holy grails – Everest or the Poles. They do very well even without any more derailments, but how long the lecture tours last depends on the quality of the derailment, the length of the book and who plays the lead part in the follow-up film. This is a once-in-a-lifetime opportunity, because after a second derailment your personal brand development will die an early death if the media decide to typecast you as merely mad and 'should be banned'.

Better still ensure that your career pathway includes Everest and a make-over, and use your delicate footwork, strength and balance to great effect on *Strictly*, but don't 'break a leg' and thus destroy the rough, tough, no-holds-barred image of climbers for all time.

For ordinary mortals it's sport at our personal cutting edge, controlling our perception of danger to feel '**life force**' running thick and fast through the body and mind. The excitement, the challenge, the risk, and knowing the true simplicity of being alive.

Those who can go the furthest are the champions and have earned the right to some cash and to know the very essence of adventure itself. Long may they prosper, pay their PAYE and never see A&E.

The Buachaille.
Watercolour: John
Mitchell.

FAR FROM HERE
Lines written from London in lockdown

... the Buachaille was less clogged with the pollutions of mortality than is normally granted to an earthly form.
— W.H. Murray, 'Mountaineering in Scotland' (1947)

Alone above a moor of lochs · bogs · boulders
a patchwork of greens · browns · greys draped over granite
there stands a stupa · a pyramid · a cone beyond the dreams of Euclid
a cathedral of stone · its pillars in parallel

      a random miracle of rhyolite.

Hard as bone · older than the first mammal
Buachaille Etive Mòr · the Great Herdsman of Etive
keeps his counsel · watching indifferently over the land.
The black hill cattle he once tended are gone
the people he cupped in his hand are gone.
Now sheep and deer graze his flanks · frogs and adders

      lurk in his grasses.

The lower slopes are home to mosses
marsh orchids · bog asphodel · bog myrtle · bog cotton
butterwort · sundew · tormentil · thyme –

      time's losses.

I first slept beneath the Herdsman's care when I was six
camped on a damp bank of tussocks backed by birches
above the place ringed with rocks and alders where
Coupall and Etive intertwine then run together to the loch below the glen
where Deirdre and her lover hid from Conchobar and his jealous rage.
The idyll ended for Deirdre in sorrow

      but not for us.

Camping when I was six meant the treat of Sugar Puffs for breakfast
picnics of hard-boiled eggs · packets of crisps with twists of salt
Dairylea Triangles smeared on Ryvita · suppers of Spam and Cadbury's
    Smash
puddings of Angel Delight · tinned prunes · tinned peaches
then a hard bed on the groundsheet · pullover for a pillow
the river gushing and bubbling us to sleep
all mixed with midges and raindrops pattering on the flysheet

the distant calls of cuckoos.

I would have been scared sleepless had I known
the Etive takes its name from *Èiteag*
a local sprite too small · too horrid for description
or that the glen is haunted by a *fàchan*
a creature with one hand out of his chest
with one leg out of his haunch · with one eye out of his face.
The Great Herdsman kept both at bay
left them roaming far from where I lay
in the late grey light of a midsummer night

      while willow warblers sang.

Five years later we returned.
In China Mao's Cultural Revolution began · by us as yet unnoticed.
Instead we thrilled to the march of progress of mother's campsite cooking.
And so we dined exotically on freeze-dried Vesta Chow Mein with
    noodles

      a sachet of soy sauce on the side.

This time we climbed the Herdsman in sun and black school shoes
scrambling up the rocks and heather on his southern side
beyond the Allt Clach nan Gillean · the stream of the stone of the young
    men.
From the summit we looked down to a thin busy ribbon
the A82 · incalculably far below the northeast face
where the broken-backed spine of Crowberry Ridge

      launched itself out into space.

I wondered then whether I would ever put on a rope and find the faith
to climb the mountain that improbable way.

      I did

by walls and ribs and fissures · grooves and steps and ledges
slabs and ramps and chimneys
all that remains of the lava that fountained and flowed like liquid flame
from the great Glen Coe volcano

      millions and millions of years ago.

The lava cooled to fine-grained reddish rhyolite

later plucked and scoured as glaciers passed
split and shattered as water froze and thawed.

I returned again and again to this ruin of geological time,
this remnant of a burning world
to Murray's *most splendid of earthly mountains* –
in summer warmth · in autumn snow · in springtime rain · in winter ice
in storm and shadow · sunlight · moonlight · torchlight
in dusk and dawn and dark · in joy and fear

anxiety and calm.

Ten years ago we scattered our parents' ashes
at the Herdsman's foot · not far from where we'd camped as kids.
They had been wise · but now they'd left
and we were there to try to plumb

an unfathomable loss.

Drizzle fell · a chill wind whipped their dust into our eyes
clouds folded and unfolded far above us
round Crowberry Gully and the Rannoch Wall.

Now far from there where my heart and past both sleep
I sing with Duncan Ban MacIntyre improvising in his exile
I long to be on the Buachaille thigh-deep in snow.[1]
In my mind's eye I look up from a sheep-cropped sward by the river
long after the sun has set · staring higher then still higher
at Crowberry Tower · a stark black thumb
a silhouette against the fading yellow of the sky
perhaps a jagged angel

or a funeral pyre.

It promises me silently I will return
vouchsafes a vision · a memory of warmth

a memory of fire.

---

[1] *Is truagh nach robh mi 'm Buachaill Eitidh*
Gu h-aird na sleisde anns an t-sneachd ann ...
Duncan Ban MacIntyre (Donnchadh Bàn Mac an t-Saoir, 1724–1812),
extemporizing in Edinburgh. The poet, better known for his *In Praise of Ben
Dorain*, added that he wished every citizen of that city would follow behind him
barefoot. The lines are quoted in Ian Mitchell, *Scotland's Mountains before the
Mountaineers* (Luath Press, 1988).

Ian Crofton (right) with his three older sisters beneath the Buachaille in 1961.
Photo: John Crofton.

Ian Crofton
8 June 2020

GROT ON GARBH BHEINN

by Phil Gribbon

TRICKLES OF ICY WATER were streaming down the buttress and draining away all feeling from our hands. Blobs of soggy snow-gunge were falling on the faint bumps and hollows rippling on the big slab, and were melting as soon as they fell. A wandering shower laced with cold, unwelcome, sleety rain had come drifting from nowhere and was dropping its unpleasantness on us.

It had become traditional to camp in early May on the level ground beside the river. The venue was most advantageously placed, a mere stroll from the old road, and had genuine natural camping qualities: it was unexploited, tidy and rubbish-free, with nearby little shallow pools for water sports where paddlers could potter, and there was sufficient dead gorse at hand to allow a wee fire to amuse any little folk in the evening gloaming. Up the glen was the curving flank of the mountain, shielding its high ridges with their grey bright walls rising above broken terraces that had been formed where the slabs curled back downwards towards the core of Garbh Bheinn. All across its shoulder was a liberal scattering of bare, exposed, pockied patches, scraped into the light of day on the bedrock. It made a hostile home – too steep, if decorative and abrupt, to grasp and hold all the world – where life struggled to exist on the unforgiving downward plunge of the mountain. It doesn't need saying that the climbing potential of such pretty little rocky surface-samplers was nigh on zilch.

Why was the weather being so uncooperative? Yesterday had been quite perfect; it had been like spring, with the bright sun warming the dry rock, and the birch trees down in the dip showing the first tinges of green. A cuckoo had been plaintively summoning a breeding partner, and its monotonous call had filtered metronomically through the glen. We were free now to recall and interpret its double-call syllables as a derogatory but appropriate comment on our present ludicrous situation. Nonetheless our behaviour continued to be irrational and ill-advised; we should reconsider hanging around perched on a miserable cliff waiting for the day to improve.

However, in spite of having nothing to do David and I clung on, leaning back to the wall, watching and waiting, to see what our dedicated, chosen, sharp-end man would decide. This was Grot, with the pet name that his pals used invariably and without causing rancour on his part. He had drawn the proverbial short straw to work out a route; and while the normal summer route, as we knew it, went on tip-toes up the centre of today's streaming slab, he had to go some other way; but for the moment he stood impassively at the end of the narrow ledge that defined the base of the slab. His only choice would be the thin, insignificant crack line that proceeded up the rock adjacent to the slab. It was all so wet that we hoped this could persuade him to give up and call it a day before it had even begun. We said nothing, but just slouched on the ledge – two damp disconsolate hang-dogs.

Yes, the crack might provide some succour if he was going to persist with this folly. We just had to wait and imagine we were somewhere else. We offered no advice, because who were we to dissuade our leader? It was his choice. We were mere appendages who had to follow his lead, if there ever was to be one, or alternatively we could set another outcome and reverse down our ledge, untie and slink back to the comfort of our tents and have a cup of tea and a good consoling dram, all in spite of it being indecently early in the day.

Unfortunately the mist was wishing to begin to disperse. The snow blobs that had landed on the rock had long since melted and had turned into its unwelcome wet trickle draining down the crack and dripping off its slightly overhanging start. With improving visibility we could now make out where the crack curved back to reach the terrace above. It still looked a long pitch. We carefully studied our leader as he made some tentative gestures and thrust his hand and fingers at the trickle and the chilly rock. Carefully he placed a boot where there might be a foothold and stepped up; he was committed. We couldn't back out now. Ever so cautiously and slowly, Grot silently kept going with neither a whimper nor a word of complaint.

Perhaps that was what I had to expect from a hardy sailing man who was given to unplanned epic voyages and fraught situations. I well knew of this because, although once I had crewed on his cramped little lively one in perfect weather, I had also experienced sudden incipient disaster that only terminated with us both looking wide-eyed at each other and still trembling. This had been the moment when Grot slid his hand behind the panelling to produce a half-bottle of unopened Black Rum; his emergency moment had come upon us, and moved on. Now, at last, the skipper could decree that after many moons hiding in the dark the bottle could see the light of day, and the world was free to sniff its beneficence. He had unscrewed the cap and we had taken a couple of good, contemplative slugs of his ancient firewater. *Ah, quelle bliss!*

I was glad I had not been that unwitting crewman who (having been persuaded to come for the ride more than anything else) was with him in heavy seas on the boundless Atlantic Ocean, and off a tiny island called Inishtrahull off the coast of Ireland, when the tiller linked to the rudder had shattered. Having jury-rigged its replacement, Grot had then endured thirty and six or more sleepless hours at the helm, limping imperceptibly into sheltered waters on the Donegal coast. All was ample proof that Grot was the stoical type for whom a few minutes navigating up a frigid sopping wet crack in Ardgour was nae problem.

David and I watched as gradually and steadily he gained height. His gear was in short supply and what little he had was of little use. His hunched silhouette slowly diminished as he gained height, and occasionally he paused to consider what he might do next and then he did it. Our team was in a manner of speaking doing it, even if there remained the sting in the tail for a couple of chilled ledge-lurkers to follow in pursuit of our hero.

My pal was next on line. It was our moment of truth, to disclose how relatively soft we were on the Grot resilience scale. David reluctantly forced himself to begin, but quickly stopped to tuck his fingers into his oxters, searching for a womb of warmth. Did this make much difference? No, it was abysmal low-temperature stuff all the way, much finger-suffering without relief until strangely it all seemed better when every sensation had vanished. It all had to be accepted because again we had no option. Away and well up there he paused, and bending agonisingly over he gave an unsettling, mournful, inhuman sound from the depths of his being – a long, deep moan of abject abandonment and martyrdom endured – and then with the comfortable security of the rope he arrived thankfully at the terrace. We had proved nothing except what we already knew: that Grot was a hard man and impervious to the cruel slings and arrows of outrageous routes. My own performance was to be little better, and that is how I know how David felt, and so the less said…

Perhaps this endurance test should have called forth a mind-over-matter transformation. Pretend it isn't happening. Escape from your own personal demons. Convince yourself that you are somewhere else. Was this adventure with Grot just one more moment of innocent pleasure? Really?

Now, years on, some moments of perfect pleasure can drift back to squeeze away that terrible crack on Garbh Bheinn. For the searing agony of that line, try substituting some joyful moments sailing with Grot.

We were moving imperceptibly up the Sound of Sleat between Knoydart and the Isle of Skye. Up there, so high and seemingly distant, the sun-brightened ridge of Beinn Sgritheall dominated the skyline. The wind was hardly noticeable, and could do no more than think of leisurely ruffling the edge of the sail; the sea was asleep, soothed as if by a magical oil spread across its mirror surface; the only sound was a faint ripple of water caressing the side of the yacht, as we moved ever so slowly along the sound, sailing on to places unknown.

Grot was dozing in the cockpit; there was nothing else to do. I was lounging flat on the deck, head hanging over the side, gazing at the water mirroring my face. In those days I was a pipe-smoker, and a gentle blue smoke-trail showed that we were moving, just and no more. Then somehow my pipe jumped from my lightly gripping teeth and plopped into the water. Okay, lean over and pick it up. I tried but missed it by millimetres. That's funny, try again, but with the same result. Come on, be serious. I was, but it was futile, because ever so imperceptibly my sentimentally loved pipe was bobbing astern. Off, like us, to shores unknown.

We all have good days and bad days. To accept both is equally valuable.

Store them up in the memory banks to be paraded when needed. Who knows when that will be?

Drifting along on this sun-baked day was ideal. When I got home I knew she would be pleased to learn that the smelly old pipe had departed and I would be spared from gobs of goo sucked onto my palate.

On the dripping sleet-soaked slab linking these tiers I waited, and then it was my turn to experience the ordeal. First though, dream pleasantly of the days of summer. Good old Grot!

CRACK ADDICT

by Olly Stephenson

WHERE TO GET HELP for drugs? A GP is a good place to start. They can discuss your problems and may offer you treatment at the practice or refer you to your local drug service. If you're not comfortable talking to a GP, you can approach your local drug-treatment service yourself.

Treatment is not without risks – dangers include mums with jogging prams, cyclists, and coxed-four rowing boats. The Crack itself is so intense it generates cosmic levels of bruising, with the backs of addicts' hands quickly rivalling those of street fighters, forcing them to restrict their consumption to just two sessions a week. Leptosirosis (Wcil's disease) is an additional risk, but it's often seen as a good thing by addicts, a potential release from the vice-like grip of this habit.

My name is Olly, I'm a Crack addict, and this is my story.

It all began in the latest Lockdown (No 3), which commenced in Scotland on 24 December 2020 and lasted four months, with virtually everything closed, draconian restrictions on movement, gatherings banned, facemasks mandatory, and all sorts of other controls in place to slow the spread of the Covid-19 virus. Much of this will seem incredible to future generations reading this story, but I can assure you it felt equally remarkable living through it too.

Exercise is restricted to starting and finishing in your local authority area which, when living in Edinburgh, never feels much of a restriction as it includes some of the best ski-touring of my life, on the coveted Pentland Skyline (>30km distance, >2300m ascent), together with plenty of bike rides, runs, swims and wild camping all on our doorstep.

The only thing lacking is inspiring local climbing, constrained at this time of year by the typically cold and damp conditions and the paucity of good rock within the boundaries of Edinburgh itself. By chance, however, and within a few weeks of the latest Lockdown starting, a goal emerges that is on my doorstep and is seriously addictive. It's just ten metres in length, probably less than all the words in this story strung together, but like the best addictions it imparts some truly memorable and life-affirming experiences.

To set the scene, picture yourself walking along a canal, in this case the Union Canal at Meggetland in Edinburgh. Joggers, cyclists and rowers hurry past as you gaze upwards at a nondescript road-bridge spanning the water above your head. The underside of this is scored like giant corduroy into half a dozen parallel roof-cracks, formed by the intervening and massive concrete beams. One crack is just about wide enough for a hand-jam: it is 10m long, and was first climbed by Robbie Phillips at the start of the original Lockdown to create *The Troll Toll*, E5,6b. Since then it has only had a handful of repeats and presumably a larger number of swims in the canal.

I'm an average climber who only just scraped into the SMC, and I feel a bit of a fraud even writing this story, but Lockdown No 3 seems the perfect opportunity to throw myself at the challenge. Problems encountered along the way include the fact that I'm weak, I'm rubbish at climbing parallel roof-cracks, I've not climbed anything even remotely at this grade for more than 30 years, and that *The Troll Toll* is just plain hard.

Training for it covers much of what I most enjoy about climbing – an inspiring line, setting a goal and working towards it, embracing the small steps forward and the lurches backwards, the intersection of physical and mental challenge, the movement – and best of all, the fact that I can share this obsession or addiction with two of my children, Jack (19) and Bella (16), who also climb.

We begin our training at a similar bridge at Murrayfield known as 'the Crack Den', with the advantage that there are lots of climbable cracks here (again, all roof-cracks, set in the underside of a bridge), and they are only 1.5m above a concrete floor. All these climbs rely on hanging upside-down suspended entirely on hand and foot jams in smooth, parallel, featureless, concrete cracks: if strength departs, it gets too painful, or any of your jams rip, you instantly fall out. The width of each crack is somewhere between a flat and a flexed hand (i.e. less than a fully clenched fist) and varies by 1cm or 2cm along its length, meaning the jams are consistently pumpy and go from quite challenging to desperate (or *vice versa*) depending on hand size and technique.

On any level Jack and Bella are completely kicking my 52-year-old ass with their climbing prowess, and I was a sorry mess trying to keep up with them, but they are patient as they transform from crack novices to crack heroes in just a couple of sessions. Meanwhile my 'I'll get this in a few sessions' optimism morphs into quiet resignation, as weeks and then two months of effort fly by with glacial progress; but I'm enjoying learning something new, and can feel the addiction taking hold.

I am possibly the only person in Scotland worrying that Lockdown will be eased too soon, specifically before I complete my self-imposed goal of *The Troll Toll*. Training continues on the easiest roof-crack at Murrayfield. Readers who have experienced the joys of crack climbing in places like Yosemite will know that 'easy' is relative: bronzed American locals routinely solo such climbs before breakfast while we Brits are on them from dawn to – well – benightment. And the guidebook mocks our siege warfare by assigning a grade of 'only' 5.9 (HVS), and all of this on cracks that are merely vertical.

Back to Murrayfield, and the easy route I'm training on is itself called *Lockdown*. It's a 20m-long roof-crack graded 5.11d (E4/5), and was first done by the bronzed local American crack-legend and Edinburgh resident, Andy Hein – in summary, not exactly a warm-up for someone like me. However, after a few sessions I'm making progress and can reliably hang upside down and sustain the jams all the way along it to about 18m. It's very pleasing to see the progress, but frustrating that the crack narrows at this point and I just can't seem to complete the final 2m. Several times I get close, touching the finishing wall with one foot, then hanging entirely on narrow hand-jams as I slowly pivot my hips and ease the second foot around, inching closer ... but then falling off as I try to touch the wall with my second foot, hands too bruised to continue, arms too tired to hold my weight, lungs bursting as if I've just emerged from a three-minute free dive. Exasperation oozes from every pore as the route only counts when both feet touch, and my children are almost in tears too just watching my efforts. Meanwhile they are lapping *Lockdown* (the climb): 'Come on Dad, keep up.'

On the plus side I am so rubbish that this really is a learning bonanza: crack gloves for example (what a godsend); stiff boots with low-profile toes to twist into the crack better; taping your thumbnail to prevent the quick blowing open under all the pressure; lots of small cuts that only heal with Savlon ... . I could go on. Family breakfast chat often involves each of us tapping the jamming bruises on the backs of our hands like karate black-belts: 'Hmm, it's still really sore, but I should be ready for more crack tomorrow.' My Crack addiction has become all-consuming.

A small local crack-climbing scene forms, and other addicts are very generous in their advice, the consensus invoking a trick called FLF, to be deployed at the point of maximum exhaustion and pain, the first two words being *fight* and *like*.

After about six weeks' effort I am consistently making it to 18.5m on *Lockdown*, but still unable to reach the very end. By trial, error, and (frankly) desperation, I discover that headphones and loud music provide a small but noticeable boost. On my next attempt I reach 19m, biceps, lungs and eyeballs all exploding, hands as flaccid and sore as rashers of bacon – and all of this now collectively hardwired in my brain to equal imminent failure, like some sort of cruel Pavlovian torture – but at the final nanosecond I remember FLF, and do the most un-British thing imaginable. It feels as if there is literally nothing else left for me to try.

I let out my very first ever power scream.

Passers-by stop and stare. Mothers clutch their children tightly. Momentarily I feel very self-conscious and stupid. I worry I'm making a scene, that I'll be kicked out of the SMC. But thankfully the music is so loud I can't hear anything, and all such negativity vaporises instantly.

And by way of full disclosure, it's actually two power screams. The shame of it. You may have heard them. Anyway, each one gives a jolt of adrenalin that is precisely equal – no more, no less – to allowing each foot to touch the finishing wall in turn, thereby completing the climb, before the dying picoseconds of hand-jam depart and I slump to the boulder mat in utter and unadulterated ecstasy.

It feels as if an elephant has been walking up and down my hands and feet for the last three minutes, but like the best climbing experiences I quickly forget the pain and instead am able to replay the route in my mind's eye for several days thereafter (minus the power screams, which being British I edit out), leaving a very profound sense of satisfaction.

Lockdown is sufficiently hard for me that it takes another week of effort just to repeat it, during which time I on-sight two further 20m 5.11d roof-cracks at Murrayfield. It transpires that hand size and technique really are key to this game, and I'm better suited to the wider hand-jamming cracks – who would have guessed?

Meanwhile Robbie Phillips and Andy Hein both warn me to 'get comfortable on the thin cracks at Murrayfield before you attempt *The Troll Toll*,' as the latter is over the canal and generally thought harder than *Lockdown*. I ignore all of this, which is perhaps why my first attempt ends in the canal.

The Troll Toll is higher off the ground and feels more committing the instant you commence hand-jamming and pull your feet up into the crack. The jams start out painfully narrow, meaning the hand-jams are poor and your toes are scarcely in the crack, so you are constantly on the cusp of falling like a sack of coal, landing on your back on the hard concrete lip of the canal 2.5m below. The roof-crack then widens over the middle of the canal to 'comfortable' (a relative term when you're hanging upside down entirely on hand- and foot-jams), and then back to sustained thin hands to finish, with the very real prospect of falling out again and smacking your head on the opposite edge of the canal. This is all done ropeless, or solo, as it's quicker and each second counts.

On the plus side I am still learning, and my first attempt at *The Troll Toll* teaches me that the canal is neck-deep in places, which is good, but the water itself is possibly even more infectious than a race-meeting at Cheltenham at the start of the pandemic. The joys and stench of knee-deep sludge probably won't be mentioned in future editions of the

The Troll Toll: seconds from a swim on the first attempt. Photo: Mary Harvey.

climbing guide, and I discover that emerging from it like a swamp monster causes something of a stir amongst the locals. But luckily no contact with jogging prams, cyclists, rowing boats, or leptospirosis thus far.

Tail between my legs, I resume training at Murrayfield. Mentally it all feels a bit hard, to be honest, and I struggle to repeat *Lockdown*. I start to lose excitement and belief in ever doing *The Troll Toll*.

And then a small miracle appears. Specifically, a calendar reminder pops up on my computer at work. In a week's time it will be my second anniversary of completing chemo. The realisation dawns that I can use the anniversary to expedite and turbo-charge my second attempt at *The Troll Toll*, and I start to tell a few friends to ratchet up the commitment.

It feels far too soon to make any further training gains at Murrayfield, and instead my next *Troll Toll* attempt will have to be based entirely on an improved mental approach – focusing on how lucky I am simply to be alive, how life-affirming it is to be back to health and doing stuff like this again, to be sharing experiences like this with my kids – hell, getting to the end doesn't even matter anymore, it'll be a memorable way to mark the day regardless of the outcome.

On 15 April 2021, my second anniversary of completing six rounds of chemo, surviving Stage 4 cancer and much more besides, I'm standing on the south side of the Union Canal at Meggetland, 90% certain I'm destined for another swim, but open to whatever the next few minutes bring.

I'm feeling that intoxicating mix of excitement and nerves, as if I am about to go on stage, but remain focused and calm as my hands reach into the roof-crack above. I squeeze hard on the jams, the concrete pressing like a vice, tensing my core to pull my body up, and twisting the tips of my toes into the crack.

The Troll Toll: seconds from success on the second attempt. Photo: Hugo Tay.

The timer on a three-minute fuse has just been lit. I know from all my training that a single second longer and I will lose all strength and fall out. I'm aware of every wisp of breeze, and enter that delicious state of focus and calm that only comes to the fully committed.

I'm hanging upside down like a bat, suspended entirely by hands and feet jamming into the underside of a bridge-crack, shuffling along as fast as I can. It's evidently not a very common sight, as mums with jogging prams stop and stare, cyclists ring their bells and cheer, and the crew of a rowing boat beneath me pause their stroke, jaws agape. The crack widens over the middle of the canal, which brings some respite, but the fuse continues to burn quickly, and I'm aware of every second as I battle along the crack for the sustained fight at the end. Muscles are flashed and I'm on the brink of imminent failure, a few desperate grunts issuing involuntarily (it's far too public for full FLF power screams) and sending a small ripple of concern through the crowd, but thankfully I avoid another swim, or worse still landing on top of them.

After precisely 10m I drop my feet, release my hand-jams, and step on to the tow path on the north side of the canal. Exhausted. Elated.[1]

It feels like a great way to celebrate my second chemo anniversary and simply being alive, how lucky I am. The NHS should prescribe this to all Crack addicts.

---

[1] A video clip of the author on *The Troll Toll* can be downloaded from this Dropbox link <tinyurl.com/pb9pupdm>. Retrieved 9 September 2021. – Hon. Ed.

THE SCOTTISH MOUNTAIN PAINTINGS
OF D.Y. CAMERON

by Donald Orr

DAVID YOUNG CAMERON WAS BORN in Glasgow in June 1865. A son of the manse, he was educated at Glasgow Academy and from 1881 attended Glasgow School of Art, where his outstanding ability at drawing was immediately obvious. Later he enrolled at the Trustees' Academy in Edinburgh in 1885 where his incisive skill in line drawing, noted as a precocious virtuosity, was directed into etching and engraving. This pursuit created many landscape and architectural subjects of a very fine quality and saw him elected an Associate of the Royal Society of Painter-Etchers (R.E.) in 1889 and a Fellow of the R.E. in 1895, being regarded as 'the most brilliant etcher of his generation'.[1] His paintings and watercolour sketches of landscape and architectural subjects of this period were partly influenced by the Glasgow School of painters who flourished during the two final decades of the nineteenth century. At that time Glasgow was the scene of a remarkable outburst of creative activity, not only in painting as architecture and the applied arts came to the fore particularly through the Art Nouveau movement and the work of Charles Rennie Mackintosh.

The group of Glasgow painters were dissatisfied with the romantic, picturesque, and sentimentally anecdotal paintings produced by their immediate elders. A new realism was the aim that they adopted, together with a rejection of the academic finish, the mainstay of the Scottish and English painters of the day. It can be seen in much of Cameron's early work that these attitudes were already instinctive and being implemented by him. Alongside this the Glasgow group displayed a growing animosity to the Royal Scottish Academy who, at that time, tended to ignore all artists not residing in Edinburgh. While the exact relationship of each artist within the group is difficult to ascertain, what can be seen is that by 1884 most of the members had studios in Glasgow around the West Regent Street & Bath Street area. Their work is defined by strong compositions, confident brushwork and a naturalism or realism sensed in the French plein air painting of the Barbizon School. This loose association of painters worked at Barbizon near Fontainebleau, and strove to elevate landscape from being a mere background for mythical or romantic scenes to a subject in its own right. Although greatly interested in the qualities of light and a looseness of handling, they were the precursors of Impressionism as their work demonstrates no concern for the translation of light into colour but with the accurate rendering of coloured tones. The Glasgow School adopted these attitudes, worked throughout Scotland, had strong ties to the New English Art Club, and

---

[1] W.R. Hardie, *The Glasgow Boys*, Part 1 (Scottish Arts Council, 1968), p. 7.

gained international fame in Europe, being associated with the Viennese Secessionist movement. Of the school of Glasgow painters Cameron 'was the only one of the group to look to the Highlands'.[2]

In 1899 Cameron and his wife moved to Kippen near Stirling where they resided for the rest of their lives, although they did own a house in London. His studio afforded him views of Ben Lomond, and this open aspect may have been a contributing factor to his greater focus on Scottish landscape subjects and a more natural treatment of colour as he moved away from the more decorative style favoured by the Glasgow School.

His prints were hugely popular, specialising again in landscape and architectural themes, and produced in small editions that were eagerly sought after and commanded high prices. His inventiveness as a painter saw more dramatic contrasts of light and a naturalness of colour in his canvases, which made a marked comparison to the romantic portrayals of Highland scenery by earlier Scottish landscape painters. By 1907 Cameron was producing landscapes devoid of people and dominated by hills. 'The Eildon Hills' (Stirling) and 'Criffel' (Edinburgh City Art Centre), both of that year, reveal 'Cameron increasingly turning to the landscape of Scotland for his inspiration'.[3] This placed him firmly within the Scottish landscape tradition established by Nasmyth, Knox and McCulloch where he pursued a natural non-decorative style – the only one of the Glasgow School to follow this format. He developed a controlled and refined handling in his paintings, relying on strong composition and natural colour rather than picturesque detail or atmospheric renderings of weather conditions. He avoided the spectacular rock formations and extreme weather circumstances, preferring to capture the stillness and character of the locality. Minor and insignificant details were eliminated from his work and an austere beauty was established. What he sought to do was express the breadth and splendour of the Scottish landscape, whether it was the stark magnificence of 'The Hill of The Winds'[4] or the complex topography of 'The Wilds of Assynt'[5] which marked the striking contrast to the romantically charged Highland scenery depicted by many Victorian painters.

The following examples form a spectrum of his work, an indication of what can be found in public galleries around the country.

---

[2] B. Smith, *D.Y. Cameron – The Vision of the Hills* (Edinburgh: Atelier Books, 1992), 68–9.

[3] B. Smith, *op. cit.*, p. 68.

[4] 'The Hill of The Winds'; 1913, oil on canvas, 46×53cm. National Gallery of Scotland.

[5] 'The Wilds of Assynt'; 1936, oil on canvas, 102×128cm. Perth Museum & Art Gallery.

D.Y. Cameron: 'The Peaks of Arran'; date unknown, watercolour on paper, 32×49cm, by permission of The Fleming Collection, London.

The Peaks of Arran

Painted in the early years of the century, before the Great War, this watercolour echoes the feel of the 'Hills of Arran' of 1903. It was created at a much higher altitude than many of his paintings, and while Cameron was no mountaineer he certainly must have climbed many of the Arran hills to achieve these views. The view would appear to be that of Cir Mhòr dominating the mid-ground with its peak at top left, and the horns of Caisteal Abhail and its east ridge forming the background. If this is the case Cameron may well have situated himself somewhere on the saddle between North Goat Fell and Cir Mhòr. There is a raised section of the saddle to the east of the low point which may well be the lighter area in the foreground. It is the dawn in the Arran hills that has drawn the artist to the serrated edge of the ridges, attracted by the linear structures he perfected in his etchings.

The picture demonstrates one of the initial palettes he employed, using sombre browns, greys and black to achieve a clarity in linear landscape under declining or growing sunlight, and depicts the stern and serious nature of the mountain environment, disclosing it as the essential structure of Scotland. This projection of a dark and serious natural world has been linked to his experience in etching and engraving that afforded him an acute sense of line in terms of structure, tone and balance, the gradations of dark and light; and these qualities are the mainstay of this piece. There is overall, however, a dark and menacing quality to many of his renditions of the Arran mountains that warns against the foolhardy approach; the mountains are part of the landscape, but for those who would enter this arena care and experience are vital. Within this his dawn and evening mountain canvases, while often dark, still offer us the promise of either an outstanding day, or that dark, silent timelessness that is an attraction to many of us.

Shortly after this he finalised his landscape style, and while his palette went through a number of phases, he established a clarity of landscape. His canvases held a sense of order and balance that was always controlled and refined. He avoided the picturesque detail, had a strong awareness of design, and achieved dramatic effects with subtlety.

Ben Ledi: Late Autumn

This prominent mountain could easily be seen from Cameron's house in Kippen and became a continuing source of inspiration to the artist, who painted it many times in all seasons and atmospheres. Simplicity and natural design are the keynotes to this specific painting. Late autumn has removed the last of the leaves from the parallel birch trees that now frame the view and concentrate the spectator's gaze towards the shapely mass of Ben Ledi.

D.Y. Cameron: 'Ben Ledi – Late Autumn'; date unknown, oil on canvas. 36× 36cm. National Gallery of Scotland.

This compositional device alongside the slightly flattened perspective may well show the influence of Japanese art (then highly popular) on this canvas, as alongside the simplicity of the scene there is also a decorative aspect that works exceptionally well. The autumnal colour scheme of the foreground locates us in that season of the year and a series of dark and light horizontal bands leads us across the farmland to low hills whose blue tones form a base for the mountain, where early snow has come down to around the 600-metre mark. The warm tones of the autumn sky hold a reflection of the foreground stubble fields that leads the eye round again to the central form of the mountain. For the mountaineer this is an invitation card and reminder to organise the winter gear for 'joyous days upon the mountain side!'

The Hills of Skye

This view taken across Glen Sligachan gives a canvas, depicted in a classic three grounds, receding to the Cuillin skyline of Sgùrr nan Gillean. It proceeds from a dark brown foreground knoll, probably Nead na h-Iolaire, creating a gap and projecting the distance to the dark blue ridge in the mid-ground. This may well be the southern wall of Coire Riabhach, whose horizontal line sets off the massif in the background where a blue-grey airiness and a back-lit ridge are the counterpoint to a sky of high,

D.Y. Cameron: 'The Hills of Skye'; oil on canvas, 107×127cm. Glasgow Museums Reserve Collection, acquired 1928.

flat cloud. The eye is easily led out across the moorland to 'a rising of glens, of gloomy corries / a lying down in the antlered bellowing' described by Sorley MacLean in his poem *Kinloch Ainort*.

While specific details of the Cuillin Ridge may be lightly indicated, what has been determined is the distance of the range, its towering verticality, and its isolation. This is MacLean's 'exact and serrated blue rampart', which stands as a challenge to mountaineers, but at the same time the physicality of the massif is a solidity, a presence in the landscape offering protection and various sanctuaries within its encircling walls.

The Wilds of Assynt

From around 1930 Cameron concentrated solely on painting Scottish mountain landscapes in oil and watercolour; this determination coincided with the death of his wife in 1931, and it was his strong interest in mountain painting that staved off many bouts of loneliness and depression. 'The Wilds of Assynt', painted in 1936, 'which Cameron regarded as his finest large oil',[6] does reflect some of the loneliness he may have felt. The land unfolds in ever increasing ridges as it recedes towards the mountain skyline; the autumnal colour scheme passes from the brightness of the foreground to the darkness of the ridges to the blue of the sky suggesting uplift and promise, in both the physical and the colour aspects of the canvas. The two diminutive figures in the left foreground appear to be in Highland dress and gaze out over Loch Assynt towards the ruins of Ardvreck Castle and the distant Quinag. The remnants of the castle coupled with the dominance of Quinag and its outliers while endorsing the magnificence of the area may also indicate Cameron's own sense of loss. His sense of devastation and bereavement represented in the austerity and isolation of the scene is balanced by his treatment of the landscape, which is full and majestic as the depiction of the 'wilds' discloses distance and an ageless grandeur that may have been for the artist a promise of the future and a consolation. Many of his late paintings display a lighter, richer palette, often depicting sunsets and secluded mountains arising out of the West Highland moorland.

Throughout his life Cameron's work was admired and much sought after, winning him many awards, medals, and memberships of academic bodies including both the Royal Scottish Academy and the Royal Academy. Much respected by his peers, he declined to be nominated for presidencies of both these academies, where he was recognised as an outstanding individual both as an artist and an administrator. In his lifetime his organisational abilities and supervision of art exhibitions and major arts projects were acknowledged and saw him receive four honorary doctorates, from the universities of Glasgow, Manchester, Cambridge and St. Andrews. From 1917 to 1919 he was appointed as a war artist for the Canadian War Memorials Fund, for which work he was knighted in 1924

---

[6] B. Smith, *op. cit.*, p. 109.

D.Y. Cameron: 'The Wilds of Assynt'; 1936, oil on canvas, 102×128cm. Perth & Kinross Council.

by King George V in the Birthday Honours List. At home he was appointed the King's Painter and Limner in Scotland in 1933.

Dramatism, rather than Romanticism, became the hallmark of his landscape canvases. He was said to have been a deeply religious man, and some have noted that his 'later landscapes express a quasi-mystical view of the majesty of the natural scene.'[7] Not a mountaineer himself, Cameron never stood on the 'torn parapets' of Leslie Stephen's Alpine Club aesthetic. While the accuracy of recording details was important to Cameron, a literal transcription of these aspects was never going to reveal the 'truth' in mountain art. It was to find 'a visual idiom to convey the essence of the thing'[8] that Cameron strove, that idea of the spirit of place; the same qualities of adventure and determination that drew mountaineers to the Highlands in the first place. Prior to this, many representations of mountains blurred the boundary between fantasy and nature, and soaring verticality was depicted merging with masses of cloud-forms that only served to remove the compositions from any kind of understanding of the natural world. Cameron emphasised the structure and skyline of a mountain against a background of bright sky which could, along with the removal of any non-essential detail, enhance the central peak with an awesome presence.

---

[7] W.R. Hardie, *op. cit.*, p. 7.

[8] S. Schama, *Landscape and Memory* (London: Fontana Press, 1996), p. 506.

There is a strong case for acknowledging Cameron as the foremost mountain painter in Scotland. While some may prefer the work of Horatio McCulloch (1805–1867) and point to his determination to overcome the difficulties of travel in the Highlands during his lifetime, it must be noted that McCulloch tended to dwell on the panoramic and atmospheric in many of his works. His breadth of handling, natural colour and form, and his removal of sentimental aspects from his canvases secure his place in the history of Scottish Art. McCulloch's innovative tutor John Knox (1778–1845), while the first to establish a naturalistic handling of landscape and accuracy of colour, still maintained a figurative presence in his scenes, a residual aspect of the Classical process. His inventiveness removed the nymphs and satyrs from his scenes but retained the occasional fisherman, stalker, or tourist in the foreground. At the time when these artists were active, the difficulties of travel in the Highlands and the vagaries of the weather made plein air painting using oil paint on canvas almost impossible. Most work recording the Highland landscape was achieved in drawings and watercolours,[9] and these were often illustrative archives of expeditions to remote parts of Britain 'before the age of photography' that might occasionally be worked up on canvas in the studio.

Cameron's output is recorded in the range of titles that includes 'Schiehallion', 'Ben Cruachan', 'Ben Vorlich', 'Glen Strae', 'The Peaks of Arran', 'Glen Nevis', 'Ben Dearg' and 'Glen Coe', amongst many others, all held in public collections. His watercolours and drawings echo these titles, many of which, like the studies of Ben Lomond and Ben Ledi, were repeated numerous times in differing weather conditions. Cameron was no great innovator in the history of art, but he was never an imitator and his honest, luminous paintings were as popular in England as they were in Scotland and overseas, particularly in Canada where the quality of his Scottish landscapes struck a chord. His was 'a powerful evocation of the beauty and grandeur of the Scottish landscape'.[10]

Today his work may seem staid and dated to some, too concerned with subject matter rather than emotional content expressed through colour, as is seen in many contemporary West Highland landscapes, but it was rarely mannered and never heavy handed. His elegant designs and subtle use of colour exemplified the environment he worked in, and his portrayal of the character and spirit of the mountains in many ways succeeded in capturing the elusive drama of the Highland landscape, its freshness and spontaneity – the aspects that draw us all to return to the mountains.

---

[9] See Robin Campbell, 'Drawing the Highlands and Islands', *SMCJ*, 47/210 (2019), 16–32.

[10] B. Smith, *op. cit.* p. 113.

A DAY OR TWO WITH ANDY NISBET

by Dave Allan

ANDY AND I WERE ON Quinag's Barrel Buttress one summer. While I was happy to be rock climbing, he was really in search of new winter routes. Having said, that I am not averse to a new winter route myself.

One of the interesting things about the day was the solar eclipse which happened that morning. We got a good view of it through light cloud and it grew noticeably darker, but what I was more aware of was the silence. There was no bird-song or other sound, as if nature was holding its breath. Up at the buttress Andy pointed out a recent Grade VIII winter route, and I spotted a line further left that might give another very good winter climb. We could pick out a line zigzagging up rightwards to near the top of the cliff, but here it was obvious there was only one possible finish, and this looked sensational. We resolved to have a closer look from the top, and later in the day after a bit of exploration we located the spot and peered over. It looked spectacular. The buttress was very steep but we could see a small patch of turf about a foot long on a narrow ledge below us. We rigged an abseil for a closer look, and I went down with a warning from Andy not to remove the turf. As if I would! Andy then went down himself and reckoned the route would go and that the turf would be the crucial hold. Having descended further than me he discovered he could not return, and had to make prusiks from his shoe-laces. I said I would ring him the next winter when I reckoned it was in condition, which would basically mean the weather being cold enough to freeze the turf.

In mid-December we had a series of frosty nights and I was fairly sure conditions would be good on the north-facing Barrel at 760m, so I gave Andy a ring and left a message. On returning home from climbing I found two replies from him. He was keen to climb on Quinag the next day as he 'couldn't think of anything better to do.' Neither could I, so I suppose that was fair enough. Andy was too tired to come up that evening but said he would get up at four the next morning, then changed that to five. True to his word, the next morning at 06.30 he was at my door – literally at my door, as the snow in my garden must have confused him and he had driven over my lawn and parked on the patio. He had surmounted a couple of minor steps in achieving this, but he is a climber after all. I just didn't realise his car was too.

We are on the hill before daylight at 08.00, and it is an overcast day with a brisk north-west wind that picks up periodically as snow showers blow through. As in much of Sutherland there is no path to follow, so we make our own way across the snow-covered heather and bog, heading for the steep edge of Sàil Gharbh just visible against the lightening sky. We gear up at the bottom of the buttress and set off, soloing the 200 metres of about Grade II, vegetated, rocky ribs towards the barrel. A pleasant warm-up for what is to follow.

Andy always liked to do the first pitch, and he started up a grassy ramp that led to a narrow chimney about seven metres high. I doubted it would be wide enough to get into, especially with a sack on, but he managed it and emerged from the top in a peculiar manoeuvre with both feet in mid-air. Directly above was overhanging and clearly impossible, so he moved left and out of sight. I knew from the slow movement of the rope that it could not be easy. Andy reappeared on a steep nose of rock that looked decidedly airy, then belayed (as he put it afterwards) 'in the middle of nowhere' and shouted for me to follow. The chimney was very tight and awkward but at least offered some security, unlike the exposed traverse to follow. An easy ledge led me horizontally left, to peter out at some shattered rock on an overhanging rib. An array of runners adorned the rib, their presence more than justified by the stomach-churning drop below. One of the nuts wouldn't budge and I had to hang out over space to dislodge it. The move round the rib was not inviting either, and I tried it once or twice on hands and axe-picks before committing to moves using handholds alone. Once around, it was no easier, with one or two very insecure balance-moves without positive holds to attain the belay. I admitted I had not enjoyed the passage round the nose much, and Andy said he didn't think I would. He asked me if I wanted to lead the next pitch and I told him I did, and that he would not put me off that easily. I suspected by his tone that he was half expecting me to say No, or maybe was just hoping I would. We had a quick chat to make sure we were agreed on the direction we were heading, although to be honest there was not a lot of choice, and I set off.

I moved up and left on rocky steps and within a few metres reached the left end of an overhung grassy ledge, along which I moved easily rightwards, placing a couple of runners as I went. Here a two-metre vertical wall barred the way to a ledge above. A metre beyond the end of my ledge though was a good foothold, which I improved a bit by kicking some loose rock off it. With a good handhold and an axe in the turf of the ledge above I stepped up, switched feet and pulled over. Not too bad – in fact, very enjoyable. Once again, as we had expected, the only way was rightwards along this ledge, which terminated in an open vertical corner. I clearly had to reach a big ledge up to my right, but how to get there? I started up the corner, and small wire runners and good axe torques got me got me up the initial step. A large stone was jammed across a gap at the top of the corner, and this was the only feasible way out. I moved as high as I could then reached up below the stone and buried my axe-pick in what I hoped was a good turf placement. It did not look too great, but I was not in a good position to test it as it was the only hold I had. I put a little weight on it and nothing happened, so I trusted it and swung my right foot up onto a small hold on the wall. I was then high enough to get my other axe over the corner of the chockstone and strenuously pull over. The moves had been harder than they should have been because of bad rope drag, caused either by bad rope management on my part or the complicated nature of the pitch. It had been another good pitch though. I had got to exactly where we had planned, directly below the steep exposed wall we knew would be the crux of the climb. Andy arrived and said he was quite impressed. He stopped beneath the chockstone to assess the situation and I suggested he hook his axe where I had, momentarily forgetting who I was climbing with.

He took the gear and moved rightwards up the ledge before disappearing above me. I shouted up to ask if he could see the top wall, and he replied that it was directly above me and he was approaching it. Minutes later I leant backwards to see him perched on the final arête in a spectacular position. Soon came the shout and I set off. Lovely turf steps led up and left to a ledge beneath a smooth wall. This was it. The situation was one of incredible exposure with fresh air and a huge drop beneath your feet. I removed Andy's two nuts and knife-blade peg and had a look at the wall. There were two thin cracks about two metres up and one would take about 20mm of an axe-pick. Some 25mm-wide ledges would provide footholds provided my front points didn't skite off their rounded edges. Quite what I would use after that I wasn't sure, for although there were reasonable footholds higher up, I could see nothing for my axes. The route I had to follow was clear: diagonally up left, to the little patch of turf we had seen in the summer, which now appeared tantalisingly out of reach. I put my right axe-pick in the crack and gave it a tap home with my other tool, then applied some weight to test it. It held. I gave a shout that I was climbing, then tip-toed up the footholds till my right arm locked off with the axe-head level with my head. The only flaw in the rock above was a vague horizontal break I could just reach with my axe. Groping with it, I searched for a hold. All I could find was a small knob of rock, and it was hard to judge how much of a hook my axe had on it. There was nothing better, however, so I would have to use it. Looking down to check the footholds I got a stomach-churning sense of exposure, but there was no mileage in worrying about that. 'Just concentrate on the moves,' I told myself. With a leap of faith I transferred my weight to my left axe and removing the right one I hooked it beside the left. 'Bloody Hell!' Crabbing my feet up and left I made a swing for the turf with my left axe. It is so hard the pick will barely penetrate but a second stab goes in half-an-inch. It will have to do; I can't hang here any longer on a knob of rock so dubious I don't even want to look at it. I run my feet across to a half-decent foothold and breathe deeply, realising I have been holding my breath. A move or two more and I am looking over the top at a grinning Andy.

I admitted I was not sure if I would have led it without knowing how good the knob of rock was, but he said he had spotted it in the summer and checked it out, the wily old dog. It was still a great lead. He asked me what grade I thought it was and I said at least V,6. He decided afterwards on V,7 and called it *Chang*. Andy must have been buzzing, as once we got packed he shot up the ridge to the summit at a tremendous pace, leaving me struggling in his wake. In fact I was blown off my feet at one stage in a strong gust and forced to crawl. A steep descent of the south-east face and two miles of bog-trotting got us back to the car.

Back home that evening we are watching Rangers play a European game on the TV, and Andy says that one of the Rangers players is an Eskimo. I express some doubt about this, but he says he has seen Eskimos and this guy is definitely one. I agree it is a cold night in Glasgow and say that maybe they are expecting him to come into his own if the pitch turns icy. Andy is unimpressed by this suggestion, and his withering glance persuades me to keep my thoughts to myself about maybe getting an igloo-building demonstration at half time.

HOPEFALL

From dawn to dusk – and earlier, and later –
we spun our new line up towards the skies,
shadows of movement in the greater silence,
a quiet but shared ardour in our eyes,
while sunlight danced from snow to loch to sea.

And then the got-it moment met our hope:
the angle fell away and the rest was white,
a walk-up to the summit, trailing ropes,
the black crag overcome, and the plan come right.

But if a fault appeared then and gaped open
and widened till it swallowed you and me,
tripped up, ensnared and swamped, so quickly taken –

that does not mean our partnership was broken;
does not annul the trust that set us free;
and does not take the sunlight from the sea.

Sophie-Grace Chappell

WRITTEN 8.2.19 IN MEMORY OF
ANDY NISBET AND STEVE PERRY
BEN HOPE, SUTHERLAND, 5.2.19

Suilven ablaze!
Photo: Kevin Woods.

WAY BACK FAR EAST

by Greg Strange

'COME ON BABY, don't fear the Reaper,' sings the American rock band Blue Oyster Cult, as we speed westwards, hood down, in the old MGB. It is early morning one Saturday in May 1980. The driving music is the choice of my young companion, Brian Sprunt, who is beginning to come to life after being woken by the rattling of chuckies against his bedroom window. We are heading to Coire Mhic Fhearchair, the great north-west corrie of Beinn Eighe. This will be the third occasion in the last twelve months we have been there to complete a climb on the steep quartzite of the Far East Wall.

It was Allen Fyffe who first spoke to me about the Far East's potential for new routes. He and Paul Williams had made an early route there, *Sidewinder*, while on a Lairig Club meet to the Ling Hut in October 1966. Years later, in June 1973, I finally visited the corrie with Rob Archbold and Johnny Ingram. Although we had no particular objective in mind, we did have a copy of the newly published Turnbulls' guide, which had a diagram of the wall with only two routes marked on it. The guide made reference to a tremendous pillar on the right, and as we approached along the lochside we could just make out a prominent groove system running its full height. The sheer unexpected joy of climbing *Groovin' High* that day remains a vivid memory. Afterwards, Rob wrote an excellent article entitled 'Westcoastin''. It featured in the Etchachan Club's *Kohouteks Klimbing Klub Komic* in 1974 and is well worth seeking out.

Over the next few years Rob and Geoff Cohen made three further impressive climbs, all more difficult than *Groovin' High*. *Sundance* took an obvious corner towards the left, *Birth of the Cool* went just left of *Groovin' High*, and *Colgarra*, the most difficult route, climbed a very steep line in the centre of the wall. All then seemed to go quiet. Most of our small group were aware of the hanging crack on the clean grey wall left of *Sundance*, but no one had made a move. I knew Brian would be up for anything new and adventurous, and after talking to him about the crack he was keen for a visit to Beinn Eighe. This was June 1979.

After a bivouac among the pines at the foot of Glen Torridon in Brian's pole-less tent, we walked round to Coire Mhic Fhearchair on what was turning out to be a dry, improving day. Beside the loch it was flat calm, and a perfect reflection of the Triple Buttresses was very striking. There was so much to look at and talk about that it took a while to wander up to the crag. Eventually we stood below the compact grey wall, lying between *Sundance* and a groove system 150 feet farther left (taken by a route named *Sting*, climbed by Johnny and myself in 1974).

Staring up the wall, it all looked so blank and improbable. I was shocked to think I had conned myself (and Brian) into believing we could find a route to the top. The crack itself, right of centre, was indeed the only obvious straight-up feature, but it bottomed out well above the narrow horizontal fault crossing most of the cliff at one third height. Below this, a multi-hued dripping wall looked repulsive, so we turned our attention to some left-leaning grooves leading up to the fault a bit left of the crack. Perhaps the quartzite really would be more accommodating than its appearance suggested.

Brian Sprunt on The Reaper (E2) on Beinn Eighe's Far East Wall, June 1979.
Photo: Greg Strange.

Expecting to be out of my depth on the wall above, I offered to take the first pitch. Pleasant climbing up left led to steeper rock and the first groove. Brian had given me some of his chalk, which I stuffed in to one of my pockets. I still struggled a bit in the groove but managed to exit right on to a small grassy ledge, in a second, larger groove. My memory recalls a good belay.

By the time Brian had joined me we were almost in the sun and there were larger breaks in the cloud. The plan was now to go up this leaning groove to the horizontal fault, then try to climb diagonally up right to gain the crack. Brian quickly dispatched the groove (good runners) and soon he was committed to the wall above. Progress was very slow owing to poor holds and lack of protection. After a while all conversation ceased and there was a real sense of tension. Eventually, he announced he didn't think he could reach the crack and that he was going to attempt to climb back. How he did not fall I will never know. I cannot recall him leaving gear; perhaps he had placed none. Future guidebook writers quoted him saying he managed to rest with his chin on a hold. He may well have done this, but I did not see it, either here or anywhere else on the climb.

For a while he stood in the fault, ashen-faced, but soon the banter returned. He decided to follow the break rightwards to below the crack, to see if he could get some protection before climbing straight up from there. In the end he continued to traverse all the way to a belay in *Sundance*. There was a fair incentive for me not to fluff the tricky moves up into the fault, then a very long horizontal shuffle re-united us. Retreat was not discussed. I handed over what gear he had placed, then he returned along the fault to a point several feet right of the downward continuation of the crack. Slowly but steadily he climbed very steep rock, placing a few nut runners until he reached better holds and was able to move left into the crack. He then continued to a niche with an excellent belay below a bulge.

That was where the attempt ended. I followed the pitch, finding it very sustained and fingery. The continuation of the crack above was wet and still looked hard, so with some relief on both our parts, we abseiled off. It was a beautiful evening as we crossed the ridge of Còinneach Mhòr, heading for a fast scree descent to the glen. We had had an exciting day and both agreed it was going to be an excellent climb. Completely dry rock would be a prerequisite for success.

Two months later, in August, we camped in the corrie, but cold weather, even wetter rock and the fact that Brian had left his rock boots in Aberdeen put paid to another attempt. We did, however, enjoy *Central Buttress*, and the next day, using a small sketch given to me by Ed Grindley, we climbed *The Black Streak* at Diabaig, Brian leading the top pitch in his trainers.

It was now nearly one year on. The weather that May morning was perfect, with everything looking bone dry. In fact, we later heard from the barman in the Kinlochewe Hotel that there had been no appreciable rain in the area for nine weeks! We pitched the tent at an idyllic spot at the

Brian Sprunt at the top of Central Buttress, Beinn Eighe, August 1979. Photo: Greg Strange.

head of the loch, had a brew and made our way up to the grey wall. It still looked intimidating, although less so now we had solved part of the puzzle. Crucially, all the weeps had gone and the air was warm.

This time the first pitch passed quickly. I now had a home-made chalk bag and was probably carrying my first three 'Friends' (Nos 1–3). They were cosmetically imperfect 'seconds' that I had acquired direct from

Wild Country. We didn't completely trust them initially. On the big pitch Brian was on fire. In the fault he traversed away right to a point below the crack (out of sight above). Here he pulled onto the wall, moved up a little, then continued rightwards to join the line he had taken before. It was a really powerful lead, and despite having climbed most of it the previous year, I still found following the pitch very hard.

Above our high point the crack formed a shallow right-facing corner. This was now completely dry and provided another sustained pitch at a slightly easier angle. It ended on a comfortable ledge at the end of the main difficulties. Less taxing climbing, following small features and a final chimney, completed the route.

For a good while we just lazed on the short vegetation and soaked in the atmosphere. Out beyond the cliff-top the view was dominated by the deep blue of Loch Coire Mhic Fhearchair and the dark profile of Sàil Mhòr. In the middle distance, the hazy peaks of Baosbheinn and Beinn an Eoin stood proud in a moorland speckled with lochans. I felt mellow and could easily have fallen asleep. We descended the little gully on the left, and as we passed back under the crag Brian spotted an obvious short left-facing corner. The single pitch *Nightcap Groove* was pleasant enough, but seemed trivial after the main event.

Next day we climbed the *Pale Diedre*, a prominent feature near the middle of the Eastern Ramparts. Robin Smith had referred to it in his route description of *Boggle*. Once again Brian was in his element, leading the superb second pitch on sight. To this day it remains one of the best pitches I have climbed. It certainly rounded off a brilliant weekend with great company in one of Scotland's finest mountain arenas. It is hard to believe this was 40 years ago and just a few years before Brian lost his life on the north face of the Matterhorn.

Later that Sunday evening, on the way home and well into another repeat of the Blue Oyster Cult track, he breaks off from singing and declares, 'That's what we should call the route on the Far East Wall: *The Reaper*.'

ALEISTER CROWLEY
Part 2: Encounters with Collie, Eckenstein and the Y Boulder
(1894–1905)

by Michael Cocker

(The first half of this article was published in the 2020 Journal, and covered the years 1890 to 1894, ending with Crowley's exploration of the cliffs at Beachy Head in the early summer of 1894. The story continues.)

IN AUGUST 1894 CROWLEY travelled with his tutor to the Austrian Alps where he completed a number of successful ascents, both with local guides and solo. He also met Ernest Maylard and they climbed the Schrotterhorn and the Vertainspitze together, which Maylard later recorded in the *SMC Journal*. This was Crowley's first season in the Alps. When he returned to England, in September, he enrolled at King's College, London, to read Medicine and Natural Sciences. At the time, Norman Collie was a lecturer in the Chemistry department and Crowley attended some of his lectures. In December 1894 Crowley was elected to membership of the SMC, at the age of nineteen. He had been proposed by A.E. Maylard and seconded by Collie.

Crowley's SMC application was seven pages long and it appears to include most (possibly all) of the ascents he had made up to that point. The document is interesting now to the mountaineering historian, but is likely to have seemed a trifle boastful to the committee at a time when most applicants, some of them very experienced, confined themselves to a single page, or two at most.

Shortly after joining the Club Crowley submitted his paper on Beachy Head, one that has always struck me as an unusually good composition for someone of his age. (Bill Brooker even considered including it in his anthology *A Century of Scottish Mountaineering*.) However, it is now clear that the article was substantially revised by the editor, William Douglas, because on 3 February 1895 Maylard wrote to Douglas:

> About Crowley's paper – it's horribly egotistical, ungrammatical, and in parts juvenile; it has however the material for a short and interesting paper, if you can get permission to cut it up as you like. I really don't think it ought to go in as it is. He would regret it himself ten years hence. It would be a real kindness to the fellow if he could somehow or other get quietly taken down. You editorial gentlemen must know how to deliver the necessary correction.[1]

Douglas amended the article and sent it back to Crowley for his approval. A letter from Crowley to Douglas, dated 28 March, confirms this and that Crowley was planning to attend the 1895 Easter meet:

---

[1] We do indeed, but feel the pain as keenly as the victim. This letter is in NLS Acc. 11538.40. – HON. ED.

Dear Douglas,

I must apologise for the delay, but I have been confined to my bed for a week and am not yet allowed out of my room. I have threatened my doctor with the worst kind of annihilation if he does not cure me in time for Fort William.

I have only made trifling alterations to your condensation… The sketch has been a trouble. I have no power of drawing (except a cheque or a chicken) and have wasted a lot of time and paper before getting a moderate result. I shall be able to borrow the negatives of the two larger photographs and will forward to you directly I get them.

Hoping to see you in a fortnight.

I am yours very truly,
E. Aleister Crowley.

Crowley did not attend the 1895 Easter meet, and the fate of his unfortunate doctor remains unknown.

It is not clear when Crowley and Collie had first met in person. In his *Confessions* Crowley says this was in Westmorland and writes elsewhere that it was shortly before Collie left for Nanga Parbat. They were both staying at the Wastwater Hotel over the Christmas and New Year period 1894-95 so this may have been the occasion. The visitors' book records that Crowley was there from 23 December to 4 January. John Robinson, O.G. Jones and Joseph Collier were also amongst the guests. The only entry in the Climbing Book during this period was one by Crowley recording what he thought was the first descent of the *Oblique Chimney*, on the Ennerdale face of Great Gable, which he made with Jones, Robinson and a Dr J. Lewkowitch. Underneath this entry is a note by Robinson pointing out that Joseph Collier had previously descended the chimney in December 1892. The frequent corrections to Crowley's inscriptions suggest he was perhaps a little too quick, opinionated and, at times, ill-informed when making entries in the Climbing Book.

Both Jones and Crowley left accounts of their descent of the *Oblique Chimney*. Jones, in *Rock Climbing in the English Lake District* (1897), is jovial and upbeat, saying 'a large party of Wasdale Christmas revellers made for the *Oblique Chimney*…the rocks were dry and very free of snow'. In *Confessions* Crowley paints a different picture:

I was only once on a rope with Jones. It was on Great Gable; the rocks were plastered with ice and a bitter wind was blowing. In such conditions one cannot rely on one's fingers. Our party proposed to descend the Oblique Chimney on the Ennerdale face. Robinson led the way down. The second man was a Pole named Lewkowitch, who was generally known as 'Oils, Fats and Waxes' because of his expert knowledge of them and personal illustration of their properties which he afforded. He was no experienced climber and weighed about sixteen stone. It was up to me the third man to let him down slowly … I soon found myself in the most difficult part of the chimney, very ill-placed to manipulate a dangling ox. I looked up to Jones, the last man, to hold my rope so that I could give full attention to Lewkowitch, and saw to my horror that he was maintaining his equilibrium by a sort of savage war dance! He was hampered by a photographic apparatus which was strapped on his back. Robinson had urged him to lower it separately. As nor Einstein nor the Blessed Virgin Mary were there to suspend the laws of gravitation I have no idea how we got to the bottom undamaged; but when we did I promptly took off the rope and walked home, utterly disgusted with the vanity which had endangered the party.

There may be some truth in Crowley's suggestion that Jones was at times vain and reckless. Most of the other accounts of Jones were written either by the Abraham brothers, who idolised him, or by Jones himself, so lack objectivity.

In the summer of 1895 Crowley climbed in the Bernese Oberland, where he made ascents of the Eiger, the Mönch, the Jungfrau and several other peaks, again often climbing solo. Martin Booth, one of Crowley's biographers, suggests this was because he felt safer climbing alone and that it brought him closer to nature. In an unpublished manuscript Crowley wrote:

> I would never climb with guides, after my first season when I discovered to my surprise and alarm that the best of them were only peasants climbing by rule of thumb. There was never a guide yet with the true scientific knowledge of mountain and weather conditions which would enable him to tackle an emergency problem. I have found guides huddled together within a few yards of a regular route in a complete panic and utterly incapable of doing anything to retrieve their situation. I have found myself much safer by relying entirely on myself.

Aleister Crowley when he started at Trinity College, Cambridge, October 1895.

Crowley started at Trinity College, Cambridge, in the autumn and at the end of the year travelled to Wasdale Head with Morris Travers, who was a colleague of Norman Collie's at London University. The visitors' book records they stayed from 27 December to 2 January. On their way to the hotel they made the sixth ascent of *Great Gully* on the Screes and, on New Year's Eve, the first ascent of an unnamed gully between *Arrowhead Ridge* and *The Sphinx* on the Napes crags. Crowley left a detailed account of the second route in the Climbing Book, which is now called *Square Cut Gully* and is described for the first time in the 2007 *Gable & Pillar* guide, with a tentative grade of Severe.

The SMC Easter Meet of 1896 was held at the Alexandra Hotel in Fort William, the notable event being the first winter ascent of the North-East Buttress on Ben Nevis by William Naismith and four others. Thirty-two members and guests attended, and Crowley's name is recorded in the Journal as one of those present. However, the weather was generally poor and there is no mention of his activities. This is the only SMC meet Crowley ever attended. He left the club in 1902. The reason for this is not known but by that time he had a base in Scotland, Boleskine House, on the south shore of Loch Ness, and was away a good deal on expeditions.

Crowley spent the summer of 1896 climbing in the Pennine Alps with Morris Travers and Gregor Grant. Around this time Norman Collie proposed Crowley for membership of the Alpine Club, and Sir Martin Conway supported the application. Collie was informed, however, that this was likely to be opposed, so Crowley withdrew the application. At Cambridge it was put about that he had been blackballed, but this was not true. Some years ago I enquired at the Alpine Club if they still had a copy of Crowley's application, but there was no record of it.

Crowley, who was rarely complimentary about his contemporaries, had an unusual regard for Norman Collie. In the unpublished manuscript mentioned above, he gives us the following assessment:

> Professor Norman Collie ... was unquestionably the finest all-round climber of his generation. He was ideally built from a physical point of view for every kind of all-round work. He had a precise scientific knowledge on every point, and besides this he possessed a savage instinct which was of the utmost value on unknown mountains, and which, I am glad to say, I share with him. For example, neither of us ever got lost in any kind of weather. It was not that we knew exactly where North was, but we knew the direction in which we had started out when setting out in the morning.
>
> In addition to this, we both possessed a quite exceptional physical memory of the details of rock climbing so that after climbing a route in the morning we would come down it again in pitch darkness, our feet automatically finding the places where they had found hold on the ascent without our eyes to guide us. I may say that such physical memory is remarkably persistent even after a lapse of several years. We could remember the minutest detail of any difficult climb.

He also included this brief anecdote:

> Collie brought back from India several pairs of puttees, and he and I both wore them at Wastdale[2]. I do not know whether anyone will be surprised, but we were both absolutely ostracised for the innovation. Nobody would believe, even on demonstration, that puttees would keep out snow.

Crowley thought that Collie's book *Climbing on the Himalaya and Other Mountain Ranges* was 'the only book on mountains which possesses any literary merit'. Of some of the other mountaineering authors he remarked:

> Mummery's is good because he really had something to say, but his style shows the influence of Collie. Owen Glynne Jones produced a patent plagiarism of Mummery's style; and when it came to the brothers Abraham, the bottom was reached. And what a bottom! In fact, two.

It is worth mentioning that Mummery's classic tome *My Climbs in the Alps and Caucasus* was published seven years prior to Collie's book!

Crowley's comments on Jones's *Rock Climbing in the English Lake District* are hardly justified as this was original in concept and possesses considerable literary merit. He was perhaps closer to the mark with George and Ashley Abraham, whose books, although valuable for their historical and photographic content, are not especially well written. George in particular was inclined to prolonged passages of purple prose.

Crowley stayed at Wastwater Hotel for a few days at the end of September 1896, and placed the following note in the visitors' book:

> Pillar Rock by Cent & W Jordans, Arete, Pendlebury's Climb & the first ascent of this rock by a dog was made by the easy way.

In his memoirs he refers to this canine ascent with characteristic attitude and embellishment:

> I took the Climbers' Record to be a serious compilation and never wrote in it without the fullest sense of responsibility. So when I found a solemn Te Deum being chanted on the fifth ascent of Pillar Rock by a 'lady', I took my dog to the top and recorded, 'first ascent by a St Bernard bitch'.

There is no record of the ascent by 'a St Bernard bitch' in the Climbing Book.

Crowley returned to Wasdale in the spring of 1898 and stayed at the hotel from 14 March to 18 April. The place was overrun with climbers including Joseph Collier, O.G. Jones, the Abraham brothers and Oscar Eckenstein. Crowley struck up a friendship with Eckenstein, who was seventeen years older and an experienced mountaineer, having already climbed extensively in the Alps and having been on one expedition to the

---

[2] 'Wastdale' (including the letter t) is the old spelling of Wasdale. Both versions are used in this article depending on the context.

Karakoram. Despite their very different personalities they on well together, finding a common interest in eastern philosophy and admiration of the explorer Sir Richard Burton.

They did some climbing together and on the off-days amused themselves throwing boomerangs. (Eckenstein was interested in the principles of the boomerang.) They also worked out a series of gymnastic

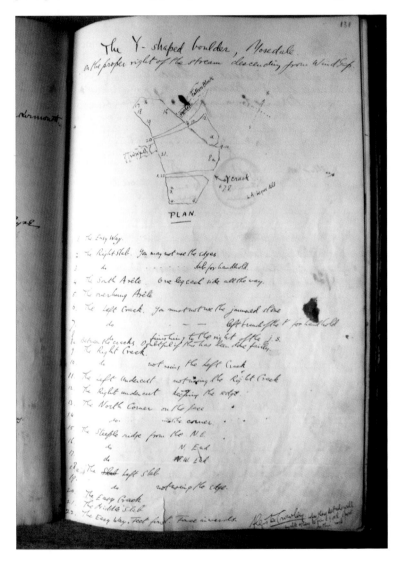

Crowley's guide to the Y boulder in the Wastwater Hotel visitors' book, April 1898. Photo by M.T. Cocker from FRCC Archives.

problems on the hotel barn wall and on the Y boulder in Mosedale. Towards the end of the holiday Crowley wrote a guide to the Y boulder in the hotel visitors' book, which included a sketch by L.A. Legros and a list of 22 boulder problems. Legros was a friend of Eckenstein's and the son of a well-known French artist, Alphonse Legros.

Eckenstein is often credited with being the first person to use boulders

Joseph Collier making his feet-first, face-in, upside-down ascent of the Y boulder, April 1898. By kind permission of ©abrahamphotographic & FRCC Archives.

to hone his technique and to develop the art of balance climbing. Crowley's guide is the first attempt to document individual boulder problems; the most innovative of these being Joseph Collier's feet-first, face-in, upside-down ascent – a feat that was recorded as Problem No 22 in the guide and captured in a photograph taken by the Abraham brothers. This, however, is not the first reference to bouldering in British mountaineering literature. T. Fraser. S. Campbell published an article 'On Boulders' in the January 1896 issue of the *SMC Journal*, in which he gives an account of the impromptu formation of the 'Boulder Society', comprising two members, and describes several boulders on Arran with suggested modes of ascent. As an SMC member Crowley would probably have been aware of this article.

Crowley left Cambridge (without a degree) and spent the summer of 1898 climbing in the Alps with Eckenstein. He returned to Wasdale briefly in January 1899, but left no record of his activities, and was back again on 22 March 1899 and stayed until 15 April. (Eckenstein was there from 22 March to 1 May.) On 10 April Crowley and Eckenstein climbed *The Curtain* and *The Arete* on Pillar Rock, currently graded Hard Severe, with a Miss von Wyss and Sophie Nichols – probably the third ascent. It is not known who Miss von Wyss was, but Sophie Nichols appears in a photograph with Mrs Bryant and Oscar Eckenstein, taken by the Abraham brothers, outside the Pen-y-Gwryd Hotel, in Snowdonia, at Easter 1897.

Group outside Wastwater Hotel, Easter 1899. Seated from left: Charles Oppenheimer, Aleister Crowley, Lehmann Oppenheimer, Oscar Eckenstein (hatless & bearded), Sophie Nichols (?), unknown, L.A. Legros (?). Ashley Abraham is sitting on the ground. The Peak District pioneer, Jim Puttrell, is second from left in the back row, while W.G.Clay is third from left in the middle row. Photographer probably George Abraham.

Eckenstein apparently had an irrational fear of kittens, and in Confessions Crowley tells the following story.

> One Easter the hotel was overcrowded; and five of us, including Eckenstein and myself, were sleeping in the barn. One of Eckenstein's greatest friends was Mrs Bryant. … She had brought her niece, Miss Nichols, who to intrepidity on rocks added playfulness in less austere surroundings. I formally accuse her of putting a kitten under Eckenstein's pillow in the barn while we were in the smoking room after dinner. If it had been a cobra Eckenstein could not have been more upset.

It was during this holiday, on 21 April, that Sophie Nichols led *Kern Knotts Crack*, with Eckenstein supporting her. She had made a top-roped ascent the previous year. This was the first female lead of a route that was technically one of the hardest in the district, O.G. Jones having made the first ascent, after several top-roped inspections, two years earlier. It is currently graded Very Severe. Eckenstein recorded this feat in the Climbing Book – the only entry he ever made. Crowley said that 'so much fuss' had been made about Jones's ascent of *Kern Knotts Crack* 'that Eckenstein took a young girl named Miss Nicholls [sic] and asked her to lead it, which she did'.

Crowley and Eckenstein climbed in the Alps together, in the summer of 1899, and met Tom Longstaff, at Montenvers, in the Mont Blanc Range. Longstaff mentions this encounter in his book *This My Voyage*, and refers to them as an 'enigmatic couple' and to Crowley as 'a fine climber, if an unconventional one'. He also remarked that, at the time, Crowley 'chose to wear full Highland dress, complete with eagle's feather, on all occasions'.

Crowley purchased Boleskine House in November 1899 and owned it until 1911. Here he styled himself as a Highland laird, entertained lavishly, walked the hills, fished for salmon in the loch and conducted magical ceremonies. On one occasion he even went to the length of organising a haggis-shoot for an unsuspecting foreign visitor who was curious about the origins of this dish. The head of the ram, which had stood in for the haggis, was duly stuffed and mounted with an engraved gold plaque underneath.

In 1901 he went with Eckenstein to Mexico, where they climbed several volcanoes. The following year they organised an expedition to K2 in the Karakoram, and in 1905 Crowley led an expedition to Kangchenjunga. The stories of Crowley's Himalayan expeditions are well told elsewhere, and only mentioned here to note that they were the first attempts ever made on these 8000-metre peaks and that the controversy surrounding his behaviour on the Kanchenjunga expedition – allegedly ignoring cries for help when some of his companions were avalanched – effectively marked the end of his climbing career. After this he was shunned in mountaineering circles and, although he occasionally did some scrambling on the hills around Boleskine and visited Wasdale again in the summer of 1909, he did no more serious climbing in Britain or abroad. It appears that Eckenstein also distanced himself from Crowley after Kangchenjunga, but the friendship survived and Eckenstein was one of the three people Crowley dedicated his autobiography to.

Acknowledgements

I am particularly grateful to the Editor for his helpful suggestions whilst revising and extending the second part of this article, and to Robin Campbell for drawing my attention to the interesting correspondence between Maylard, Douglas and Crowley.

References and Sources:

Booth, M., *A Magick Life, A Biography of Aleister Crowley* (London: Hodder & Stoughton, 2000).

Campbell, T.F.S., 'On Boulders', *SMCJ*, 4/19 (1896), 52–6.

Cocker, M., *Wasdale Climbing Book* (Glasgow: Ernest Press, 2006). (Facsimile & commentary on climbing book kept at the Wastwater Hotel 1890–1919.)

Collie, J.N., *Climbing on the Himalaya and Other Mountain Ranges* (Edinburgh: David Douglas, 1902).

Crowley, E.A., application for membership of Scottish Mountaineering Club (1894).

Crowley, E.A., unpublished manuscript sent to the author by C. Warren.

Jones, O.G., *Rock Climbing in the English Lake District* (London: Longmans, Green & Co, 1897).

Longstaff, T., *This My Voyage* (London: John Murray, 1950).

Mummery, A.F., *My Climbs in the Alps & Caucasus* (London: T. Fisher Unwin, 1895).

Rigby, P.C. & Reid, S.J.H., *Gable & Pillar* (Fell & Rock Climbing Club, 2007).

Symonds, J. & Grant, K. (editors), *The Confessions of Aleister Crowley* (London: Routledge & Kegan Paul, 1979).

Wastwater Hotel Climbing Book 1890–1919.

Wastwater Hotel Visitors' Books 1891–1894 & 1894–1901.

PATHS

by Peter Biggar

THE DESCENT FROM CAIRN GORM to the plateau above the Northern Corries is like a miniature slice of the desert, denuded of vegetation, sprinkled with lumps of pale granite gnawn by ice and endlessly scuffed by boots which crunch and slither on the scree. The path which continues along the rim of Coire an t-Sneachda and out to Ben Macdui, echoes the desert theme: hard, gritty, arid, like an early Roman road designed to get the traveller as directly and speedily as possible to the summit and perhaps success.

Only descend a little from this path and the experience changes. Especially in autumn one is aware of colour at one's feet; deep crimson of the sphagnum set off by yellowing vegetation. Clear water trickles over black moss; the deer grass fringing the little pools looks as though it has been dipped in blood. Frost crystals cling to the fronds. The ground under one's feet becomes soft and springy; one moves silently in a different world.

Approaching the plateau from further to the east on the well-engineered path towards Lurcher's, the same transformation is found just a few yards off the gravelly way. Reds, golds, livid green of moss, yellow and white lichen on pink and black spotted rock, and cushioned silent textures underfoot. A few feet away the legions kick up the dust.

Some paths seem designed to do maximum damage to the traveller. One such is the path up An Cabar on Ben Wyvis. Considering the number of people who wish to climb the mountain, this path like those on Cairn Gorm is necessary, and a stone staircase is just about all right in ascent, but if you value your knees and your hips find another way down.

We seem to have a strange compulsion to follow paths. It afflicts us in life as on the hill. We talk about 'career paths'. Religions stress the value of following 'the true path'; we are exhorted to 'keep to the straight and narrow'. Paths like these can also damage us.

Consider the ambition of climbing all the Munros. A glance at our 'Munro Matters' will tell you that there are many different ways of following this path. I followed mine slowly, accruing summits rather as a stone gathers moss. Still, on my fiftieth birthday I earnestly believed I had completed my round on Ladhar Bheinn, graced by Brocken Spectres and Glories. On reviewing my records, however, this minor satisfaction fell to bits: it seemed that there were two summits I had definitely not climbed, another I felt unsure about, and one about which I felt equivocal.

I thought I had climbed Càrn Bhac in the southern Cairngorms, but I had failed to spot that the name of the hill on the map was printed on a lower top and not on the summit. Barry Hard and I were too intent on the next summit and dashed on unheeding. A cool misty day in October with stags roaring put that right. I had climbed Beinn Avon on a freezing winter day, but hadn't climbed the summit tor because it was iced. I felt equivocal. After all, the Inaccessible Pinnacle in Skye used to be ignored in favour of Sgùrr Dearg, but that was a poor excuse. A long cycle with Roger Robb, a gentle wander over a plateau alive with nervous ptarmigan and their young followed by an easy scramble up the tor set the record straight.

Meall nan Tàrmachan in Perthshire I had climbed many years ago in a snowstorm and I wasn't sure if I had reached the top. My revisit one April had echoes of the past. Only two days earlier I had enjoyed a warm, sunny traverse of the Lawers group. Off-guard. Now, up at Lochan na Lairige the cloud was down and it was cold and drizzling. Up in the steep little corrie below the summit crags snow was lying. The soles of my walking boots were worn. I had no axe or sticks. As I gained height the drizzle turned to sleet and then snow. I tried to go up a steepish runnel but found it too dodgy. To the right there was a rounded grassy spur covered with a slippery skin of fresh powder. Up this I went – looking back nervously as I got above crags, and looking up as the angle persisted in steepening. My hands were in the snow but I just made it to the crest of the ridge, turned left and followed indistinct wisps of path to the summit cairn on the rim of the plateau. No view, snow falling, wind blowing.

There were footprints, some human and some dog, but their marks went down a snow-clad grassy chimney I didn't want to follow. I retreated along the summit ridge, now really wintry. I needed open slopes of reasonable gradient. I went a fair way and thought I had found an escape route, but I looked and looked and the angle increased as it tends to do when one is doubtful, so back I came. This manoeuvre was repeated several times, but at length I came back to the chimney I had initially rejected, was slightly heartened by the signs of previous traffic, and very gingerly climbed down, gaining easier slopes below with a great sense of relief. An interesting day to be sure, but in context unnecessary, because I became convinced that I had reached the top before: I remembered the position of the cairn on the corrie rim.

The path to completeness now led to Skye. Arriving late on a fine April evening in Glenbrittle I went up towards Coire Lagan in the last of the light, cooked my dinner and slept by a boulder. Morning brought the threat of lowering cloud. I traversed the hillside and gained the path to Coire a' Ghrunnda. As I went up, the cloud and rain came down to meet me. I went on to just below the crags that guard the entrance to the corrie before turning back. It was plain that Sgùrr Dubh Mòr would have to be courted more assiduously. One does not, of course, have to climb this mountain while traversing the main Cuillin Ridge, and I had ignored it: a mistake, or perhaps a happy accident.

In May Barry and I drove round from Torrin to Glenbrittle. We enjoyed a stiff scramble through the crags that guard the corrie. Today the hill was alive with other parties, most of whom seemed to be making for Sgùrr Dubh Mòr. Avoiding them we skirted round the loch on huge red-brown

boulders and climbed the gully which took us under the gigantic
chockstone and on to the col between the Caisteal of Coire Garbh and
Sgùrr Dubh na Da Bheinn, the scramble up the latter exhilarating but not
hard. Looking over to Sgùrr Dubh Mòr confirmed my impression that I
hadn't climbed it. A miniature Edinburgh Castle defended by a bristling
arête, not easily forgotten.

While scrambling across this intervening ridge we were overtaken by
what I'd guess were guided parties who seemed to be intent on making
the ascent as hard as humanly possible by including every pinnacle on
the way – the ascent of some of these looked precarious, especially when
the holds above were occupied by boots and those below by fingers.
Ignoring these antics, Barry and I made our way along tenuous paths on
scree-rattling ledges which clung to the side of the ridge. Various people
were descending the final pyramid; it didn't look straightforward. We
explored round the steep-sided base of the tower, but were no nearer to a
solution when we were hailed by a man who turned out to be a guide with
a nervous looking client in tow.

'If that's no good,' he said, 'Try this way – most guides use this way.'
And he climbed steeply up a slab, advising his client where the holds
were. They were using a rope and the guide was climbing in short pitches
and bringing the client up. With all this activity going on around us I lost
focus and became undecided. To compound my uncertainty a few
snowflakes fell. Today was not the day. This path had led to an
unimportant failure.

'You may regret this,' said Barry, already on his third round.

However, consolation was at hand for we decided to lengthen our day
by descending the Garbh Corrie and going round the coastal path to
Camasunary and out to the Torrin road at Robostan.

Retracing our steps to the bealach, into the Rough Corrie we plunged.
I hadn't been been there since the late 1980s and what I remembered as a
pristine boulder-slope has now developed its own little path of sorts. On
the way down – still a bone-shaking experience – we briefly caught up
with a party of young people who had just done the famous Dubhs Ridge,
the obvious and best way to climb Sgùrr Dubh Mòr.

We struggled down the corrie and then made the mistake of going too
far right and getting involved in the little cliffs and bluffs of Meall na
Cuilce, but we extricated ourselves and gained the path by Loch Coruisk.
In pleasant evening sunlight we crossed the stepping stones and took the
shoreline way round the coast.

A day it seemed to be for being overawed by ordinary obstacles. The
Bad Step in either direction, wet or dry, with or without a large pack, had
never bothered either of us. This time the step onto the slab, high above
the ebb-tide, seemed perilous, and neither of us was prepared to make it.
Instead we traversed the loose and loathsome avoiding path which has
developed above the Step. A cuckoo was calling on the hillside.

Much later we slithered across the slimy seaweed in the Camasunary river, refilled our water bottle and sat on the bank. The tide was out and no sea-trout jumped in the pools below the ruined bridge. The house here used to be the most stylish bothy in Scotland. Now, reclaimed by its owner, it stands empty and on the verge of ruin. I looked through one of the broken windows. Cement bags were scattered around the dirty floor but nothing had been done. As Will Rowland noted in last year's *Journal*, the building constructed by the MBA away at the other end of the bay doesn't even have a fireplace … . On we went over the soft green machair dusted with pale orchids and tiny violets.

Barry went ahead on the stony track over to Robostan in hope of a lift to his car at Torrin, while I followed more slowly. Once at the road I had only gone a few hundred yards when headlights approached through the dusk.

'First car that came,' he said with a huge grin. 'I didn't think they'd stop.'

Paths are odd things. Sometimes obvious, sometimes barely discernible – a mere suggestion in the grass. Happiness has a relationship with paths. We seem to need paths in the sense that we need goals to pursue which give our lives meaning. At the same time it seems important to get off the path, stop pursuing, and appreciate what lies to either side.

In Tolstoy's *War and Peace* the aristocrat Pierre Bezúkhov is caught up in the fall of Moscow and thrown into prison. All his life Pierre has been searching for some way to give his life meaning. He tries debauchery, intellectual activity and freemasonry, but none of them brings fulfilment. In prison he meets the simple peasant Platón Karatáyev and learns from him that life 'is the living of it'. In our terms it is seeing the blood-red grasses fringing the little streams, hearing the croak of the ptarmigan, seeing the tiny flowers on the machair, feeling the soft spring of the ground under our feet, and delighting in these things.

JUST FOR A PHOTO

by Noel Williams

AS A TEACHER IN HIGHLAND REGION I was very fortunate every February to get a long weekend (Friday–Monday) as a half-term break. On numerous occasions I took advantage of this short holiday to pay a visit to Barrisdale in Knoydart. There is some fine winter climbing in Coire Dhorrcail and the remote setting means that you normally have the place to yourself at that time of year.

The usual approach, along an undulating path on the south side of Loch Hourn, is varied and delightful though it can seem a long way when carrying climbing gear as well. However, on a couple of visits I went in by boat and I must confess that if this can be arranged it is certainly the quickest option.

As a complete non-swimmer I've always been a bit wary of water, but on an early trip there I was persuaded against my better judgement to venture in by canoe. This remains my one and only journey anywhere by canoe. The school had two ancient fibreglass KW7s which we took to Kinloch Hourn strapped to the roof of a car. I struggled to keep up with my much more experienced companion, and I found the tide-race through the narrows at halfway a little too exciting for comfort. By an amazing stroke of good fortune, however, we arrived at Barrisdale Bay on the flood tide and managed to paddle to within a short distance of the bothy. We took steak and a bottle of wine with us in a watertight compartment.

Canoeing into Barrisdale, February 1982. All photos by the Author.

The only other other trip I've done by water was in Douglas Anderson's inflatable, which had a 45hp outboard motor. We blasted along Loch Hourn and seemed to get there in no time. We then moored the boat on a running line just near the end of the vehicular track on the south side of the bay. This left an easy walk of just over two kilometres to the bothy.

Having helped with the Knoydart section of *Northern Highlands South* I promised Neil Adams I would try to get new digital images of Coire Dhorrcail this winter for the new South-West selected winter climbing guide. We had a good dump of snow in January this year and the weather remained cold for several weeks. As a result of the coronavirus lockdown Ben Nevis was unusually quiet, although a party from Glasgow had to be rescued from *Minus Two Gully* and were fined by the police for their pains. I managed to get a dramatic photo of the rescue from my house with my new telephoto lens. (See page 282.)

For a resident of Highland Region the coronavirus travel restrictions have hardly been onerous and in theory I could 'exercise' anywhere from John o' Groats to Bridge of Orchy. I kept my eye on the forecast and prayed the snow wouldn't disappear. In early February a good weather window of several days was predicted, with clear blue skies but very low temperatures. This was my chance.

I knew the bothy at Barrisdale would be closed so I planned on bivvying out. I have a good sleeping bag and decided to take just a bivvy bag rather than a tent. I left home just after midday and drove at a leisurely pace along the single-track road towards Kinloch Hourn. The road was clear as far as Tomdoun but by the time I'd climbed up to the Quoich dam the road was covered in thick snow with deep icy ruts. The stretch of road on the north side of Loch Quoich proved to be the crux because a lot of snow had drifted onto the road where it ran through a long stretch of rhododendron bushes. My wheels started spinning and I slewed to a halt on an uphill section. I kicked myself for not bringing my shovel, but after backing up and rocking to and fro I managed to break out of the ruts and gained traction again. Deer were plentiful, so I had to look out for them as well. The narrow and twisty road down to Kinloch Hourn itself is always a little worrying in winter, but fortunately it was completely free of snow and there were no other vehicles about.

I parked in the parking area, put my boots on, left some money in the honesty box and set off on the last 750m of tarmac to the road end. It soon became obvious that I would have to be extremely cautious on the path that day. The ground was rock hard, any lying water was frozen solid and most rocks were covered in verglas. I wasn't expecting to see anyone else and the last thing I wanted was a mishap.

I recognised the early tunnel through rhododendrons from the return leg on my previous trip. On that occasion I had given my friend Willie Jeffrey my spare headtorch while I went back to find the camera I'd stupidly left at our last stop. Rechargeable batteries are a good idea but they don't hold their charge very well. He had cursed me as he groped his way through the tunnel in the pitch black.

The ice-covered approach path along Loch Hourn.

There are a couple of big up-and-down sections on the path, which avoid tricky crags overlooking the shore. On one trip I was amazed to see the light of one of our party behind me as he fought his way along the shore having missed the path. On another occasion walking into Barrisdale late at night a friend immediately in front of me stepped off the path into space. He was only saved from plunging headfirst into the

sea because he got caught upside down in a tree. He was grateful that I was able to help him extricate himself.

On this year's visit I managed to do most of the approach in daylight and only had to get my torch out for the final descent to Barrisdale Bay. I hadn't set any records, but had enjoyed every minute of it. There were no signs of life as I passed Barisdale House though I noticed that it had acquired a fine dry-stone wall since my previous visit. An outside light flashed on automatically as I passed the keeper's cottage, but I kept going. A diesel generator was belching fumes as I passed the end of the building with the bothy.

In order to save weight I hadn't bothered taking a map or compass with me. I thought I could find the stalkers' path to Coire Dhorrcail blindfold but I was wrong. Immediately after crossing the bridge over the River Barrisdale I knew to turn right, but I was thrown by a newly improved track that seemed to be heading out towards Barrisdale Bay. My memory was playing tricks on me and after following the track for a short distance I decided to head off leftwards over boggy ground. This was a big mistake. The ground wasn't frozen as I'd assumed it would be, probably because

Coire Dhorrcail and Ladhar Bheinn, 9 February 2021.

it was salt marsh, and the next thing I knew both boots had filled with water. I scuttled back to the track and decided to see where it lead. It eventually petered out by a small stream. I crossed over the stream and found a small walled enclosure where I could shelter though the ground inside was very uneven. I still needed to gain height so that I'd be in position to get photographs early the next day. So I drank some coffee from my flask and then decided to slant diagonally leftwards up the steep hillside.

I discovered the following day that I'd actually been in the right place, but the stalkers' path heads a long way left at this point. I failed to find the stalkers' path that night but after gaining a fair bit of height I decided to settle down for the night on a flattening behind a small knoll. I took my boots off and dried my feet and put on a spare pair of dry socks. It was bitterly cold so I kept my clothes on and got into my sleeping bag. I ate a couple of rolls and some chocolate and slugged back the remainder of my coffee. I didn't have a stove so that was the last warm drink I had. I made another mistake by not taking my boots inside my Gore-Tex bivvy bag with me. The wind got up from time to time and it seemed to roar around in the trees just above me. A tawny owl hooted as I looked up at the stars. I zipped my bag closed and soon fell fast asleep.

I slept as sound as a bell and woke up just before 8. At least in the daylight I could tell that I was in roughly the right place. I had a good view of the north face of Luinne Bheinn, and although it was in deep shadow I could make out the amazing descent route I had found many moons ago when I'd had the longest and best standing glissade of my life.

It turned out it had been the coldest night of the year so far and after eating a roll for breakfast I tried to put my boots on. They were frozen absolutely solid as were my wet socks. It took me twenty minutes and a huge amount of effort before I managed to get my feet in them. I set off uphill trending slightly left and was delighted to soon join the stalkers' path where it began to level off. At the high point on the shoulder I had a great view of Beinn Sgritheall across Loch Hourn.

I now decided to stash my rucksack and sleeping gear and continue with just my camera kit. These days I'm rationed to only two bottles of Cherry Coke per outing and this is when I discovered that my spring water – the healthy option I'd been forced to take – was frozen completely solid. I was very grateful that my Cherry Coke was merely slushy.

The path descends slightly from the shoulder before turning leftwards into the mouth of Coire Dhorrcail. This in one of the most dramatic corners in the Highlands. A few hundred metres further on the magnificent headwall of Coire Dhorrcail comes into sight capped by the shapely summit of Ladhar Bheinn. Although there was little snow to speak of where I stood, the distant face looked in splendid winter condition.

The sun was quite low but the right-hand part of the headwall was well illuminated and I took lots of photos. It was tricky crossing the icy stream in the floor of the corrie, but this allowed me to also take photos of the north face of Stob a' Chearcaill. I spent a couple of hours altogether taking pictures above the snowline.

I then headed back down the corrie and rescued my rucksack. My spring water was still frozen solid so I had to drink more Coke with another roll. I then followed the stalkers' path I'd missed the night before as it zigzagged down the slope. It wasn't as easy to follow as I'd remembered because much of it was covered in dead bracken. I eventually reached the end of the track that led me back to Barrisdale.

By the time I got back to the car it was dark and when I took my boots off I found I'd developed some spectacular blisters on both feet, mainly because of the unforgiving ground. I drove as fast as I dared on the snow-covered section of road to make sure I maintained momentum on the uphill icy stretches. Once I reached the dam I knew I was more or less home and dry.

The day after I got back I learned that Tom Prentice had broken his leg when out taking photos in Pollok Park. It goes to show that you can't be too careful. I lost both big toe-nails in the days that followed and my blisters took an age to heal, but I had the photos I was after.

THE WINTER MUNROS

by Kevin Woods

SOMETIMES THE BEST IDEAS creep up from nowhere, building in the background until they can't be ignored any longer. In the summer of 2013 I did the Munros in a three-month trip, which at the time greatly expanded my abilities. It was a fantastic summer. It was hard, I learned a lot, and by the end I was getting around the hills very differently from the way I did when I started.

The Winter Munros sat in the back of my head for years, casual at first but an idea that turned more serious with each passing winter. I started looking at the fine details of the weather, noting daily forecasts and readings from December to March. I tightened up on my navigation and increased my volume of winter climbing. I'd do days on the winter hills, then compare them against the weather station readings, probing for the upper limit. Maybe surprisingly, that limit was a lot higher than I'd first thought.

What started as a vague idea morphed into a full-blown, hard ambition. I was excited to be unravelling the pieces while bowled over that it meant I would actually have to go for this some time. And what a thought that was – an awesome cocktail of flying imagination, thrill and pit-of-the-stomach fear.

I worked out the theory behind the Winter Munros long before I had the life circumstances to support it. Sorting out life's priorities and finances was one of the last things to fall into place.

I considered going for the round in the 2018–19 season. In the end it seemed I might gain by delaying one year, and it was just as well: the winter gave little in the way of hard conditions, and autumn seemed to roll over to spring. Tragically it was also the year the Scottish mountaineering community lost Andy Nisbet, Steve Perry and Martin Moran. Thus two people who had already done the Winter Munros were gone, and although I knew neither of them it felt like a punch in the gut. I'd read essentially everything Martin wrote on the Scottish mountains, and related massively to his sentiments and aesthetic of place. Steve had revealed less on his monstrous four-month winter backpack, but a trawl through the internet revealed some in-depth podcasts. In the end, having previously set a target to begin in December 2019, the losses of that year did not blunt my wishes at all.

A late change to plan was to go for the vehicle-based round. I'd planned the whole thing in backpacking terms, then dropped that for multiple reasons: partly social, partly in flexibility to choose mountain ranges, but also nutritional. The backpacking approach might have built on what had gone before, but I would lack regular support and did not wish to lean so heavily on Glasgow-based family. Lastly I did not care to substitute a steady diet of whole foods for three months on processed food fit for

The auld year: Bidean nam Bian on 31 December 2020. Photo: Kevin Woods.

backpacking. I enjoyed being reactive to conditions, eating well and travelling lighter. So I bought a van, did a basic conversion, and on the shortest day of 2019 started my winter on Ben More on Mull.

From the beginning I was in the right headspace. I considered my options as far as the weather forecast allowed, and no further. The trip may have been months in duration, but I settled into a day-to-day pattern around the Southern Highlands. As is typical for December, the snows were transitory and the daylight rarified. Wall-to-wall westerlies ensured a daily drenching.

And I loved it; allowing this distilled, intense focus of years to emerge. Each day, I did as much as I felt able while supporting myself; every day formulating a plan for the next based upon the forecasts. Having wrapped up the Etive and Coe area, I moved towards Glen Lochay and Glen Lyon for a period that would see the Southern Highlands completed.

Daylight was limited but the storms were transitory, short and sharp. There were many incoming depressions, but the calm between them didn't always coincide with daylight. In the middle of January, I waited out 24 hours of torrential rain in Killin then walked through a night, a day and the following night to complete the Southern Highlands on a pre-dawn Meall nan Tàrmachan. It was worth skipping sleep for this: the forecast gusts were high enough to put notions of the high tops to bed.

The second part of the winter began with a run across the Glen Shee hills in blizzarding weather. I had a freezing mid-winter trip into the Tarf Hotel with Lorraine McCall. Here was full-blown mid-winter desolation with the river freezing over, deep snow and incoming weather fronts: exactly how you'd want the Tarf in the depths of the season.

Crossing to the Cairngorms, I did a four-day traverse with Helen

Kevin Woods traversing southwards on Bruach na Frìthe. Photo: Dave MacLeod.

Rennard, from Invercauld to Feshie. The first couple of days were in sun, high winds and on crunchy, firm snow. Stepping out of Corrour bothy on the third morning revealed the hills entirely stripped of snow. Up high there were only the mist and drenching quantities of drizzle! We continued over the western summits to Feshie, and I was finally in Strathspey.

Momentum gathered as I went westward. With the support of friends, I built the mileage through Lochaber to the highest winter totals. I felt I was on a roll, each day a range in itself: the Mamores in one, the Grey Corries to Nevis in one. The six Ben Alder hills took a beautiful long day culminating in a wander over the Alder plateau on a calm and clear evening – walking on crunchy, firm snow with the moon rising and the sun fizzling out in the west. In fifty days, and by summit tally, I was almost two-thirds through the trip.

I would have loved to have kept going at pace, but the weather had other ideas. In the second week of February the storms intensified such that it became difficult to get anything done. I'd seen nothing but westerlies since starting and had run out of 'sheltering' eastern hills. There was nothing but to face up to the North-West when the weather was at its very worst. A virus put me on my back – literally – on top of Ben Klibreck of all places. I was now grappling to maintain momentum.

Conditions didn't settle for the rest of February. I plugged away in Glen Shiel in the meantime; there were spectacular conditions with towering snow showers moving through. Wind and spindrift all conspired to create magnificence, a place to feel small among the mountains and very great forces. But I also wanted to move.

I stole an afternoon of calm weather on the Cuillin crest with Mike Lates. I'd met him in his hostel the previous night.

'When are you doing the Cuillin?' he asked.

'Not sure,' I said.

'Go tomorrow!'

And that was it; a plan made out of nowhere, and half the ridge complete. Leading off up the In Pin was a real winter highlight for me, something I had thought about long before. If you were going to face up to the whole Winter Munros, get that pitch done in winter! Soon after, I returned to complete the ridge with Dave MacLeod on another stolen day of calm.

Going into March, conditions did gently ease. Any time the sun was out, the hills seemed to be loaded under piles of powder so I was still restricted from the deepest ranges.

Covid built in the background like a lead weight, then in the middle of the month the sun finally emerged. It was the first time conditions ever came good for more than a day, perhaps two. That elusive combination of settled weather and snowpack quickly got me through Mullardoch, Monar and Fisherfield. At last I could put the foot down on the big days while the outside world was on the cusp of shutting down.

With a handful of summits left, the world finally stopped. I knew perfectly well what had been going on, but seemed wedged between my need to finish the winter round and the fact that, for the first time in a couple of generations, going to the hills was forbidden. I went out to Seana Bhràigh on a day of eerie silence and a ceiling of grey cloud, draining the colour from the land. On this, my penultimate Munro, I was low and getting lower. I'd left Ben Lomond for my last, an obvious symmetry to my first ever Munro in 2001. But now it seemed difficult to justify.

In March 2020, many had much bigger problems than me in my self-imposed predicament. I never want the hillwalking to be anything but enjoyment for myself; why should it be more? It is, after all, just great fun. But there's no denying it had gone well beyond that. Now I was facing abandonment of the Winter Munros one summit short of the last. It was not good for the head; I had to finish, even just for myself. Nobody need know, but I needed to know. A couple of days later, I headed out just before dawn and finished my winter on top of Ben Lomond, there myself with the mist.

And what else to do now, except go home, enjoy the spring sun, head out on the bike? I could at least be glad that I finished the thing I started a rather long time ago.

THE MORNING AFTER THE NIGHT BEFORE

by Geoff Cohen

Never sees horrid night, the child of hell,
But, like a lackey, from the rise to set
Sweats in the eye of Phoebus, and all night
Sleeps in Elysium…
— Shakespeare, Henry V.

AS WE AGE AND BECOME less active on the hill it is pleasant to beguile ourselves with reminiscence of the excitements of yesteryear. Our *Journal* is full of such looking back and I hope I may be forgiven for adding to the genre. While attempting to do so I have to confess to a dreadful memory, so that the few vignettes I want to describe are represented in my mind by only the vaguest of 'screenshots'. Since much of what I'm talking about took place in the dark, even these screenshots are pretty empty!

I am a great believer in enjoying the mountains in the evening. I'm prepared to risk a few hours stumbling in the dark in order to maximise the time spent high up with a view of a beautiful sunset. Contrary to the calumnies spread by my so-called friends I do not actively seek to suffer unplanned bivouacs, but they have admittedly sometimes occurred, and in retrospect they provide the most vivid memories.[1]

In 1993 I crossed the Atlantic for the first time to climb in the Canadian Rockies. Ian Rowe, with whom I had climbed in Scotland in the early 1970s, was our excellent host. From his base in Golden he showed us not only the superb Bugaboos but also some very impressive and little-known walls in the 'Welsh Lakes' range. On the day before I was due to return home Ian and I set our sights on the East Ridge of Mount Temple. At one time this was considered among the 50 best climbs in North America. I can only hope they have found a few better ones since.

After a long haul up to the ridge (during which we were able to admire the north face, which has been likened to the Eiger) we embarked on a traverse of various gendarmes. We lacked a detailed description, and all I recall is a fair bit of complex up and down climbing. After many hours we reached a point where we needed to ascend towards the summit snowfields, and here we encountered the loosest rock I have ever had to deal with. It was not technically difficult but belays were purely psychological as every single thing we touched seemed to move. Past this we had a pleasant snow-ice pitch to circumvent a cornice, and emerged on a gently inclined slope just as darkness fell.

Never mind, it was a fine night so we just scooped out a bit of a ledge in the snow and sat down. Instead of cuddling up together we sat facing

---

[1] For memorable bivouacs in bygone days, see 'Night Up There' in *SMCJ*, 22/131 (April 1941), 277–86. – HON. ED.

each other, feet to feet. I don't think I had any spare clothing. The lights visible below, and the stars above, twinkled pitilessly all night as I shivered in my anorak. Conversation was surprisingly sparse, given that Ian has plenty of Canadian adventures to relate. Dawn arrived and we ambled up to the summit then hastened down the easy descent, reaching the cars about noon. I should have explained that we had driven independently: Ian had come in his car as he had to return west to Golden, while I had a hire car that I needed to return to Calgary. I had thought that my flight was late afternoon, but on opening my car I checked and found to my horror that departure was in about two hours' time. I leaped into the driver's seat and sped off. Getting to the airport through the busy highways around the unfamiliar city was horribly tense – a single mistake at a junction would mean missing my flight. I drew up with some ten minutes to spare and opened the boot. No rucksack! I'd left it in Ian's car, but had the detritus of three weeks' holiday strewn about my car. Stuffing everything into plastic bags I rushed to check in and just had time to phone the hire company and tell them where the car was. (It was supposed to be returned to their city depot; this was long before mobile phones of course.) Somehow I made it to my flight still in the sweaty clothes that had helped me survive the night. My rucksack and climbing gear arrived home many months later, courtesy of Ian's brother-in-law, a pilot.

A couple of years later I took a holiday in Wadi Rum with Andy Tibbs and Helen Shannon. The magnificent sandstone walls of Jebel Rum loomed over the campsite. We spent a good week exploring Bedouin routes and doing excellent climbs in different parts of the range. Towards

Helen Shannon and Geoff Cohen getting ready to bivouac at the top of Renee van Hasselt (Wadi Rum). Photo: Andy Tibbs.

the end of our stay we decided to climb one of the longer routes directly up the face above the campsite (*Renee van Hasselt*). Challenging long chimneys and steep fingery walls led after about ten pitches to a point of no return. From a hopelessly inadequate belay it was necessary to traverse out on the lip of an overhang over a huge drop. The 'chicken-head' holds were good, so that technically it was only about Severe, but there was awesome exposure and no protection until after about 40 feet we reached a ledge with a tree. There was more hard climbing above and finally as darkness approached we squirmed up a final deep chimney. There was now no alternative to a night out. Andy and Helen were able to huddle together, while I lay out on a neighbouring slab, clad only in a tee-shirt and light fleece. It was Easter time, and desert nights can be quite cold at over 1700 metres, so a decent amount of shivering ensued, while trying to elevate the spirit by losing one's thoughts in the infinite starry spaces above.

But again what remains most in the memory is the following morning. Andy was always the one to get us off the mountain. On previous climbs he had successfully deciphered the maze of domes that conspire to cover the summit of Jebel Rum. On this occasion it was not far at all to our chosen descent – by abseil down a route named *King Hussein*. This climb consists of a series of horrendous chimneys at a standard far harder than anything we could climb. So it was essential not to get the abseil ropes stuck. Andy and Helen having gone first, I gingerly lowered myself to the lip of a huge roof and peered down at them a hundred feet below. Very fortunately it was one of the rare times in my life when I displayed some common sense. Observing a leering crack in the lip, prudence took hold. I hauled myself back 25 feet to the abseil anchor and constructed enough length of line to take the abseil point over the lip. Clutching the line till I was over the lip I was able to abseil free down the chimney, confident that the rope would pull and we would not have to attempt the impossible task of climbing (or prusiking!) up the roof. More wild abseils followed – I have a vivid memory of Helen perched on a tiny ledge in the middle of a huge wall. By the time we reached the bottom in mid-morning our friends had organised a camel party to carry us the twenty-minute walk back to the tents.

I had an even harder night out a decade later. Dave Wilkinson, Steve Kennedy, Des Rubens and I made an expedition to Peru's Sierra Vilcanota. Towards the end of the trip Steve and Des elected to climb an elegant ridge (the 'Scottish Spur') directly above our base camp, while Dave and I went off to explore a face we could not see on a peak of about 5900m with the strange name Ninaparaco. After a day trudging up a broad glacier before branching up another tributary, we camped with a partial view of our face. Unfortunately we discovered next morning that a lower portion of the face had been entirely hidden from view. Some relatively complex route-finding took us to the base of the face proper, where a dangerous-looking icefall appeared to bar the way. Dave was undaunted

Ninaparaco, showing the route taken. The unplanned bivvy was near the rocks, about half way up, below and a bit right of the pronounced arête. Photo: Geoff Cohen.

however and soon pushed us through to the shelter of a dripping ice cave. From here a series of interesting ice and rock pitches on a diagonal line took us after a couple of hundred metres to open snow slopes. We laboured up these, gaining a narrowing couloir to the summit, which we reached about 4 p.m. Afternoon cloud swirled about, giving the scene a wild Andean atmosphere. We rapidly began retracing our steps, but Dave was soon well ahead. At a certain point, having come down perhaps 300 metres, I traversed right to what I thought was our diagonal line. There was no sign of Dave and it was beginning to get dark. I shouted but got no response. I am not sure why, but I began to think that I had lost him for good. For some reason the trauma of losing my great friend George Gibson on the Ben a decade earlier played on my mind. I imagined that Dave had gone the same way.

   Playing safe I just sat down where I was on an outward sloping rock-shelf between snow bands. The only belays I could find were poor, but gradually I divested myself of crampons and other accoutrements and made myself as comfortable as I could, in a not very convenient sitting position. The night comes quickly at these near-equatorial latitudes, and (unlike the summer Alps) it lasts a full twelve hours. But it was not long after dark that Dave's head torch appeared a few hundred feet below me. We established shouting contact, but I felt it was unwise to try and reach him in the dark. So we each had to settle into our own exiguous nook for

Dave Wilkinson in a '...wild Andean atmosphere' amid late-afternoon cloud at the summit of Ninaparaco. Photo: Geoff Cohen.

the long night. The moon rose and shone for hour after hour on the exquisite face of Callangate (6110m) opposite. But time passed extremely slowly as I shivered away, wondering how, at the supposedly mature age of 57, I had managed to get myself into this pickle.

Finally the sun rose again, and with infinite care I packed up and made my way down to join Dave. We were both exhausted by the long night out. Retreat down our diagonal line and icefall went without incident, but once on the glacier the effects of sun and lack of sleep really began to tell. I was unbelievably slow, barely able to put one leg in front of the other. A snail's pace descent got us back to the tent, where we had to spend another whole day recovering before we could muster the reserves to pack everything out to base camp.

This night out had been entirely my fault. I had forgotten a slight traverse that we had done on the ascent. Dave had followed our ascent line correctly, whereas the point where I had been seeking to traverse was too high. Had I joined him just as the light was fading, it is likely we would have had the energy to continue the descent by torchlight. The unplanned bivouac not only inflicted the slow tortuous descent in the sun next day but so depleted us as to require two extra days on the mountain. Bivouacs are all very well – it is afterwards that the problems start.

SCOTTISH SEA STACKS:
THREE OLD MEN AND TWO YOUNG ONES

by Richard Ive

Four extraordinary days. An accidental new route. And it all started so innocently. With a window of opportunity in September 2016 between finishing my postgraduate degree and starting the law conversion course, a Scottish climbing extravaganza with Rob Moorcroft, my friend and climbing partner, seemed like the ideal adventure.

The Old Man of Hoy

We made the long journey north from Manchester to Tongue in early September. After a couple of days in the local area – one spent on Ben Hope and another on the majestic Ben Loyal – we decided to head across to Hoy via Stromness. By this point, Rob was overflowing with enthusiasm. I suggested we should keep an open mind; visit the headland overlooking the Old Man of Hoy and 'Take a look'. Rob, who was by now familiar with this turn of phrase, translated it as 'Let's go for it!'

On the ferry across to Stromness, our spirits were high but, on reaching the port, high winds and torrential rain put a dampener on everything. We had promised a woman working on the ferry that we would wave to her from the top of the Old Man the next day. That promise was starting to look like wishful thinking. As we walked from the ferry terminal to the campsite on the peninsula in the pouring rain, we were struck by the gloominess of the scene on that dark and dispiriting night.

On arrival at the campsite, we realised just how exposed the peninsula was. Our thoughts turned immediately to finding a suitable spot for the tent – one where it would not be flattened in the night. Next morning the storm, to our relief, had abated. The walk to the ferry terminal presented Stromness in a different light: pleasant, cobbled streets lined with quaint shops and pretty houses with colourful doors. The gloom of the previous night had passed. Things were looking up – or so we thought.

On arriving at the quay for the Moaness Ferry, we were met by a despondent looking captain: 'The ferry won't be going today. This morning, the wind was so strong we snapped one of the warps.' A melodramatic gesture revealed the line in question. It looked as if our adventure had met its end before it had even begun.

Rob and I quizzed the captain. Our question, 'Is there another way of getting to Hoy this morning?' elicited just the one word: 'Houton'. 'Houton, Captain?' His manner softened imperceptibly: 'A ferry from Houton will take you to Lyness.' 'And when might that ferry leave?' The response '20 minutes' spurred Rob and me into action. We jumped into a taxi and arrived at Houton just in time to see the ferry leaving the harbour. We caught the next one, but time was now nail-bitingly tight.

While on the ferry, Rob managed to book a taxi to take us up from Lyness to Rackwick – the attack point for our mission. On arrival, we scanned the scene in vain for anything that might resemble a taxi. Nothing. Then the door of a dark green, 1990s 5-series BMW slowly opened. A 'mature' man, well into his seventies, got out. He was wearing a deerstalker.

'Mr Williams?' Rob ventured.

'Aye,' came the response.

Mr Williams's driving was as unconventional as his appearance. Whilst he was regaling us with one of his many stories, the taxi crept along. But in the (rare) moments of silence, he would unexpectedly put his foot down and the taxi would leap forward at incredible speed. During one of the slower moments, he opened all the car windows, pointed to some large rocks in the distance, and told us they had previously been people's houses. Were we being taken for a ride in more than just the literal sense? It turned out that, although he was a native of Hoy, he had spent some time in 'the Deep South' – Fife.

He had taxied many famous climbers over the years. Had any of them been unsuccessful on the Old Man of Hoy? 'Yes. Two. I knew they were not going to make it.' How had he 'known' that that particular pair were not going to 'make it'? 'I just knew.'

'Will we "make it"?' Silence. And then, after what seemed like an eternity, a gentle nod of the head. I caught the reflection of Mr Williams smiling furtively at me in the rear-view mirror. That was enough. We had the blessing of the Gatekeeper to The Old Man of Hoy. He was to be our good-luck charm. Our parting was graced by one final flourish of eccentricity: 'Mr Williams. It's not my only name, you know.' He proceeded to explain that he sometimes used a pseudonym.

Time was now tight. It had just turned 15.00. That did not give us much time to get down to the base of the Old Man of Hoy and climb its five pitches before we were due to wave to the woman on the ferry. We hurriedly dropped off the tent and the camping gear at the Rackwick bothy, giving us just enough time to read the warning sign:

CLIMBERS ARE HEREBY WARNED THAT THERE IS NEITHER SUITABLE RESCUE EQUIPMENT NOR EXPERIENCED ROCK CLIMBERS IN THE VICINITY. CLIMBERS THEREFORE PROCEED AT THEIR OWN RISK.

This was a sobering welcome.

The next two hours just evaporated. It was 17.00 as I set off, leading. Two pitches up, I had to persuade Rob that we should retreat: the mist was coming in, rain had started to fall with more persistence, and the light was continuing to fade as dusk rapidly turned to night. Retreat, in practice, meant undertaking a 60m free-hanging abseil back to the base of the sea-stack. We abseiled down, made our way back to the tent, and bedded down for the night on our rucksacks (we had had to leave a lot of things in the car on the mainland), hoping that the next day's weather would be better.

Unfortunately, the following morning we were woken by the sound of rain loudly battering down on the tent. As the pattering continued (*pit-a-pat, pit-a-pat, pit-a-pat*) throughout the morning, we became increasingly dejected. It looked as if our hopes of climbing the Old Man of Hoy were about to be dashed – again. Finally, at 13.00, the pattering on the tent stopped. Rob ventured to poke his head out. 'Rich,' he exclaimed, 'the rain has stopped and the sun is out.' I could not quite believe what I was hearing, so frantically unzipped the other side of the tent and forced my head out. Rob had not been playing some kind of cruel joke. The rain really had stopped, and the sun really had come out. Now was our chance. We both knew that we had to act fast if we were to seize it. This time, we managed to start climbing by 15.00.

We knew we had six or so hours of daylight. The ominous clouds of the day before had long since departed. Rob and I were in high spirts at the end of Pitch 3. The crux was behind us, we were making good time, and we joked that, if we kept this sort of efficiency up, we would arrive at the top too early for our waving extravaganza. We spoke too soon.

Above the third belay ledge are two chimneys. The description that we were using advised us to follow the 'obvious' chimney. This presented us with something of a dilemma. Both chimneys looked equally 'obvious'. We plumped for the left one. I led up, and up, and up. Eventually, after a short, rightwards traverse, I reached some in-situ gear: a golden screwgate, a couple of big hexes, and a large nut. It looked as if another party had reached this point and then thought better of it, deciding instead to abseil off. Rob agreed. It seemed that on the last pitch we had gone off the original *Original Route*. Poking my head round the corner, I could see the infamous crack of the final pitch. A short, 10–15m rightwards traverse across a smooth, vertical face would take us to it. We could see a way forwards – or at least sideways – in the form of virgin rock. The traverse was tremendously exposed and delicate; equally exhilarating for both leader and second.[1] By this point, the sun – which had started to drop – was shining through the crack in the middle of the stack. A short sprint up the final pitch took us to the top. Mission accomplished!

It was as we basked in the early evening sun on the summit of the Old Man of Hoy that Rob and I were able to enjoy a firm handshake and take in our magnificent surroundings. Not only had we reached the top, but we had – as promised – managed to wave to the woman on the ferry. Whether or not she had seen us was another matter. Perhaps more significantly, we had avoided being projectile-vomited upon by any fulmars – despite their best attempts.

By the time that Rob and I turned our thoughts to the descent, the sun was setting into the sea – a beautiful sight. The final, free-hanging abseil was undertaken in the silence of the dark with the assistance of our headtorches – an eery experience. Upon touching down, Rob turned his

---

[1] For details of this new route, *East Face Chimney Variation*, see *SMCJ*, 45/208 (2017), 170. As noted in the New Routes section of this year's *Journal*, it has now been renamed *We Spoke Too Soon*.

Old Man of Hoy: Richard Ive leading crux pitch and Rob Moorcroft belaying. Photographer unknown.

head to the darkness consuming the sea. He was fixated on a flashing light. 'Look, Rich,' he called out, 'someone is lost out there. They're sending an SOS.' I turned my head and counted the flashes – six quick, one long. He was right. There was a light flashing. Six short flashes followed by one long one. Repeat. Our lost soul was a self-respecting South Cardinal Buoy, transformed in the imagination by the intensity of the dark and the adrenalin-fuelled effort of the past few hours.

We made our way back up the cliff on the mainland, from where we could begin our walk, under a clear starlit sky, back to the tent. Happy and triumphant, we unzipped the doors of the tent sometime after midnight, feeling delighted that we had climbed the infamous Old Man of Hoy. It was an experience that we knew we would never forget.

The following day, Rob called our taxi driver, Mr Williams. We had asked him to drop us off at Moaness. As soon as we got into the taxi, Mr Williams asked us if we had 'made it'. 'Yes,' we replied. His response meant more than the climb itself: 'I knew you would.' Then, as if an afterthought, 'Did you have any champagne?' We confirmed that we had omitted this from our emergency equipment. Was he about to produce some? No! It was a lead-in to another of his stories: a helicopter, three glamorous waitresses and an unforgettable birthday party on the top of the Old Man, told with such gusto that he surely must have been there himself!

The ferry back to the mainland passes the Old Man of Hoy. We cast it a final glance. By virtue of our inadvertent first ascent, we felt that we had become a part of its history. Just after we had passed the Old Man, we found the woman of our outward voyage. She thanked us for waving, and assured us she had waved back. As the ferry steamed along, we thought about the next few days. Rob had to be back in Manchester in three days' time. 'What about Am Buachaille and the Old Man of Stoer?' I asked. Rob grinned. A plan was formed.

Am Buachaille

The next morning, the alarm went off at 6am. Our tent was pitched just a few miles away from Am Buachaille. Yesterday's rain seemed trivial in comparison with that morning's thunderstorm. Clearly, the rock would take some time to dry out. We rolled over, quite happy for an excuse to press the 'snooze' button on the alarm. Thankfully, the thunderstorm passed as quickly as it had arrived. In no time at all, we were up and off.

A team of nine – three female climbers and six men (a dad and the film support team) – arrived opposite the base of the stack shortly before we did.[2] They were aiming to climb the same three sea-stacks as us, over the course of three days. Am Buachaille was their first. Rob and I mentioned that we had climbed the Old Man of Hoy a couple of days earlier. Rob – ever keen for 'crag-swag' – proudly announced that he had 'rescued' some old gear. This struck a chord with one of the women, who referred to the Old Man of Hoy as her 'nemesis'. She had, she explained, had to retreat a couple of years ago, after she and some friends had gone off-route.

'What gear did you leave?' asked Rob.

'My lucky golden screwgate and my favourite blue hex,' came the reply.

Rob and I laughed. 'Would you like them back?' The answer was a resounding 'Yes!' Climbing really is a small world.

The three women swam across first. (There is a narrow gap between

---

[2] The three women – Vicki Mayes, Natalie Feather and Jennifer Rogers – were raising money for *Urban Uprising*. The film of their climbing journey won the 2017 BMC Women in Adventure Film Competition.

Am Buachaille. Photo:Dave Linnett.

the mainland and the stack that, even at low tide, requires a short swim.) Minutes later, Rob and I followed. We were thankful for the warming sun. We scampered up the stack's landward side. At the first belay, halfway up the stack, the three women were somewhat perplexed as to where the next pitch went; it was not at all obvious. They asked us if we wanted to nip past. Feeling a little chilly, we accepted their offer. Thankfully, after a minute or so of feeling around for good holds, I pulled myself up from the belay ledge and got cracking on the top pitch. The initial difficulties gave way to trouble-free climbing. I soon reached the top, swiftly followed by Rob. Am Buachaille's summit was much smaller than the Old Man of Hoy's, and we perched precariously like sea-birds.

We abseiled past the three women, who were by now almost at the top themselves. A quick, exciting swim took us back to the rocks beneath the mainland cliffs. The tide was now coming in fast, with waves starting to crash against the seaward side of the stack. Before turning our backs, we spared a thought for the first ascensionists, who had misjudged the timings and were forced to spend a cold night on the stack. Thrilling as that must have been, we had places to be and another sea stack to climb: the Old Man of Stoer.

The Old Man of Stoer

After a drive along the coast, Rob and I pitched up next to the Stoer Lighthouse. The following morning, a short walk along the cliff top took us to a viewing point for the Old Man of Stoer – an impressive and inspiring sight. We abseiled to the base of the cliff and made our way to the ropes that marked the start of the Tyrolean traverse. There we found two ropes and the three women from Am Buachaille. They had made an early start, climbed the stack, and were soon to be on their way to Hoy. One of the ropes looked as if it had seen better days. They assured us that the better of the two ropes was safe: 'Oh, it's fine,' they assured us, with a confidence borne of heading in the opposite direction.

The Tyrolean traverse was great fun and surprisingly trouble-free. We soon found ourselves at the first belay on the stack. The occasional wave

Old Man of Stoer. Photo: Dave Linnett.

threatened to give us a soaking, but the sea-state by now was settled. I led us up the Original Route, and after several highly enjoyable pitches, we found ourselves on the top. 'Hurrah! We've done it!' But then the crash of a wave 50 metres below reminded us that the task was only half-done.

We needed to get down and across safely before the tide trapped us. One long abseil took me down to the first belay, from where I could make myself safe. And then nothing happened. What was taking Rob so long?

'Hurry up, Rob! The tide is coming in – fast,' I shouted.

'I am trying, Rich, but I can't,' he shouted back.

'What do you mean, "you can't"?'

He bellowed a reply over the sound of the crashing waves: 'The screwgate connecting me to the anchor at the top is stuck. I just can't get it undone.'

Boom! Crash! Waves were starting to splash my feet now, each more vigorous than the last.

'Get yourself attached to the abseil ropes, and cut the sling to free yourself.'

'Done it, Rich!'

I pulled myself back across the Tyrolean to the mainland. From the end of the rope on that side, I was able to watch Rob make his dramatic journey back. And then there he was – next to me. We were both safe. We had done it. Despite the best efforts of the weather, fulmars and badly behaved screwgates, Two Young Men had climbed Three Old Ones in the space of just four days. A new route had even been thrown in for good measure. Now for the celebrations. We were without champagne (sorry, Mr Williams), but some kind soul had left two cans of coke and two caramel bars on the windscreen of my car. Never have a coke and a caramel bar tasted so good.

If anything, reflecting on this trip has reminded me that climbing is as much about the friends you go with (thanks, Rob), the places you visit (the stunningly beautiful, rural Scotland), and the people you meet along the way (the eccentric Mr Williams, the woman waving on the ferry, and the three women we met on Am Buachaille) as about the climbing itself.

So, from Two Young Men to Three Old Ones: thank you for happy climbing memories that will last a lifetime. All three of you were magnificent – and, I might add, are looking remarkably good for your age. SMC Members, if I may: I wish to finish with an exhortation. Climb these spectacular stacks before they fall into the sea!

THE SHARD

by Callum Johnson

HOW COULD IT BE? I glanced rightwards, distracted from my current pursuit; something had caught my eye. Staring for a few seconds, a line of granite ripples came into focus, rounded edges twisting their way up the otherwise blank wall. My eyes scanned from bottom to top, trying to link the pieces together in my mind. Surely it was not possible? It would have been climbed already. I continued up the steep line of *Haystack*, enjoying the subtle movement on the Cairngorm granite. At the next belay I stood facing outwards, gazing the length of calm Loch Avon, my head swirling with possibilities. I would have to come back.

I wasn't the only one who had seen the possibilities; speaking with Guy Robertson I found he was keen to have a look, so a date was set. We were keen to try and climb on sight, ground-up. We started on the lowest rocks of the Shelter Stone Crag's main bastion, weaving our way up enticing grooves and thin cracks. On only the second pitch, however, our ground-up attempt ground to a halt, at an overlap and a bold slabby section neither of us was willing to commit to. We escaped leftwards up a couple of pitches of *Citadel*, then moved back right to check out the pitch: it was thin but was all there. We moved left again, and I climbed The Pin, then returned right to check out the upper sections of our line, linking pitches of other routes and looping round. Opting for a more logical and direct route I realised our line would not take in the enticingly rippled wall that I had seen – that pitch would have to wait.

Guy abbed the second-last pitch, a soaring crackline, where a wobbly block was wobbled free. Triple checking below before setting it loose, I held my breath – the block flew unhindered 200m to the base of the crag, just scraping the lowest tongue of slabs before shattering to fragments. 'Woah!' We topped out, happy with a good adventure on a big cliff – not quite the day we had hoped for, but we came away confident we had figured out our line, checked the pitches we needed to, and cleaned the sections that required attention. My eyes were now opened to the possibilities that lay before them; even on what I thought to be a well-established, all-climbed-out crag there were new lines to find. We must return soon.

'Same rack as last time?'

'Yep.'

We approached over the plateau, as before, to stash our bags at the top of the crag, enjoying warm morning sun whilst the Loch Avon basin was like a bathtub full of clouds, wisping eastwards on a gentle breeze. There was a lightness to our step as we rock-hopped across the trickling Feith Buidhe; it had been a warm, dry summer in 2018, but we filled our bottles and drank deeply. Bags stashed, we descended, reaching the lowest rocks

Callum Johnson on the penultimate pitch of The Shard (E5,6b) on Shelterstone Crag.
Photo: Guy Robertson.

again, and this time it felt more familiar. We had agreed the order: I would lead first, and we would swing leads from there.

I rack up whilst Guy flakes the ropes.

'Guy, do we have more draws? We've only got six …'

'What?'

We both pause, and nervous laughter ensues. I realise my mistake: I haven't packed my half of the extenders, thinking that Guy was taking them all.

'Woops, sorry; glad we've got some at least!'

We laugh at our position – above us 200m of climbing up to E5, and only six quickdraws. Prusik loops, spare slings and any surplus karabiners are hastily linked together to add to our collection, making it up to nine-and-a-half extenders. I rack the assemblage on my harness and set off, padding up the clean granite. The morning sun has burnt the cloud away. I gain a shallow groove; the climbing is familiar from last time, and I move smoothly but know this is just the warm-up. Guy follows, then sets forth on the technical and bold second pitch. With knowledge that the holds don't completely run out and there is more gear – perhaps just one move further than you would really like – the pitch is dispatched with a deftness that can only be gained from many years moving on this stone. I look up from this position, the main bastion rearing over us like a huge tidal wave of rock, impressively steep and an exciting playground to spend the day on.

Guy's on-sight of a tech 6a pitch through roofs at half-height is impressive, this being one of the few pitches we hadn't inspected on our last visit; leaving something as a bit of a mystery is quite appealing. The pitches continue to flow, excitement builds, and at every belay we laugh as we swap the rack, then focus again as we remember the way ahead.

The soaring crack on the second-last pitch, of intimidating exposure and arm-sapping steepness, is my lead. The crack starts as a pin scar emanating from the top of a niche, and gradually widens with height. It seemingly reaches a crescendo of difficulty where the width has gone from fingers to ring-locks then to tight hands, just as the crag arches back to its steepest angle. With only space below my feet all the way to the loch, or so it seems, forearms burning, fingers uncurling, the battle is won when a good hand-jam is reached, leaving only a few more moves before the angle relents. A moment to take in the position; I glance down to Guy on the belay and smile. The crag drops further below to the boulder-field, putting our position into perspective. My eyes are drawn out past the rocks that scatter their way to the little beach at the head of the loch, and beyond.

We trotted back across the plateau and down from the mountains, watching the midsummer sun sink towards the north-west horizon, heads full of the day's adventures. A proud new route right up the front face of one of the best mountain crags in the country. *The Shard*, E5,6b, lives long in the memory.

The granite ripples had to wait. That night I drove to the west coast ready for an early departure to St Kilda, for three weeks of conservation volunteering with the NTS. Meanwhile Guy returned to the Shelter Stone for the first ascent of that line, creating *The Heel Stone*. I managed to get back the following May to make the second.

MOUNT KENYA REVISITED

by Niall Ritchie

Time and tide wait for no man.

IN THE BLINK OF AN EYE, it is close on thirty years since climbing Mount Kenya. Time to reflect on a trip to a wonderful mountain, towering over the equator in east Africa, in the company of Donald Bennet, Mike Taylor and a more youthful Jas Hepburn. Donald and Mike are no longer with us and are sorely missed, having left an indelible mark on the history of this Club and upon Scottish mountaineering in general.

Jas and I had not been beyond the Alps before and knew little about the area to be visited nor indeed had any inclination to go there. The opening proverb tells us to seize the chance when it comes. We certainly have no regrets that we did.

Mike must be thanked for that opportunity, asking us to join him for a rematch on the peak, having attempted it two years earlier. Success was denied on that occasion when one of the party suffered as a result of altitude. Although not of Himalayan proportions, Mount Kenya at 5199 metres above sea level has a reputation for mountain sickness and punches well above its weight in this regard.

To our trip, and drawing on Donald's 'SMC Abroad' account published in the 1992 *Journal*:

> Mike Taylor and Donald Bennet arrived at the Kibo Hotel on the south side of Kilimanjaro in mid-December to take part in the seasonal pilgrimage of hopeful high-level hillwalkers to Africa's highest summit. The November rains had not ended, and parts of the route were reminiscent of the CIC path. Five days later, after a short diversion to the Mawenzi Hut for acclimatisation, we reached Uhuru Peak on a grey morning. The sun rose from a sea of cloud which seemed to stretch across the continent, and promptly disappeared into a higher all-enveloping cloud cover. The famed views of Africa at dawn were denied to us.
>
> Several days later, reinforced by young bloods Niall Ritchie and Jas Hepburn fresh from their Deeside gymnasia, we were on the lower slopes of Mount Kenya, toiling up through the Vertical Bog, still black and glutinous from the November rains that lasted until December.

The previous day had been Christmas Eve and saw us camped at the Meteorological Station, having been driven up from Naro Moru River Lodge by Land Cruiser; a bumpy ride with at least one stop for an overheating engine. We shared this clearing in the forest at 3050 metres with playful colobus monkeys and a team of German climbers. After dinner, a thimbleful of Glenfiddich was dispensed, and carols quietly but tunefully sung by candlelight in both German and English. '*Stille Nacht, heilige Nacht*' competed with nature's sounds of the forest.

Next morning, Christmas messages and gifts from the younger members' wives-to-be were opened in a melancholy spirit. There were no smart phones back in those days. This feeling of self-pity was short-lived, however, as a truckful of porters arrived and a scramble for the lightest packs commenced in a cloud of dust. With substantially more red blood-cells coursing through their veins, our local friends sped into the distance, to be met again for payment, job done, as we 'peched awa' only halfway along the trail. It being Christmas, double-time was the agreed rate in Kenyan shillings, and Paymaster Taylor handed over a wad of notes that was gratefully received and divvied amongst the members.

There is no memory of glutinous vertical bog, but a clear recollection of remarkable vegetation zones with the most peculiar-looking flora and fauna, some of which are found only in this part of the world: ten-metre-high heather, giant groundsel and ostrich-plume lobelia, all having adapted to an incredibly harsh environment that can have a daily temperature range of 20°C. There is the feeling of being next to the coal fire until sundown, then being thrown into a cold store for the next twelve hours, until the welcome arrival over the horizon of dawn at 5.30 next morning. With park life including buffalo, elephant, spotted hyena, leopard and lion (none of which we saw), it's the stuff of David Attenborough.

With steady progress made along the Teleki Valley to the Teleki Lodge campground at 4200 metres, stunning views of the south side of Mount Kenya grab your attention, in particular the famous lines of the Ice Window and Diamond Couloir. The latter is known for its hardness of ice and leads to the magically sounding 'Gate of the Mists', which splits the twin peaks of Batian (5199m) and Nelion (5188m). These are named after two former Maasai warriors.

This was to be our base for the week. Our gear awaited our arrival and lay piled on the dirty, dry ground. Provisions were not light and included tins and tins of bully beef. Our week's menu consisted of bully-beef Smash, curried bully beef and bully-beef risotto, to name but three dishes. I think it may have even been on the menu daily, with Oxo cube soup for starters! Little wonder it was close to a quarter of a century before I could set eyes on a corned beef sandwich.

A porter by the name of Castro remained with us for the duration as our *askari*, ensuring all was well in camp while we were on the mountain. A regular visitor to camp was the alpine rock-hyrax; this small rodent is not only an enterprising thief but a taxonomic anomaly, in its distant relationship to the elephant. Something to be witnessed was Donald launching sizeable rocks to shoo one off our dining table – the hyrax, that is, not the elephant – while a passing Italian screamed over in pidgin English, 'Why you do this? Why you do this?'

> After two days of acclimatisation on Point Lenana and Point Pigott, we settled in to a very comfortable bivouac at the foot of the start of the climb.

At 4985m, Lenana is a popular trekking peak above the Lewis Glacier and gives fine views of The Aberdares and across to Nelion and Batian. At this point, Jas became Mallaig's highest man, and photographs were taken of us in matching Braemar Nordic Ski Centre T-shirts – for no obvious reason. Thirty years on, Mr Hepburn retains this honour though not the T-shirt, which last fitted some considerable time ago.

Point Pigott was a different kettle of fish – a more technical training climb, and one we did not get the better of. Slow going owing to altitude, the cold, and the problem of it starting to snow with a long way to the top, led to us backing off. Some down-climbing on slabs and several abseils brought us back to solid ground and a long slow trudge back to camp. At the time it felt like a tough Scottish winter day out.

Any aspiration of tackling the Diamond Couloir or Ice Window was only a dream. Neither feature was close to being formed, and anyway posed far too great a challenge for us at this time. With the mountain almost directly over the equator, climbing seasons are unique. When the sun reaches its zenith in March, what has been in summer condition becomes winter, and *vice versa*. There are also snowfall variations on the east and west sides owing to prevailing weather. Glaciers are either receding fast or have disappeared altogether, seven having suffered this fate since Sir Halford Mackinder's first ascent of the mountain in 1899. Mike on his previous trip had made a solo circuit of Mount Kenya in a long day, and said it was one of the finest days he ever had in the mountains.

A couple of days later we walked up to the Austrian Hut and Top Hut and crossed the Lewis Glacier towards our main objective. A short and easy scramble to Point Melhuish (4880m) before dinner gave us the chance to see at close quarters the route to be tackled in the morning, and to photograph a misty, moody sunset. The rocky spire of Point John came and went from view in the swirling cloud, adding to the atmosphere. A tiny red spec of a climber in descent was visible halfway down the face and gave some perspective of scale.

> The following morning by great misfortune MT succumbed to respiratory problems, for which Mount Kenya is infamous, and had to descend immediately. More climbers suffer from AMS (acute mountain sickness) on Mount Kenya than on any other mountain, so we are told.

It had been a beautiful sunrise. Lenana was silhouetted before a deep red sky in the still, bitterly cold morning, and looking south, the tops of Kibo and Mawenzi of Kilimanjaro could be seen peeping above the clouds, almost 200 miles away: truly a *wow!* moment that was brought crashing to earth by Mike's plight. He awoke with sharp pains in a lung and, being a doctor, self-diagnosed early signs of pleurisy – surprising in that he had climbed Kilimanjaro in great shape less than a fortnight earlier.

The three survivors climbed Nelion by the E face and SE ridge, which

Donald Bennet & Jas Hepburn below Baillie's Bivouac at 5000m on SE face of Nelion, Mount Kenya, December 1991. Photo: Niall Ritchie.

is the *voie normale* at that time of year. NR and JH continued to Batian and returned to the summit of Nelion at sundown where DB had dinner ready for them in the tiny tin hut which serves as a shelter there.

Climbing on the sun-kissed volcanic syenite rock was enjoyable and straightforward, helped by near-perfect conditions. The route, first done in January 1929 by Shipton and Wyn Harris, follows terraces, exposed ledges, delicate traverses, gullies and chimneys leading to Baillie's Bivi. This is a doorless, ice-filled tin shelter at 5000 metres, which was built by Rusty Baillie in the early 1960s and is the halfway point, reached in around three hours. Route-finding becomes a little more complex from here, but Donald had the beta and pointed us youths in the right direction. After turning Mackinder's Gendarme on the left, we chose *De Graaf's Variation* (IV inf.) to unlock the steeper section to an interesting amphitheatre, a steep wall, and some easy ground leading to the summit in six hours.

Donald, very content with his morning's work, relaxed at the Howell Hut on the summit and sent the pair of us off to ascend Batian. Although only 11m higher and just 140m away, it involves an abseil descent of almost as many metres into the Gate of the Mists. Crossing the top of the Diamond Couloir and ascending a snow-filled gully in rock-shoes numbed the feet, though thankfully warmer rock soon returned on the southern side and remained till the summit of Africa's second-highest peak. Jas had a smile as broad as the nearby Great Rift Valley as he pulled up to join me on top. We about-turned after a handshake and the briefest of stops to take in the moment. With the sun rapidly dropping below the

Jas Hepburn in evening sunlight at the Gate of the Mists, Mount Kenya.
Photo: Niall Ritchie.

horizon it became extremely cold as we returned to Nelion using a rope left in place. Retracing our steps with haste to catch the last remnants of daylight, we reunited with Donald, who had been following our progress over the past three hours or more.

The Howell Hut is a contender for the eighth wonder of the world. To quote the guidebook author, Iain Allan:

> This magnificent bivouac shelter was built by Ian Howell in February 1970 after five loads had been successfully parachuted onto the Lewis Glacier. In a feat that can only be described as remarkable, Howell then made thirteen solo ascents of Nelion as he gradually carried the materials to the summit.

It is a godsend to climbers doing both tops, making it a far more feasible proposition.

> Next day being Hogmanay, we had a leisurely descent (almost entirely by abseil) and a stroll down to the Teleki valley camp to reunite with MT. Any possibility of a New Year celebration was ended by NR's exotic oriental cuisine, which kept half the party on the trot, but not first-footing, throughout the night.

I have no memory of an attempt to kill off the team but cannot swear it was all in Donald's imagination. NR's cooking skills have greatly improved over the past 30 years, and now stretch well beyond Oxo soup and bully-beef Smash – honest!

We touched down on the Lewis Glacier after eight abseils and made our weary way back to camp. Mike and Castro came some way along the track to meet us and offer congratulations on getting up and down the mountain safely. For our part we felt mixed emotions: delighted to see Mike on the road to recovery and very pleased with our achievement, but desperately disappointed he had missed out again and was unable to share in this good feeling. I clearly remember him saying, 'You guys look like you have aged ten years!'

Time and tide wait for no man.

NEW ROUTES

The simplest way to submit a new route is to use the proforma at
<www.smcnewroutes.org.uk>. This will input the route description directly into
a holding area of our database. The route will then be checked and verified, and
you will receive an email confirming receipt of the description and whether it
covers new ground. The proforma can accept multiple route descriptions.

Alternatively, send an email to to the New Routes Editor at
newroutes@smc.org.uk. Please ensure the description includes information in the
following order: area, crag, route name, length, grade, suggested stars, first
ascensionist(s), date, route description. Please include first names of first
ascensionists.

Submission of diagrams and topos is strongly encouraged. These are kept on file
for future guidebook authors.

The cost of publishing the New Routes Section in the *Journal* is supported by the
Scottish Mountaineering Trust. Their ongoing support is gratefully acknowledged.

The deadline for sending route descriptions for the 2022 *Journal* is 31 May 2022.

OUTER HEBRIDES

LEWIS, Aird Mhòr Mhangarstaidh Central, Magic Geodha:
Flannan Zigzag 35m HVS **. Michael Barnard, Lucy Spark. 2 Aug 2020.
1. 15m 5a As for *Flannan Slab Left-Hand*.
2. 20m 5a Take the small slabby ramp up left and continue leftwards up the
slanting crack to finish as for *Campa Crack*.

Michael Barnard notes that the difficulties on *Campa Crack* are not confined to
the first 5m as the guidebook suggests.

LEWIS, Aird Mhòr Mhangarstaidh North, Painted Geodha:
Michael Barnard notes that *Gravity Man* was thought E1 5b, *The Painted Wall*
and *The Dreaded Dram* both E3 5c.

LEWIS, Rubha Cuinish, Creag Liam:
Michael Barnard notes that *The Bernera Prow* was thought to be E3 5c.

Abortive Arête 20m E2 5c *. Michael Barnard, Alan Hill. 28 Aug 2020.
The arête between *Barnacle Butter* and *Conception Corner* has more protection
than first impressions would suggest.

LEWIS, Ard Dalbeg, Dalbeg Buttress:
Space Truckin' 40m E4 5c ****. Michael Barnard, Alan Hill. 31 Aug 2020.
A brilliant sustained pitch linking *Neptune* with the soaring upper cracks of
Tweetie Pie Slalom. Although the pitch contains little new ground it was thought
worth recording as it opens up a lot of great climbing to those operating below

E5. Climb *Neptune* to the obvious horizontal break; handrail along this to gain the large flake of *Neptune a Calling*. Climb the shallow groove of *Neptune a Calling*, then move up to the roof. Follow *Tweetie Pie Slalom* to the top.

LEWIS, Rubha na Beirghe:
Michael Barnard notes that the lower part of *Internal Exam Crack* appears to have possibly fallen down, or the description is lacking, but either way doesn't look E1.

Blended Learning 25m E2 5c **. Michael Barnard, Lucy Spark. 31 Jul 2020.
Immediately right of *Internal Exam Crack*. Climb the steep crack which widens and goes through a bulge into a V-groove.

LEWIS, Bernera, Creag nan Urrabhaichean (NB 153 378):
This west-facing crag lies across the lochan from the road junction to Tobson with nice short routes 4 minutes from the road. There is room for a car beside the first passing place south of the junction. Walk round either side of the lochan; there are stepping stones to the south of the lochan. There is a jumble of boulders below the crag so walk up to either end, not directly up to the centre.

Stand Off 9m HVS 5a *. Colin Moody, Cynthia Grindley. 28 Aug 2020.
Start 7m left of *Pussy Riot* below short wide crack in the upper wall. Climb up through the crack to finish up short right-facing corner.

The Riot Act 9m HVS 5a **. Colin Moody, Cynthia Grindley. 28 Aug 2020.
Climb the wall to finish at short right-facing corner.

Pussy Riot 9m H.Severe. Colin Moody, Cynthia Grindley. 28 Aug 2020.
Start below twin cracks. Go up then follow ledges to the left and finish at steep corner crack.

Rubber Bullets 8m HVS 5a *. Colin Moody, Cynthia Grindley. 27 Aug 2020.
Start as for *Pussy Riot* and climb twin cracks. There is a hold at the top to the right of the cracks.

Bernera Riots 9m HVS 5a **. Colin Moody, Cynthia Grindley. 27 Aug 2020.
Climb the right-slanting crack.

Tear Gas 8m E1 5a *. Colin Moody, Cynthia Grindley. 27 Aug 2020.
Clamber on to the left side of the block. Climb the wall on the left to finish up a right-slanting crack.

Burning 10m VS 4c **. Colin Moody, Cynthia Grindley. 27 Aug 2020.
Climb left-facing corner then the right-slanting crack.

Looting 10m VS 4c *. Colin Moody, Cynthia Grindley. 27 Aug 2020.
Start between two short corners. Climb the flake crack then a right-slanting ramp.

Shooting 8m H.Severe. Colin Moody, Cynthia Grindley. 28 Aug 2020.
Go over bulge at right end of crag, follow the crack to finish past a heather ramp.

PABBAY, Small Buoys Geo:

Original Sink 15m E1 5b *. Ellis Ash, Niall Grimes, Nick Wallis. 22 May 2021.
The arête between *Spare Rib* and *First Groove* on its right side. From the ledge,
follow a thin crack then the fine sharp arête to a crux at the top. Step right above
and finish up a groove.

MINGULAY, Rubha Liath, The Point:

The Gull Who Shagged Me, Chicken Dinner Finish 25m E2 5b ***. David
Wood, Nathan Adam. 18 Aug 2020.
A great variation that lowers the grade but not the quality of climbing. Where the
original route goes right at the crux, take the excellent handrail leading left to
reach a rounded crack. Climb this directly, or more easily by stepping into a short
corner left again, before following short ledges to the top.

Rubha Liath, Seal Song Wall

They Came From Above 40m VS * 40m. Pitch 1: Nathan Adam, Matthew
Rowbottom 1 Aug 2019. Complete ascent: Nathan Adam, David Wood 16 Aug
2020.
Start from the triangular ledge of *Ocean Wrath*.
1. 20m 4c Climb off the ledge by a helpful but green crack on the right. Cross
Walking on Waves and head right to reach a short corner leading to a broad bulging
wall. Climb this to belay on the good ledges below the final pitch of *Spitting Fury*.
2. 20m 5a Take the obvious diagonal fault going right past two steep steps. Where
the continuation goes right (loose), climb a short way up a left-leaning crack
before making steep moves on the left wall to reach the top. (Topo provided.)

INNER HEBRIDES AND ARRAN

CANNA, Upper House Crag:

Smidge 18m E4 5c ***. Jamie Skelton, Morag Eagleson. 14 Aug 2020.
Technical bridging up the left-facing corner in the dark area of rock right of
Missing the Boat. Climb to the ledge and continue up the corner which has good
gear after initial bold moves passing a rotten peg.

The Big Cat 25m E4 6a **. Jamie Skelton, Morag Eagleson. 14 Aug 2020.
An independent and more sustained start to *Aristocrat*. Start right of that route by
scrambling up the middle of the rotten band to projecting nose of rock. Head up
the left side of this (gear on the right side) to a roof. Move left of the roof and
make tricky moves that continue up towards the top groove of *Aristocrat*.

Downsizing 15m E1 5b. Morag Eagleson, Jamie Skelton. 13 Aug 2020.
Move up onto a ledge just right of the short pinnacle of *The Privileged Few*. Climb
the crack above to a ledge and easier ground.

Land of Opportunity 20m E4 6a *. Jamie Skelton, Morag Eagleson. 13 Aug
2020.
At the left end of the rotten band is a groove that leads directly towards a large
diamond-shaped roof at half-height. Pass this on the right and make an insecure

stretch up to a good cam slot on the right side of the groove. Move up and back left (crux) to gain the ledge just below the top. High in the grade.

The Fortress:
Canna Believe It 25m E2 5c **. Jamie Skelton, Morag Eagleson. 15 Aug 2020.
Right of *The Bastille* lies a shallow depression. Follow the twin cracks in this to reach a small roof at the end of the depression, swing round into a groove on the left and continue up to finish left of the prow as for *The Bastille*.

Canna and I'm Gonna 25m E4 5c/6a *. Jamie Skelton, Morag Eagleson. 8 Sep 2020.
Follow *Canna Believe It* to the small roof, make a tricky move right and continue up to a big flat hold just right of the prow. Make ever more committing moves along a line of holds leading diagonally leftward to edge of the prow and the top.

Andrew's Crag:
Stone Racer 22m E2 5c **. Jamie Skelton, Morag Eagleson. 6 Sep 2020.
Left of the alcove and *Remember, Remember* is an obvious right-facing corner/crack. Climb the crack and make a tricky move to gain the corner; at its top swing left and climb over a bulge to finish.

SANDAY, Sputain (NG 2674 0408):
A small protruding buttress of very compact rock with ample natural belays. The routes sit on a partly tidal ledge but can be accessed at any time in calm sea states. Approach: Head up the initial steep section of Finlay's road. Just before the first houses there is a left-hand bend in the track and a gate on the right. Head through the gate and across the fields heading to the coast, the crag protrudes out towards the sea and is easy to spot. About 15 to 20 minutes from the Sanday bridge.

Larven 12m H.Severe 4b. Morag Eagleson, Jamie Skelton. 10 Sep 2020.
On the left side of the main buttress is a small door-shaped cave or hole. Start just left of this, climb a short wall to a big ledge and finish up the groove above.

Tallabac 12m E4 6a ***. Jamie Skelton, Morag Eagleson. 9 Sep 2020.
Just right of the small door-shaped cave is a thin curving crack. Follow this over a small overlap until a final tricky move right can be made to jugs in a niche just below the top.

RÙM, Kilmory:
The following routes lie on the same promontory as *Double Trouble*. The first one is a real classic and a must-do for Reiff aficionados.

The Reiff Teleporter 15m E2 5b ***. Michael Barnard, Alan Hill. 22 May 2021.
The line of least resistance on the seaward face. Immaculate rock and reasonably well protected with a good selection of cams from micros to Camalot 1. Start on the left and take a right-slanting crack to the first break. Step right slightly and move up to the higher break, then hand traverse this to near the left arête. Move up, pull left onto the arête for a few moves, then pull back right to finish up the fine top crack.

Escape from the Deer Botherers 15m HVS 5a *. Michael Barnard, Alan Hill. 22 May 2021.
The corner line right of *Double Trouble*.

COLL, Creag nan Clamhan:
The rock is perfect, and the recorded routes are naturally lichen-free. Climbing might not be possible in spring because of a nest. North of the crag is a fence which leads NW towards the road. North of the fence is a short quick-drying crag that faces the main crag. 5 minutes from the road and SW-facing.

Penny Banger 7m Severe. Cynthia Grindley, Colin Moody. 5 Nov 2020.
Start below the hanging flake crack. Go up left and climb cracks up the wall.

Jumping Jack 7m VS 4c. Colin Moody, Cynthia Grindley. 5 Nov 2020.
Climb the shallow corner just right of the hanging flake-crack.

Hogh Rocks, Beginner's Slab:
Bourbon Girl 8m Severe. Colin Moody, Cynthia Grindley. 6 Nov 2020.
Between *Izzy Whizzy* and *Battenburg Boy* with a bulge near the top.

Tiree Wall:
This is in front of the north end of The Slab. To the south is Mingulay Buttress and between them at a lower level is Black Wall.

Luxury 10m Diff. Colin Moody, Cynthia Grindley. 6 Nov 2020.
Climb a crack then flake-crack left and up.

Warmth 10m Diff. Colin Moody, Cynthia Grindley. 6 Nov 2020.
Crack to the right.

Seafood 7m Severe. Colin Moody, Cynthia Grindley. 6 Nov 2020.
The rib left of the diverging wide cracks with a step left.

Jarl 7m Diff. Colin Moody, Cynthia Grindley. 6 Nov 2020.
The fine rib right of the diverging wide cracks.

The Slogh:
Brasso 8m Diff. Colin Moody, Cynthia Grindley. 6 Nov 2020.
Start up *Bottleneck* then move left below the overhang to finish just left of *Bold as Brass*. Note: *Bold as Brass* no doubt goes diagonally right not left.

RP 8m Diff. Colin Moody, Cynthia Grindley. 6 Nov 2020.
Right of *Bottleneck* is a recess. Climb the crack to the right of the recess with an undercut start.

Brass Rubbing 8m Diff. Colin Moody, Cynthia Grindley. 6 Nov 2020.
The next crack to the right also with an undercut start.

MULL, Calgary, Dark Side:

Rendezvous 8m E1 5b *. Pete Whillance, Cynthia Grindley, Colin Moody. 2 Aug 2020.
Climb the corner crack in the yellow tower. This is well left of *Dark Corner*.

Longer 10m VS 4c *. Colin Moody, Cynthia Gridley. 12 Jul 2020.
Climb *Shorty* until just short of the easy section. Step left, climb the groove then the groove just right.

Creag na Bà (NM 402 454):

Park west of Torloisk, just east of a burn NM 403 457; room for two or three cars (or drive down the track and find somewhere off it to park). Walk down the track and take the left fork to cross a bridge above the turbine house. Then walk down to the top of the crag overlooking the burn. Less than 10 minutes.

Burnside:

The west facing walls overlooking the burn. The first route has a tree belay and the others share a stake. Short routes on perfect rock, which perhaps should have bouldering grades.

Arboretum 6m Severe *. Colin Moody, Cynthia Grindley, Pete Whillance. 1 Aug 2020.
Start down left of the other routes. Climb the crack past a small tree.

Foot and Mouth 7m VS 4b. Colin Moody, Cynthia Grindley, Pete Whillance. 1 Aug 2020.
Up right of *Arboretum* is a buttress with a shelf on the left-hand side. Pull onto the nose then follow the shelf left and climb the short wall.

Highland 6m Severe *. Colin Moody, Cynthia Grindley, Pete Whillance. 1 Aug 2020.
Climb corner cracks just right of the edge.

Belted Galloway 6m VS 4b *. Colin Moody. 13 Jul 2020.
At the left-hand side is a 4m-high oak tree; right of this is a slightly overhanging arête. Climb the arête right again.

Bovilis Huskvac 6m VS 5a *. Colin Moody, Dot MacLean. 6 Aug 2020.
Climb the bulging wall.

Little White Bull 6m Severe. Colin Moody. 13 Jul 2020.
Bridge up the fault, passing a large chockstone.

Stampede 6m V.Diff *. Colin Moody, Dot MacLean. 25 Jun 2020.
Climb the face.

Milk Shake 6m V.Diff *. Colin Moody, Dot MacLean. 25 Jun 2020
The honeysuckle finger-crack just right of *Stampede*.

Milk Marketing Board 6m V.Diff. Colin Moody. 13 Jul 2020.
Left-facing corner.

Blessed are The Cheese Makers 6m VS 4c *. Colin Moody, Dot MacLean. 25 Jun 2020.
Climb the steep crack left of the overhang.

Butter 6m V.Diff. Colin Moody. 13 Jul 2020.
Rib then groove right of the overhang.

Estuary Walls:
Between Riverside and Estuary Walls is an easy path. West-facing. Stake belay.

Suckler 6m VS 4b. Pete Whillance, Colin Moody, Cynthia Grindley. 1 Aug 2020.
The wall just left of *Calf.*

Calf 6m Severe. Colin Moody. 14 Jul 2020.
Climb the shallow corner with thin crack.

Cows Lying Down 7m Severe *. Colin Moody, Cynthia Grindley. 3 Jul 2020.
Climb the face which is slightly proud of the crag.

Heelan Coos 7m VS 4c *. Colin Moody. 14 Jul 2020.
Aim for cracks with a bulge to start.

Dragonfly Eggs 7m Severe 4b *. Colin Moody. 24 Jul 2020.
The crack left of *Curd* with an undercut start.

Curd 7m Severe. Colin Moody. 13 Jul 2020.
The left-slanting crack passing a prow.

Maverick 10m HVS 4c. Pete Whillance, Cynthia Grindley, Colin Moody. 1 Aug 2020.
Start up the rib on the left side of the large buttress. Move right and climb up left to the top.

Cattle Grid 7m VS 4c *. Colin Moody, Cynthia Grindley. 17 Jul 2020.
About 30m right is an obvious corner between two buttresses.

Main Wall:
To the right is a small burn, right of which is the mostly west-facing Main Wall. The central section is steep and lacks cracks so might give some hard sport routes.

Last Roundup 10m HVS 5a *. Pete Whillance, Colin Moody. 3 Aug 2020.
Left of the central section is a slabby bay. Climb the corner-crack at the left side.

Wild West 10m HVS 5a **. Pete Whillance, Colin Moody. 3 Aug 2020.
Right of the steep central section the wall turns to face south (easy access up the cliff just before). Climb the jam-crack, on the south wall, slanting up left, then the bulging crack on the left.

Western Wall:
Right (south) of *Wild West* is a steep south-west-facing wall behind oak trees.

There is access at the left end over a boulder and a path at the right end.

Cowboy Boots   9m   H.Severe 4b *. Colin Moody, Billy Hood. 18 Jul 2020.
Start at pointed block 1m back from the crag. Climb the rib to a shelf then move left, climb the bulge and finish up the grassy corner.

Rawhide   10m   E1 5b **. Pete Whillance, Cynthia Grindley, Colin Moody. 1 Aug 2020.
Right of *Cowboy Boots* for 8m the cliff base is overhung; start just right of this and step onto easy rock. Climb the corner to the roof and move left to pass it. Continue up easier but poorly protected rock.

My Horse is Lame   9m   VS 4c *. Colin Moody, Cynthia Grindley. 2 Aug 2020.
Start 7m right of *Rawhide*. Climb the right-slanting crack just right of a very steep finger-crack.

It's John Wayne   9m   VS 4b. Colin Moody, Cynthia Grindley, Pete Whillance. 1 Aug 2020.
To the right is a grassy gully. Start 6m right of the gully, climb an awkward block then the corner-crack past the roof.

The Broch:
A V.Diff was climbed right of *Niche Crack* by Colin Moody around 2000.

Creag an Eoin:
Five Mile Rule   12m   H.Severe *. Colin Moody, Cynthia Grindley. 2 Jul 2020.
A crack left of *Pinnacle Crack*.

Creag an Eoin South:
The following routes are two minutes' walk south from the other routes on the crag marked as Creag an Eoin on the map. Look out for the occasional loose hold especially at the finishes.

Goose-step   10m   VS 4c. Colin Moody, Cynthia Grindley. 3 Jul 2020.
Start near the left side of crag. Climb up to platform then up jam-cracks.

Grey Goose   8m   VS 4c *. Colin Moody, Cynthia Grindley. 3 Jul 2020.
A few metres to the right climb two cracks, a prominent crack and a shallow corner-crack just left.

Goose Bumps   8m   VS. Colin Moody, Cynthia Grindley. 3 Jul 2020.
Just right climb cracks up the left side of a pillar where the crag changes direction.

Goose Grass   8m   VS. Colin Moody, Cynthia Grindley. 3 Jul 2020.
Climb the recess round to the right.

Gander   8m   VS *. Colin Moody, Cynthia Grindley. 3 Jul 2020.
Twin cracks just right.

Goose Fat   8m   VS *. Colin Moody, Cynthia Grindley. 3 Jul 2020.
The crack up the left side of the rib.

Creag Mhòr (NM 467 393):

This long crag consists of a series of buttresses starting south of the houses. The rock is very rough, like gabbro, and there is probably a lot of bouldering potential. The earlier routes were not recorded so the crag was forgotten about and missed out of the guidebook. The first two routes overlook the burn at the left end of the crags.

Access There is a car park near the high point of the road to Ulva Ferry from Salen, where a track leads up to an aerial NM 469 396. Walk west down the road for 100m then head downhill to the crag, crossing the fence. 10 minutes.

Second Round 12m HVS 5a *. Colin Moody, Paul Gillies. 21 Apr 2014
Climb up to the cracks on the right-hand buttress (just right of the main rib) then step left and continue up.

Rowan Rib 8m V.Diff. Colin Moody, Calum Black. 1999?
There is a rowan tree to the right. Start just right of the tree and climb the rib.

Left Flake Crack 6m V.Diff. Colin Moody. 1999?
About 10m right is a flake; climb the left side.

Right Flake Crack 7m V.Diff. Colin Moody. 1999?
Climb the right side.

Further right the crag forms two tiers.

Upper Tier:

Big Drop 6m VS 4c. Steve Kennedy, Cynthia Grindley, Colin Moody. 27 Sep 2020.
Climb the short steep crack above *Chalky Wall*, so not a good solo.

Detached Flake 6m Severe. Colin Moody. 1 Jul 2020.
The flake is left of *Ivy Chimney* with a steep start.

Ivy Chimney 7m V.Diff. Colin Moody. 1 Jul 2020.
The chimney left of the old ivy, a bit hollow on the right.

The Move 7m HVS 5a. Colin Moody, Cynthia Grindley. 9 Aug 2020.
Round to the right is a corner-crack with a wide bulging crack to start.

Fish Box Corner 7m Severe. Colin Moody, Martin Kafka. 7 Jun 2020.
Climb the corner crack at the back of the bay.

Lower Tier:

Block Wall 8m VS 4c. Steve Kennedy, Colin Moody, Cynthia Grindley. 27 Sep 2020.
Start left of *Chalky Wall*, climb up to a right facing corner crack then follow it.

Chalky Wall 8m HVS 5a *. Colin Moody, Cynthia Grindley, Steve Kennedy. 27 Sep 2020.
A nice line following a right-slanting crack with edges to the right.

Scruffy Left Corner 8m H.Severe. Colin Moody, Calum Black. 1999?
A reasonable route up a left-facing corner crack just right of *Chalky Wall*.

Return 8m E1 5b *. Colin Moody, Cynthia Grindley. 25 Sep 2020.
To the right is a buttress then a wall with a steep crack. Climb the steep crack.

White Van Man 8m HVS 5a *. Colin Moody, Cynthia Grindley. 9 Aug 2020.
Round right again climb the wide crack in the right-facing corner.

Rose Crack 8m VS 4c *. Colin Moody (back rope). 19 Jun 2020.
To the right is a curtain of ivy. Climb the crack just left of the ivy, with surprisingly varied moves. Probably will need some pruning before climbing.

White Streak 7m E1 5b *. Colin Moody, Cynthia Grindley. 25 Sep 2020.
Climb the thin crack in the white streak.

Still 7m HVS 5a *. Colin Moody, Cynthia Grindley, Steve Kennedy. 27 Sep 2020.
The bulging recess and crack above.

Oak Rock:
Oak Tickler 7m Severe *. Colin Moody, Cynthia Grindley. 2 Jul 2020.
Climb to the corner, follow this to the top then move left and finish. Nice climbing, probably unprotected.

Shelf Rock:
Tiny Rowan 7m Severe *. Colin Moody, Calum Black. 1999?
Climb the bulge then follow the groove.

Shelf Rib Left 9m VS 4b. Colin Moody, Martin Kafka. 7 Jun 2020.
Start up *Shelf Rib* then move left and climb the other rib.

Shelf Rib 8m VS 4b *. Colin Moody, Martin Kafka. 7 Jun 2020.
Climb the rib left of the shelf.

Shelf 7m HVS 5b. Colin Moody, Martin Kafka. 7 Jun 2020.
Climb up to the shelf at the right side of the buttress, gain the shelf then the top using a small loose flake.

Overhang Rock:
Ferry Crack 9m HVS 5b *. Steve Kennedy, Cynthia Grindley, Colin Moody. 27 Sep 2020.
The crack on the left of the overhang, going up slightly left.

Fishnish Time 7m Severe 4b. Colin Moody, Steve Kennedy, Cynthia Grindley. 27 Sep 2020.
The last ramp on the right-hand side of the buttress.

Tram Lines 7m V.Diff *. Colin Moody. 26 Jul 2020.
Right of Overhang Rock is an easy angled buttress with twin cracks up high. Climb onto the shelf then continue up the scoop just left of the twin cracks.

Bus Lane 7m V.Diff *. Colin Moody. 26 Jul 2020.
Climb onto the shelf and climb the scoop just right of the twin cracks.

Acharonich Crag (NM 471 395):
This is the name given to the crag on UKC with *Locals Don't Wave* E2 5c. Going
from Salen to Ulva Ferry. Just before the high point on the road are some boulders
above the road and a cliff below. Park at the old quarry just west of the boulders.
Walk back to the cliff below the road, less than 5 minutes.

Free of Tourists 10m V.Diff. Colin Moody. 7 Jun 2020.
A burn runs down the west end of the crag; part of it runs down the face and part
runs down a slanting gully. Climb the slanting gully over a chockstone, drought
conditions being helpful.

Locals Don't Wave 15m E2 5c. Paul Bedford, Rebecca Edwards. 5 May 2018.
Start in an obvious recess 4m left of the fence line. Climb broken rock past a
sapling into a broken crack. Step left onto a small ledge under a bulge. Make a
strenuous move over the bulge. Continue direct up the delicate slab.

Stac Liath, East Face:
Two routes not far right of *Let There be Light*. Left to right, same lower-off.

Ant Attack 12m 6a *. Colin Moody, Cynthia Grindley, Pete Whillance. 31 Jul
2020.

Formic 12m 6a. Colin Moody, Pete Whillance. 3 Aug 2020.

Caigeann Mhòr:
Neither 15m VS 4b *. Colin Moody, Cynthia Grindley. 9 Jul 2020.
A line just right of *Clegs Then Midges*.

Fionnphort, Fidden, North-West Face:
A nice slab of pink granite that gets the sun from early afternoon is seen on the
approach to the other routes. The original routes were given bouldering grades;
most were cleaned, led and given alternative grades in 2020. Protection can be
poor.

Dead Tree Groove 8m V.Diff. Colin Moody. 21 Jul 2020.
Start left of the dead tree at the left end of the crag. Move up right and climb the
groove above the tree.

Another Rat 8m Severe. Colin Moody. 21 Jul 2020.
Climb the groove right of the dead tree.

Post 9m Severe. Colin Moody, Cynthia Grindley. 10 Jul 2020.
Left of the pink slab is another slab; climb the left-hand line.

Passing Place 8m V.Diff *. Colin Moody, Cynthia Grindley. 10 Jul 2020.
The right-hand line.

Small Rat   7m   Severe. Colin Moody, Cynthia Grindley. 10 Jul 2020.
Climb the discontinuous crack-line between two grassy cracks.

Big Vole   8m   Severe *. Colin Moody, Cynthia Grindley. 10 Jul 2020.
The line just left of *Black Streak*.

Black Streak   8m   VS 5a **. Ole Kemi. 28 May 2016.
Follow the streak, thin climbing to a small crack (cam) then easier above.

No Colour Wall   8m E1 5a **. Ole Kemi. 28 May 2016.
The fine wall to the right, climbed without using holds on other routes.

Field of Cracks   8m   VS 5a *. Ole Kemi. 28 May 2016.
Climb cracks.

Another Colourless Wall   8m   E1 5a **. Ole Kemi. 28 May 2016
Climb the wall without using holds on other routes.

High Crack   8m   VS 5a *. Ole Kemi. 28 May 2016.
Gain and climb the crack on the right.

Right Crack   9m   V.Diff *. Ole Kemi. 28 May 2016.
Climb the left-slanting crack to the easy-angled slab. There is a good belay crack
well up on the right.

Right Wall   7m   Severe 4c *. Ole Kemi. 28 May 2016.
The crack to the right has a thin start.

ISLAY, Geodha Uamh nam Fear, Fin Wall:
Eagle Arête   15m   Hard V.Diff. 15m. Nicholas Hurndall Smith, Paul McWhinney.
24 Sep 2020.
The arête which forms the left side of the wall. Step under a large prow to the left
of *Above the White*, climb up with the prow on your right, and swarm up the ridge
above it in an exhilarating position, keeping to the arête.

Am Burg Defile (NR 192 648):
The main defile between Am Burg and the mainland links to another, shorter,
defile running in from the west, thereby isolating the stack. On the landward side
of the latter defile is a striking slim corner with a wide, slabby, left face. The rock
in this area is often covered with a fine film of dust, effectively eliminating what
little natural friction the rock has. Dry conditions are therefore essential for
climbing, and mid to low tide is best.

Slate Modern   13m   E3 6a *. Graham Little (unseconded). 10 Jul 2020.
Climb the desperate corner for 3m (crux) then move left onto the slabby face.
Climb it and then easier, slightly vegetated, rock above. The only good belay is
about 30m back from the top of the crag. NOTE: a well inflated fishing buoy is
an essential bit of kit – required as a launch-pad to reach the first hold! The route
was practised on a top-rope.

South-West of Saligo Bay:

The coast to the south-west of Saligo Bay holds a number of short but good meta-sandstone walls. To access them go through the gate just south of Saligo cottage and walk along the coast.

A distinctive prow of banded rock lies on the coast at NR 203 661, seaward of where a small burn hits the shore. Mid to low tide required.

Jugular 4m Severe **. Graham Little. 8 Aug 2020.
Climb the steep prow on generous holds.

Choker 4m Severe *. Graham Little. 20 Sep 2020.
Climb the steep banded face on big holds.

Jammed Log Geo (NR 202 660):

This atmospheric narrow geo holds a clean little south-west-facing wall with a collection of enjoyable lines. It can be accessed from the head by scrambling over a boulder at a constriction. It is a mid- to-low-tide venue. The routes are described from right to left, as approached. (Topo provided.)

Flogged 6m 5a *. Ryan Little, Graham Little. 19 Sep 2020.
After scrambling over the constriction boulder there is a nose of rock on the right where a little gully joins the geo. Climb the awkward nose and slabby rock above to a bollard belay.

Boulder Rib 5m Moderate. Graham Little. 13 Jul 2020.
Start on a large, flat boulder and climb the rib to the right of the groove demarcating the right side of the clean wall.

Logged On 5m Difficult *. Graham Little. 13 Jul 2020.
Climb the wall just left of the groove described above.

Logarithm 5m V.Diff *. Graham Little. 13 Jul 2020.
Climb the wall to the right of the slight step in the wall.

Logged Off 6m V.Diff *. Graham Little. 8 Aug 2020.
Climb the edge of the slight step in the wall.

Driftwood 6m 4c **. Graham Little. 8 Aug 2020.
Start at the very end of the low intrusive dyke and climb the clean face.

Loggia 5m 4c. Graham Little. 8 Aug 2020.
Step left from the start of the previous route, move up and take a diagonal crack to a ledge just below the top.

Black Boot Block (NR 201 659):

Just landward of a squat pinnacle at NR 201 659 is a boot-shaped block of dark, slaty rock. It is backed by a sinister pool of brackish water.

Instep 4m 4c *. Graham Little. 8 Aug 2020.
A direct line to the left of centre.

Backstep   4m   4b **. Graham Little. 8 Aug 2020.
A diagonal line to the right of centre.

The Amphitheatre (NR 201 660):

A quite remarkable natural amphitheatre lies to the north of Squat Pinnacle at NR 201 660 complete with stage, stalls and circle. The right flank (looking up) of the amphitheatre is, in part, undercut with a big roof. There are four bouldering-type routes, described from left to right. First ascent of all routes by Graham Little on 20 Sept 2020. (Topo provided.)

Stage Fright   3m   4c *. A strenuous pull over.
Act One   4m   5a * Fingers in pockets!
Curtain Call   4m   5a **. Layaway and pray!
Standing Ovation   5m   5a *. Pull up on a quartz pocket, step left and finish straight up (easier without the step left).

The slabby wall further right gives a couple of short, pleasant, lines at around Difficult standard.

ARRAN, Cir Mhòr:

Kev Howett notes that pitch one of *Insertion Direct* has been described incorrectly in the past. A revised description follows:

Insertion Direct   95m   E5 **. Mark Charlton, Kevin Howett. 6 Jun 1986.
Incredibly bold padding at the limit of adhesion, with the sting in the tail. Start about a metre to the right of a broad crack which is about 8m right of *Hammer*.
1. 50m 5c   Climb straight up a steep slab to an overlap. Surmount this, then climb direct passing through a diagonal quartz line of pockets (unfortunately no protection) into a scoop in the centre of the slab. Climb this, and as it steepens teeter up and right to under the roof above. Hanging belay.
2. 25m 4c   Gain the big corner on the left and exit the roof at its top onto slabs. Head up and left to belay below a steep wall under a massive roof.
3. 20m 5c   The bulging wall contains a large pocket. Gain and pull past it and smaller pockets above to swing round the edge and climb upwards onto the very edge of the ridge. Head up to join *South Ridge Direct* after pitch 7. Follow this to The Terrace.

SKYE THE CUILLIN

SGÙRR SGÙMAIN, West Face:

In April 2021 a worryingly large flake on pitch 4 of *Sunset Slab* & *Yellow Groove* caused a team to back off.

SRÒN NA CÌCHE, Cioch Buttress:

Crembo Cracks, Pitch 3 Variation   35m   E1 5b **. Michael Barnard, Alan Hill. 9 Aug 2020.
A fine pitch, low in the grade. Traverse right from the belay and climb thin flake-cracks just left of the arête to reach a ledge. Step right around the arête and go rightwards up a ramp to gain and follow a left-trending fault. Continue up to join *Cioch West*.

SGÙRR MHICCHOINNICH, North Face:

Mongoose Direct 195m VIII,8 ****. Jamie Skelton, Tim Miller. 10 Feb 2021.
A brilliant and sustained winter route based on the summer line and taking the main corner feature up the centre of the cliff. In good conditions useful ice forms on the right wall of the corner on pitch 1.
1. 45m Tackle the steep layback crack for 25m to the first sloping shelf (possible belay). Continue by the corner line before crossing a thin slab left to belay (made easier with snow and ice build-up on the slab).
2. 40m Climb the right wall of the corner by a steep crack. Move back left into the corner, which is followed to a ledge (20m). Head across the ledge to an easier groove (*Dawn Grooves*) and climb this till 10m below the obvious overhung corner ahead and belay.
3. 45m Move up to the base of the corner and climb this with poor feet (crux) to a niche on the left (possible belay). Climb the overhanging chimney above for 15m and belay on a big shelf below a chimney.
4. 50m Climb the tight chimney to an overhang then traverse out left. Move up and right and climb the final awkward corner.
5. 15m Easy scrabble to the top.

Michael Barnard, Doug Bartholomew and Graham Wylie repeated *Hanging Slab* on 15 Aug 2020 and thought it merited E2. Below is a new description and possibly an improved version of the climb:

Hanging Slab 180m E2 **
This route takes the slab above the overhangs left of *Exiguous Gully*. Scramble up the belay on a large block at the base of the gully.
1. 45m 5b Traverse left and move up through the right end of the bulging wall to gain the slab. Go up to good nut runners then step down leftwards, then boldly left along the slab until possible to move up and left to gain a right-trending crack or groove. Climb this, moving right near the top, and continue up to belay above the centre of the traverse.
2. 15m Walk left to belay below a slightly right-trending crack.
3. 30m 5b The innocuous-looking crack.
4. and 5. 90m Continue more easily to the top.

COIRE A' GHRUNNDA, Sròn na Cìche, South Crag:

Moonrock 110m (to Pinnacle Rake) VS 4b *. Steve Kennedy, Colin Moody, Cynthia Grindley. 19 Sep 2020.
The leftmost of the obvious corner/groove systems on the face right of *Trap Dyke Route*. Start on Stony Rake above and left of *Hell-Broth* below a roof with a groove running up its right side. Not to be confused with a smaller roof just below.
1. 55m Climb the steep slabby wall just right of the roof and continue up the groove above to a grassy recessed area which is climbed by cracks on the right.
2. 55m Continue up cracks and grooves to reach the large recessed area near the left end of Pinnacle Rake. A finish was made by traversing horizontally left along the rake to reach the upper section of Stony Rake (easily descended to the base).

Hell-Broth 140m VS 4c **. Steve Kennedy, Colin Moody, Cynthia Grindley. 15 Aug 2020.
The next left-facing corner system between *Moonrock* and *Wytches' Brew* (*SMCJ* 2019).

1. 50m Start close to the foot of Stony Rake, directly below the line of disjointed corners about 15m left of the start of *Wytches' Brew* and just left of a grassy ledge. Climb slabs directly, crossing parallel faults, to the initial corner and continue in the corner line above to a ledge.
2. 55m Continue up a slab leading to a pale left-facing corner then take a fairly direct line up easier ground via corners and cracks.
3. 35m Finish by scrambling up and rightwards to reach Pinnacle Rake above *White Slab*.

Smitch   30m   VS 4b *
Steve Kennedy, Colin Moody, Cynthia Grindley. 15 Aug 2020.
The bold rounded arête left of *Smidgen* (*SMCJ* 2019). Start up the arête, moving temporarily onto the slabby left wall at about mid-height, to reach a ledge below a bulge. Surmount the bulge and continue to a further ledge and possible belay. An alternative block belay and abseil point is located about 10m to the right near the end of the ledge.

Steve Kennedy on the FA of Jupiter (E1,5b), Coire a' Ghrunnda. See SMCJ 2020, p. 156. Photo: Colin Moody.

BLÀBHEINN, Winter Buttress:
Vaccination 40m IV,4 **. Ian Hall, Katharina Lenz. 6 Feb 2021.
The blocky right-facing and right-slanting corner on the buttress above *Escape From Colditz*. Approach via the ledge above *Escape From Colditz* or as a continuation from that route. The corner contains four bulges, of which the third is the crux. The bulges are all well protected and give tremendously satisfying climbing. Chockstone belay immediately above the final bulge.

SKYE SEA CLIFFS & OUTCROPS

STAFFIN, Southern Cliffs, Tempest Buttress Area:
Andy Moles comments that the 'easy gully' approach to Tempest Buttress has a bad step which is manageable with care, but the traverse is extremely dangerous. He reversed it having abseiled the wall and was able to stay on the rope, but wouldn't dream of doing it unroped. Access has to be by abseil, but there are no stakes in situ at present (or they have disappeared under the heather) and no other anchors. He recommends two stakes as the turf is only a couple of feet deep.

Northern Cliffs, Staffin Slip South:
Agent Cooper 35m E3 5c ***. Douglas Sutton, James Sutton. 14 Jun 2020.
The crack between *Captain Patience* and *Glorious Five Year Plan*. Climb the crack to where it pinches out, and move left to gain another crack which opens up just when you need it. Getting established in the left crack is the crux.

KIMALUAG AREA, Balmacquien:
Demijohn 15m Severe. Nicola Bassnett, Roger Brown. 20 Sep 2020.
An abseil gains the stance of *Golf Girl* to give this pleasant, consistent route. Follow the rightwards-slanting groove and blunt arête to good belays on the ledge. The name commemorates exactly 50 years of climbing by John Holden, of the Penrith Mountaineering Club, and was a simultaneous synchronised project with his long-awaited repeat ascent of *Flying Buttress* at Stanage – a situation that was determined by Covid restrictions.

RUBHA HUNISH, Meall Deas:
Michael Barnard notes that pitch 1 of *The Knowledge* was thought solid HVS (perhaps even low E1), so the combination mentioned in the guide would not be possible at VS, and really is not as good as just climbing both pitches of the route.

The Black Book 65m E3 ***. Michael Barnard, Alan Hill. 19 Sep 2020.
Two quality pitches. Pitch 1 follows the topo line on p.118 'Skye Sea Cliffs and Outcrops' for *The Knowledge*, which does not fit the description for that route (but the line is correct on the p120 topo). Start 5m right of the most direct groove line to the chimney, below the next cracked groove right of it.
1. 40m 5a Move up to climb using a combination of the crack in the groove and another crack in the column just left of it, and continue through the break in the overhangs as for *The Knowledge*.
2. 25m 5c The left crack, passing an old in situ nut (crux).

Ice Cream and Jellyfish 90m E3 **. Michael Barnard, Alan Hill. 18 Sep 2020.
1. 55m 5b Start as for *Minch and Tatties*, but then step left and go up to climb the
centre of three cracks right of a square-cut roof, pulling into the right-hand one
above its vegetated section. Continue more easily, traverse left to a slight rib and
make thin moves up this, then boldly up to below the headwall. Move up and left
to belay as for *The Knowledge*.
2. 35m 5c Move up to below the left crack, then traverse right to climb the right
one (slightly easier but more sustained).

Michael Barnard notes that the top pitches of *The Black Book* and *Ice Cream and
Jellyfish* take the parallel hanging cracks mentioned in the description for *The
Knowledge*. They are excellent jamming pitches and would be well worth
abseiling in to do in their own right. Take at least two Camalot 2 and 3 for either,
and at least one Camalot 4 for *Ice Cream and Jellyfish*.

Colin Moody on the FA of Glue Cuts (E1,5b), Bornesketaig, Skye. See SMCJ 2020, p. 157.
Photo: Steve Kennedy

Bornesketaig, Organ Pipes:

Falling Time   22m   HVS 5a *. Colin Moody, Cynthia Grindley, Steve Kennedy. 23 Aug 2020.
The crack approximately 5m left of *It's a Shame* starting from a large block and with a small overhang low on the right.

Andy Moles suggests *Power to Believe* is E1 5b **.

Bornesketaig, Gully Walls:

Ghost Net   16m   E2 5b. Steve Kennedy, Cynthia Grindley, Colin Moody. 30 Aug 2020
Twin cracks right of *Glue Cuts* to the same lower-off.

Box of Frogs   16m   E1 5b ***. Colin Moody, Steve Kennedy, Cynthia Grindley. 30 Aug 2020.
Perhaps 10 to 15m right of *Ghost Net* are obvious striking twin cracks, just right of a squat pillar. Climb these cracks finishing on the left-hand crack.

Creelman   18m   HVS 5a **. Steve Kennedy, Cynthia Grindley, Colin Moody. 6 Sep 2020.
Located about 50m west of Poly Wall on a projecting spur about 15m left (east) of a disintegrating basalt pinnacle. Climb twin cracks on the left side of the spur, moving into the right-hand crack below a small overhang in the upper part to finish at a lower-off.

Andy Moles offers the following opinions on grades and stars of recent routes: *Tripoli* E1 5b ***, *Polysexual* E1 5b **.

NEIST POINT, Upper Cliffs, Gritstone Reminiscence Buttress:

Callum Johnson notes that *Seven Days* (*SMCJ* 2014) is very good and worth three stars if not four!

Stone Wall Buttress:

Twegolapps Direct   20m   VS 4c. Nicola Bassnett, Roger Brown. 8 Jul 2020.
Start as for *Twegolapps*, then take the left-hand crack at the V. Step left onto the buttress, to follow the crack to a steep awkward finish left of the groove of the original route.

Poverty Point, North End:

Italian Arête   18m   E2 5b *. Mike Mason, Lucy Spark. 14 Oct 2020.
Below the upper part of *Italian Job* is a blank wall and large flat platform. Use the left arête of this wall to gain the same finish as Italian Job.

Poverty Point, Boulder Cove:

Tim Miller and Andy Moles repeated *The Poverty Trap* and felt it was hard 6a and solid E4 **.

Vagrants   25m   E5 6a **. Andy Moles, Calum Muskett. 15 May 2021. The nicely featured wall between *Rhubarb Crumble* and *The Poverty Trap*. Start just left of *The Poverty Trap* and swing out left to jugs. Move up boldly but easily, then step right into a niche. Climb directly up via a layback flake and small groove (good cam on the right between these) to gain a tiny ledge. Make a blind crux reach to gain the hanging flake above, and climb this to reach a big flat hold. Step left to finish. Take a selection of micro gear.

Urchins   25m   E1 5b *. Calum Muskett, Andy Moles. 15 May 2021.
Towards the right side of the wall, just right of a steep and blanker section, is a shallow right-facing corner. Climb up a big flake to gain the corner, and follow it to a ledge. Finish more easily up the crack above. Good climbing in the lower half, but a bit boomy.

Otter's Arcade   30m   E2 5c *. Andy Moles, Calum Muskett. 15 May 2021.
The main corner at the right end of the wall, just left of the tunnel through the headland. A crux layback section at two-thirds height is the highlight. Prone to being greasy. Top out with care, and belay well back on the grass ridge.

The Bays:
Callum Johnson notes an ascent of *Freeze Dried*, which was thought to be E3 5c.

Callum Johnson notes an ascent of *Hot Blast*, which was probably E4 and would be **** if topping out onto the ridge didn't involve pulling on a few loose blocks (much easier climbing by this point). The rest of the rock on the route is very good. Recommended gear: 1 x BD#0.3-1, 4 x BD#2, 2 x BD#3, 2 x BD#4, set of wires, 8 extenders, some alpine draws. The two stakes described in the guide for the descent are only just OK. They can be backed up with a couple of wires 15m higher up the slope. An 80m rope would be enough to descend the ridge to the top of the crag. A further 35m abseil gains the ledges below the routes.

Andy Moles notes that a rockfall appears to have removed the top of the route *Trilobite Groove*, and possibly *Agfa* as well.

South of the Steps, Pinnacle Flake Area:
Bartizan   30m   E4 6a *. Jamie Skelton, Morag Eagleson. 9 Jul 2020.
A striking line up the middle of the pinnacle which is slightly let down by friable rock. Tackle a low crux and hopefully gain juggy pockets on the wall left of the crack. Carry on until standing on the big hollow block in the middle of the crack (bold). From here climb direct or go out left and back right again. At the summit continue as for *Golden Flake*.

Bartizan Arête Finish   30m   E4 6a *. Jamie Skelton, Morag Eagleson. 9 Jul 2020.
From the hollow block at half-height move right into a hand crack and continue up the arête in good position to the top.

Power Bells   30m   E3 5c ***. Jamie Skelton, Morag Eagleson. 9 Jul 2020.
A well protected test of jamming just right of *Bluebell Groove*.

Jamie Skelton notes that *The Old Man and the Sea* (*SMCJ* 2017) should be 28m not 18m.

RAASAY – ARNISH and TORRAN, Little Diabaig, Near Dome:
Lizard   10m   Severe 4a. Jack Copland. 25 Apr 2021.
Climb the twin diagonal slanting cracks just right of *Tooth Fairy*. Some thin feet

in the middle, but good hands and protection throughout. Finish on good jugs over the top.

Caravel   12m   Severe. Jack Copland, Patricia Carvalho, Steve White. 25 Apr 2021.
On the approach to Little Diabaig (from Ocean-Going Cliff), a fine strip of Lewisian Gneiss marks the left side of the natural corridor up towards Little Diabaig's Near Dome. This is the first route here, with plenty of potential for more routes. The climb starts at the obvious protruding prow. A high step as first move gains the prow to easier ground above. Follow the crack right of the triangular block at half-height.

NORTHERN HIGHLANDS NORTH

ARDMAIR, Dancing Buttress:
Just Add Lib, Direct Finish   35m 10m   E1 5c. Andy Moles, Tom Powell. 23 Aug 2020.
From the arrival point on the Dance Floor, move up directly (as for *Primitive Dance*). Make a steep pull into a groove on the left, and follow this to a careful heathery exit.

Beast Buttress:
Michael Barnard notes that where the holds turn to slopers near the top On the *Western Skyline*, reaching right into *Neart nan Gaidheal* to avoid the slopers makes the route a very good E2 5c pitch.

Big Roof Buttress:
Optical Delusion   25m   E5 6b *. Ian Taylor, Tess Fryer. 27 Sept 2020.
Climb the wall right of *Tunnel Vision* to a small roof and make a hard move up a disappointingly holdless groove, to gain good holds above. Swing left and follow a flake to a rest below another roof. Move very awkwardly left until able to bridge out into *Tunnel Vision*, then pull back right and climb a thin crack to a ledge (optional belay). Finish up a short corner.

KEANCHULISH, Camas an Lochain Crag:
Fly with the Wind   30m   E2 5b/c **. Callum Johnson and Tom Shaw. 18 Sep 2020.
Start between *Keanchulish Crack* and *Slotting the Eunich* at a thin crack (about 1m right of the left arête of the front of the buttress), climb direct up the crack to join *Slotting the Eunich* where it traverse in from the left. Climb up flakes following a small right-facing corner and continue direct. Cross *Keanchulish Crack* before that route pulls into the V-groove, move right along a wide break then pull up to climb sensationally up the left-hand side of the upper arête via breaks, briefly moving onto the right-hand side, before pulling back left and surmounting the final steepening by a crack and block.

The Tides of Time   18m   E3/4 5c ***. Callum Johnson, Tom Shaw. 18 Sep 2020.
Climbs the arête between *Tricky's Route* and *Carefree*. Low tide required. Start directly beneath the arête. Climb thin flakes and pocketed breaks (crossing the

barnacled traverse break of *Carefree*) to gain cracks on the left-hand side of the arête, climb these on improving holds until they join the arête at 10m. Finish easily up the right-hand side of the arête.

Skimming   6m   Severe 4b. Callum Johnson. 18 Sep 2020.
Just south of the descent and left of an overhanging wall is a corner with cracks and flakes. Gain the corner by a tricky step then continue steeply on good holds.

Callum Johnson notes that he was unable to locate *Scary Jellyfish* (*SMCJ* 2019) and believes there to be some confusion. There is not a north-facing wall right of *SAF Route*, so assume a misidentification of the chimney mentioned in the guide as *SAF Route*, which would mean that *Scary Jellyfish* actually takes the existing line of *Tricky's Route*, which would fit the description.

SGÙRR AN FHÌDHLEIR:
South Buttress   100m   III,4. Dan Moore. 3 Jan 2021.
Climbs the ridge overlooking *South Gully* on the small buttress south of the main wall. Start left of the gully and climb steepening turf until possible to move onto the ridge overlooking *South Gully*. Continue up this and tackle the summit tower direct (crux – also possible to walk into the gully at this point). (Topo provided.)

Iain Young offers an improved description of the classic *Direct Nose Route*:

Direct Nose Route   365m   HVS ***.
The base of the buttress is very broad and broken, so the lowest rocks and the crest are hard to define. Look for a line of grassy grooves that slant up the centre, heading slightly rightwards. At the base of these on the left (looking up) and directly below two triangular overhangs, is a clean slab. Start at the base of this slab. You can tell people have been this way before, but it's not a path.
1. 60m 4b Climb diagonally right across the slab, move onto turf and then follow the grassy grooves, with occasional rock, to belay on a large block on a terrace.
2. 55m 4b Above is a large protruding block with the continuation of the grassy grooves to its immediate right. Follow these grooves to belay.
3. 50m 4b Follow the line of grooves, with more rock climbing, to belay below slab dotted with light grey lichen, the 'First Pale Slab'.
4. 30m 4a Continue in the line of the grooves, passing rightwards past a prominent overhang, to belay on blocks festooned with ancient tat under another roof.
5. 15m 4a Traverse left, beginning with a line of turf at hand hight, on insecure slabby footholds left to belay on a large block on the crest. This is the 'Hansom Cab' stance. There is protection to be found on this traverse, but a confident second will help.
6. 40m 5a Now the good rock climbing starts. Above is a bulge above a steep, cracked slab. Climb to the bulge, pass this on the left, then climb the wall above just left of the crest to belay on a fine ledge.
7. 15m 4c Above is a clean rib, with cracks on its slabby left side and a grassy groove left again. Climb the cracked slab to belay on another ledge.
8. 15m 5a Above is an old ring peg in an alcove; ignore this, step just right and make a hard move up onto the slab, go up cracks to another ledge, then move left to belay at a notch on the crest, or continue the first few metres up the next pitch and belay on a little ledge.
9. 25m 4c Step right and surmount the overlap by two old peg runners. Climb

the cracked slabs above just right of the arête, which steepen, to gain a small ledge and belay in a fine position.
10. 20m 5a More cracked slabs lead to a short wall climbed by finger cracks. (A tricky pitch but there's a secret.) Belay below an obvious V-groove above.
11. 40m 4c One tricky move in the V-groove quickly leads to easy ground. Run it out to belay in a fine position on the shoulder.
180m of scrambling lead to the summit.

CAIRN CONMHEALL, Acheninver Pinnacle:
Mistdemeanour 105m Severe. Chris Dickinson, Anna Guy. 15 Aug 2020.
Start on the leftmost (western side) pillar of rock on the main tier.
1. 40m 4a Climb the fine 'laid back' pillar on the left edge and continue by cracks in the centre to easier ground.
2. 40m Step right and climb continuous rock, occasionally loose, to reach a horizontal ledge. Follow this to a huge belay boulder platform on *Acheninver Pinnacle Original Route*.
3. 25m 4a Climb a vertical crack up a steep perched pillar just left of the crest to gain a huge belay boulder. Finish up the arête above to the summit.

BEN MORE COIGACH, Fred's Crag:
Fred's Crag is the obvious, grooved cliff that you can see on the left looking up the line of the Garbh Allt. In addition to the three new routes mentioned here, *Right Said Fred* was repeated and thought to be worth two stars. The crag has great climbing in a beautiful setting. The gully between the crags provides an easy descent. (Topo provided.)

Yabba Dabba Doo 30m VS 4c *. Iain Young, Kenny Brookman, Simon Osborne. 1 Sep 2020.
This route takes the blunt arête forming the left edge of the main crag. Start up the initial bulge and then climb directly up the rib to belay on the huge block on top of the crag.

Boss Bird 35m HVS 5a *. Kenny Brookman, Simon Osborne, Iain Young. 1 Sep 2020.
Five metres right of *Right Said Fred* is a short, shallow, left-facing corner. Climb this then to a ledge at 5m, then head directly up the cracked wall above trending left at the top and finish up a short slab.

Wilma 40m Severe. Iain Young, Simon Osborne, Kenny Brookman. 1 Sep 2020.
Takes a line on the slabby crag just to the right of Fred's Crag and mentioned as being more obvious on the approach in 'Northern Highlands North'. Start on the right, just left of a heather-topped pillar leaning against the slab and climb directly to a right-to-left-trending weakness; follow this to its end, then climb directly to the top.

CÙL BEAG, Lurgainn Slabs:
Friends Galore 12m VS 4c **. John Mackenzie, Neil Wilson, Ian Douglas. 15 Aug 2020.
Left of *Rogue Ripple* is another flat-faced buttress with a prominent steep left edge. Climb the near-vertical left edge directly for maximum enjoyment. The best of the Lower Tier routes by far.

John Mackenzie on the FA of Rogue Ripple (E1,5b), Middle Tier, Cùl Beag.
See SMCJ 2020, p.159. Photo: Andrew James.

Friends in Need 20m Mild Severe *. Neil Wilson, Ian Douglas, John Mackenzie. 15 Aug 2020.
This takes the arête of the rib left of *Friends Alone* directly and pleasantly.

Absent Friends 20m HVS 5a *. John Mackenzie, Ian Douglas. 15 Aug 2020.
This is the leftmost and scruffiest looking rib but is better than it looks. Start in a hollow below the rib and climb steeply to gain a shelf. Climb the wall above via a flake and stand on this to exit up a rippled slab on the left which has a juniper and grass finish.

Misanthrope's Groove 85m HVS 5a **. Stephen Venables, John Mackenzie, Ian Douglas. 24 Aug 2020.
A fine route that takes the crack-lined groove cutting through the big roof left of the *G.F.C.* Good protection and positions and some very pleasant climbing.
1. 35m Climb the slab as for *Breakout* and *Breakthrough* but move up and right to belays by a juniper ledge.
2. 20m Climb the cracks, crux, to the big roof and break through this on great holds and position to belay below a short steep V-groove.
3. 30m Climb the short V-groove to the slab above. Follow the shallow groove to a prominent triangular overhang, step up right over this to climb to the top. Good thread belays at the top of the *G.F.C.* (Topo provided.)

Tarantula Assault Course 10m Severe. Rosie Rothwell, Joseph Barlow. 19 Sep 2020.
Approximately 50m right of the *Paper Tiger* lies a short wall split by a crack. The crack has a horizontal break running just above half-height. Start on a platform at the base of the main crack and climb it direct. The name of the route comes from the number of large spiders encountered on the route. (Topo provided.)

Smiling Buttress 75m HVS 5a **. Andrew James, John Mackenzie. 30 May 2021.
This is the narrow buttress on the left of the Top Tier, left of the crack of *Breakthrough*. It has an enigmatic yet alluring stone smile created by a curved concave smooth section. Due to the overall steepness of the ground below the crag, there is considerable exposure right from the start.
The excellent second pitch is protected by smallish cams. The climb starts up a slope from the main slab reached by a grassy corner. The start of the climb is right of a steeper section where a corner with a heather patch has a small clean ledge at the base.
1. 20m 4a From the little ledge climb into the corner on the right and exit more awkwardly to a very constricted semi-hanging stance directly below the crack of *Breakthrough*.
2. 20m 5a Climb the horizontal ripples left of the edge and move up left, skirting 'the smile' and climb up the middle in a great position to a surprise crevasse at the top. Belay on the far left side of this.
3. 35m 4b Climb up then slightly right past a triangular block without using it. Move up a slab above and step right into a block-topped corner. Climb this or easier, step right and up to the same place. Move left into a rather grassy groove and so to the top.

Sunset Ridge　60m　Moderate to Difficult. Andrew James, John Mackenzie. 30 May 2021.
Above the Top Tier and on the left is a disjointed ridge which is open to variation and with much scrambling. If a midway crack and the top tier are taken directly then some climbing can be had on excellent rock.

STAC POLLAIDH, No 1 Buttress:
Michael Barnard notes that *Non Compos Mentis* & *Felo de Se* as suggested (*SMCJ* 2015) make a good consistent combination, perhaps worth ** overall. Pitch 1 is 45m.

Pinnacle Basin:
Pollaidh Peapod　15m　E2 6a. Michael Barnard, Alan Hill. 25 Apr 2021.
Immediately right of The Irascible Porcupine pitch 1. A classic piece of climbing, with the crux arriving at a similar point as on its more famous namesake. Take care with some blocks near the top.

No 3 Buttress:
Michael Barnard notes that the *Jamalamadingdong* wall actually lies here, just right of *Summer Isles Arête* and near *Outrageous Fortune*. For such obvious cracks, the description is rather confusing. The wall would be better described as having two main crack-lines, with *Jamalamadingdong* taking the left one and Highland Spring starting up a short crack just to its left. *Jamalamadingdong* was thought ***, one of the best single-pitch lines in the area.

Moving right from the *Jamalamadingdong* wall, the next small buttress is easily identified by a small pinnacle at its base. It features a fine crack with a rightward kink past a bulge.

Who Shot Fardel's Bear?　10m　E1 5b. Alan Hill, Michael Barnard. 25 Apr 2021.
Left of the curving crack is an easier groove. Climb the jamming crack left of this.

Wild Beaver　15m　E2 5c **. Michael Barnard, Alan Hill. 25 Apr 2021.
The curving crack; easy up to the kink and much trickier above!

Magnum O'Puss　15m　VS 4c. Alan Hill, Michael Barnard. 25 Apr 2021.
The crack right of the above has a difficult start and some suspect rock near the top.

Consider the Lillies lies more like 100m right of *Summer Isles Arête*, not 40m. Just left of that wall is a smaller tower with a fine curving flake-crack on its front face.

Sunday Service　20m　HVS 5a **. Michael Barnard, Alan Hill. 25 Apr 2021.
The wide flake-crack (large cams required).

Saturday Sun　20m　VS 5a. Michael Barnard, Alan Hill. 24 Apr 2021.
Move up to below the flake-crack, then traverse left to climb a corner crack. Finish up the arête.

Michael Barnard on the FA of Beggar's Bouquet (E2 5b), Stac Pollaidh. Photo: Alan Hill.

Schrödinger's Goldfish   15m   Severe 4b *. Alan Hill, Michael Barnard. 25 Apr 2021.
Around the corner to the left, climb twin cracks near the right edge (the 'other side' of *Saturday Sun*'s corner-crack), moving left into another crack once past its vegetated section.

Consider the Lillies was thought E1 5b *, and the crux is definitely before the top ledge (the final flake-crack around on the right is about 4a).

Beggar's Bouquet   25m   E2 5b *. Michael Barnard, Alan Hill. 24 Apr 2021.
Start down and right of the right-hand crack in the *Consider the Lillies* wall. Move up to the crack, step left into the left one and climb this to the top ledge. Continue up the crack above.

REIFF, Roinn a' Mhill, Bouldering Cliff:
Frog Arête   15m   E6 6b/c. Callum Cunningham. Sep 2015.
The arête right of *Toad in the Hole* climbed direct.

Rapacious   20m   E6 6b. Iain Small, Murdoch Jamieson. 3 May 2014.
Start up *Crack of Desire, Direct Start* then break out right to climb the wall, by hard moves, to gain the big break below a roof. pull through the roof and move up on undercuts until along move right gains a jug on the arête. Micro cams in small flake below. Make committing moves up the arête and pull left to a hidden pocket to finish up arête.

The Point:
Routes are from right to left, starting just after *First Twin*. (Topos provided.)

Second Twin   4m   H.Severe. Rory Brown, Emma Atkinson. 11 Aug 2020.
The wall between *Pollock Shuffle* and *First Twin* with some great pockets.

Pollock Shuffle   4m   Diff. Emma Atkinson, Rory Brown. 11 Aug 2020.
Immediately to the right of the 'deep wide crack descent' is a faint arête. Climb the featured arête through a mini sentry box low down.

The next routes are on the wall between *Treat* and *OH Crack*.

On Point   8m   V.Diff. Rory Brown, Emma Atkinson. 11 Aug 2020.
To the left of *Treat* the next wall is quite featured but has a distinct right-slanting crack or ramp line starting about one-third height. Climb directly to the start of the crack or ramp and then follow it on great holds. Lots of seaweed on the starting footholds.

On Point Direct   7m   Severe. Rory Brown, Emma Atkinson. 11 Aug 2020.
Start up *On Point* but continue straight up the wall where it goes right.

C Rack   7m   Severe 4b. Rory Brown, Emma Atkinson. 11 Aug 2020.
Left of *On Point* is a short crack set in a very thin groove. Climb this to the big horizontal break and then finish straight up.

A Roof 6m   VS 5a. Rory Brown, Emma Atkinson. 11 Aug 2020.
To the left of *C Rack* climb a steep flake-crack that leads to a small roof. Pull through this to an obvious jug and head direct to the top

The next routes are on the north-facing wall with *Minkie*.

Point Scoop 5m   H.Severe 4c. Rory Brown, Emma Atkinson. 11 Aug 2020.
The scooped wall to the right of *Rampline* with a tricky start and a sloping finish.

Horizontal Happiness 10m   VS 4c. Rory Brown, Emma Atkinson. 11 Aug 2020.
Start up the *Rampline* to the second big horizontal break. Hand traverse this all the way left to finish up *Nanny State*.

An Stuir, Sugar Kelp Bay:
Furbelows Holdfast 10m   Severe. Alan Hill, Michael Barnard. 27 Sep 2020.
The next crack left of *Sugar Plum*.

Boring Piddock 10m   Very Difficult. Alan Hill, Michael Barnard. 27 Sep 2020.
From the base of *Guttie Groove*, step up and traverse right to climb the bottomless groove around the arête.

The Talus Man 10m   HVS 5a *. Michael Barnard, Alan Hill. 27 Sep 2020.
From the base of *Guttie Groove*, climb a steep left-trending crack to gain a hanging slab. Continue up the slabby wall above.

The Wondering Albert Ross 6m   Severe. Alan Hill, Michael Barnard. 27 Sep 2020.
A short vertical crack in the centre of the wall left of *The Talus Man*.

The Hipster 10m   HVS 5a. Michael Barnard, Alan Hill. 27 Sep 2020.
Around the corner left of *The Wondering Albert Ross* is a fine easy cracked slab. Around the next corner is a steeper black slab. Climb steeply up the right side of the slabby wall.

Do You Have a Licence for that Minke? 10m   Difficult *. Alan Hill, Michael Barnard. 27 Sep 2020.
The next feature left of *The Hipster* is a fine left-slanting hanging groove.

All Things Nice 10m   E1 5a *. Michael Barnard, Alan Hill. 27 Sep 2020.
Starting a few metres left of *Do You Have a Licence for that Minke?* climb a short left-slanting groove to its top, make a long reach for a ledge then pull up right to finish on the arête.

The following routes are described from right to left. (Topo provided.)

Don't forget the Cam 9m   Severe*. John Higham, Kenny Brookman. 2 Sep 2020.
Above the pool and to the right of the alcove mentioned in *SMCJ* 2019, a broken crack-line splits the wall between a slab and some overhangs. Climb this.

Take a Cam 9m   H.Severe. John Higham, Kenny Brookman. 2 Sep 2020.
Climb the right-hand side of the deep corner that lies directly above the pool.

Devil's Apron   8m   VS 4b. Iain Young, Simon Osborne. 2 Sep 2020.
To the left of the alcove is short wall broken by a central overhang cut by a prominent crack. Gain and climb the crack.

Around the corner to the left is a crack-seamed slab where the two most prominent cracks provide enjoyable routes.

Left-Hand Crack   6m, V.Diff *. Kenny Brookman, John Higham. 2 Sep 2020.

Right-Hand Crack   6m   V.Diff. Kenny Brookman, John Higham. 2 Sep 2020.

Impostor   8m Diff. Iain Young, Simon Osborne. 2 Sep 2020.
The little gulch running past the slab mentioned above ends in a steep-looking crack corner. Climb this, much easier than it looks.

Wheat Puffs   9m   Severe. Kenny Brookman, John Higham. 2 Sep 2020.
To the left of *Impostor* is a short wall right of a deep gulch and wide crack. Climb the wall over a small bulge.

The rib to the left of *Impostor* was soloed by Iain Young at about Diff.

Slabby Ramp   8m V.Diff *. Simon Osborne, Iain Young. 2 Sep 2020.
Around the next corner is a steep wall split by an overhung slabby ramp. Gain and climb this. Excellent.

Sea Belt   8m   HVS 5b. Iain Young, Simon Osborne. 2 Sep 2020.
Left again is a short slab topped on the left by a V-shaped, overhung alcove. Gain the alcove and make a tricky move to turn the lip.

Iain Young notes that *The Talus Man* looks to come round the arête from the right and finish as for *Devil's Apron*. *The Wandering Albert Ross* is the crack to the left of *Devil's Apron* (or they might be the same thing.)

An Stuir, Hidden Walls (NB 968 165):
There are some hidden, short, and largely slabby west-facing walls just south of the little bay at Sugar Kelp Bay. Most are easily reached by traversing around and in from the north at tide level until you reach a large non-tidal platform backed by slabs and a steep little wall. The centre of this short cliff takes the form of a fine, undercut slab on the left, separated from bulging walls and then more slabs to the right by a prominent right-angled corner. (Topo provided.)

Good to be Back Crack   8m   V.Diff. Iain Young. 27 Apr 2021.
The prominent right-angled corner.

Off Key   8m   E1 5b. Iain Young, John Higham. 28 Apr 2021.
Immediately left of the central corner is a fine slab. Climb this just left of a hairline crack.

Three Tier Slab   8m   V.Diff. John Higham, Iain Young. 28 Apr 2021.
Left again is a slab with a block at the base and a break at two-thirds height. Climb over the block and up the slab via the faint arête.

Descent Corner   6m   Diff. Iain Young, John Higham. 28 Apr 2021.
The black corner at the left end of the crag.

Slanting Crack   14m   V.Diff. John Higham, Iain Young. 28 Apr 2021.
To the right of the central corner is a bulging wall then an obvious diagonal break running up from a recess. From the recess, gain and climb the fine, slanting thin crack.

Big Boulder Slab   12m   V.Diff. Iain Young, John Higham. 28 Apr 2021.
Right again is a boulder-filled gulch. From the large boulder at its base, climb directly up the slab above.

Offshore from here is a long fin of rock. Two routes were climbed on the seaward face of this fin. At low tide, a moderate scramble via ledges leads along the base of the slabby seaward face, or it can be descended by an obvious ramp and moderate down-climb.

Offshore Rule   8m   Diff. Iain Young. 28 Apr 2021.
The prominent V-groove.

Tide Race   10m   Severe. Iain Young, John Higham. 28 Apr 2021.
Take the centre of the fine slab to its the overhung top. A perfect hold allows a straightforward pull over onto steps that lead to the top.

Rubha Coigeach, Golden Walls:
Midge Fighter   15m   E3 5c. Ian Taylor, Tess Fryer. 6 August 2020.
An eliminate line up the arête left of *Rite of Spring*. Start up *Sweet Chasity*. At a good ledge move right onto the arête and follow it direct to the top.

Rubha Coigeach, Amphitheatre Bay:
The Shoogly Corner   10m   VS 4c. Tess Fryer, Ian Taylor. 23 Jul 2011.
The most obvious corner on the smaller NW-facing wall left of the main Amphitheatre.

The Swinging Sixties   20m   E1 5b *. Michael Barnard, Alan Hill. 15 May 2021.
A line up the left side of the main amphitheatre. Start a couple of metres right of *The Shoogly Corner*, below an undercut crack. Climb this (crux) and move out left to a ledge. Gain the next ledge above, step right and go up a flake-crack before hand-traversing right to reach another ledge. Gain the next ledge up and right, then finish up cracks directly above (stakes in situ).

The Furious Fifties   25m   E4 5c *. Iain Small, Sam Williams. May 2014.
Steep cracks and even steeper corner line about 20m left of *Roaring Forties*. A classic grovelfest at the crux.

Lip Trip   30m   E6 6b. Iain Small, Niall McNair. 10 Apr 2018.
Climb *Minjeetah* to the big jug below its easy top corner then launch hard left along a break-line traverse through very steep ground under the capping roof. Pull out left onto the headwall and finish more easily. Care should be taken to extend most runners. A double set of cams is required.

Ian Taylor on the FA of Midge Fighter (E3,5c), Golden Walls, Reiff. Photo: Tess Fryer.

Michael Barnard thought *The Roaring Forties* was overgraded but vastly underrated – E2 5c ***?

Rubha Coigeach, Rubha Ploytach:
Caddy 24m E2 5c **. Connor Henley, Harrison Connie. 9 Oct 2020.
Start directly below prominent upper face in the small alcove 7m to the left of *First and Ten*. Go through the lower roof to climb up a broken slab arriving at a large break. Head directly up the bulging roof above onto the prominent slabby wall and climb direct up the upper wall.

Third Horn 20m E1 5b *. Connor Henley, Harrison Connie. 9 Oct 2020.
Start one metre left of *First and Ten* and head up the open corner to stand on a block. Go through the roof trending rightwards to finish directly.

BREABAG, Coirean Bàn, Upper Buttress:
Little Top 45m VS. Rob Archbold, Greg Strange. 21 May 1977.
Moving up and left from the left end of the 'Lower South-East Cliff' (p. 213 of 'Northern Highlands North') there is a steep wall with overlaps and a small waterfall on its left. This route climbs the left edge of the wall, overlooking the waterfall. Start up a pale ramp and its continuation groove, then trend steeply up rightwards on good holds to the top.

LOCHINVER CRAGS, Creag Rodha Mòr:
Glittering Girl 30m E2 5b ***. Michael Barnard, Alan Hill. 1 May 2021.
A link-up of *The Shiner*, *Read My Lips* and continuing to join and finish up *Small Time Girl*. Not much new ground but excellent steep juggy climbing up the diagonal flake-line.

Andy Moles notes that *The Melting* was more E1 than E2.

LOCHINVER CRAGS, Achmelvich Campsite Crags:
Andy Moles notes that if the upper half of the arête of *Flawless* is climbed on its left side, the route is more like E6 6b *** and hard for the grade if you're less than average height. *Flawless Left-Hand* is worth a separate guidebook entry. As far as he knows it was first climbed this way by Richie Betts in 2009.

Andy Moles notes that he climbed the remaining upper corner of *Calypso* via the lower arête of *Flawless* on 29 May 2021. He thinks this is the first ascent since the giant block that defined the lower half of the route fell out and considers it now top end E4 6a **, maybe E5. Climb *Flawless* as far as the foot ledge, then move left around the arête and span the gap to gain the corner. The original advice about two RP2s was not helpful as he didn't place any. There is a key small wire halfway up the corner, which is bombproof but tricky to get in. He doesn't think one move of new climbing merits a change in name, but it would be fun to name the new version *Collapso*...

POINT OF STOER, Old Man of Stoer South Stack (NC 015 350):
The impressive stack approximately 200m south of the Old Man of Stoer. It is largely hidden from view in a steep geo, but even so, it is surprising it had not been climbed before. It had most likely been overlooked in the rush to bag the Old Man and was possibly the highest unclimbed sea stack on the Scottish

mainland west coast. The stack is unnamed on maps and the name has been taken from the database of British and Irish hills.

South Face 40m Severe. Mark Robson, Simon Richardson. 30 Aug 2020.
Access is difficult in all but the calmest seas. Descend the cliff as for the Old Man of Stoer and traverse to the most southerly point of the shelf at the base of the cliff until opposite the stack. Make a 30m swim across to the stack and land on a platform on its west side. Move across the platform and traverse right along ledges to gain a right-trending crack-line up the centre of the south face. Climb this on excellent rock – easier than it looks. Abseil descent and reverse the approach.

CANISP, North Flank:
North Rib 90m II/III. John Higham, Iain Young. 7 Dec 2020.
A prominent rib drops north from the summit shelter. On this occasion this was gained by dropping west from the summit to a shoulder then north down a snow gully (Grade I) to below the steep portion of the rib. Traverse on to the rib at NC 202970 188290 and then climb it in two pitches to the summit. Much variation possible, but a superb setting and high enough to be wintry when other places are not. Of interest for starting on Torridonian sandstone and finishing on Cambrian quartzite.

One Too Many 50m II. John Higham, Iain Young. 7 Dec 2020.
The sandstone buttress to the west of *North Rib* was climbed by a line of turfy grooves towards its right side.

QUINAG, Sàil Garbh, Barrel Buttress:
Beefheart 60m VII,7 ***. Andy MacKinnon, Callum Johnson. 28 Dec 2020.
A winter ascent following the summer route throughout. A good winter line, well protected, steep with an 'out there' feeling. Conditions were very good, with turf well frozen and a lot of snow around.

CAPE WRATH, Clò Mòr Cliffs:
Callum Johnson notes that if an abseil approach is used to approach *Clo Mor Crack* the first pitch will only be accessible an hour either side of low tide, with a calm sea. The birds need to be away for access to pitch 1 as well (they were gone by 6 September in 2020). Johnson's party climbed from pitch 2 up. Pitch 2 was cleaned on abseil. Approach was possible with 100m static and 80m static. Rebelaying several times is recommended. They also climbed a pitch right of *Clo Mor Crack* pitch 4 – an obvious crack up a slabby area of rock; Guy Robertson and team also climbed this pitch earlier in the summer.

Ceannabeinne Beach:
Giraffes and Swans 12m HVS 5a **. Mike Lauder, Susan Guest. Aug 2008.
Start from the top of an obvious block (a paddle at high tide). Climb past two breaks before heading left then back right to a small ledge. Careful with the grassy top-out. Fence-post belay.

Crocodiles and Elephants 12m HVS 5a **. James Milton, Sophie Jacobs. 12 Jul 2020.
Starting in the niche just right of *Giraffes and Swans*, climb up to the highest point of the small roof. Continue up before reaching out right to some cracks and finish easily.

Mark Robson on the FA of South Face (Severe), Old Man of Stoer South Stack.
Photo: Simon Richardson.

Karen Latter on the FA of Do You Expect Me to Talk (Severe), Ardmore View Crag.
See SMCJ 2020, p.163. Photo: Gary Latter.

NORTH CAITHNESS CRAGS, Brough Stacks (ND 221 742):

Access: Parking at Brough Harbour Trust parking (enough for four cars). Sheltered bay which is good for open water swimming, paddle boarding and exploring caves to the east of the bay. The two stacks are accessible by foot when tide is at 3.3m or less (check tide timetables for Scrabster). The outer stack is smaller and has much better rock than the inner stack, and provides good scrambling and bouldering. The impressive looking stack on the east side of the bay at ND 224 741 was climbed by its easy north ridge (Moderate) by Mark Robson and Simon Richardson, 29 Jul 2006 after a swim approach (probably climbed before).

The inner stack has some good scrambling and bouldering on its the eastern side (facing the outer stack). This can be used to access the top and set a hanging belay for the routes on the north face.

South Face   20m   Diff. Richard Hunt, Sandy Hunt, Darren Sutherland. 27 Mar 2021.
Follow the obvious corner crack for 10m and link exposed tiers of rock to the top.

The following two routes lie on the 20m-high north face which has good rock for the first 12 to 14m.

Nae Crack   20m   Severe. Richard Hunt, Sandy Hunt, Darren Sutherland. 27 Mar 2021.
Follows the prow of north face edge and to the left of the nose at top. (Topo provided.)

'e Craic   14m   Severe. Richard Hunt, Sandy Hunt, Darren Sutherland. 27 Mar 2021.
Start left of *Nae Crack* and follow the obvious left to right sloping crack line until rock gets too loose at about 14m and leader bottles it. (Topo provided.)

Longgeo Wall (ND 298 747):

Access: Park on verge opposite house/campsite above Long Goe farm and walk along edge of field to caves. The wall is tidal and can be accessed by abseil or walking in 150m from the east. Although very short, the climbs are on a clean wall with good cracks. Routes are named after John o' Groats Brewery beers and described from left to right. (Topo provided.)

First Footing   5m   V.Diff. Richard Hunt, Louise Hunt. 27 Jul 2020.
Good holds following crack up corner to top.

Swelkie   5m   E1 5a. Richard Hunt, Louise Hunt. 27 Jul 2020
Clean crack-line direct to top.

Liddel Eddy   5m   E1 5a. Richard Hunt, Louise Hunt. 27 Jul 2020
Using ledges climb direct to top using cracks either side for protection.

Deep Groat   5m   Severe. Richard Hunt, Louise Hunt. 27 Jul 2020
Follow obvious curving crack-line to top with good protection where needed.

St John's Point (ND 402 753):
St John's Stack   10m   V.Diff. Richard Hunt. Summer 2018.
The short sea stack at ND 400 753 climbed by its landward face.

Port Vasgo:
Mokoshi   20m   E3 6a/b **. Callum Johnson, Andy MacKinnon. 8 Sep 2020.
Takes the roof crack between *Satari* and *Highline*, through the widest part of the
top roof. Start as for *Satari* until past the roof at the bottom of the crag, then step
right into the line of right-facing corners and small overhangs to the upper roof
and crack. Hard well-protected moves lead to the top.

SOUTH HEAD OF WICK:
Selkie   10m   E2 5c **. Callum Johnson, Andy MacKinnon. 9 Sep 2020.
Halfway between *Lightness of Being* and *Wick and Feeble*. Start at a left-facing
corner and climb the wall to gain parallel cracks in the upper wall. Finish pulling
into the notch, which is just left of the change in height of the crag.

SARCLET, Occam's Buttress:
10 O-Clock Shadow   30m   H.Severe 4b *. Alan Hill, Michael Barnard 17 Apr
2021.
A line of left-slanting grooves left of *Thrumster Regatta*. Climb the initial slabby
corner of that route, then step left to continue up the slanting grooves.

Find the Cost of Freedom   35m   E1 5c *. Michael Barnard, Alan Hill. 17 Apr
2021.
A line of cracks and grooves right of the arête. The lower section is good but some
of the rock on the headwall is suspect; after the crux it may be better to move left
onto *The Ugly Bug Ball*. From a stance on the arête, step right and climb
rightward-trending cracks and grooves to below an overlap. Step right and
surmount this, then move back left past a roof (crux) to gain a groove. Continue
more easily up the groove. Climb a steep blocky crack just right of the main roof
and traverse left on the lip to finish up flake-cracks in the arête.

Another Day at the Office, Left-hand Finish   10m   E1 5b ***. Michael Barnard,
Alan Hill. 25 Oct 2020.
On reaching the top roof, traverse left under it and finish up the cracked wall.

Djapana Buttress:
Regal Wall   25m   E2 5b ***. Michael Barnard, Alan Hill. 17 Apr 2021.
A future Sarclet classic up the fine wall left of *Arch Rival*. Abseil from the
tombstone block to gain a good ledge on the left edge of the wall (up and left of
the base). From the left end of the ledge, go up a steep cracked groove. Climb to
a couple of metres below the roof, then move out right to gain a rest ledge.
Continue boldly up a shallow right-facing groove, and on to the top.

Unknown Buttress (ND 342 419):
Michael Barnard notes that the following routes lie on the edge of the next
promontory south of Tilted Ledge. Non-tidal. North-east facing. It is unsure how
these relate to Gloup Ledge, but Simon Nadin doesn't recognise the photos and
the descriptions don't seem to fit. An old in situ nut was found at the bottom of a
difficult tight groove, so it seems likely the easier lines have been climbed before

(and not recorded); certainly the VS will have been. A large black non-tidal ledge lies below the routes, gained by abseil through the finishing groove of the VS. The routes are around 25–30m long. In the upper section, left of the main groove, is a nasty-looking tight groove (E2?). The main groove has two parallel cracks in its left wall. These can be climbed with a step left into the easier finishing groove at VS 4c *. The back of the main groove, moving right into another short groove to finish, is possibly HVS. The steep cracks up the arête on the right are HVS 5a **.

ULBSTER, Whaligoe, Ellens Geo:

Girdle Your Loins 65m E3 ***. Michael Barnard, Alan Hill. 26 Oct 2020.
A sensational traverse. A triple set of cams from Camalot 0.5 to 2 may be found useful. Start as for *The Cat's Outta the Bag* (*SMCJ* 2020).
1. 20m 5a Follow *The Cat's Outta the Bag* up the sandstone and a couple of metres up the conglomerate, then move up left into the crack-groove immediately left of it, and climb this to ledges.
2. 25m 5c Take the obvious rising break out right, crossing *Stratagem, Brains as well as Brawn* and out to the arête of *Third Degree* (crux). Move up to arrange a semi-hanging belay.
3. 20m 4c Step back down and continue the traverse past *Hundreds and Thousands* and *So this is Summer* to finish up the short final crack of *Treading Water*.

Michael Barnard notes a more independent finish to *Cat Burglar* (*SMCJ* 2020) keeping it independent of *Guest Pass Violation*:

Cat Burglar 35m E2 5c **
Follow *The Cat's Outta the Bag* up the sandstone and a couple of metres up the conglomerate, then move left via a line of knobbly holds towards a short slanting undercut crack. Use this to gain the steep groove out left and climb this to ledges. Take the left-trending conglomerate flake-crack above to join and finish up the top arête of *Gagging Clause*.

Oliver's Travels 80m E3 5c ***. Rory Brown, Peter Herd. 10 Aug 2017.
A wild girdle taking the continuous pale diagonal break from left to right, with increasing difficulty and exposure. Start below the easy starting corner of *Brains as well as Braun*.
1. 25m 5a Climb the corner to access the pale diagonal fault line. Follow breaks right to a spacious belay on the arête, immediately left of the corner of *Where the Taught Wave Hangs*.
2. 25m 5b Leave the ledges and continue along the break across the wall. Airy moves around an arête lead to a small belay ledge in the corner of *Non Stop Nitty Gritty*.
3. 20m 5c Tricky moves of the belay lead to better holds and a rest once around the arête. Continue on the line with a further tricky section as the break crosses an innocuous looking wall. Belay just after this on an obvious ledge in the corner of *Layer Cake*.
4. 10m 5a Finish up the corner of *Layer Cake*.

Michael Barnard notes that he thought *Non Stop Nitty Gritty* E2 5b **** and the best line on the crag.

Michael Barnard on the FA of Squeal Like a Pig (E2,5c), Ellens Geo, Ulbster.
See SMCJ 2020, p. 168. Photo: Alan Hill.

MID CLYTH, Sgaps Geo:

Callum Johnson and Andy MacKinnon thought *Deep Joy* and *Sunny Side Up* were superb but probably E3 5c. *Spummin Marvellous* was just that, but thought to be E2/3 5c. *Big Sky Country* tricky E4 or soft E5 6a. *Cauliflower in the Soup* felt E5 6b, with micro cams being essential. All routes were 3 stars though! (Routes not reported in Journal so far, but topo provided.)

Clythness North (ND 292 364):

This is the area just north of Clythness (Mid Clyth) Lighthouse. Access is from a lay-by on the main road at ND 286365. Walk along the grass verge northwards and turn down the lighthouse access road. At the bottom of the road follow the John o' Groat's Way for 100m or so northwards before cutting down to the huge crazy-paving slab via a small rocky bluff. The first major feature on the seaward side of the slab is a square-cut slot, a few metres wide, that cuts into the slab. The first couple of routes are on a small promontory just south of the slot.

Centre Line 20m VS 4c *. Mick & Kathy Tighe, John McClenaghan. 8 Feb 2013.
Abseil down to a black triangular ledge well above the sea. Climb the fine system of short cracks and corners in the middle of the crag.

Centre Left 20m VS 4b. Mick & Kathy Tighe, John McClenaghan. 8 Feb 2013.
A couple of metres left of *Centre Line* climb a similar system of cracks and corners. N.B. There is an interesting looking slab on the right of the crag with a slot and steep headwall above – not climbed.

There is a grand little V.Diff up the back corner of the slot approached by abseil or scrambling down the south corner. North from here is a series of hanging grooves. The following route takes the most northerly one, just before the big overhang.

Ludgy Pot 40m E1/2 5b ***. Mick Tighe, Doug Lee. Aug 2014.
Approach via a tricky traverse from the bottom of the slot, climb the steep black wall, excellent runners, to gain the upper groove. Abseil approach possible, but you need to swing in or go for a swim!

A further 30 to 40m beyond the slot there is a much smaller one that leads down to a large platform with several shallow pools formed by the sloping flagstone. Below the platform is a large recess/bay. Routes are described starting at the southern end of the bay which has a steep wall facing north – unclimbed.

The Seam 15m HVS 5a ***. Mick & Kathy Tighe. 25 Aug 2019.
The excellent stepped groove or crack-line on the southern (seaward) edge of the bay i.e. the left edge of the steep, north-facing wall.

Kath's Corner 20m Mild Severe *. Kathy & Mick Tighe. 25 Aug 2019.
This, and the next climb, are in the north corner of the bay. Abseil down to the good ledges above the tide line. Climb a lovely, black, narrow slab, just left of *The Hoodie* groove, and continue up to a short corner to finish.

The Hoodie   25m   V.Diff. Mick & Kathy Tighe. 8 Feb 2013.
Start at the same place as Kath's Corner and climb the obvious inverted V-hoodie groove. Go up and right along an easy ledge to finish up an exposed edge above a chasm – see next routes.

At the north end of the big ledge there is a smaller bay, 'he chasm'. The following three routes start from a good ledge at the bottom – abseil approach and no easy way out!

Left Wall   20m   E1/2 **. Mick Tighe, Doug Lee. Aug 2014.
This is the fine left (north-facing) wall of the chasm. Climb the steep, seaward side of the wall on good holds to a diagonal ramp line that goes up right to the top of the crag.

The Great Escape   20m   E1/2 *. Mick & Kathy Tighe. 13 Apr 2019.
Climb the crack-corner line at the back of the chasm up to the overhang. Good, small Friends under the overhang allow for a safe traverse left, up and around the corner to the top.

The Sting   20m   HVS 5a. Mick Tighe, Ian Robertson, Robert Veitch. 20 Aug 2017.
Climb the fine slab on the right side of the chasm and the 5m V-groove at the top, which is the sting.

The Sting finishes in a small bay which can be accessed from the main ledge by a short, scary traverse, or by going around the top and scrambling in from above. The next two routes are accessed via this wee bay by abseil.

Vertical Vice   20m   VS 4c **. Mick Tighe, Ian Robertson, Robert Veitch. 20 Aug 2017.
This route finishes pretty much in the middle of the small bay. Abseil down the line to a fine little ledge above the tide-line. Climb back up the tight groove-chimney line.

Bypass   20m   VS 4c *. Mick Tighe, Ian Robertson, Robert Veitch. 20 Aug 2017.
A few metres right of *Vertical Vice* another cracking groove-corner line leads to a small overhang which is avoided by stepping out left onto the wall, and back right above.

The huge crazy-paving slab keeps going until it ends in a geo. There's a little inset wall where the cliff turns into the geo with a couple of exciting routes – not led. Back south a few metres there is another little ledge a few metres down on the seaward side. There is an excellent corner below, flanked by a smooth wall to the north and overhangs to the south.

Bodach Bell   20m   HVS 5b ***. Mick & Kathy Tighe. October 2016
The fine corner-line gives an excellent excursion, tricky in the middle; exit right at the top.

Clythness South (ND 289 362):
Approach as for Clythness North as far as the lighthouse. There is a barbed-wire

fence approximately 100m south of the lighthouse, and a further 100m south a very narrow ledge at the extreme edge of the cliff leads to a much bigger ledge which is the depot for the first crop of routes (ND 28921 36176). There is a fine double-overhang corner at the southern end of the big ledge (unclimbed), after which, going back north, there is a buttress with an overhang at two-thirds height. The first route climbs the fine recess just north of this buttress immediately below the ox-eye daisy patch.

Daisy Root 20m VS 4b***. Mick & Kathy Tighe, Morten Hansen. Jul 2019.
Abseil down to the big ledge well above the sea and climb the excellent crack in the back of the recess.

The Link 40m HVS 5a ***. Mick & Kathy Tighe. 19 Jul 2019.
Climb halfway up *Daisy Root* before traversing left along the fabulous bedding lines under the overhang. A small ledge on the arête allows for a belay to avoid rope drag. Finish around the corner up the top part of *Double Overhang*.

Lack-a-Daisy 15m VS 4b **. Kathy & Mick Tighe, Morten Hansen. 19 Jul 2019.
There's a fine little corner-crack-line in the upper part of the wall 8 to 10m right of *Daisy Root*. Start on a higher ledge system up and right of *Daisy Root* and make a bold pull up the initial bulge to gain the fine groove or crack.

Oops-a-Daisy 15m VS 4c **. Mick & Kathy Tighe. 8 Aug 2020.
Start a couple of metres right of *Lack-a-Daisy* and pull through just left of the start of the black overhangs. Climb the fine wall above.

Cleft Asunder 20m MVS 4b *. Mick & Kathy Tighe, Morten Hansen. 19 Jul 2019 .
A big ledge runs along north from the start of the Daisy routes, finishing where a deep cleft cuts into the rock. Disappear into the cleft and reappear a few metres higher up. Fine ledges lead to the top.

Heading back towards the lighthouse there is a cluster of large boulders topped with yellow lichen, the Seven Stones. Below is an excellent, gently overhanging, wall rippling with big holds – Muscle Wall – on which two routes have been top-roped, not led. There are two routes just south of Muscle Wall.

Arms Dealer 20m VS 4c. Mick & Kathy Tighe. 8 Aug 2020.
Abseil down from the Seven Stones to good ledges just above the high tide line. The left (south) side of Muscle Wall is defined by a deep cleft topped by an overhang. Climb the wall left of the cleft for a few metres then go diagonally left through a steep, slabby section to finish in a small recess just south of the Seven Stones.

Armalite 20m VS 4b. Kathy & Mick Tighe. 8 Aug 2020.
The wall just left (south) of the above, finishing in the same place.

Heading back towards the barbed-wire fence there is a large, coffin-shaped stone just south of the corner post. Good anchors underneath for an abseil down the groove-line opposite to ledges north of a big cave.

Offshore Wind   20m   VS 4b/c *. Mick & Kathy Tighe. 17 Sep 2020.
Climb the prominent crack in the fine black wall to a big ledge. Go up the steep, slaty section, finishing up the groove-corner line.

Stack Area – Skerry Mòr:
Callum Johnson agrees with Steve Perry's comment that *Doomsday* is E6 6a and ***. The crucial cam in the pocket is good but strenuous to place.

ORKNEY, Old Man of Hoy:
Richard Ive notes that *East Face Chimney Variation* (*SMCJ* 2017) has been renamed *We Spoke Too Soon*.

NORTHERN HIGHLANDS CENTRAL

BEINN A' MHÙINIDH, Bonaid Dhonn:
South by South-East   V,6 *   65m. Rob Giddy, Tim Miller, Callum Johnson. 4 Feb 2021
A winter-only line that climbs the obvious corner on the left side of the crag between *Netsky* and *North by North-West*. Two pitches; belay three-quarters of the way up the corner on a ledge on the left.

GRUDIE CRAGS (NG 974 664 to NG 969660):
The line of the main crags can be seen on the hillside from the road at Bridge of Grudie. One could approach from here to maintain a good visual of the various sections, however a slightly more direct approach is from the large parking bay overlooking Loch Maree at NG 982 671. Cross the road and head directly up through some trees onto the open hillside of Meall a' Ghiuthais. Head south-west up the hillside, following a rocky band just left of the edge of the hillside proper. A couple of bouldering outcrops are passed en route. At approx 200m the hillside flattens out into a small plateau. Cross this flat area, aiming for the next rise approx 50m right of where another rocky band joins from the left; the Main Crag starts just over this rise. (30min).
   These sandstone cliffs lie at an altitude of 300 to 350m and are mostly west to north-west-facing. Routes are described left (east) to right (west), unless stated otherwise. (Topos provided.)

Eastern Sector, First Wall:
Descents for this sector are either to the east (joining the approach route), or at this sector's western end via a steep heathery bay. The first (most easterly) continuous section of rock, approx 100m in length.
Left Crack   15m   VS 4c. Ben Sparham, Dave Porter. 23 May 2010.
The leftmost of two obvious crack-lines near the right-hand side of the wall.

Right Crack   15m   VS 4c. Ben Sparham, Dave Porter. 23 May 2010.
The next obvious crack-line 5m to the right of *Left Crack*.

Eastern Sector, Upper Tier:
Moving west, the crag line is 'interrupted' by a much browner, easy-angled

sandstone section 30m wide. (Brown Wall – no routes.) Just right again, the highest wall of the crag has a slightly lichenous veneer and a green undercut right-hand side. (Big Wall – no routes.) The ground rises past the end of Big Wall, and one can then switch back above to access a tier of cleaner sandstone (Upper Tier) or continue up to a steep heathery bay bounded on the left by a heavily striated but compact wall (Compact Wall). The routes on the Upper Tier are described right to left (west to east) as this is the order in which they are met.

Midgy Arête 8m Severe. Ben Sparham, Dave Porter, Maurice O'Connell. 1 Aug 2019.
Climb the short right arête of the detached pillar, the first main feature left of the compact wall.

On No Account 10m HVS 4c. Ben Sparham, Dave Porter 10 Apr 2010.
Left of *Midgy Arête*, this is the corner formed by the left side of the detached tower. Protection could be better.

Pass Book 10m HVS 5a **. Dave Porter, Simon Clark. 10 Apr 2010.
The obvious open-book corner set into the arête. Strenuous and well-protected.

Continuing along the upper tier terrace, past broken and vegetated ribs, in 30m you come to a clean light-brown slab.

New Account 15m VS 4c **. Dave Porter, Simon Clark, Ben Sparham. 10 Apr 2010.
Very pleasant climbing up the slab, using intermittent cracks.

Western Sector, Buttress Area:
Cutting directly across the heathery bay, from the edge of the Eastern Sector, Upper Tier, the main crag line is joined once more after about 300m at a short grey wall on sloping ground, split by a steep jam-crack. Just round the corner are a series of buttresses, beyond an initial slab and roof-corner-crack (unclimbed) and a couple of vegetated faults. Descend via a shallow gully into the central bay between Buttress Area and Hidden Buttress.

'Yorkshire VS' 15m E1 5c *. Simon Clark, Dave Porter. 15 Aug 2020.
On the first buttress, climb the deceptive crack just left of centre on the lower wall, then step right and fight up the hanging corner-crack. Will be more pleasant after brushing the hanging crack.

Statement of Middle Age 16m HVS 5a *. Ben Sparham Dave Porter. 4 Sep 2010.
On the next buttress, climb the obvious crack line up centre of buttress before moving slightly left to tackle the top crack above a bulge. Escapable at bulge, so loses a star.

Mossemite 16m Severe Ben Sparham Simon Clark Dave Porter. 10 Apr 2010.
The corner to the right of *Statement of Middle Age* – a bit manky!

The right wall of the Mossemite corner forms the left side of the first of a pair of prows. These prows form a bay which contains a clean slab of immaculate sandstone. The two corners of the bay are both unclimbed, the left corner being off-width.

Run, Parthians, Run   20m   E2 5b **. Ben Sparham, Dave Porter. 23 May 2010. Start at the base of the left-hand corner of the bay. Move up to an Australia-shaped block on the side of the prow, level with the square-cut roof in the front face. Use the edge of the prow above and face holds to move up to a pocket on the arête. Swing left from this around onto the front face of the prow at a ledge. Move up the prow to finish.

To the right, the clean immaculate inset wall is defined by a series of thin shallow cracks running up the centre of the wall. These provide fine climbing with adequate protection. It was led with pre-placed gear and awaits an ascent in better style. Probably E5 6a for the on-sight.

Beyond the second prow, the final section of the Buttress Area contains a buttress with a prominent prow at half height (Pig Prow) and beyond this a vertical crack (unclimbed).

Tarvie's Six-Million Dollar Man   15m   HVS 5a *. Ben Sparham Dave Porter. 20 Sep 2010.
The thin crack to the right of Pig Prow.

After this a wide bay opens out (descent comes down here). The right side of this bay contains a large cracked buttress with many potential routes (dirty). From here, continue westwards around a corner to find Hidden Wall.

Western Sector, Hidden Wall:
The west facing Hidden Wall is composed of a central corner, flanked by left and right walls. The left wall is more extensive, forming a reverse L-shape against the central corner. The lower left side of the left wall is made up a series of flutings and cracks running up the face and finishing on the ridge making up the limit of the Hidden Wall. The upper left wall is more compact and square-cut and only makes up the upper right side of this wall.

Hitting the Sack   20m   HVS 5b *. Simon Clark, Dave Porter. 15 Aug 2020.
Start as for *Gift for Laura*, but trend left up the wall, passing through a shallow niche to reach the right end of ledges. Now move right and climb the left side of the square recess in the upper wall.

Gift for Laura   20m   E1 5b **. Ben Sparham, Dave Porter, Simon Clark. 10 Apr 2010.
Start 5m left from the central corner, below an obvious crack in the upper wall. Surmount the lower wall via a slim right-facing corner and bulge to gain a central ledge. Follow the upper crack, which is initially a slim left-facing corner, pulling through a small roof to gain the upper crack.

Jenny's Gem   20m   VS 4c ***. Dave Porter, Simon Clark, Ben Sparham. 10 Apr 2010.
The excellent big central corner with short deviations to the right at mid-height. May weep in places, but these can be avoided.

Jenny's Gem, The Exit Cracks   10m   E2 5b *. Simon Clark, Dave Porter. 15 Aug 2020.
A left-hand variation finish to *Jenny's Gem*. Halfway up the corner, move left into cracks in the smooth wall, finishing more easily above.

Sedgehog   18m   Severe. Simon Clark, Dave Porter, Ben Sparham. 10 Apr 2010.
On the right side of the right wall, 10m right of the corner. Climb the prominent clean arête, on its right-hand side, passing a break at one-third height.

Further right is another clean buttress with a series of cracks running up it.

Memory Loss   20m   Severe. Simon Clark, Dave Porter, Ben Sparham. 10 Apr 2010.
Start 20m to the right of *Sedgehog*. Go up an easy crack on right side of a black water-mark to reach a steeper crack splitting an arête above. Follow this to the top.

POOLEWE & TOLLAIDH, Loch Tollaidh Crags, Upper Tier:
Rab Anderson notes that the following routes were inaccurately described in 'Northern Highlands Central'. Corrected descriptions are given below.

Fetish Crag:
Bound and Gagged   35m   VS/HVS 4c. Rab Anderson, C.Anderson. 23 Jun 2001.
Towards the left end of the crag is a black area of waterwashed rock with a corner. Climb the corner and the ensuing wall to reach a diagonal crack then follow this round the left side of a small roof to finish up heathery ground and a short wall.

Silky Smooth   30m   E3 5c ***. Rab Anderson, C.Anderson. 24 Jun 2001.
A superb route (when it was climbed 20 years ago!) taking the crack left of *Stiff Egg White*. Start at the edge of the buttress beside the heathery fault. Climb to the crack and follow this to the horizontal break at the roof. Step right and surmount the roof left of *Brewers Droop*.

Rubberist   30m   E3/4 6a **. Rab Anderson, C.Anderson. 24 Jun 2001.
The cracks in the orangey wall between *Viagra Falls* and *Lewd Behaviour*. Climb the corner on the right to the roof (gear) and swing left onto the wall (the big block does not need to be handled!). Continue up cracks and pull over a steepening to a break (semi-decent Camalot 3). Finish up easier slabs and walls.

Thong and Dance   30m   VS 4c *. Rab Anderson, C.Anderson. 23 Jun 2001.
It is not certain how this relates to *Large Libido*, which predates it. Right of *Prickly Pair* on the rightmost side of the crag, climb to a flake and instead of climbing the right-slanting groove pull up left onto the wall and climb nice rock to the top.

Buttock Buttress:
Little Cuss   E2 5b/c *. Rab Anderson, C.Anderson. 17 Jun 2001.
It is not certain how this relates to *Balls of Fire*, which predates it. The awkward groove just right of the sharp arête on the right section of the crag, left of *Yabbandit*, leads to a choice of easy finishes.

Kuhjo Crags:
Andy Moles notes that the grades generally feel harsh, and some wouldn't be a pushover if they were a + grade higher – particularly *Spiderman* and *The Green Solution*.

RUBHA MÒR, CAMAS POINT:
Flump 15m H.Severe 4b. Joe Barlow, Rosie Rothwell. 30 Aug 2020.
Climb the thin vertical crack 2m to the left of *Niece Wall*. Follow this to the ledge and climb direct through the bulge above.

Seal Slab 10m V.Diff. Joe Barlow, Rosie Rothwell. 30 Aug 2020.
Start 2m left of *Escalator* and climb direct up the slab through the large horizontal break.

BEINN LAIR, North-East Face:
SMCJ 2008 carries a correction stating 'The winter ascent of *Right Wing Butterfly Buttress*, as described in Northern Highlands Central was an ascent of *North Summit Buttress*.' This correction is misleading as the route was a wholly independent ascent of this very wide buttress (i.e. didn't follow the summer route at all) and so should have a distinct name. An amended description follows:

Glaodh an Iar 600m III **. John Higham, Iain Young. 20 Feb 2005.
Start at the lowest rocks on the right-hand side of the buttress uphill from a huge rectangular boulder and directly below a pointed top (pt830m on the 1:25,000 map). Climb more or less directly upwards following grooves, chimneys, arêtes and with a zigzag on open snow slopes between one-quarter and one-third height. Finish just right of pt830m with a belay on the prominent cairn. (Topo provided.)

GRUINARD BAY CRAGS, Gruinard Crag:
Paradise Direct 50m E2 5b **. Nathan Adam, Morna Baillie. 29 Apr 2021.
Enjoyable bold climbing, low in the grade. The second pitch is less good and possibly coincides with the original route. It may be be better to abseil from the block at the top of the first pitch or scramble off right.
1. 30m 5b Follow the original route past the chimney to the ledge on the right and arrange protection. Step left and up to a good foothold before making some hard moves on slopers (bold) to a good ledge and gear. Continue direct to join the rib leading to the jammed block.
2. 20m 5a Step off the block and move up left across the red wall (hidden holds) to reach a ledge. Climb up the short arête before trending back rightward to the top.

Dog Crag:
Whining Dog Climb 50m Severe. John Mackenzie, Eve Mackenzie, Colin Tarbat. 3 Apr 2021.
Climb the quite bold slab well right of the crack of Pluto to a heather patch. Cross this rightwards to a blocky groove which is climbed to an easing. Move right again and climb the top wall of Wanderlust to finish.

AN TEALLACH, Glas Tholl:
The Flying Fox 90m VIII,8. Callum Johnson, Tim Miller. 3 Dec 2020.
1. 30m. Start as for *The Silver Fox* (very bold and serious) and continue up the

steepening groove until it is possible to balance right on ledges to gain the groove leading to the obvious left-facing corner. Belay at the base of the corner.

2. 30m. Climb the superb vertical corner, move right 2m and climb a shallow groove straight up to an easing in angle, belaying in a bay below a series of roofs.

3. 30m. Climb straight up a wide steepening groove to below a roof, step right on ledges to climb a shallow groove for 4m then step right again and climb another easier angled groove to the top.

LITTLE LOCH BROOM, Badrallach Crag:
Pillar of Society, Direct Start   5m   VS 4c. Iain Young (solo). 12 Aug 2020.
Climb straight up the overhanging bulge directly below the crack. Probably adds a star to the complete route which is then almost as good as *Poacher's Prize*.

Fresher at Seventy   25m   VS 4b. Iain Young, John Higham. 12th August 2020.
The rib squeezed in between *Fresh at Forty* and the groove to its left. Finish up *Fresh at Forty*. Eliminate, but fun.

Up and left of the main crag (left again from *Crack 'n' Rib*) is a shorter crag with well-defined grooves and arêtes. The rib on the left side of the most prominent groove was climbed at V.Diff and the overhanging crack just to the right of the left-most rib was climbed at HVS 5b by escaping onto the rib after a few moves.

Much further left (north) and a little lower at NH 10620 91485 are two clean slabs with a superb outlook over Ullapool. The following three routes lie on the right-hand slab that has a prominent, shallow crack line just left of centre with other crack lines to the right and left. (Topo provided.)

Trepidation   12m   VS 4b *. John Higham, Iain Young. 12 Aug 2020.
Climb the right-hand twin cracks to start, then finish up and slightly leftwards. One runner at mid-height.

When The Boat Comes In   10m   Severe. Iain Young (solo). 12 Aug 2020.
Follow the central crack-line.

Dance To Your Daddy   8m   Severe. John Higham (solo). 12 Aug 2020.
The left-hand crack-line.

Loopallu   25m   VS 4b. Iain Young, John Higham. 12 Aug 2020.
This route lies on the left-hand slab. Start up the shallow scoop on the right then continue up past a prominent block to finish up the upper slab above a grassy break. (Topo provided.)

STRATHCONON, Glen Marksie Crag:
Callum Johnson notes that he cleaned *Deimos* (on abseil) and *Callisto* (on lead) in spring 2019.

Dam Crag:
Bottling the Bulge   18m   E3 5c. Gaz Marshall. 8 Jun 2020.
A bold, but logical way through the smooth arching bulge. Place gear low in the groove of *The Gulf Crisis* then climb into the middle of the arch to pull through the bulge at its left end, using the short arête that forms the right side of *The Gulf*

Gaz Marshall on the FA of Bottling the Bulge (E3,5c), Dam Crag, Strathconon.
Photo: Jenna Bisset.

Crisis corner (old peg). Then pull onto the slab above using the odd bit of old quarrying metalwork and finish direct.

Meig Crag:

Callum Johnson notes that the first pitch of *The Birch* was cleaned by Gaz Marshall in spring 2019, and is still clean.

Creag Ruadh, North-East Face:

Triple Decker Buttress   115m   III,4. John Mackenzie, Ian Douglas. 12 Apr 2021.

Near the left of the face and right of *Creag Ruadh Corner*, and identified by a triangular top buttress on the skyline. The base is quite high up above an upper ramp line, and a large horizontal boulder marks the start. Easy ground leads to a rock step and nut belays. Well frozen turf and ice on this ascent but little natural protection. Good climbing on the three tiers but easy ground between.

1. 55m Climb the rock step and head to a prominent short icefall. This is 75 to 80 degrees, too thin for screws on this occasion and climbed to a solid turf exit. A slab immediately right would be easier if it had climbable ice. An easing leads to an easier icefall which is climbed to another easing and hidden nut belays below a boulder.

2. 45m. Head straight up to the triangular top buttress which has a flaky lower wall with a poor spike. Either climb the wall to turf or climb the corner just right and step back left, (good nut runner), to the same place and finish up the middle on turf.

RED ROCK:
This small but imposing schist crag lies 800m east of Ravens Rock. The approach through the forest below is tedious but the best way is to follow the private road past the sawmill for 20 minutes just past a group of pines at NH 47421 60306 and a small roadside cairn, and follow the orange tree markers to the crag, an adventure in itself – Pendragon Way. Allow an extra 30 minutes or so from the road. The base of the crag lies at around 165m; once out of the trees, keep high on a track to cut up steeply to a rock step. To reach a fine ledge – The Belvedere – scramble the little rock step then move up left to the ledge. Older locals sometimes called the crag King Arthur's Castle which, when it is shrouded by low mists, seems apt. There are no restrictions on access. Trees currently hide the crag from below, and despite its north-facing aspect it dries very quickly as it stands well clear of the plantation below. Allow a day after rain in summer. The crag appears much larger than it actually is. Overall, it is wedge-shaped with central overhangs and general steepness. The Moine schist is heavily folded into an anticline which has created holds and ramps that slant up to the right, giving climbing that is both delicate and, in places, strenuous. Exposure is out of proportion to the size of the crag due to the routes starting from a height and the undercut nature of the rock. However, the often parallel crack systems give excellent cam protection. (Topo provided.) Descents are to the left looking up, or right looking down. A convenient but exposed scramble to reach The Belvedere from the descent is to traverse right from a small pine near the bottom of the descent, keeping high, and then a short ascent to a small nose that is crossed to descend and traverse to the top of an easy slab next to The Belvedere. This is all quite exposed and care is needed if damp.

Guinevere 30m E1 *. John Mackenzie, Andrew James. 1 Jun 2020.
A fine and very airy route lies right of the central overhangs at the base of a lower wall, taking the upper anticlinal wall. Will be worth two stars with traffic and weathering. *Guinevere* is a little bold but can be won over quite easily by the 'right sort'….

1. 10m 4b The easy looking short wall isn't, but is climbed to a midway ramp that has a hidden jug to reach the ledge up on the right (big cam).

2. 20m 5a Now the fun starts! Step left from the ledge and climb up past parallel cracks to the right side of the overhang and step right onto the nose in a great position. Reach for jugs and a jutting spike and continue more conventionally up the wall to a right slanting break below a small tree. Climb through the break by

a tree to step left between the trees to cleaned shelves and tree belay above a mossy ledge. Either abseil off or scramble right then up to the summit in 20m.

Camelot   35m   E2 **. John Mackenzie, Ian Douglas, Neil Wilson. 18 Jun 2020. Probably the route of the crag. It has a distinctive crux, but is well protected by cams from 0.5 to 3. A vital 2 and/or 3 above the roof calms the nerves. The route takes the centre of the roofs in a wild position above an alcove before following the upper ramp rightwards.
1. 3b 10m Above the lower wall is a very prominent rightwards-leaning ramp. Follow this to the ledge and large cam belay.
2. 5c 25m Step left and climb the wall to below the roof. Move left to a constricted alcove and surmount the roof using a sharp 'keyhole'. Mantel onto the ramp above – there are at least two methods of doing this. Follow the ramp rightwards to a rib which is climbed to the same tree belay as Guinevere. Scramble right and up to the top for a further 20m or else abseil off.

BEN WYVIS, Glas Leathad Beag, Diamond Buttress (NH 499 721):
This small, but striking, diamond-shaped buttress is situated high (altitude 700m) on the subsidiary spur of Fiaclach above Loch Glass. The crag, easily seen from afar, faces north-east and is very steep with a series of turfy lines reliant on a plentiful supply of bulldogs for protection. Routes are described from right to left. (Topo provided.)

Winter Skills   70m   V,5. Mark Robson, Neil Wilson. 3 Jan 2021.
Start at the toe of the buttress beneath the central of three apparent lines of weakness.
1. 25m Turfy ledges lead to steep moves past a small protruding block on the left and so to the central ledge system.
2. 45m Avoid the large roof above by traversing right to a steep ramp, then up, before returning left along higher ledge system. Short turfy groove to finish.

Cycle of Doom   95m   IV,5 *. Mark Robson, Neil Wilson. 15 Jan 2021.
Tackles the obvious challenge of the left-slanting ramp beneath the largest of the overhangs.
1. 35m Zigzag over ice bosses and turfy ledges to gain the ramp, which is followed to a belay ledge.
2. 25m Steeper moves lead to a big ledge and wall above. Climb this on ice, then more easily to a belay below a small roof.
3. 35m Continue rightwards up easy ground to finish.

Six Finger Gully   75m   II. Neil Wilson, Mark Robson. 3 Jan 2021.
Start high on left side of the crag beside the massive fallen block split by a crack.
1. 45m Climb over blocks to wide ledge which leads right, under a large roof, into the open gully. Follow line of least resistance to belay under small roof on right.
2. 30m Step back down and left, then continue up turfy ramps and ledges to finish on summit crest.

STRUIE HILL CRAG:
David Allan notes the following revised descriptions:

Achilles Chiel   20m   VS 4c **.
Climb a left-slanting rib then a short arête to a slab. Trend left to a small slanting overlap and follow the thin crack leading from it. This is a re-write and renaming of *Achilles Left-Hand*. The existing *Achilles Chiel* description should be removed.

Le Cadeau   20m   VS 4c **.
Climb the recessed corner to the right of the slanting rib of *Achilles Chiel* to an overhang. Follow the crack above to the slab and finish by a miniature right-facing corner.

NORTHERN HIGHLANDS SOUTH

LOCH ARKAIG, Beinn Bhàn, Coire Dubh:
Stair Rods   120m   II. Simon Richardson. 17 Feb 2021.
Coire Dubh is cut by a wide snow gully starting at NN 1359 8601. Climb the gully for 50m then bear right up icy grooves cutting through the left side of the inverted triangular headwall. (Topo provided.)

LOCH LOCHY, Allt na Molaich (NN 216 903):
Allt na Molaich   200m   IV,4. Will Rowland, James Cooper. 10 Feb 2021.
The gorge at NN 216 903 provided some pleasant ice climbing with a sustained 30m cascade in its upper half. Approach by cycling from Clunes.

GLEOURAICH, Garbh Choire Beag:
Corona Arête   200m   II/III. Chris Dickinson, William Wilson, Anna Guy. 28 Nov 2020.
The prominent ridge descending north-east from the summit. Approach by downclimbing 15 minutes into Garbh Choire Beag from just east of Gleouraich summit and start where the ridge steepens at NH041055. Turn the first steepening by slabs on the left to a wide ledge below and very steep wall. Pitch two traverses round onto the west side and back up left. One easier pitch then leads to the final arête and snowfield, leading to the summit cairn. An interesting climb in a magnificent position. (Topo provided.)

GLEN PEAN, Beak Wall (NM 889 899):
Vanishing Crack   55m   E1 5c *. Alastair Rose, Spencer Noble. 14 Oct 2020.
The buttress at NM 889 899 has a large projecting beak or roof. This route climbs the crack-line leading up to the roof and out left. The crack is visible from afar but weirdly not when one is standing underneath it.
1. 20m 5c Climb the crack to where it steepens to layback and stemming. Pull out right onto the flake and belay.
2. 35m 5a Pull left, back into the crack system and follow till the crack peters out. Follow the mossy chimney to the top. (Topo provided.)

KNOYDART, Ladhar Bheinn, Coire Dhorrcail:
Tir na Og, H2R Finish   100m   V,5. Robin Clothier, Doug Hawthorn, Uisdean Hawthorn, Richard Bentley. 5 Mar 2018.
A finish left of the stepped chimney line of the normal exit. From the final terrace climb a wall and groove into the continuation gully above. Climbed in error during poor visibility.

Beinn an Aodainn (Ben Aden):
Don't Follow the Lights 80m VS 4b. Alistair Docherty, Sarah Reed. 24 Jul 2020.
On the SW face of Ben Aden there is an obvious steeper buttress at around 680m elevation (NM 895 986). This is easily seen from the River Carnach. Left of the main steep buttress are some vegetated slabs. This climb follows a line of least resistance up these slabs and ribs. From below the main buttress, scramble up and left on grassy terraces. Start at a left-slanting vegetated crack in a slabby rib. (Topo provided.)
1. 30m 4b. Climb the crack to a ledge at 10m. Step left and climb detached pillars to a steep move up and right back onto the slab. Poor belay on a ledge behind a sharp bolder.
2. 50m Move up and right to perched boulder and surmount a ledge. Then continue straight up grass to a belay on blocks well back (50m). Not the best – mostly a grass pitch.

NORTH GLEN SHIEL, Creag Lundie, Slab One:
Biden Time 45m Severe 4a. Chris Dickinson, Anna Guy. 7 Nov 2020.
The final continuous crack-line left of *Thirty Below*. Climb the crack line to the first grassy ledge and its continuation to a second grassy ledge. Climb the fine slab above starting left and making a delicate rightward traverse to reach the top. (Topo provided.)

Slab Three:
Just above and to the right of *Instagram* is a separate higher slab. A descent route from that route angles down past it. The following nice route starts up this towards the left side.

Social Distance 15m Diff *. Chris Dickinson, Grace Peach Perry. 9 Jul 2020 .
Climb up featured rock, with good protection, until a move up and right leads into a recess. Climb out of the recess on the left side and then up the slab above to the top.

Far Eastern Zone:
Beyond the gully of *Firewall* is another gully (Far Far East) where you can find the following routes:

Extension 30m Severe *. Chris Dickinson, Grace Peach Perry. 18 Jun 2020.
Make steep moves through an overhang (crux) and then onto the easier slab above trending up and rightwards. Top belay is scarce, so belay well back.

Between the gully of *Firewall* and the gully of *Extension*, there is a very clean looking wall of granite high up that gives the fine route *George Floyd*.

George Floyd 20m VS 4c *. Chris Dickinson, Grace Peach Perry. 18 Jun 2020.
This exciting route is well protected. Climb the right-hand and very obvious diagonal crack. Where the crack becomes vertical make hard face moves right into twin flared cracks which lead to the top.

Allt Coire Lundie:
Above and to the right of the bottom of the main falls is another small stream. Tweedle Slab, on its left, looking up, has four nice short routes. A belay can be

arranged at a crack on the rib above, before the gutter of water behind is reached. Routes described from left to right.

Tweedle Dum 15m V.Diff. Chris Dickinson (solo). 20 May 2020.
Start left of the pool and climb the clean slab to the top.

Tweedle Dee 20m Severe *. Chris Dickinson (solo). 20 May 2020.
Start below the pool and climb round the rock hanging over the pool, make thin moves diagonally left on the slab and then climb the slab directly to the top, just right of *Tweedle Dum*. A nice outing.

Humpty 15m Diff. Chris Dickinson (solo). 20 May 2020.
Climb up the left slanting recess and where it finishes go straight up.

Dumpty 15m Diff *. Chris Dickinson (solo), 13 June 2020.
Start as for *Humpty*, but this time take the clean steep crack on the right and follow to the top.

Front Zone West:
This area lies below the Belvedere and comprises various areas of slabby granite, some small and some a full pitch long. Th best approach is to take the normal route up, and before you reach the elevation of the Belvedere, traverse east across the top of the steepest ground. Alternatively descend from the Belvedere. The first climb reached is identified by a massive boulder perched right on the top of the slab below you. It is an easy scramble down to the boulder. One can either arrange a rappel to get to the foot of the route or scramble down further east. This route can be approached from the road below.

Amazing Grace 40m Mild Severe *. Chris Dickinson, Grace Peach Perry. 13 June 2020.
Climb the slab, left of a corner feature, with occasional runners. Climb up beside a grassy patch and then continue up the fine slab above to the great boulder. A satisfying stroll with little protection in the upper part. Beautiful outlook over Loch Cluanie.

About 200m further east a dome of fine rock can be seen protruding from the hillside. The next two routes climb a double slab behind and above this feature, to a prominent boulder. The final route climbs a steep slab below the dome, finishing up on top of the dome.

Perrywinkle 30m Mild Severe *. Grace Peach Perry, Chris Dickinson. 13 June 2020.
Climb the left side of the lowest slab to a grassy ledge. Awkward moves with protection surmount the short wall on the left side. Continue up the easier angled slab above to finish at the boulder.

Chrisgraceful 30m Severe *. Chris Dickinson, Grace Peach Perry.13 June 2020.
Start about 5m right of *Perrywinkle*. Climb directly up the right end of the lower slab, joined to the wall above by some rocky bulges. Climb the steeper wall and then the slab above, finishing on the cleanest part of the slab directly below the obvious boulder. Belay using the boulder, or better, use belays up and left.

Black Lives Matter   40m   Severe **. Chris Dickinson, Grace Peach Perry. 13 June 2020.
Descend easy ground to the right, looking down, from the rocky dome. Cut back left to the foot of a steep slab with a weep in the centre at the bottom. This route gives beautiful climbing despite its appearance. Ascend the right side of the slab, moving into the centre, on nice holds, with good protection. Pull onto the grassy break, runners on right side above, and then take the fine leftwards slanting features, before moving slightly right to climb onto the top of the rocky dome. Sneaky belays just to the right side. (Topo provided.)

Front Zone Central:
This area lies just to the west of Central Gully. Best approach is directly from the road below or by descending Central Gully from areas higher up.

Track and Trace   45m   * Diff *. Chris Dickinson (solo). 21 Jul 2020.
A pleasant route with varied situations that takes the best line up the right-hand side of the rock formations that lie to the west of Central Gully. Start at a small ramped slab that leads left to the edge. Each time the edge steepens, climb the right wall to regain it. Then follow a slab rightwards on the edge and rightwards to a finish. Belay on threaded boulder in a dip.

Ella's Route   60m   VS 4c. Chris Dickinson, Anna Guy. 2 Aug 2020.
1. 35m Start some 40 metres left of *Track and Trace* at the base of an obvious slab, bounded on the left side by a steep wall that curves round the top of the slab. Climb the slab to runners on the left wall (15m), then step right and continue up a thin, sometimes wet, slab (4c) to reach a runner, before making an awkward step up left (4c) onto a sloping ledge. Climb to heather and then onto the slabs above. Continue without further protection until you reach a sparse stance before a steepening.
2. 25m Climb the slabs above by the easiest line with little or no protection. Finish by a fine final steeper slab to a good belay at two obvious boulders. A serious excursion, best undertaken after a couple of dry days.

BEINN LOINNE, Ceann Druim na Garbh-Leitir (NH 173 083):
This crag is the same granitic mass as Creag Lundie and outcrops on south side of Loch Cluanie on the eastern top of Beinn Loinne. The rock is similarly good but some areas have sparse protection. (Topo provided.)

Bunloinn Grooves   70m   H.Severe **. Chris Dickinson, Anna Guy.10 Aug 2020.
1 35m 4b Climb the prominent and very fine groove system on the left side of the right-hand mass of granite on the main cliffs above the Great Ledge. Climb the groove directly until forced to move right. Step back left to regain the groove and make a stance. The only belay protection of any note here is in cracks on the slab on the right side of the groove above.
2 35m 4b Climb these slabs and the bulge above, then trend left across the top of a very large slab that comes from down left and climb a stiff cracked corner to gain easier rock and thence to the top.

Second Wave   45m   Severe 4a. Chris Dickinson, Anna Guy, Grace Peach Perry. 27 Sep 2020.
Start part-way up the grassy gully on left side of the main face, about 40m left of

Bunloinn Grooves. Climb the short wall by a fine crack to gain a long and fine slab that runs diagonally rightwards across the face, all the way to the top. Climb the centre of the slab, trending right towards the top to gain an exposed edge to finish. Where the route trends right, it crosses *Bunloinn Grooves*.

Twinkletoes 25m V.Diff *. Chris Dickinson, Anna Guy.10 Aug 2020.
Climb the left edge of the fine slab by a crack where it steepens and leads onto a fine upper part of the slab.

Pyramid 45m Severe 4a **. Chris Dickinson, Anna Guy.10 Aug 2020.
Climb the right side of the fine slab by a crack, a scoop, exiting right and then straight up to a fine arête and beyond that an intriguing final pyramid. Wonderful rock.

Two Step 25m V.Diff *. Chris Dickinson, Anna Guy.10 Aug 2020.
Climb up unusual steps to the first ledge (unprotected) and then tackle the final wall.

SÀIL CHAORAINN, Coire Mheadhoin:
This corrie is quite remote. Easiest access is by bike from the A887 past Ceannacroc Lodge. Where the River Doe splits, at two new micro hydro power stations, a new road continues rightwards and then left steeply up into Coire Mheadhoin, reaching the hydro intake at 450m. A very rough track including some river crossings continues to 550m. This latter part might be easier on foot. It would also be possible to approach from Loch Cluanie by climbing over the summit of Sgùrr nan Conbhairean and continuing on to Sàil Chaorainn, dropping rightwards into the corrie before the summit. Two hours with bike and then on foot; nearer three hours from Loch Cluanie on foot. Routes are described in relation to an easy leftwards slanting snow gully in the centre of the Coire. Easiest descent is to walk south-east onto the ridge that leads to Càrn a' Mhadaidh-ruaidh and descend snowfields back into the corrie. (Topo provided.)

Corridor Of Covid 400m I/II. Chris Dickinson. 13 May 2020.
At the snowfield where the diagonal gully starts, climb the gully that continues directly up the face, passing two steeper sections, trending slightly right on the final pitch under the summit rocks. Finish close to the summit cairn.

Wuhan Blues 400m I. Chris Dickinson. 10 May 2020.
About 200 metres left, climb the obvious wide snow gully until it opens into a wide upper basin. Head sharp right along a rising ledge system until a final steep gully heads towards the top.

Lockdown 150m I. Chris Dickinson. 13 May 2020.
This route starts in the wide upper basin, mentioned in the previous route description. Climb this striking and steep snow gully directly to the top.

South-East Buttress:
Stirling Moss 60m VS 4b. Ken Applegate, Chris Dickinson. 20 Jun 2020
The rocks on this mainly broken buttress on the left side of the corrie are continuous on the right side (looking up). Start at a micro gully and climb onto

and round the rocky rib to easier slabs. The steep wall ahead is the crux and requires careful climbing, leading to slabs and some short bulges and the top.

Coire Lochan Uaine, Prince Charlie's Buttress (NH 135 149):

The buttress lies on the south side of the ridge from *Stirling Moss* on the South-East Buttress of Coire Mheadhoin and overlooks the Uaine lochans. Approach as for *Stirling Moss*. The buttress faces south and has magnificent views of Sgùrr nan Conbhairean. Descend from a little way to the west to the foot of a 'flying' rib, which is steep and overhanging at the bottom. Go into a cave on its left side. This is the start.

Prince Charlie's Crack 35m VS 5a *. Chris Dickinson, Ken Applegate. 20 Jun 2020.
Make a hard couple of moves out of the cave by moving right under the huge chockstone (well protected) to reach a fine slab. Proceed up this via a cleft to the horizontal arête in a fine position. Above, a thrutchy hanging V-groove, on the left, gives access to the final easier arête. A pitch of considerable interest.

KISHORN:

Colin Moody notes that the prominent waterfall on the north side of the road from Lochcarron to Kishorn (*SMCJ* 2011 p462 and *SMCJ* 2012 p187) was climbed by Morris Macleod solo in 1978 (and not with a partner as previously recorded).

MEALL GORM, Creag a' Chumhaing:

Greg Strange notes that a recent exchange of old photos with Rob Archbold brought about memories of a climb they did in 1977 on the 'Eastern Buttress' of Creag a' Chumhaing. 'The previous day we had climbed Super Direct on A' Chioch. The midges were desperate so we camped that night above the hairpins at the top of Bealach na Bà. In the morning we were intrigued by the steep profile of Meall Gorm's skyline buttress (Eastern Buttress) and decided to investigate. At the parking spot below the *Sword of Gideon* we met a lad called Keith (I later discovered his surname was Chadwick). He was working at the Kishorn yard and had come up on spec. We told him what we were planning to do, and he actually seemed interested (in conversation he said he had recently climbed *Vector* at Tremadoc). The three of us traversed across the broken face and started the route from the obvious spiral terrace (now a Grade II winter climb). We each led a pitch up steep vegetated sandstone and later sent a note for the 1978 *SMCJ* Northern Highland Notes. The climbing was not great, hence the note and not a detailed description. Anyway, the purpose of this ramble is to name the route and suggest that it is mentioned in the next 'Northern Highlands South' guide, if only from a historical point of view.'

Skyline Route 140m VS. Greg Strange, Rob Archbold, Keith Chadwick. 21 Aug 1977.
The eastern crest of Creag a' Chumhaing. Approach via the winter line of *Spiral Terrace* and climb the crest in the three full pitches. The climbing is mostly in grooves and is steep, vegetated and loose. The relationship to the upper section of the winter route *Peace on Earth* is uncertain, although the routes must be close. (Topo provided.)

DIABAIG, The Domes:

Kevin Howett notes that he led the first ascent of *The Con-Con*.

Colin Moody notes that the second pitch of *Plunge* is above the belay tree which is about 7m right of the *Bromide*, not 3m as stated in 'Northern Highlands South'. The left-hand start to *Bromide* was added by Andy Nisbet and partner. The original line is worth a star, and *Plunge* is also worth a star.

Loch Diabaigas Àirde, Windy Crag (NG 820 592):

This crag is situated just to the east of what can be called the Valley of the Slabs (see *SMCJ* 2018). It consists of a row of blocky buttresses on its eastern side descending towards the loch. Whereas the Valley of the Slabs catches the sun in the morning, Windy Crag gets it in the afternoon. It is very useful in the midge season. At the top of the defile is a square-cut buttress with two routes and many more possibilities.

Safari Crack 15m V.Diff. Roger Robb, Peter Biggar. 8 Sep 2019.
The left-hand of obvious twin cracks. Steep, well protected.

Isosceles 20m V.Diff. Peter Biggar, Barry Hard, Roger Robb. 19 Sep 2020.
In the middle of the buttress is a triangular cavity. Climb the previous route to gain a pedestal, move delicately left across the wall to the cavity, step left to a curving crack, gain a ledge and scramble up easier rock.

Further down the slope is an obvious ridge composed of bulging boulders. This provides a series of disconnected problems at V.Diff. Further down still one comes to a ridge with a prominent rib running up its right flank.

Sidestep 20m Severe. Peter Biggar, Peter Macdonald. 24 Aug 2016. Climb the rib, awkward but well protected, until it is possible to make a difficult step left onto a holdless, gritty slab. Climb this and an easier slab to finish. Low in the grade.

Down the hillside one comes to an area of blocky arêtes: one is particularly worth mention because of its fine upper cracked slab.

Split Slab Arête 25m Diff. Roger Robb, Peter Biggar, Peter Macdonald. 24 Aug 2016.
Start up a rather dirty crack and gain ledges. Go right onto the blocky arête and climb the right-hand side of the slab above until it is possible to traverse a thin ledge into the very pleasant final crack.

Valley of the Slabs (NG 818 592):

This is the area referred to above. At the foot of the valley containing *Broadband* and *Exchange Line*, there is a curving slab which ends in a heathery nose over a drop above slopes leading down to the loch.

Curving Slab 30m Diff./Severe. Roger Robb, Peter Biggar. 23 Jun. 2016.
Starting from a grass ledge either, boldly climb the crest of the slab, unprotected, or more cautiously go up left to a cracked area and then step right and continue

up the slab finishing by short walls above. (Unpleasant in damp conditions; no belay at foot of climb above drop).

Twin Slabs Area (NG 806 598):

Roughly halfway along Loch Diabaigas Àirde (NG 810 600) the loch thins to a narrow stream crossed by a rickety bridge. Approach from the road where a car can be parked with care by the entrance to a field on the north side of the road. (Do not block access.) Access the field above the loch by a gate, cross the bridge and head up heathery slopes bearing to the right where two long slabs can be seen on the eastern exposures of Meall Ceann na Creige.

Left Slab   30m   V.Diff. Roger Robb, Peter Biggar. 11 May 2017.
Take a rightward trending line up the gently steepening slab to finish up an area seamed with cracks, not all as useful as they look.

TORRIDON SANDSTONE CRAGS, Seanna Mheallan West:

Iain Young Notes that *Queen of Hearts* was first climbed by John Higham and Iain Young on 2 Jun 2012.

About 20m left of *Wilma* is a separate buttress with an obvious black streak on its left-hand side.

Stickleback   16m   E1 5b *. David Porter, Ben Sparham. 29 May 2021.
The obvious crack-line on the right of the buttress with a shallow roof at one-third height. Gain the crack and use an undercling to reach a hold beneath the roof. Pull through the roof (crux) and continue up the crack with sustained interest to the final steepening which has some sharp flake holds.

Barney Rubble   124   H.Severe 4b. Ben Sparham, David Porter. 29 May 2021.
Start between *Wilma* and *Pebble* and follow a crack rightwards up a rib to gain the left side of the *Pebble* alcove. Step out left onto the wall and follow the left edge of the cracked buttress to the top.

Fence Crag, Right Wing:

Left of *Fence Crack* is a corner with a rowan tree. The wall left of this.

Under Surveillance   8m   H.Severe 4b. David Porter, Ben Sparham. 3 Apr 2021.
Climb the middle of the wall, just right of a small C-shaped groove. Finish up through blocks.

Dunk's Magic Bum Cream   6m   VS 4c. Ben Sparham, David Porter. 3 Apr 2021.
Climb directly up the centre of the slab between *Marmot* and *Flying Footless*.

Far Right Wing:

Bleach Drinker   10m   Severe. David Porter, Ben Sparham. 3 Apr 2021.
The crack just right of *More Fascist Than Hitler*.

On same terrace level as Triangular Niche Buttress, and about 100m west, is a small outcrop with an undercut base and prominent vertical cracks.

Downwind Danger 6m   VS 5a. David Porter, Ben Sparham, Maurice O'Connell.
3 Apr 2021.
Start at a niche at the right-hand side of the undercut wall. Follow the right-hand
crack. Short but not without interest.

Triangular Niche Buttress:
Below is Triangular Niche Buttress a small buttress with three prominent clean
vertical cracks. The central and right-hand ones are the most prominent.

Central Fissure 8m   Severe 4a. David Porter, Maurice O'Connell, Ben Sparham.
3 Apr 2021.
The central crack.

Creag nam Leumnach:
Miss Piggy 30m   E3 *. Michael Barnard, Alan Hill. 5 Oct2020.
1. 15m 6a The crack immediately left of *Gift Horse*, moving left to finish on the
left side of the big block.
2. 15m 5b As for *Muppet on a String*.

Muppet on a String 30m   E3 *. Michael Barnard, Alan Hill. 17 Oct 2020.
1. 15m 6a The next crack left of *Miss Piggy*; a hold out left may help near the
top. Continue to a belay next to the big block.
2. 15m 5b Walk left 5m. Starting on the left, climb the steep but thankfully juggy
crack.

Dodgy Transaction 25m   E2 5b. Michael Barnard, Alan Hill. 5 Oct 2020.
The shallow right-trending groove left of *Cross Dressing* and joining that route
just before its traverse. Nothing too hard but very bold in the middle; take RPs
and micro-cams.

Michael Barnard notes that the layback crack on *Gift Horse* is unremittingly
strenuous and overall the route was thought E3 5c ***.

BEINN ALLIGIN, Na Fasreidhnean, South Face:
Salt n Pepper 200m   III *. Adrian Gaughan, John Higham. 10 Feb 2021.
Two intersecting gullies are formed in a south-east facing break in the cliffs on
the south face of the Na Fasreidhnean ridge of Coire nan Laogh (NG 858 592).
This route takes the lower left-hand gully and the buttress to the left of the upper
left-hand gully (*Saltire Gully Right to Left*). Climb the lower left-hand gully
through two short steep steps. At the intersection of the two lower gullies it is
possible to break out left onto the buttress and climb through sandstone bands to
join the top of the upper left hand gully. Easy slopes lead to the ridge crest. Note:
from the intersection of the lower gullies, it is also possible to continue up the left
to right gully line on easier snow slopes at Grade I. (Topo provided.)

BEINN EIGHE, Coire Mhic Fhearchair, Far East Wall:
Groovin' High 90m   VII,8 ***. Tim Miller, Jamie Skelton. 28 Dec 2020.
Start 6m to the right of the obvious chimney of *Ling Dynasty* at a series of corners.
1. 35m Climb these via awkward steps to a big ledge where one could traverse
in from the right. Climb the two-tiered steep wall above to another big ledge at
the base of an inviting corner.

2. 20m Climb the corner via brilliant cracks to a belay below a roof.
3. 35m Make an awkward step to the right into another corner system and enjoy more positive hooks to the top.

Eastern Ramparts:

Never Never Land 100m VIII,8. Callum Johnson, Tim Miller. 4 Dec 2020.
Start roughly 8m right of *Fairytale Groove*, just left of a tricky step on the lower girdle ledge.
1. 45m. Climb up corners and ledges, taking in a superb 8m left-facing corner. Trend slightly left onto the upper girdle ledge to belay below the centre of the white wall.
2. 35m. Move right 4m to make committing moves into the base of a groove (at the right edge of the white wall) which leads up to a small roof with a prominent wide crack splitting its left-hand side. Climb the crack strenuously around the roof. Continue up the wide crack then shallow groove, taking a line of twin cracks up a wall to a good ledge.
3. 20m. Climb the open-book corner and pull slightly right onto the crest of *East Buttress*. (Topo provided.)

East Buttress:

Iain Young notes that he made an ascent of *East Central Gully* with Simon Osborne on 11 Feb 1978. The route is uncredited in 'Northern Highlands South' so this may have been the first ascent.

Central Buttress:

Pigott's Route Variation 5m VS 5a **. Michael Barnard, A.N.Other. 31 May 2020.
On the top tier, after pulling up left to the flake. Instead of stepping left from here, climb the steep crack through the bulge. Gives a good direct finish to *Central Buttress – VS Route*. Possibly climbed before.

West Central Wall:

Wall of the Winds 110m VII,8. Peter Flanagan, Sam Ley. 13 Mar 2021.
A winter version of the summer line. The third pitch covers new ground and the fourth pitch is the crux pitch of *Mistral*. These two pitches replace summer pitch 3. Start 10m left of *Mistral*, halfway between the initial corner of *Mistral* and the pinnacle of *Twilight Zone*.
1. 10m Climb an easy blocky groove.
2. 35m Continue up the groove and chimney above to the top of the pinnacle. Steep climbing up the corner leads to the lower girdle ledge. (The crack in the steep slab to the left is also possible). Belay at the far right of the bay.
3. 20m Step around the arête at the right side of the bay and climb the exposed bottomless rib to the upper girdle. (The right corner of the bay can also be climbed direct to the upper girdle). Ascend to a large belay ledge 5m above the girdle.
4. 20m Climb twin parallel cracks to below a fin-shaped capping roof with large crack at its left edge. From 3m below the roof delicately traverse right to a projecting block. Climb directly up mossy cracks with thin placements (*Mistral* crux) and exit leftwards to belay under the final chimney.
5. 25m Finish up the *Wall of the Winds* chimney. (Topo provided.)

THE CAIRNGORMS

COIRE AN T-SNEACHDA, Fiacaill Buttress:
Callum Johnson notes an ascent of *Omerta* (VIII,9) on 8 Dec 2020 with Guy Robertson. Both thought grade IX might be more appropriate. A good route with some technical climbing and small gear and exciting Peckers!

LOCH AVON BASIN, Craig Raibeirt:
Thunderbolt Crack 70m H.Severe. Jonathan Preston, John Lyall. 18 Jul 2020.
As for the winter line.

STAC AN FHARAIDH, West Flank, Lookout Buttress:
The following two corner lines are situated the left-hand base of the leftmost buttress of the three that make up the top tier left of the West Flank of Stac an Fharaidh. Approach as for *Wobble Block Chimney* in Chasing the Ephemeral. Routes are at the base of the 'short gully' descended 'to reach the terrace below the upper tier'. This left-hand of the three buttresses is quite extensive and was first climbed by the winter line of *Lookout Buttress*.

Loch A'an Corner 35m HVS 5a **. Jonathan Preston, John Lyall. 24 Jul 2020.
The right-hand of two obvious corners just up from the bottom left-hand base of the buttress (on the westernmost wall, facing towards Shelter Stone Crag). Start below and right of the corner. Climb diagonally leftwards to get established in the corner and climb it with interest to the top. Block belays well back. High in the grade.

The Ladder 25m H.Severe 4b **. Jonathan Preston, John Lyall. 18 Jul 2020.
The left-hand of the two corners, stepped up into from the left and climbed direct. High in the grade. (Fàradh in Gaelic means 'a ladder'.)

Lookout Buttress 60m V.Diff. Jonathan Preston, John Lyall. 24 Jul 2020.
As for the winter line.

CNAP COIRE NA SPREIDHE, Mhearad's Fall Area:
On the left side of the Cnap Coire na Spreidhe is an area of icefalls. (Topo provided.)
Mhearad's Fall 120m I to III. Ron Walker and Fi Chappell. 5 Jan 2017.
Several lines climbed including a very short escapable but much harder chimney finish at around Tech 4.

Mhearad's Right Edge I/II. Ron Walker and Notts Uni Students. 5 Feb 2017.

To the right of *Mhearad's Right Edge* are several icefalls (II to III) climbed various dates from winter 2017 solo by Ron Walker.

Lower Tier:
The following routes lies on the lower tier of Cnap Coire na Spreidhe. (Topo provided.)

Capricorn Birthday Boys   250m   III,4. Ron Walker, Fi Chappell, Scott Flett. 22 Dec 2019.
The line of icefalls on the left side of the lower tier starting at NJ 01778 04549.

Central Left Chimney Groove   300m   II/IV. Ron Walker, Scott Flett. 5 March 2019.
The wide groove left of *Central Couloir*.

Central Couloir Direct   300m   II/III. Ron Walker, Shaun Williams. 19 Mar 2018.
A right-hand start to Central Couloir starting at NJ 01781 04656.

Amphitheatre Chimney   40m   IV,5. Ron Walker, Scott Flett. 11 Jan 2018.
The steep chimney right of the crux pitch of *Goulotte Cachée*. On this ascent it was approached by *Rampline*.

Upper Tier:
Upper Central Ridge   150m   II/III. Ron Walker. 23 Jan 2017.
The well-defined ridge right of the upper snowfields of *Central Couloir*. Start from a flat area just below gendarme on the LHS of the ridge and take the easiest line before moving onto the centre of the ridge via short ramps and grooves. There are several variations at the start including a squeeze tunnel. (Topo provided.)

Upper Central Ridge, Direct Variation   20m   IV,4. Ron Walker, Fi Chappell. 8 Mar 2018.
Climb directly up the smooth slabby wall on the second pitch. (Topo provided.)

Wee Central Gully Finish   150m   I/II. Ron Walker. 23 Jan 2017.
The defined gully on the LHS of *Upper Central Ridge*.

Abline   100m   I/II. Ron Walker. 23 Jan 2017.
The line of an abseil approach from the plateau.

Summit Crags, Torr Buttress:
Ron Walker notes he climbed *Dodger Ramp* (*SMCJ* 2019) with Fi Chappell on 5 Jan 2017. The route was called *LHS Rampings* (II).

Slab and Flake Chimney   35m   Severe. Ron Walker, Fi Chappell. 20 Sep 2020.
A summer ascent of *Brain Melt* incorporating the lower slab.

Summit Crags, Pinnacle Ribs:
This crag lies 50m right of Torr Buttress. The central line is *Cleft Ridge* (*SMCJ* 2019). (Topo provided.)

Left Groove and Rib   35m   I/II. Ron Walker. Winter 2017.
The leftmost line.

Squeeze Chimney   35m   III,4. Ron Walker. 6 Feb 2020.
The narrow chimney left of Cleft Ridge. Rope solo.

Hookers Wide Chimney   35m   III,4. Ron Walker. 6 Feb 2020.
The chimney right of Cleft Ridge. Rope solo.

Right Groove and Rib   35m   I/II. Ron Walker. Winter 2017.
Follow the groove and rib on the right flank of the buttress.

Summit Crags, Slabby Ribs:
Slabbering   35m   II/III. Ron Walker. 6 Feb 2020.
Climb the centre of the buttress that lies approximately 70m right of Pinnacle
Ribs. (Topo provided.)

El Alamein Slabs:
Zig Zags   100m   III. Ron Walker, Hugo Heagren, Finn McCleave. 8 Jan 2020.
Climb icedslabs above the El Alamein bothy. The whole area banks out quickly
but can provide thickish ice early season. Andy Nisbet climbed a line hereabouts
but the details were never recorded.

CREAGAN CHA-NO, International Rib:
International Rib   65m   Moderate. Roger Webb, Simon Richardson. 28 Jun
2015.
Follow the winter line.

Mainmast Area:
Short Ridge   50m   Diff. Simon Richardson. 22 Aug 2015.
Follow the winter line.

Another Pointless Eliminate   35m   III,4. Gary Kinsey, Roger Webb. 22 Nov
2020.
Climb the wide crack between *Mainmast* and *Cutty Sark* to a platform. Step right
and finish up the left-hand of the twin faults in the upper corner of *Cutty Sark*.

Chimney Rib:
Chimney Rib   60m   Diff. Roger Webb, Simon Richardson. 28 Jun 2015.
Follow the winter line.

Anvil Buttress:
Flaked Out   50m   HVS. Simon Richardson, Roger Webb. 12 Aug 2015.
Follow the winter line in two pitches (5a, 4b). The first provides a strenuous
struggle similar to winter.

Plundered Crack   18m   E1 5c *. Andy Townsend, Bill Strachan. 19 Aug 2020.
Crack just left of centre on the wall right of *Anvil Gully*. Start left of block pillar,
sustained moves up and left gain the obvious jam crack. Strenuously follow to
small ledges and the top. (Topo provided.)

Second Prize   22m   E1 5a *. Bill Strachan, Andy Townsend. 19 Aug 2020.
The rightmost crack on the wall right of *Anvil Gully*. Start by climbing the right-
facing corner of the large rectangular block pillar to gain the slightly left-trending
crack. The arête on the right provides some good holds low down. Follow this to
top. (Topo provided.)

Anvil Corner   60m   VS. Roger Webb, Simon Richardson. 12 Aug 2015.
Follow the winter line in two pitches (4c, 4b). An enjoyable route.

Arch Wall:
Jenga Buttress   70m   V.Diff. Roger Webb, Simon Richardson. 28 Jun 2015.
Follow the winter line.

Right-Hand Ribs:
Boundary Ridge   180m   Diff. Roger Webb, Simon Richardson. 28 Jun 2015.
Follow the winter line. Rock at first then heathery scrambling.

LURCHER'S CRAG:
Rottweiler, The Mongrel Mutation Finish   60m   V,6. Erick Baillot, Dave Kerr. 6
Dec 2020.
Start 25m up pitch 2 of *Rottweiler* immediately at the end of the steep climbing
at an obvious small platform.
1. 20m Step up and left into an obvious groove immediately right of the crest.
Follow continuation cracks curving left over ledges to join the corner of
Shapeshifter and the offwidth crack-corner to belly flop top-out. 2. 40m Continue
up Grade I ground for 30m to the top of the next step, and exit easily to the top of
the crag. (Topo provided.)

Erick Baillot and Dave Kerr consider *Rottweiler* to be V,6 overall. They also
climbed *Shapeshifter* on 4 Jan 2021 and thought it merited VI,7.

BRAERIACH, Coire Ruadh:
Trumped   80m   II/III. Simon Richardson. 4 Nov 2020.
Start 5m right of *Birthday Treat* and follow grooves weaving between ribs to gain
a snow bay at two-thirds height. Finish up the open groove right of the final tower.

Long Shot Ridge   40m   III. Simon Richardson. 4 Nov 2020.
The short ridge left of the crag that contains *Enterprise Corner* etc. has a small
triangular-shaped tower at its foot. Climb the steep front face up stepped grooves
on good hooks until a ledge leads around the left side of the tower. Finish more
easily up the ridge crest to the top.

BEN AVON, Creag na h-Iolaire:
The Nose of A'an, Right-Hand Start   15m   VS 5a. Michael Barnard, Alan Hill.
18 Jul 2020.
The wide crack.

Michael Barnard notes that the 'unclimbed offwidth corner-crack' is considerably
harder than E1 (6a?) and remains unclimbed. The 'very steep and hard 12m crack'
is a king line and after a quick clean could give a potential three star E5.

Clach Fiaradh, Easter Island Boulder:
Eggsquisite   8m   E4 6a **. Julian Lines. 4 Jul 2019.
The centre of the slab to the left of *The Lone Stone*.

Eggcentric   8m   E3 6a **. Julian Lines. 4 Jul 2019.
The left arête of the east face. Start up *Eggsquisite* for a move (crux) and improvise
left to the arête.

Julian Lines notes that he descended these routes by down climbing *The Lone Stone*, which was thought to be E1 5b with the crux at the bottom.

LOCHNAGAR, Central Buttress:

Moonshadow, Direct Variation 40m V,5. Dan Moore, Martin Stephens. 28 Dec 2020.

From the good ledge at the end of Moonshadow pitch 2, climb straight up a small awkward buttress to belay on the crest below a smooth slab to left of Giant's Head Chimney Direct. Follow a line of turf going right to left cutting across the lower left-hand part of the slab and continue up the rib bounding the left of the wall. At its top, step left into a groove and climb a tricky wide crack behind a big block leading back to the crest where the angle eases. A great pitch in a fine position. (Topo provided.)

The Stack:

Cac Spout 70m IV,4 *. Will Attridge, Cameron Richardson. 27 Mar 2021.
An icy mixed line on the left wall of *The Black Spout*. The first ascensionists think it lies right of the icefall of *The White Spout* but the lines may partly coincide.
1. 35m Start on the left-hand side of *The Black Spout* in an obvious bay above The Stack. Climb an open corner of ice, followed by a delicate traverse left under a niche with good rock gear. Follow the snow slope above to a belay under an overhang.
2. 35m Pass the overhang on the left and traverse right to follow iced slabs straight up to the cornice. This was passable on right and left. (Topo provided.)

West Buttress:

Western Passage 125m III,4. Dan Moore, Ana Fleming. 11 Dec 2020.
1. 50m Start just right of *Western Slant* and climb easy ground first right then back left to belay at the bottom of a long slabby wall.
2. 50m Continue straight up alongside the wall before traversing up and right into a small bay below a steepening.
3. 25m Climb up through the obvious slot onto the snow field above to gain the base of the upper tier. Possibly climbed before. (Topo provided.)

Coire Loch nan Eun, The Stuic:

Didgeridoo 50m III. Simon Richardson. 23 May 2021.
The break in the wall midway between *Glottis* and *Deesider*. Climb easily up to short square-cut gully. Climb this (ice on the first ascent) and pull over a bulge to a ledge. Finish up and right. (Topo provided.)

Deesider 50m II/III. Jamie Greig, Will Attridge, Cameron Richardson.
The second gully left of *Stegosaurus Rib*. It twists from right to left at the top through mixed ground and an iced corner exit. (Topo provided.)

Bone Wars 50m II. Simon Richardson. 23 May 2021.
The short gully immediately left of *Stegosaurus Rib*. (Topo provided.)

Spoon Bow 60m II. Simon Richardson. 23 May 2021.
The rib right of *Whaleback*. The smooth-looking headwall was climbed using hidden steps leading right to left.

EAGLES ROCK, A Likely Story Slab:

Graham Tyldesley notes that a couple of the route lines on the Eagles Rock topo (p. 421 of 'The Cairngorms Rock and Ice Climbs') are incorrect. *Ripping Yarn* crosses over *A Likely Story* where it is shown joining it. It joins just below the final overlap. The line of *The Stretcher* is completely wrong. It starts up *Fraud Squad* and continues traversing left beyond where that route starts going up. Then it takes a direct-ish line to under the steep nose. (Topo provided.)

GLEN CALLATER, Creag Leachdach:

Sheep Bone Slab   60m   Severe. Simon Richardson, Sophie Grace Chappell. 8 Sep 2020.
The lower tier of slabs on the south face of Creag Leachdach provides an attractive sweep of granite. This route takes a line up the right side of the slabs. The direct line up the left side of the slabs was climbed on a top rope, but unfortunately there is no protection.
1 25m Start at the left toe of the slabs and climb a crack to a small, stepped roof. Traverse right under the roof (crux) and continue up easier ground on the right flank of the slabs to gain shallow cracks.
2 35m Follow cracks up and left passing a vegetated ledge to a steeper finish on the sloping terrace at the top of the tier. (Topo provided.)

LITTLE GLAS MAOL, North Facing Buttress:

After Church Arête   130m   II. James Lamont, Dave Slade. 6 Dec 2020.
The first buttress immediately east of the north-facing cliff containing The Ramp and *Slanting Ramp*. The route starts at NO 177 761 and tops out at NO 177 760. The approach was from Glen Shee, over the summit of Glas Maol and then descending a gully to the east of the route.
1 50m Start in a bay below the buttress. Go straight up a series of rocky steps that wind around some rocky bulges for around 30m before coming to some easier ground for 20m. Belay here.
2 50m Take the left-hand line up more rocky steps to a narrow arête (crux) and continue along the arête to second belay.
3 20m Continue up easier broken ground to finish up a short rocky step. (Topo provided.)

CAENLOCHAN GLEN, Druim Mòr, Creag Caorach (NO 190 769):

Unusually late season snow brought this south-facing cliff into winter condition. (Topo provided.)

XYZ Rib   160m   II. Simon Richardson. 7 May 2021.
The well-defined rib right of *Y Gully* starting from NO 1908 7695. Climb the rib over two steps. The second narrows to a knife edge and can be climbed by turfy grooves just to its left.

Caorach Gully   200m   II. Simon Richardson. 7 May 2021.
The shallow narrow gully starting right of *XYZ Rib* at NO 1913 7687. Possibly climbed before.

GLEN CLOVA, Corrie of Bonhard:

Secret Staircase   80m   III,4. Simon Stewart, Grant Farquhar. 19 Dec 1986.
The left nose of the buttress taken by *Mystery Ramp*. Start immediately right of

the depression or icefall defining the left edge of the buttress and follow the natural line veering left under a pronounced prow near the top. (Topo provided.)

Dreish, Winter Corrie, Waterfall Buttress:

Get Into The Groove 60m III,4. Dave Slade, James Lamont. 28 Dec 2020.
The steep cracked buttress to the immediate left of a Grade I blocky gully, 40m left from *The Waterfall*.
1. 25m Climb the crack direct until progress is halted by a steep wall. Traverse left below the wall on good hooks and torques to a bay with a block belay.
2. 35m Climb slightly right onto the top of the previously mentioned wall, step across the gap before trending left across easier ground (the route follows Waterfall Buttress Direct from this point) to the base of the final short but airy wall. Climb this direct on positive hooks to block belay. (Topo provided.)

Note: *Waterfall Buttress* mentioned on p. 430 of 'The Cairngorms' guidebook was first climbed by Graham Penny and Tommy Sutherland in 1992 and named *Work Ethic* (IV,4).

GLEN MARK, Couternach:

Simple Interest 30m Severe. Iain Young, Kenny Brookman. 25 Apr 2021.
More straightforward and old-fashioned than *Speculation*. Climb the obvious corner right of the Central Buttress in its entirety, sticking to the inside of the corner in the smooth lower section. Enjoyable.

Iain Young notes that *Speculation* was excellent – definitively worth a star or two.

NORTH-EAST OUTCROPS

FINDON CLIFFS, The Shark Fin:

Kelpie 20m 8b **. Gordon Lennox. 17 Aug 2019.
Climb Mako then traverse left to finish up *Snakehead*.

The Orchestra Cave:

BawBags 30m 8b ***. Gordon Lennox. 13 Sep 2019.
Climb *Blobstrop* and follow the *Encore* finish to above the main roof, then climb up and left to the *Dangleberries* pitch 1 belay and continue up the *Dangleberries* pitch 2 to the top of the crag.

Piledriver 30m 8c ***. Gordon Lennox. 17 Sep 2019.
Climb *Magnum Opus* to the junction with *What the Funk*. Make the dropdown move to reverse the crux of *What the Funk* and join *Blobstrop*. Follow this and continue as for *BawBags* to the top of the crag. An epic if slightly eliminate link-up which takes in all the hardest climbing to the top of the crag.

MEIKLE PARTANS, Crabs Wall:

Sweep's Chimney 5m V.Diff. Mark Bannan, Ian Hamilton. 29 Jul 2020.
The obvious chimney right of the VS 4c crack-line (rightmost of the four crack-lines mentioned in 'Northeast Outcrops'). Good rock and protection.

NORTH HAVEN AREA, The Red Wall Quarry:
Bolt 20m 8b **. Gordon Lennox. 12 Oct 2019.
Climb the The King to its top crux deadpoint to the pocket in the top break. Make hard moves to traverse the break right into Dracula True Finish.

LONGHAVEN AREA, Buchan Walls:
This multi-pitch crag lies in the inlet south of Meackie Point, only about 100m from the road near a clifftop house. Only one route has been previously recorded (*Gold Dust* HVS 1977) despite the crag's sunny aspect and generally good clean rock. There are a few kittiwake and cormorant nests on the lower left side. A couple of abseil stakes have been placed and these are also useful for belays. It is also possible to access the non-tidal base of the cliff via steep grass to the east, near Meackie Point.

Gold Placer 40m E1 **. Keith Milne, Ian Milne. Mar 2017.
1 25m 5b This route takes the straight groove above the orange slab. It may be necessary to remove a few nests near the start. Climb directly up the lower wall using side pulls to gain the ramp (no protection, but can be bypassed on the right). From the ramp, the first few moves are on the left wall, reaching right into the groove to a place a good wire. Above this there are some marginal runners with intricate climbing. After a small ledge, the line continues with solid runners in a wonderful clean granite corner. Belay below a small overhang.
2 15m 5a Climb the overhang with difficulty using reachy side-pulls to an easy-angled slab which finishes on the left.

The following three lines were climbed on sight with some minimal cleaning on lead; there is still some gritty and potentially loose rock in places but overall the rock is clean enough and solid. With some repeats it should clean up nicely.

Wild Frontier 40m E4 6a **. Russ Birkett, Keith Milne. 14 Sep 2020.
An excellent adventurous climb taking the left arête of the main wall right of *Gold Placer*. Start at the base of the easy right-trending ramp, or better from the flat guano ledge part way up (which can be accessed directly by abseil). A left-trending slab ramp cuts out across the steep lower wall. Balance a few metres along this then pull directly up through a bulging wall heading for a narrow hanging groove. Step left to the arête and follow this to below a downward-pointing spike roof (cam in high pocket). Pull through this and continue direct to the final overlap below the slab, trend up and right through the final overlap following good slots and edges on the slab to finish.

El Dorado Groove 35m E4 6a **. Russ Birkett, Keith Milne. 17 Sep 2020.
The black groove, roof and corner in the centre of the wall. Starting from the guano ledge on the easy ramp, bridge up this rightward a few moves to pull through a bulge leftward to gain the base of the narrow groove. Move up this easily to just below the roof where a step left onto the wall leads up to the weakness in the roof. Awkward and difficult to protect moves lead through this to a standing position on the ledge. Climb the corner direct to swing out right at the top. Move rightwards across ledges to finish over the roof and up the finger crack in the final slab.

Gold Fever   35m   E3 5c **. Russ Birkett, Keith Milne. 17 Sep 2020.
The rib right of *El Dorado Grooves* gives another fine pitch following the line of undercut flakes and hairline crack. Start as for the previous route but move up the easy ramp to step left onto the wall below the undercut flakes. Climb directly to reach easier ground common with *El Dorado Grooves*. Finish as for that route or the groove on the right.

The next routes start at the lowest point of the wall. There are occasional nests, but not on the routes.

Prospector   45m   HVS *. Ian Milne, Keith Milne. Sep 2016).
1 20m 4c Start just right of an overhanging wall. An interesting pitch. Climb a few metres of steep steps until it is possible to move up right into a clean niche. With feet low, make a few moves left and then up short cracks to a ledge. With a high runner on the right, move back left and climb the slab to reach broken ledges.
2 25m 4c Climb the corner crack on the left. Slightly crumbly rock. Move past a doubtful block by moves on the left wall and then a few moves back right, finishing up a short wide crack (or the clean slab with a thin corner crack).

End of the Rainbow   50m   E1 *. Keith Milne, Ian Milne. Apr 2017.
1 30m 5b A few metres right is a steep wall with good holds. Up this and onto easier ground. Move left into a shallow groove and crack system which leads up to an overhanging wall. Climb this initially on the right using small ledges (one doubtful block on left) and move back right and finish on jugs. Belay at the bollard.
2 20m 5b Move right around the nose and traverse to the base of the corner. Climb the short overhanging gritstone-like crack to a mantelshelf. Finish easily up a slab. Large cam useful to protect the mantelshelf, but normal cams can be placed in the middle section of the crack.

Nuggets   40m   E2 **. Keith Milne, David Bird. Mar 2017.
1 30m 5a Climb the same initial wall and slab as the previous route. After a few metres step left and mantelshelf onto the nose. A short crack leads to delicate moves onto a sloping shelf. Move up and left past a smooth nose to a good bollard stance. Excellent rock.
2 10m 5c Step left to below a thin crack (reach up to place cam protection, sometimes damp). Move left and up strenuously on rounded holds to reach a good crack. Continue steeply onto a final shelf just below the top.

Panning for Gold   55m   H.Severe **. Ian Milne, Keith Milne. Mar 2017.
1 30m 4b From a broken ridge at the right side, a few easy steps leads to an enjoyable clean corner-groove. Belay on a ledge 3m below the main overhang.
2 25m 4b Step up left onto the slab on the left and move around the nose (possible belay). Traverse 5m left onto a slab. Take a wide crack to finish (or a strenuous alternative past a jutting block just to the right, 5a).

COVESEA, Stack Bay:
Apocalypse Pickle   12m   E3 6a *. Ted Collins, Robert Giddy. 4 Sep 2020.
Right of *Slyme Crime*. Move up and right to gain hanging corner. Climb up to the roof then traverse leftward to finish up *Slyme Crime*.

REDHYTHE POINT, John Wood's Hole Stack (NJ 5721 6697):
South Face Crack 12m HVS 5a. Mark Robson, Simon Richardson. 8 Nov 2020.
The stack is spit into two and can be reached by crossing boulders except at high
tide. Climb the right-facing corner in the centre of the face then move up and right
to a ledge. Finish up the short corner above. A good steep climb on excellent holds.
The lower north summit can be gained by descending easily to the west until it is
possible to traverse onto the west side of the south stack. Finish by climbing left
of the rift separating the two stacks (Diff). (Topo provided.)

Skedam Cliff (NJ 5704 6682):
The east end of the easy-angled sweep of slabs of Skedam Cliff presents a
diamond-shaped face of good rock. Approach by abseiling down the slab to below
the face. (Topo provided.)

Mermaid's Purse 12m V.Diff. Simon Richardson, Mark Robson. 8 Nov 2020.
The corner defining the left side of the diamond.

Hongeohoe 12m VS 4c. Simon Richardson, Mark Robson. 8 Nov 2020.
The steep black corner left of centre. Climb the corner to a roof at half-height then
make an awkward move up and right to gain the corner-crack in the slab above
on the right.

Sea Skate 12m VS 4c. Mark Robson, Simon Richardson. 8 Nov 2020.
Take a zigzag line up the centre of the cliff with a difficult exit into a slab at two-
thirds height. Finish up the short corner above.

Shelf-ish 15m V.Diff. Mark Robson, Simon Richardson. 8 Nov 2020.
Move right along a shelf and climb the right edge of the diamond on good holds
to a slabby finish on the right.

CLACH NA BEINN:
Solus 's na h-Uamhan 20m IV,6. Ed Hamilton, Ewan Paterson. 8 Jan 2021.
The gully left of *Crack o' The Mearns*. Start 2m left of the summer line then
continue up this to the top.

Southern Groove 20m Moderate. Simon Richardson. 26 Aug 2020.
A summer ascent of the winter line (the prominent left-facing groove left of *Eagle
Buttress*). Almost certainly climbed before.

PASS OF BALLATER, Eastern Section:
Erebus 24m VS 5a *. Peter Henry, Sam Burgess. 2 Dec 2020.
Start 4m down from Larch tree and rockfall at *Chopped P.O.R.G.* Climb the short
steep wall then traverse left along the edge of the terrace to reach the base of the
obvious arête above (12m possible belay). Tackle the arête directly to belay on a
small slab at the top (tat and maillon on tree nearby). (Topo provided.)

AN CADHA DUBH:
The Blackening 20m HVS 5a. Iain Young, Trevor Jones. 16 May 2021.
There is a hanging, black corner in the right arête of *Dirty Thing*. Start from the
base of that route and gain a pale green scoop by using a protruding square block.
Move up into the hanging black corner, step right towards its top and back left to

a short, hand crack. After that easier climbing leads to the top. (Possibly climbed before).

Clean as a Whistle 20m H.Severe. Iain Young, Trevor Jones. 16 May 2021.
Takes the clean, slabby wall on the immediate left of *Dirty Thing*, joining that route for its final few metres. Enjoyable, but escapable. (Possibly climbed before).

These two routes, together with *Dirty Thing* (which is better than its name implies), can all be made to finish at a large pine tree which makes for a convenient belay and abseil.

BENACHIE, Mither Tap:
Mither Diedre 10m VS 4c. Mark Bannan, David Jabaroo, Jo Jabero. 29 May 2021.
On the lower buttress, facing Oxen Craig, climb the obvious well-protected corner. Worth a star when clean (top section a bit dirty). Possibly climbed before.

SIDLAWS, Black Crag:
Gorse Groove 15m H.Severe 4b. Joe Barlow, Rosie Rothwell. 31 May 2020.
Start half way between *Abernyte Corner* and *Windy Gap Groove*. Climb up to the base of a black overhanging corner, then step right around the arête. Climb up the left side of the hanging slab to finish up the corner above. Nice exposed positions but some loose rock and gorse about.

No Gorse 20m H.Severe 4b. Dave Slade, James Lamont. 18 Jun 2020.
Start as for *Gorse Ramp* up obvious ramp in centre of face. After approx 2m make a committing step out right around small overhanging bulge and take an airy step up on good holds. Finish at the obvious block.

Pinnacle Face Direct Finish 10m HVS 5a. Dave Slade, James Lamont. 18 Jun 2020.
Start as for *Pinnacle Face* but take direct line slightly further left rather than line on the right. Good holds, you just need to find them! There are a couple of bold moves in quick succession above the runner so best to move swiftly!

HIGHLAND OUTCROPS SOUTH

WEEM CRAGS, Aerial Crag:
Thunderstruck 18m E4 6a *. Jamie Skelton, Morag Eagleson. 21 Jul 2020.
The right arête of the sidewall. Start as for *Saving Up for a Rainy Day* to a jug at the top of the finger-crack. Stretch up towards the next break and protruding ledge at the bottom of the arête. After mounting the ledge, exposed turbo jugs on the very edge lead to the top. (Topo provided.)

KNAPDALE, Creag nam Fitheach:
The Spirit Screen 25m E6 6b *. Jamie Skelton, Morag Eagleson. 25 Sep 2020.
The wall to the right of *Crucifixion Crack*. Climb *Crucifixion Crack* to the top of the ramp and place a high runner, move right and onto the ledge below the wall.

Boldly move up the flake-crack (RPs) and wall directly above to a good slot. Continue up and left, pulling over the arête of the buttress just below the top.

Letter From America   25m   E1 5b **. Alex Thomson, Clár Nic Giollabháin. 21 Mar 2021.
Climb the starting groove and cracks of *America* as far as the high break. Follow a line of jugs up and left in a fine position to a small stance and gear below the nose. Finish steeply over the top.

MULL OF KINTYRE, Midships Crag:
Jamie Skelton and Morag Eagleson note a free ascent of *Blood on the Cracks* at E3 5c on 23 Sep 2020.

OBAN CRAGS, Gallanach, Ardbhan Craigs (NM 841 289):
The following climbs are found on the cliffs above the road to the Kerrara ferry. The first climb takes the large corner 100m past Kilbowie House, visible from the road.

Cotyledon   35m   E1 5a **. Al Thomson, Andy Corbe. 29 May 2021.
The huge corner system above Kilbowie House. Start up an easy slab to a ledge. Small wires and a cam in a pocket out left protect steep moves up and into the corner system. Follow the corner to a large ledge (optional belay), then up to a roof. Rock on to the slab above from round to the left and continue up to atop the pinnacle. Step right and top out delicately through the undergrowth to a tree belay. Absorbing climbing, well protected with small cams and micro wires.

The next climb is found on the last big buttress before the Rockies Cottage and the slipway. Follow faint paths from the road up towards the huge leaning wall and corner.

The Braid   35m   E1 5b **. Al Thomson, Clár Nic Giollabháin. Apr 2021.
The corner systems and slab 5m left of the bolts. Follow the clean right-hand corner for 5m. Step left below the chossy roof to below the second corner-crack. Climb this with the help of some surprising holds. Follow the crack above trending left and stepping left into another crack when needed. Weave up the easy slabs above, aiming for good finishing cracks and the small tree at the top. An excellent journey.

The next climbs are found on the final buttress before the ferry, above the Rockies Cottage. An obvious clean wall is visible from the road, bounded by a corner and fin on the right. Approach via a path from the previous climb, or from abseil from above by taking the track up from the ferry slipway (stakes).

Beer Engineer   25m   HVS 5a **. Al Thomson, Joe Turner. Sep 2020.
The hanging crackline in the centre of the wall. Start right of centre at the base of a grassy crack, follow the crack diagonally left and then up to the left-facing corner below the hanging slab. Step right on to the slab and up to the roof, then step left and up the crack to the top. Belay on stakes.

Kerreran Curry   25m   H.Severe *. Al Thomson, Solene Giraudeau-Potel, Joe Turner. Sep 2020.

The great left-facing corner of the wall right of *Beer Engineer*. Quite 'traditional'.

ARDNAMURCHAN, Ring Crags, Dome Buttress (Creag an Fhir-Eoin):

Greta Thunberg 30m H.Severe 4b *. Scott Kirkhope, Dave Anderson. 14 Apr 2021.
Start at the left toe of the slab and make a rising traverse right following the crack, to make the final moves of *Rum Do*.

ARDNAMURCHAN, Meall Meadhoin (NM 492 676):

The following routes are located on the collection of crags on the north side of the Allt a' Choire on the south-west side of Meall Meadhoin. Best to start from a small gravel parking spot a few hundred metres before (south-east) the usual approach to the ring crags. Follow a faint path heading north, via a deer fence, then diagonally rightwards across the hillside. The crags are generally south-west to west-facing and enjoy any afternoon sun. Approximately 45 minutes.

Pancake Slab:

The lowest of the crags described, roughly in the middle of the hillside and featuring a right trending ramp. Well left of and at a lower elevation than Papal Slab.

Crepe 13m V.Diff *. Steve Kennedy, Cynthia Grindley, Colin Moody. 27 Feb 2021.
Start at a block on the left. Climb slabs rightwards to a smooth slab which provides a nice finish up the middle.

Waffle 15m Diff *. Steve Kennedy, Cynthia Grindley, Colin Moody. 27 Feb 2021.
The right side forms a steeper wall with parallel cracks leading leftwards. Continue up the slab and finish up a prominent crack.

The Papal Slab:

A small, clean crag split by a groove and corner with a steep, undercut wall on the right. Routes are described from left to right.

Basilica 10m Diff *. Steve Kennedy. 24 April 2021.
The diagonal crackline running from bottom left to the far right of the slab.

Fumata Bianca 9m Severe *. Steve Kennedy, Cynthia Grindley, Colin Moody. 28 Nov 2020.
Climb the slab left of the deep groove, join the corner, step right and climb the blunt rib.

Sistine Chimney 9m V.Diff *
Steve Kennedy, Cynthia Grindley, Colin Moody. 28 Nov 2020.
The deep groove and corner above.

Three Puffs or Four? 9m V.Diff *. Steve Kennedy, Cynthia Grindley, Colin Moody. 28 Nov 2020.
Start at the foot of the deep groove and climb the slab on the right to a steepening. Finish up an easy slab.

King Billy   9m   HVS 5a *. Steve Kennedy, Cynthia Grindley, Colin Moody. 24 Apr 2021.
The undercut crack just right of *Three Puffs or Four*. A meaty start leads to much easier climbing finishing up the right-hand crack.

Enclave   8m   VS 4b *. Colin Moody, Cynthia Grindley, Steve Kennedy. 24 Apr 2021.
The steep groove on right side of the undercut wall leading to a continuation crack and slab.

About 80m to the right, at about the same level, are the following crags:

Egg Crag:
The rightmost, west-facing slabby buttress with a flat top and a curious egg-shaped feature on the south-facing wall on the right. The west-facing routes lie on either side of a grassy groove. Routes described left to right.

Humpty Dumpty   12m   Severe. Steve Kennedy, Cynthia Grindley, Colin Moody. 24 Apr 2021.
The vague crack and slab above taking a direct line just left of a white splodge.

Egg White   12m   Severe *. Steve Kennedy, Cynthia Grindley, Colin Moody. 24 Apr 2021.
Take a direct line up the slab 2m right of *Humpty Dumpty*, finishing just right of the white splodge.

Breggsit   12m   HVS 4c **. Steve Kennedy, Cynthia Grindley, Colin Moody. 24 Apr 2021.
The clean edge immediately left of the grassy groove, finishing up thin cracks. Poorly protected.

Clutch   12m   V.Diff. Colin Moody, Cynthia Grindley, Steve Kennedy. 28 Nov 2020.
The first crackline 4m right of the grassy groove (sometimes damp). Climb the crack and rib above.

Cock   12m   Severe *. Colin Moody, Cynthia Grindley, Steve Kennedy. 24 April 2021.
Start 2m right of Clutch and climb a right-facing corner and cracked slab to a ledge. Finish up the open book corner.

Egg Tooth   12m   HVS 4c **. Steve Kennedy, Cynthia Grindley, Colin Moody. 24 Apr 2021.
Below the slabby wall, on the right, is the wall containing the 'egg' feature. Enter the egg and break out awkwardly onto the left edge. Climb cracks directly above to a ledge and finish up the crack right of the corner.

Chicken or Egg?   12m   Severe *. Colin Moody, Cynthia Grindley, Steve Kennedy. 6 Dec 2020.
Enter the egg and climb the steep groove on its right side. Step left across the wall and finish up a groove and wall.

Victor's Crag:

Situated below and slightly left of Egg Crag. Characterised by a large flake leaning against the right side.

Twirl 7m VS 4c *. Steve Kennedy, Cynthia Grindley, Colin Moody. 6 Dec 2020.
The left side is undercut with a curving left-facing corner and crack running leftwards. A burly start leads to the crack and slab above.

99 7m V.Diff *. Colin Moody, Cynthia Grindley & Steve Kennedy. 6 Dec 2020.
Climb the front of the large flake and slab above.

Sunset Walls:

Above and left of Egg Crag lie some steep walls topped by an attractive looking cracked slab. The upper slabs contains a number of crack lines which provide the following routes. With the exception of the first route described, all the routes start from a grassy ledge descending leftwards along the base of the slab. The ledge is most easily gained by scrambling up from the right just beyond Egg Crag. Descend on either side.

Pretzel 15m VS 4c *. Steve Kennedy, Cynthia Grindley, Colin Moody. 24 April 2021.
This route lies on the left (west) wall of the upper slabs. Climb a ramp rightwards to a ledge and finish up a thin crack near the right edge leading to the whaleback ridge.

Choux 10m Severe *. Steve Kennedy, Cynthia Grindley, Colin Moody. 6 Dec 2020.
The thin crack running up the left side of the slab (left of a left facing corner). Climb the crack all the way to the sloping ridge.

Filo 13m VS 4c *. Steve Kennedy, Cynthia Grindley, Colin Moody. 6 Dec 2020.
Start below a prominent crack about 3m right of *Choux*, just left of a left-facing corner-groove, Climb the crack, passing a large incut hold, to a rightward trending crackline running across the slab. Finish directly up the slab above.

Suet 12m Severe *. Steve Kennedy, Cynthia Grindley, Colin Moody. 28 Nov 2020.
The next prominent thin crack on the right, starting above a step in the ledge. Climb the crack, crossing the right-trending crack system, and finish up a wider crack directly above.

Puff 10m V.Diff *. Colin Moody, Cynthia Grindley, Steve Kennedy. 28 Nov 2020.
Start up a right-trending crack near the far right end and move left to below a bulging wall. Step left and finish up a left-facing corner.

AWOL Slab:

A small slab situated well above The Papal Slab (approximately 10 minutes), characterised by a prominent central crack.

Looking for a Body   10m   VS 4b *. Steve Kennedy, Cynthia Grindley, Colin Moody. 12 Dec 2020.
The seam running diagonally left to right across the slab, finishing at the far right.

Nurse in a Burn   8m   VS 4b *. Steve Kennedy, Cynthia Grindley, Colin Moody. 12 Dec 2020.
The unprotected slab left of the central crack, starting from a large boulder.

Missing in Action   8m   V Diff *. Colin Moody, Cynthia Grindley, Steve Kennedy. 12 Dec 2020.
The central crack.

Wild Goose Chase   8m   VS 4b *. Steve Kennedy, Cynthia Grindley, Colin Moody. 12 Dec 2020.
Start up the slab 2m right of the central crack, move leftwards along a break then directly.

Hide and Seek   7m   VS 4c *. Colin Moody, Cynthia Grindley, Steve Kennedy. 12 Dec 2020.
An eliminate line starting as for *Wild Goose Chase* and climbing the unprotected slab directly on small flakes. No palming off the right edge!

ARDNAMURCHAN, Meall Sanna:
A number of routes have been done on the small crags scattered on the south-west slopes of the hill south of Meall Sanna (south of a small lochan), above and north-west of the Bealach Ruadh (NM 454 677). Park just before the eastmost house in Achnaha and follow a rough, waymarked path leading south-west to the Bealach, initially crossing boggy ground and then running close to the fence line on the right, This is the path leading from Achnaha to Achosnich. About 25 minutes to the closest crag.

The crags closest to the Bealach comprise a prominent slab with a crack running up the middle and a blocky buttress to the left (NM 453 679).

Frigg   14m   Severe *. Steve Kennedy, Cynthia Grindley. 3 Apr 2021.
Climb the central crack in the slab to a ledge and finish up a steep groove containing a block directly above.

Odin   8m   VS 4b *. Steve Kennedy, Cynthia Grindley. 3 Apr 2021.
The obvious left-facing corner-crack on the right side of the blocky buttress.

The following routes are situated on the higher crags a few hundred metres to the left (NM 450 681). High on the left, directly below and close to the summit cairn, is a slab with right-slanting cracks and an undercut base. Routes are described left to right.

Helga   8m   Severe *. Steve Kennedy, Cynthia Grindley. 3 Apr 2021.
About 3m up and left of the undercut base is a short corner. Start up the corner and climb the slab and cracks directly above.

Erika 10m VS 4b *
Steve Kennedy, Cynthia Grindley. 3 Apr 2021.
Start at the lowest point below the undercut. Climb the slab to a heathery crack, move right below the upper wall and finish up a deep groove behind.

Astrid 10m VS 4c *. Steve Kennedy, Cynthia Grindley. 3 Apr 2021.
Start below a short corner or alcove on the right and climb a right-slanting crack then go directly up the slab above to a sloping ledge. Finish up the steep jagged crack just left of the pale speckled wall.

Ardnamurchan Point, Main Wall Area:
The Moral Consequences of Limpet Genocide 5m VS 4c *. Oliver Skeoch, Katie Boyle. 19 Aug 2020.
The steep corner 5m right of *Whoosh*, finishing through the slot.

Pillar Thriller 5m HVS 4c. Oliver Skeoch, Katie Boyle. 19 Aug 2020.
The inverted stepped pillar to the left of the previous route and to the right of *Whoosh*. No gear but a good landing.

POLLDUBH, Polldubh Lower Tier, Repton Buttress:
Colin Moody notes that *Bullet* is 28m in length.

The Alp, SW Buttress:
Colin Moody notes that *Fred's Delight* passes right of the niche not left. This was correct in 1978 and 1985 guides, but not in 1998 and 2016 editions.

Styx Buttress:
Read Between the Lines 30m E4 6a *. Jamie Skelton, Morag Eagleson. 2 Jul 2020.
A logical line through the middle of the west wall with sustained interested and good gear after the bouldery start. Climb *Doomsday, Direct Start*, then wiggle your way up the well protected wide crack directly above above to join *Black Friday, Right-Hand Finish*.

Polldubh Upper Tier, Nameless Crag:
Electronic Omission 20m E1 5b **. Nathan Adam, Garry Campbell. 11 Jun 2020.
The fault left of Cathode Smiles. Climb the left side of the quartz-studded wall into a right-facing corner. Go up this to the roof and climb the excellent crack above to a short corner and the top.

Anode 20m E1 5b. Jamie Skelton, Morag Eagleson. 1 Jun 2020.
This route climbs the vertical fault line between *Cathode Smiles* and *Triode*. Move up the lower wall to a small bay below the crux groove. Jam or layback this to the top.

Triode, Direct Finish 20m E5 6a **. Jamie Skelton, Morag Eagleson. 1 Jun 2020.
The direct finish is technical but only half a grade harder than the original. Stuff small gear in the *Triode* overlap, step right and commit to the short headwall above.

Lightbulb   14m   H.Severe 4b **. Morag Eagleson, Jamie Skelton. 1 Jun 2020.
The obvious crack line right of *Diode*. Climb up and onto a small ledge before
stepping left into the crack. Follow this over a small bulge to the top.

High Crag:
Jamie Skelton notes that *Quartzite Cruiser* on the Middle Tier of High Crag lies
between *Kinloss Grooves* and *Hot Tin Roof* rather than to the right of *Hot Tin Roof*
as shown in the topo on p. 239 of 'Highland Outcrops South'.

Crown Buttress:
Reason to Believe   14m   E2 5c *. Nathan Adam, Garry Campbell. 3 Jun 2020.
A good route, bold at the top, but easily escapable at a few points. Start 2m right
of *Palpitation* at an undercut crack-line. Boulder steeply up the crack to reach a
good hold on the right, and cross *Palpitation* to reach the left side of the large
detached spike. Climb the steep left side of the spike to the horizontal break above,
placing a load of gear in this (last protection). Undercling the roof, and reach for
a hidden hold high up before making committing moves left across the small
hanging wall on quartz holds to reacha good rail and rock-over to finish. Thread
belay back on right.

Tiara Buttress:
Hidden Gem   15m   H.Severe 4b *. Nathan Adam (solo). 29 May 2020.
Just right of the leftmost left-facing corner is a steep slab leading to a small
overlap. Climb a small crack to the overlap and continue on good holds to a small
ledge. Step right and go up the edge overlooking the corner. (Topo provided.)

Car Park Area, Buccaneer Crag:
The Blockaneer   20m   E4 5c *. Jamie Skelton, Morag Eagleson. 12 Jun
2020.
The cleanest sweep of grey rock on the crag can be gained by climbing the first
few metres of *Pieces of Eight* and hand-traversing the right-trending crack before
heading for a rightwards-jutting hollow block. Stuff suspect gear behind this and
make a big move up to a cruical RP placement, then continue up the wall above
trending first right and back left to finish. Poorly protected.

Phantom Crag:
Second Slice of the Pie   20m   E3 6a. Jamie Skelton, Morag Eagleson. 12 Jun
2020.
The very well protected arête on the left side of the lower tier has some good crack
climbing but some flaky rock in its lower half. It can be climbed via the strenuous
hand-and-fist crack to the top of a big pinnacle. After placing high gear climb the
leaning finger-crack and arête on the right (crux) to an easy finish.

Steall Area, Gorge Crag:
Confrontation   35m   E2 5c **. Jamie Skelton, Morag Eagleson. 8 Jun 2020.
Superb exposed climbing up the steep wall above *Conscription*. Start as for this
route to the point at which it goes horizontally right. Instead of going rightwards
climb up and slightly left across the wall to gain a layback crack at the right end
of the big ledge system. Continue up wildly on big holds to a ledge, and finish
either directly or via the left-leaning crack.

LOCH EIL, Gleann Fionnlighe, Uachan Slab (NM 958 822):

This gneiss slab is visible from the track up Gleann Fionnlighe above the buildings at Uachan. From afar the left-trending white streak looks like a well-cleaned crack cutting through the crag. Walk up the main track which crosses the river. After this bridge is a stone building. Take the disused vehicle track behind the building up and right to reach a landslide. Walk uphill until above the tree line then traverse right to the slab. The climbing is easy for the grade though committing. The rock is perfect (with a little moss in places) and the outlook over the hills is pleasant. Belays are difficult to find – there are plans to add a couple of stakes before spring 2022. Routes are described from left to right. (Topos provided.)

AstraZeneca 12m VS 4b *. Colin Moody, Steve Kennedy. 2 May 2021.
The slab left of *Local Feeling*. There is a slot for a belay about 6m up left from the top.

Local Feeling 30m HVS 4c *. Alastair Rose (solo). 20 Jun 2020.
The first continuous line up the slab, bypassing a large garden of grass just to its left in its upper half.

The White Streak 45m HVS 4c **. Alastair Rose (solo). 20 Jun 2020.
The left-trending streak.

Sputnik 45m HVS 5a **. Steve Kennedy, Colin Moody. 2 May 2021.
The slab between *Local Feeling* and *Protect the NHS* joining and following *Protect the NHS* at about 28m.

Protect the NHS 30m VS 4b *. Alastair Rose (solo). 20 Jun 2020.
A counter diagonal to *The White Streak* crossing it at two-thirds height.

Pfizer 45m HVS 4c **. Steve Kennedy, Colin Moody. 2 May 2021.
Start right of *The White Streak*. Climb up left, crossing *Protect the NHS*; very badly protected.
Phase 3 20m H.Severe 4a. Alastair Rose (solo). 20 Jun 2020.
The left side of the clean sweep of rock on the right side of the crag.

GLENFINNAN, Dome Buttress:

Aurora 8m Severe * . Steve Kennedy. 26 Jul 2020.
About 20m beyond and above *Overhang* and *Groove*, where Dome Buttress changes direction to face west, is a rounded arête. Climb the slabby wall on the left side of the arête.

Evening Star 8m Severe *. Steve Kennedy. 26 Jul 2020.
Climb the wall immediately right of the arête via a small ledge.

Celeste 8m V.Diff *. Steve Kennedy. 26 Jul 2020.
Approximately 20m right of *Evening Star* is a slab featuring a quartz vein, which is taken by this route.

The short walls between *Aurora* and *Celeste* provide numerous short bouldering routes on beautiful rippled rock, mostly in the lower grades.

Squat Buttress (NM 867 812):

The long, compact buttress situated about 50m right (south) of *Celeste*, comprising a slabby lower section topped by a steep wall.

Acadia 15m HVS 5a **. Steve Kennedy, Cynthia Grindley, Eileen Blair. 23 Jul 2020.
Start below an alcove (below a roof) in the centre of the crag. Pull into the alcove from the right and move left across a slab to reach a rock 'ear'. Continue up slabs and finish up a jagged, rightward-trending quartz fault on the steep headwall.

Paloma 15m VS 4c *. Steve Kennedy, Cynthia Grindley, Eileen Blair. 23 July 2020.
Start 3m right of *Acadia* at a cleaned flake. Climb the flake rightwards, pull over a small roof, and continue up the slab and over a bulge at the right end of the headwall, left of a small tree.

Felix 15m VS 4b *. Steve Kennedy, Cynthia Grindley, Eileen Blair. 23 Jul 2020.
Start at an embedded flake 2m right of *Paloma*. Climb the initial slab rightwards over a small roof to a heather ledge. Continue up the slab above, left of a slanting crack and via a scoop just right of a small tree.

Beatrix 11m Severe *. Steve Kennedy, Cynthia Grindley, Eileen Blair. 23 Jul 2020.
Located on the rounded buttress about 40m right (south-west) of Squat Buttress. Climb the slab on the right (just right of the rounded edge) and finish left of a prominent crack.

The following route lies on the prominent, west-facing elongated slab located approximately 100m right (west) of *Beatrix*, the top of which is at a slightly higher elevation (NM 866 812).

Luna 12m E1 5a **. Steve Kennedy. 20 Jun 2020.
Start at the lowest point, close to the left end of a rightwards-slanting roof. Climb to a sloping ledge and follow a flake-crack to the left end of a further small roof. Make thin moves passing a horizontal break to the easier slab above. Fine climbing but unprotected.

GLENFINNAN, Ranochan Walls, Ranochan West:

The Seat 8m Severe. Colin Moody, Steve Kennedy. 13 Apr 2021.
The wide left-leaning crack down and left from *Blue Velvet*.

Colin Moody notes that *Pinch Beck* and *Clover Field* were cleaned and considered E1 5b * and E2 5b ** respectively.

LOCHAILORT, Craiglea (NM 7822 8330):

A south-west-facing slab with a fine outlook south to the hills and west down to Lochailort. Head west from Fort William on the A830 towards Mallaig. Pass Glenfinnan and Loch Eilt to the small Lochan Dubh with a pine tree covered island. There is a house and railway yard on the right, at a left bend. Park after the bend on the left, the crag being seen above the parking; this is one mile before Lochailort. A direct approach involves crossing the railway, so walk back east to the railway yard at the corner. Follow the footpath under the railway, then walk up left to the crag (15 minutes). Most routes have lower-offs.

Alarm   14m   F6a *. Colin Moody, Steve Kennedy. 6 Mar 2021.
The left-hand slab.

The Hole   16m   F6a+ *. Steve Kennedy, Cynthia Grindley, Colin Moody. 11 Apr 2021.
Start at a hole. Climb the slab up left to join *Alarm*.

Brown Crack   8m   VS 4c *. Colin Moody, Steve Kennedy, Cynthia Grindley. 21 Apr 2021.
Belay up right on a huge spike or block. To descend, go right then down.

Molar   10m   F6b **. Colin Moody, Steve Kennedy, Cynthia Grindley 11 Apr 2021.
Climb through the tooth-mark.

Hollow Shield   12m F6a+ **. Colin Moody, Cynthia Grindley, Steve Kennedy. 19 Mar 2021.
Climb through the shield.

Big Crack   12m   E1 5b **. Colin Moody, Cynthia Grindley, Steve Kennedy. 20 Apr 2021.
Climb the crack. The start is shared with *Great Wall*.

Great Wall   12m   F6c **. Steve Kennedy, Cynthia Grindley, Colin Moody. 19 Mar 2021.
Start as for *Big Crack* and go up to the break. Move right to a foothold below the spring then climb the wall.

Cry Wolf   12m   E1 5b **. Colin Moody, Steve Kennedy. 1 May 2021.
Climb up to the scoop of *April*, move left and climb the crack to the top of *April*.

April   14m   F6a **. Steve Kennedy, Cynthia Grindley, Colin Moody, Billy Hood. 22 Apr 2021.
Start by moving right into the scoop then climb the rib slanting slightly leftwards.

ARISAIG, Ardnish Peninsula, Lizard Crag:
The Adder   10m   E1 5b. Morag Eagleson, Jamie Skelton. 18 Jun 2020.
Start up the left-slanting crack just left of *The Snake* and continue up the shallow left-facing groove to reach the arête and easier ground.

ARISAIG, Druim Fiaclach, Gleann Màma Slabs:
The Mystery Machine   35m   E3 5c **. Nathan Adam, David Wood. 2 Oct 2020.
Follows the obvious left-leaning diagonal cracks above the grassy bay just right of centre; scramble up the bay to approach. Excellent, steep and well protected climbing; carry a double set of medium to small cams. Start up a short left-facing corner and rock over onto a good ledge. Follow the crack leftwards on reasonable underclings along the dwindling ledge to a good hidden hold at waist height. Make difficult moves across the wall (crux) and reach left to a small quartz hold in a

corner. Make one more tricky move to stand on a ledge, exit left and continue up the fine slab above, first leftwards before going back right to finish at a block on top of the cliff.

Courthouse Blues   40m   E3 6a **. David Wood, Nathan Adam. 2 Oct 2020
Start 5m down and right of *Scooby Dubh*, at an overhung left-facing corner. Boulder steeply up the corner and pull out right (hard) onto the stepped slab, then climb this to a steep wall and crack. Go up the crack with the help of the left edge of the wall, continuing steeply through the overlap above (crux) to join the slab of *Scooby Dubh* and the corner alcove (*Scooby Dubh* belay). Climb directly out of the corner by a steep crack before heading right to finish up a quartz slab.

ARISAIG, Loch Beag Slab (NM 72636 83671):

A pleasant south-facing slab with a steeper west wall. The slab is near a house; please avoid going near the house. Park as for Gleann Màma Slabs and walk down to the track leading south west towards Ard nam Buth house. Take the track under the railway arches but turn left before the house to respect their privacy. Walk over the slight hill to reach the shore, then follow the shore right (west) to the slab. 15 minutes.

Blue Waters   14m   E1 5a **. Steve Kennedy, Cynthia Grindley, Colin Moody. 25 Apr 2021.
Fairly serious climbing on the west wall, start round left of the slab at a pointed block and clamber up to the left-facing corner. Move up the corner then go left to the rib, place two dubious crucial small cams then climb the hanging corner.

Kittyshaw   12m   H.Severe 4b **. Steve Kennedy, Colin Moody, Cynthia Grindley. 7 Feb 2021.
Start 1m right of the left edge of the slab. Climb up just right of the edge.

The Vennel   12m   VS 4b **. Steve Kennedy, Colin Moody, Cynthia Grindley. 7 Feb 2021.
Start 2m right of *Kittyshaw*. Climb the crack up slightly right to a hole with plants. Follow the ramps up left under small overlaps to finish near Kittyshaw.

Flashwood   10m   Severe *. Colin Moody, Cynthia Grindley, Steve Kennedy. 25 Apr 2021.
Climb the slab left of the heather crack.

Blair and Kersland   10m   VS 4b **. Colin Moody, Cynthia Grindley. 9 Feb 2021.
Right of the heather crack is a niche a third of the way up the slab. Climb into the left side of the niche, move up left and continue to the top.

Lynn   10m   VS 5a *. Steve Kennedy, Cynthia Grindley, Colin Moody. 17 Apr 2021.
Climb into the right side of the niche, thin. Continue up.

Doggartland   12m   Severe. Colin Moody, Cynthia Grindley. 9 Feb 2021.
Climb to a small ledge then follow the crack up leftwards using the ramp on the left for feet.

Mount Pleasant 12m Severe. Colin Moody, Cynthia Grindley. 9 Feb 2021.
Start just right of *Doggartland* and climb to the same small ledge. Climb slightly rightwards past a small triangular overhang.

Highfield 12m Severe. Colin Moody, Cynthia Grindley, Steve Kennedy. 7 Feb 2021.
The crack left of *The Den*.

The Den 12m Severe. Colin Moody, Cynthia Grindley, Steve Kennedy. 7 Feb 2021.
The right-hand crack on the slab.

ARISAIG, Clach a' Phrionnsa (Prince's Stone):
In keeping with the rest of the crag, A4 stainless steel glue-ins have been used to equip the following routes.

Squeezing It Out 6m 7a. Jamie Skelton, Morag Eagleson 21 Apr 2021.
A good but very short route on the far left side of the upper wall.

HRH 15m 6c+ *. Jamie Skelton, Rory Brown. 10 Apr 2021.
The furthest line left on the West Wall. Climb *Jugobite* to the third bolt, break left and continue up the overhanging wall on positive holds.

Jugobite 14m 6c **. Morag Eagleson, Jamie Skelton. 19 Mar 2021.
Start as for the first bolt of *The Last Stand* but continue up the groove and overhanging wall above.

Picnic Pleaser 16m 7a *. Jamie Skelton, Morag Eagleson. 19 Mar 2021.
Takes the obvious cave-like feature just right of the West Wall. Pull a few burly moves through the overhang and gain the groove above. Finish on the left side of the arête as for *Jacobite Rebel*.

Honnold of the North 11m 6b+ *. Jamie Skelton, Rory Brown 10 Apr 2021.
Jamie Skelton, Rory Brown. 10 Apr 2021.
A direct line up the right hand side of the slab on the South Wall. Struggle over the large roof-overlap and follow *Jacobite Trail* up the pleasant slab above.

Dogs on the Run 8m 6c *. Morag Eagleson, Jamie Skelton. 21 Apr 2021.
A very steep left-trending line on the right side of the upper wall.

All the Way Over There? 18m 6c+ **. Jamie Skelton, Morag Eagleson. 21 Apr 2021.
Go up *Pass the Snacks* to the good holds on the arête and move round the corner to finish up *Dogs on the Run*.

Pass the Snacks 12m 6b+. Morag Eagleson, Jamie Skelton. 21 Apr 2021.
Climb past the overlap on *Jacobite Gold*. Move out left onto the slab and stretch to good holds near the arête. A steep pull gains the *Jacobite Gold* anchors.

Jugzilla 11m 6c *. Jamie Skelton, Morag Eagleson. 21 Apr 2021.
The very steep tiered arête on the right side of the buttress.

The Bonnie Traverse 30m 6a**. Nathan Adam, David Wood. 21 Apr 2021.
A left-to-right girdle of the crag, starting up *Jacobite Rebel*. Climb past the first two bolts to a large break, traverse right into the niche of *Highland Laddie* and struggle out of this. Make a slight descending traverse to reach the slab and continue along the thin horizontal crack. Go round under the nose on the arête and up to the lower-off on *Young Pretender*. (Bring across second and abseil from here.) Take some medium cams for the crux on *Highland Laddie*, but the rest borrows bolts from the other routes.

MALLAIG CRAGS, Creag Mhic a' Ghille-Chaim:

Shakey Ridge 30m VS 4c. Alastair Rose, Matt Rowbottom. 26 Jun 2020.
The narrow ridge or buttress to the right of the main buttress containing *Edge of Perfection*. Step onto the sharp ridge and follow this up to an awkward move to gain a scoop. Continue up the buttress to a thread belay. (Topo provided.)

ARISAIG, Borrodale Crags:

A number of crags have been developed a short distance east of Borrodale Beach, close to the headland of Rubha Aird Ghamhsgail, to provide a collection of worthwhile sport and trad routes. The crags are generally south-east to south-west-facing, quick drying, and offer routes in the lower to middle grades. There is also some decent bouldering nearby. The vitrified fort on the headland may also be of interest.

Approach from the parking area at Druimindarroch (NM 6858 8442) by the old boathouse (as for Black Rock). Parking is limited at the boathouse but additional parking is available close to the A830 junction near the start of the single track road. Wellies are recommended for the approach, which involves a burn crossing. From the boathouse, cross the bay heading south and then follow a well-established path leading left (east) for a few hundred metres before eventually dropping down to the grassland above Borrodale Beach. Just before the shingle beach, cross the Borrodale burn on the left and follow a vague path through ferns to a fence. A prominent boulder (The Gatehouse) will be seen on the left. Continue on the path beyond the boulder via some boggy ground to reach a rocky bay. Approximately 15 minutes.

The Gatehouse (NM 6931 8418):

The prominent west-facing boulder seen on the approach provides a number of good problems above a flat, grassy landing in the V1 to V2 range.

The Bastion (NM 6938 8417):

The prominent projecting buttress overlooking the rocky bay, accessed from some large boulders below. Nice short routes in a beautiful setting. The routes are bolted with the exception of one trad route. Routes described from left to right.

Escape Line 8m V.Diff *. Colin Moody, Cynthia Grindley, Steve Kennedy. 18 Oct 2020.
The wide crack on the left side.

Booby Trap 9m 6b+ **. Steve Kennedy, Cynthia Grindley, Colin Moody. 18 Oct 2020.
The steep wall immediately right of the wide crack. Pulling into a sloping alcove provides the crux.

Baker Street 9m 6b **. Steve Kennedy, Cynthia Grindley, Colin Moody. 18 Oct 2020.
The strenuous wall to the right of *Booby Trap*. Start by moving rightwards before stepping left at the top of the right-facing corner.

Czech Connection 10m 5b **. Steve Kennedy, Cynthia Grindley, Colin Moody. 13 Oct 2020.
The slabby front face. Pull onto the slab from the left side and climb directly via an overlap, trying to avoid the edges.

Fortress Wall (NM 6938 8417):

The steep, quartz-studded wall situated a short distance right of The Bastion. Approach either by walking beyond the rocky bay and accessing the right end of the crag by a clearing or, alternatively, through the trees from The Bastion if climbing there first. Some minor seepage occurs after a prolonged wet spell. The base rises in steps from the right end and an intriguing hole will be seen about mid-way leading into a small cave under the crag. Routes are described from left to right.

Carry on Spying 9m 6a *. Steve Kennedy, Cynthia Grindley, Colin Moody. 23 Sep 2020.
Start on the far left, just left of a deep crack at a small platform. Move up rightwards (or climb the crack directly) below a bulge into a sloping recess. From the recess, traverse hard left below the wall to gain the left edge and finish out right.

Guerrilla Warfare 12m 6b+ **, Steve Kennedy, Colin Moody. 1 Oct 2020.
Start below the thin crackline 3m right of *Carry on Spying*. Generously bolted. Climb the crack to some quartz and continue to a small roof. Step left into the recess (joining *Carry on Spying*) and move up to its apex. Make awkward moves out right onto the edge and finish out rightwards.

Spirit of Resistance 12m 6a+ **. Steve Kennedy, Cynthia Grindley. 20 Aug 2019.
Climb a crack 2m right of *Guerrilla Warfare*, trending right to the prominent quartz shield and make an awkward move into the groove above. Continue to the small roof, step left, climb the slab above to the headwall and finish out right.

Special Operations 13m 6a+ **. Steve Kennedy, Cynthia Grindley. 26 August 2019.
Start 2m right of the hole at a raised platform. Pull out rightwards and follow a fault line, joining a left-trending crack. Finish up cracks just right of a small roof.

Ministry of Ungentlemanly Warfare 14m 6a *. Steve Kennedy, Cynthia Grindley. 26 Aug 2019.
Start at the lowest point on the right side, close to the tree. Flat holds lead via a crack to a quartz shield near the edge. Climb the wall and groove above.

Wire Crag (NM 6956 8415):

A pleasant sea cliff located a few hundred metres east of Fortress Wall comprising a short west-facing wall and the main south-east-facing wall just beyond to the east. It has pleasant trad routes in the easier grades in a fine setting, and dries quickly. Mostly tree belays at the top, situated well back. A spare rope is useful.

Approach as for The Bastion and Fortress Wall. Leave the path about 40m after the clearing leading to Fortress Wall, pass between two bent trees and continue eastwards across broken ground to reach the shore. Continue a short distance along the shore, crossing an old wire fence, and drop into the bay containing the West Wall. Routes are described from left to right.

West Wall:
The first crag reached on the approach, situated at the back of a small rocky bay. Descend by scrambling on either side.

Flush Cutter   8m   VS 4c **, Steve Kennedy, Cynthia Grindley. 1 Apr 2021.
Start on the left side of a block. Move onto the block, climb the wall directly above to join the left slanting crack running up the middle.

Clipper   8m   VS 4b *. Steve Kennedy, Cynthia Grindley. 1 Apr 2021.
Start on the right side of the block. Climb up and rightwards to a prominent edge which is followed, moving leftwards to finish.

Main Wall:
Reached by scrambling along the shore from West Wall. The easiest descent is on the left side.

Top Rung   11m   V.Diff *. Lucy Prins, Phill Thompson, Steve Kennedy. 27 March 2021.
Near the left end is a grassy corner above a large pointed block. Climb the left side of the block, move right then climb the cracked slab just left of the corner.

Tripwire   10m   Severe **. Steve Kennedy, Cynthia Grindley, Colin Moody. 21 Mar 2021.
The arête on the left, just right of a pointed block. Climb on right side, palming off the edge.

Multicore   10m   Severe *. Steve Kennedy, Cynthia Grindley, Colin Moody. 21 Mar 2021.
The prominent crack on the slabby wall immediately right of *Tripwire*, finishing directly.

Barbed   10m   V.Diff. Colin Moody, Cynthia Grindley, Steve Kennedy. 21 Mar 2021.
The left-facing, grassy corner 2m right of *Multicore*. Finish by pulling into thin parallel cracks on the left wall.

Touch of Stile   10m   Severe *, Lucy Prins, Phill Thompson, Steve Kennedy. 7 Nov 2020.
Follows the cracks on the wall immediately right of *Barbed*, staying close to the edge and finishing just right of a V-groove.

Razor 10m VS 4c *. Colin Moody, Cynthia Grindley, Steve Kennedy. 21 Mar 2021.
The next line of cracks about 2m right of *Touch of Stile*, starting up a short corner and finishing directly (crux).

Electron 10m Severe **. Steve Kennedy, Cynthia Grindley, Colin Moody. 21 Mar 2021.
The pale wall right of *Razor*. Start just right of a short corner and climb the wall directly with a sloping finish.

Heliax 12m V.Diff *. Steve Kennedy, Cynthia Grindley, Colin Moody. 18 Oct 2020.
The wall 2m right of *Electron* between two grooves, moving rightwards at the top above a block.

Snare 10m Severe *. Colin Moody, Cynthia Grindley, Steve Kennedy. 18 Oct 2020.
The edge on the far right above the narrow gully. Start just left of the edge below a small overhang. Make a few moves then pull steeply right onto the edge, which is followed directly, finishing up a hanging slab.

The Fin:
Below the right side of the main wall is a projecting rocky fin containing the following routes.

Full Metal Post 8m Diff *. Phill Thompson, Steve Kennedy, Lucy Prins. 27 Mar 2021.
Takes a line starting just right of the left edge up the smoothest area of rock.

Five Bars 8m V.Diff *. Lucy Prins, Phill Thompson, Steve Kennedy. 27 Mar 2021.
The compact area of slab on the far right side.

A pleasant Moderate route climbs the cracked slab between the above routes.

On the far right of the Main Wall is a section of clean slab above and right of a prominent pointed flake. Descend via blocks on the left.

Neutral 12m V.Diff *. Steve Kennedy, Lucy Prins, Phill Thompson. 27 Mar 2021.
Climb the right side of the flake, bridge the flared groove, and finish up the cracked slab above.

Earth 12m Severe *. Steve Kennedy, Cynthia Grindley, Colin Moody. 21 Mar 2021.
The slab to the right, starting at the lowest point. Climb rightwards towards the right edge, then up the slab.

GLEN ROY, Eigh-shruth Geal (NN 31908 90741):
This south-east-facing cliff is the most obvious crag in the area, and can be easily seen on the left when nearing the end of the Glen Roy road. It is comprised of

gneiss and lies at an altitude of 490m. Although small, it has some good rock climbs and a brilliant outlook. Park below the crag at a good layby on the right, just beyond a left-hand turn and passing place. Follow vague paths directly up the hillside to the crag – allow 40 minutes. (Topo provided.)

Natural Selection 25m VS 4c *. Nathan Adam, Garry Campbell. 18 Jun 2020.
Start one metre left of *Darwin's Delight* at a left-leaning crack. Climb this on good holds to a tiny ledge and the base of a longer crack in the slab above. Go up this with interest to the top.

Darwin's Delight 25m VS 4c **. Morag Eagleson, Jamie Skelton. 14 Jun 2020.
Good crack-climbing splitting the middle of the buttress.

Parallel Roads 25m E1 5b **. Jamie Skelton, Morag Eagleson. 14 Jun 2020.
Right of *Darwin's Delight* is a slightly wider crack. Climb this until forced onto the slab for a couple thin moves to gain the first horizontal break. The wall above can then be climbed, finishing just right of the perched block. (Nathan Adams notes that instead of going left at the top and then back right, it is possible to climb more directly at the top section. Both finishes are marked on the topo).

Parallel Roads, Direct Start 25m E3 5b *. Jamie Skelton, Morag Eagleson. 14 Jun 2020.
Climb directly up the slab via off-angle crimps and smears with no runners. The route can be made more friendly by some side-runners in either of the adjacent lines.

Cap Deigh (NN 3234 9124):
This south-east-facing gneiss crag sits high above the glen at the very top of an area of short slabs and boulders at an altitude of 550m. It lies 800m further along and 50m higher on the hill than Eigh-shruth Geal. The area is easily located on the left when reaching the end of the Glen Roy road. The nature of the rock means that cams are a necessity and the routes are not overly well protected. Park just before the wooden bridge that crosses the River Roy. Walk up the hillside and through the jumble of small slabs to the crag. Allow about an hour.

Little Iceberg 6m Moderate *. Morag Eagleson. 14 Jun 2020.
A pleasant solo up the disjointed cracks on the far right of the buttress. finishing on a good ledge.

Ice and Echoes 12m H.Severe 4b. Jamie Skelton, Morag Eagleson. 14 Jun 2020.
On the right side of the buttress lies a hanging crack, just right of *Ninth Mile*. Climb the lower slabs and tackle the crack head-on.

Ninth Mile 12m Severe 4a *. Morag Eagleson, Jamie Skelton. 14 Jun 2020.
A good route up the middle of the buttress. climbing just right of the central bulge before stepping back left (crux) and on to the top.

Braeroy Cowboy 12m Severe. Morag Eagleson, Jamie Skelton. 14 Jun 2020.
Left of the central bulge is a vague right-trending crack-line. It is bold but straightforward.

Darwin's Rest 10m Moderate. Jamie Skelton. 14 Jun 2020.
The rib at the left end of the crag.

BINNEIN SHUAS, Western Sector, Blaeberry Wall:
Rattle that Lock 25m H.Severe 4c. Michael Barnard. 18 Apr 2020.
This lies on the shorter wall at the top of the descent gully, up and left from
Cowberry Wall etc. Start up steep quartzy cracks just right of a big black groove.
Continue up to the black arête above then step round left and go up, stepping back
right to gain the upper slab. Finish up and right.

Western Sector, The Fortress:
Behind Enemy Lines 35m E2 5c ***. John Aisthorpe and Masa Sakano. 27 Sep
2020.
This is the well-protected crack to the right of *Delayed Attack*, climbed in three
pitches. Start up the easy ramp, placing gear in the wall to the left, and belay below
the vertical finger-crack (Camalot 3 or 4). Climb the finger-crack and then follow
the widening crack left. Keep traversing left until some jugs, then climb straight
up the unlikely overhang above, shared with *Farewell to Arms*. Good holds and
gear are found in hidden breaks. Belay on the ledge under the roof (Camalot 3
and many small to hand-sized cams are useful). Finish with a very short and easy
traverse-pitch leftward, to The Garden.

CREAGAN SOILLEIR, Right-Hand Crag, Middle Tier:
Kara 10m E3 6a/b. Jamie Skelton. 16 Jul 2020.
The overhanging crack just right of *Eternal Optimist* as mentioned in 'Highland
Outcrops South'. Moving around the bulge to gain the slab is the crux. Climbed
solo after top-rope practice.

GERGASK CRAIG (NN 612 953):
These two SSE-facing crags on the hillside west of Creagan Soilleir are visible
on the approach to that venue and could be combined with it. Instead of heading
across the bigger field, stay on the track which crosses the river and soon after
that head up the hillside. Go through the gate in the deer fence and continue up to
the crags. 20 minutes.

Scarface Claw 25m E2 5b. Michael Barnard, Alan Hill. 14 Sep 2020.
A worthwhile route up the centre of the left-hand crag; nice and clean through the
crux. Go up to the steep section of wall and climb through this on small holds
(bold). Move out left (cam), then back up right (bold) to a heather-pulling top-
out.

The next three routes lie on the right-hand crag.

Twitter and the Monkey Man 25m E2 5b *. Michael Barnard, Alan Hill. 14 Sep
2020.
On the left side of the crag and lying just right of a rowan tree is a short corner
with a flake-crack on its right wall; start below and just right of this. Move up to
climb the cracked corner, hand traverse the top of the flake and step right again
to pull onto the short steeper wall above using a quartzy hold (crux). Continue up
to the headwall then move out right to finish as for *Gorilla Warfare*.

Dave MacLeod on the FA of Mind Riot (E10,7a), Binnein Shuas. See SMCJ 2020, p.188.
Photo: Ed Nind.

Gorilla Warfare 20m E1 5b **. Michael Barnard, Alan Hill. 14 Sep 2020.
This route ascends a flake-crack through the steep central section of the crag. Go up to the flake line and climb it strenuously to pull into the groove above at a protruding block (keyed-in). Climb past the small aspen and continue up the crack above to a heathery finish.

Diddling Baboons 20m HVS 4c *. Alan Hill, Michael Barnard. 14 Sep 2020.
Start near the right end of the crag, directly below a crack in the upper half of the wall. Climb up into a groove, then step right and go boldly up the wall to reach the crack. Climb the crack, then move out right and up to the rowan.

DIRC MHÒR, Shining Wall:
Here's Johnny! 40m E3 6a ***. Tim Miller, Jamie Skelton. 26 Jun 2020.
An excellent route that follows the right-slanting crag in the lower centre of the face. When the crack peters out, follow holds back left into the centre of the face before finishing up right in a slight recess the same as *Nature's Raw*.

The White Tower:
Where's Johnny? 15m H.Severe 4b *. Jamie Skelton, Tim Miller. 26 Jun 2020.
The prominent crack to the right of *White Tower*.

CREAG DUBH, Bedtime Buttress:
Peigneur 25m E1 5b *. Gary Latter, Karen Latter. 6 Sep 2020.
A good direct line cutting through Negligee. Start 3m left of that route, at square cut groove. Up this to pull through roof at good crack to join *Negligee* on the ledge. Step right and climb directly up the wall (left of *Quickie*) to finish on ledge directly beneath the abseil block.

Bedtime Buttress, Upper Tier:
Contagion 15m E5 6b **. Gary Latter. 2 Oct 2020.
The direct finish to *Subjugation*. Follow that route to the good break where it escapes left. Move up past large sidepull, then using sidepull on right make hard moves to good break, finishing at two short cracks onto ledge.

Lower Right Wall:
Just in Thyme 40m E1 5b *. James Thacker, Kris Hill. 2 Jul 2020.
Start 4 metres left of *Man on Fire* and climb directly to an area of quartz. Step up and right to move up to a small overlap (thread) which is passed using an obvious V-slot, before climbing the green headwall close to a thin vertical crack.

KINGUSSIE CRAG, Upper Tier:
Hold and Seek 8m E3 5c *. Nicholas Wylie. 20 Jul 2020.
Start up the wall just to the right of *Finale*. Surmount the overlap and move on up until holding two small blocks above the quartz pockets. Reach out right to a disguised mono-pocket and use this to step up rightwards into a blind hold before continuing on good holds to the second peg of *Leftover*. From the peg, cut back up and left to finish. This route is effectively a right-hand finish to Steve Grosdanoff's route (*SMCJ* 2016) which goes straight up this wall after the overlap with a removed peg to protect it.

STAC GORM, Frank Sinatra Walls:
Callum Johnson notes that he cleaned *Vagabond Direct*, *My Way* and *Let's be Frank*. He thought *Let's be Frank* is worth E5 for the on-sight.

STRATHSPEY, Wee Farletter:
Short and Sweet 5m Diff. Alfred Roth, James Miller. 10 Jan 2021.
At the far left end of the crag there is an obvious line of good holds leading to a small ledge where the only protection of the route is available. Place it and then finish the climb, topping out to trees above.

I Put Coffee In My Coffee 10m V.Diff. James Miller, Jack Reade. 11 Jan 2021.About 5m right of the start for the routes leading to the small roof there are some ledges. Step up and left onto the wall, working towards a
small corner on the left at half-height. From here go directly up the wall above. Small nuts are and shallow cam placements.

Far Right Matt 12m Moderate. Matthew Bridgewater, James Miller. 12 Jan 2021.
At the far right end of the crag are some large ledges. Step up and right before taking a groove which trends slightly leftwards towards the top. Slings useful.

DUNTELCHAIG, Dracula Buttress:
Peter Herd notes that *Wolfman* is E6 6b ** and now clean.

Over the Top Crags:
Peter Herd notes that *Frothing Farmers* and *Fire Burnished Night* are both 6m long, merit one star and are worth a visit in their own right. The following route lies to the right.

Hyperborea 7m E7 7a ***. Peter Herd. 28 Apr 2021.
The beautiful leaning wall. The route was pre-practised. Pads were used to protect the first 5m (Font 7C crux) whereafter a small cam slot provides runner protection. Probably Font 7c+ overall and possible to highball as the landing is flat.

Knife Wound Wall:
Takoba 12m E3 5c *. Peter Herd, Murdoch Jamieson. May 2020.
The diagonal crack in the buttress right of Knife Wound Wall gives a fine and quick-drying pitch protected by small or medium cams. Start on the right side of the wall and climb boldly to start of the crack, finishing up the groove and slab. The anchor is far back so it is worth carrying some spare rope to pre-rig.

CONAGLEANN, Raven's Roost:
Callum Johnson notes that the upper slab sections of *The Raven*, *Croak* and *Toad's Arête* were cleaned on lead, so are now more amenable. He moved right at the heather ledge to finish at the abseil point above The Falcon, which is still in good condition having been replaced in 2019. He found the description for The Falcon slightly misleading and it could be better described as: 'Climb the flake to half height where a traverse left can be made to gain a vague groove right of toads arête, climb this to join that route near its top.' Probably E3 5b because of thin gear and the potential for a big swing.

BEN NEVIS, AONACHS & CREAG MEAGAIDH

BEN NEVIS, CMD Arête Headwall:
Unnamed 70m IV,6. Mark Robson, Simon Richardson. 7 Apr 2021.
The attractive narrow buttress on the right side of the headwall at the head of Coire Leis approximately 100m east of the Grade I slopes leading down from the Càrn Mòr Dearg Arête. The route climbs through a notch to the left of a prominent shark's fin-shaped flake that can be seen on the skyline when looking up from the base.
1. 40m Climb a groove on the left side of the buttress to reach a terrace. Ascend a short wall on the right then move right for 3m below a vertical wall along an awkward sloping shelf. Climb the groove on the left (crux), which leads through the notch to a good stance on the crest left of the shark's fin.
2. 30m Surmount a short wall and climb easily to the top on good blocky holds.

First Platform:
Mavericks 210m V,5. Robin Clothier, Simon Richardson. 20 Jan 2021.
A varied line starting right of *Raeburn's Arête* finishing up the well-defined left-facing corner up and right of the narrow finishing chimney of *Newbigging's 80 Minute Route*.
1. 40m Start approximately 30m right of *Green Hollow Route* directly in line with the prominent ice groove of *Bayonet Route*. Climb a shallow gully to the snow terrace of *Bayonet Route* then trend up and left over snow to a good block belay.
2. 50m Continue directly up to a large block. Surmount this on the left then continue up thinly iced slabs before making a 5m leftward traverse across snowy slabs. Gain a short groove leading to block belay of *Raeburn's Arête*.
3. 40m Move up and left to gain the groove system (third from the right) that leads up to a snow terrace.
4. 40m Continue up the right of two grooves to the crest of the buttress.
5. 40m Finish up grooves and short walls to gain the First Platform (as for *Newbigging's 80 Minute Route*).

Observatory Buttress:
Never-Never Land, Direct Start 40m VI,6. Wojciech Polkowski, Damian Goncerz. 6 Mar 2021.
Start 10m left of *Observatory Buttress* and climb directly up a vertical narrow crack until the original route is reached.

Douglas Boulder:
Stay Home, Save Lives 45m E2 5b *. Alastair Rose, Alistair Docherty. 24 Jun 2020.
The wall left of *Cutlass*. Climb the scramble start to the first belay on *Cutlass*. Pull out left through a small overhang to get established on the face and climb this to the mid-height ledge (possible belay), then carry on up the wall to gain the arête at an obvious blob. Follow this to the top. Low in the grade.

Secondary Tower Ridge:
The Final Fowl 95m IV,6 *. Huw Scott, Nathan Adam. 4 Jan 2021.
On the right wall of *West Gully* is a steep capped chimney that is slightly below the ramp that leads onto the *South-West Ridge* of the Douglas Boulder some 15m

up. Thuggish and well protected on the first pitch and delicate and bold on the second.
1. 30m Easy snow leads to the chimney; climb this and back-and-foot around the roof on good hooks (crux) to reach a ledge. Climb a short corner on the right and trend back left to the spike belay on *Inception*.
2. 45m Go left for 3m to a left-facing corner and climb this to a small bay. Go straight up a wide crack at the back of the bay to reach a prominent arête and climb this (bold) to another ledge, then traverse left to belay below the final easy slopes.
3. 20m Easy ground leads to *Tower Ridge*.

Badlands 150m VI,5. Simon Richardson, Robin Clothier. 17 Jan 2021.
The line of grooves between *Italian Right-Hand* and *Bydand*. Start midway between *Italian Climb* and *The Chute*.
1. 30m Move up to the steep wall above and make a rising traverse left on snow to belay on a prominent block. Spike runner above.
2. 60m Step left and climb the slabby groove bounding the left side of the wall to its halfway point where a hidden sloping shelf cuts across the wall to the right. Traverse across this (bold and delicate) for 10m to gain a narrow icefall. Climb this then move up and left across the snowfield above towards a prominent slanting groove. Belay on a good block 5m up and left.
3. 50m Step back right into the slanting groove and follow it to a small triangular snowfield. Take the right-hand of two grooves and climb to an overhung niche. Step left and make an awkward move into the final V-groove that leads to the top of the buttress. Either continue up *Italian Climb* or abseil the line of ascent.

That Untravelled World 300m IV,4. Robin Clothier, Simon Richardson. 22 Feb 2021.
An interesting expedition up the rarely visited area of cliff between *The Chute* and *Broad Gully*. Similar in style and standard to *The White Line*, but more serious as it finishes halfway up *Tower Ridge*. Start 30m below the top of *Garadh Gully* just right of the icefall taken by the *Indirect Finish*.
1. 40m Climb an icy corner then trend up and left up steep snow to belay on a rock island below the broad squat buttress above.
2. 70m Move left around the island and make a steep move into the left facing corner running up the buttress. Climb this to its top and belay on the right.
3 and 4. 100m Continue up snow to the next band and climb mixed ground to gain the sloping snow shelf of Secondary Tower Ridge. Belay below the steep headwall above.
5. 40m Move right for 20m to gain the prominent weakness cutting through the headwall. Zigzag left then right to a belay below a small roof on the right.
6. 50m Step back left and climb the icefall and its wide continuation gully to the top of the Little Tower on *Tower Ridge*.

Into The Wild 340m V,5. Simon Richardson, Mark Robson. 5 Mar 2021.
A parallel line left of *That Untravelled World*. Excellent climbing – more sustained and a little more difficult. Start 60m up *Garadh Gully* below the *Indirect Finish*.
1. 60m Climb the initial ice groove of the Indirect Finish then trend up and left to belay on the rock island of *That Untravelled World*.
2. 50m Traverse 5m left to gain the left-facing corner system running up the left flank of the squat buttress. Climb this, taking interesting mixed grooves to belay on the right.

3. 60m Continue up the line on icy slabs, cross a terrace and continue up the ice smear in the buttress above.

4 and 5. 70m Move right and climb an icy groove in the wall above. Continue up snow crossing the snow shelf of Secondary Tower Ridge and belay below the steep headwall.

6. 40m Move right for 25m and climb the right side of the prominent icy weakness taken by *That Untravelled World*. Climb ice grooves parallel and right to gain the belay below a small roof.

7. 60m Continue up and right up a steep icy slab and finish up a series of corners to gain the top of the Little Tower.

Pinnacle Buttress of the Tower:

Stringfellow, Auf Wiedersein Pet Variation 50m VI,5. Will Rowland, Jim Cooper. 5 Mar 2021.

From the belay below the crux corner (pitch 4) of *Stringfellow*, move to the left end of the ledge and step around onto the slab. Climb boldly to a block and then continue up right into an iced groove to regain the line of *Stringfellow*.

South Trident Buttress, Upper Tier:

Lost Horizon 80m III,4. Simon Richardson, Richard Bentley. 26 Feb 2021.

The two-tiered gully system bounding the left side of the steep section of the Upper Tier. Start 30m down and left of the icefall of *Shangri La* where a broad gully cuts through a subsidiary lower tier.

1. 40m Climb the gully (often iced), cross the left-trending ramp of *Number Four Gully Buttress* and ascend the continuation gully above to a ledge.

2. 40m Continue up the gully for 15m and finish up snow slopes on the left.

Shangri La 90m V,5. Robin Clothier, Simon Richardson.12 Jan 2021.

The short bulging icefall left of *Poseidon Groove*.

1. 50m Climb a shallow icy groove to a ledge. Move up and right to the icefall and climb it on its right side. Exit into a short gully and climb to the snowfield above.

2. 40m Continue in the same line up a shallow groove in the left flank of the easier-angled buttress above. Exit left below the steep wall at the top to finish (as for *Titan Cracks*).

Central Trident Buttress:

Metamorphosis 100m IX,10. Tim Miller, Jamie Skelton. 10 Dec 2020.

A complete ascent of the summer line. The 2009 winter ascent started via the *Cranium* start to *Heidbanger*. Climbed ground-up over multiple attempts, with the successful ascent being made on the third day.

1. 45m Start at an overhanging crack in a steep wall to the right of the *Cranium* crack. The short corner above leads to a slab; climb this direct initially, pass an overlap, then make balancy moves right and up to the base of a corner. Climb this, then follow easier short corners to a big ledge belay as for the top of the second pitch of the *Cranium* start. From here, the route follows the 2009 line of ascent.

2. 30m Make bold thin moves up and right to gain the flake-line. Struggle to the top of the huge flake, then launch up the blank-looking wall above, leading to easier ground.

3. 15m Climb to easier ground. (Topo provided.)

Number Five Gully Buttress:
High Five 120m III. Simon Richardson. 3 Mar 2021.
A central line up the mixed tier directly above Number Five Gully Buttress. Start from the foot of the terrace that slants right from *Number Five Gully* defining the top left boundary of Number Five Gully Buttress. Move up into the corner on the left side of a distinctive narrow buttress and climb an icefall to easier ground. Move right, continue up snow and exit up a short wide gully to gain the summit of Càrn Dearg.

North Face of Castle Ridge:
The Last Ridge 190m IV,4. Simon Richardson, Robin Clothier. 9 Feb 2021.
The well-defined right edge of the gully of *La Petite*.
1. 55m Start 5m right of *La Petite* and climb ice (steep snow on the first ascent) to gain a short left-facing corner after 20m. Climb this (or the rib on the left) to gain the easier-angled broad crest above. Follow this to belay on a terrace.
2 and 3. 70m Continue up the crest via a series of short grooves and belay just beyond where the gully of *Le Mechant* comes in from the right.
4. 50m Step right around the crest and climb diagonally up and right to join a prominent left-facing corner. Continue up this to where the angle eases and a belay on a large block on the left.
5. 15m Easy ground leads to the top.

Of Mice and Men 150m IV,4. Simon Richardson. 31 Jan 2021.
An icy mixed line up the right side of the triangular buttress climbed by *Le Mechant*. Start 40m right of *Le Mechant* and climb a 20m ice pitch to gain a broad ramp slanting right below a steep wall. Cross the wide terrace above and zigzag first left then right through the headwall to a steep exit. Finish up easy-angled mixed ground above.

Midnight Blue 120m V,5. Simon Richardson, Helen Rennard. 23 Jan 2021.
A direct line up the front face of the steep buttress left of *Red Gully*. Start below a right-trending open groove slanting slightly right through the initial tier.
1. 50m Climb the groove to a terrace at the top of the first tier (30m). Trend right and climb a steep short wall to gain a horizontal break leading left for 5m to a prominent block (well seen from below).
2. 45m Continue up the left-slanting groove above (just left of a pronounced rock rib), surmount the wall above and step right around an awkward jutting block to gain easing ground slanting left to a snow bay. Above is a stepped headwall cut by a short gully and topped by a prominent fence post. Enter the gully via a steep step and exit on the right at its top. Belay on the post.
3. 25m Continue up the snow slope above to easier ground and the top.

Cherry Red 120m IV,4. Simon Richardson. 19 Jan 2021.
An ingenious line finding the easiest way up the steep buttress left of *Red Gully*. Climb the broad right-facing corner to the left of *Red Gully* for 20m then break out left onto the steep buttress on the left. Follow a narrow ledge left to where it fades then cut back right on a higher right-trending diagonal ledge. Follow this for 5m then climb up and left to gain a horizontal ledge. Traverse left along this to its end below two parallel V-grooves. (These are separated from the line of *Midnight Blue* by the 'pronounced rock rib'.) Climb the right-hand of the two V-grooves (crux) then slant up left then right to easing ground (junction with

Midnight Blue). Avoid the final headwall by breaking through the final rocks on the left to gain the second of two fence posts and the final snow slope leading to the top of the cliff.

Coire Ghaimhnean:

Paradox Buttress 150m III,4. Simon Richardson, Mark Robson. 14 Apr 2021. The prominent buttress high up on the south side of the corrie. Climb the right fork of *Five Finger Gully* for 130m to the foot of the buttress on the right. This is about 30m above the first step up the narrow groove.

1. 50m Climb a short groove for 5m then traverse right for 5m to join a series of corners running left of the crest. Climb these to their end and continue along a narrow crest to belay below a steep wall.

2. 50m Surmount the wall on excellent holds and continue in the same line to a ledge below a prominent left-facing corner.

3. 50m Climb the corner, and the one above, to exit on an easy-angled ridge. Follow this to the summit plateau.

Mark Robson and Simon Richardson note an ascent of the right fork of *Five Finger Gully* on 14 Apr 2021. It provided 300m of climbing with two steep steps. The difficulty will depend on the amount of snow present, and on this occasion the route was thought to be III,4.

Coire Eoghainn:

Strike While The Iron Is Hot 230m IV,4. Will Rowland, James Cooper. 15 Jan 2021.

Left of the toe of the buttress a vague rib of rock leads to broken ground and a hidden ramp. The route takes a slightly contrived line in what is quite an open face but has plenty of interest and lovely views.

1. 70m Climb the rib.

2. 35m Continue up and left across easy snow to belay at the foot of the hidden ramp.

3. 35m Climb the pleasant ramp and belay at the crest.

4. 50m Trend 10m left then straight up to belay below steep icy rocks.

5. 40m Climb the icy steps direct (easier alternatives possible) to easy ground which leads to more steep icy steps. Climb these by a left-trending rock-ramp and icicle. Belay at a large boulder after 40m and continue up to easier ground. (Topo provided.)

Unnamed 300m IV,4. Simon Richardson, Helen Rennard. 11 Apr 2021.

The central of the three gullies to the right of the central buttress. The difficulty will depend on the amount of ice on the first pitch. On this ascent the steep lower part of the pitch could be bypassed by stepping off the lip of a 5m-high bergschrund, but the icefall above was thin and delicate.

1. 30m Climb the icefall from left to right following a line of short vertical steps.

2. 70m Continue up the snow slope above to the upper icefall.

3. 50m Climb the icefall to its top and belay on blocks on the right.

4. 50m Continue up easier ground to where the angle eases.

5 and 6. Easy snow leads to the Tourist Track at the top of *Gardyloo Gully*.

Sloc nan Uan (NN 172 708):

The centre of this shallow corrie on the east flank of Ben Nevis is cut by the wide

Uan Gully. To its left are two well-defined granite buttresses. Approach from Glen Nevis by crossing Bealach Cumhann and following the south bank of the left branch of Allt Sloc nan Uan.

Blackface Rib 100m   III. Mark Robson, Simon Richardson. 7 Apr 2021.
An enjoyable route up the north-east crest of the left-hand buttress starting at NT 172 707. Low in the grade. Follow the rounded crest for 60m to an easing below a steepening. Climb this directly on the left and continue more easily to the top.

Rosemary 80m   II. Simon Richardson, Mark Robson. 7 Apr 2021.
The triangular buttress immediately left of *Uan Gully.* The right edge is steeper but provides more secure climbing than the lower-angled slabby rock in the centre of the buttress.

Uan Gully 100m   I. Mark Robson, Simon Richardson. 7 Apr 2021.
The wide gully starting from NT 172 708.

MEALL CUMHANN, West Face (NN 177 694):
Asylum Gully 280m   III. Simon Richardson, Robin Clothier. 10 Feb 2021.
A good adventure taking in some interesting scenery. It needs a heavy snowfall to bring it into condition. The entry gully is the summer approach *Druim* and *Croch* on Meall Cumhann Summit Crag. Climb the entry gully (50m) then continue up the slabby corner on the right to the snow slope above (40m). Traverse right below subsidiary rock wall (50m) and move right into the mouth of the gully (50m). Climb the gully for three pitches (130m) to exit on easier ground at the broad col between the two summits of Meall Cumhann.

South-East Face (NN 178 689):
Calluna and Erica 140m   IV,4. Robin Clothier, Simon Richardson. 7 Jan 2021.
This cliff lies on the right flank of the rock spur comprising Meadow Walls and is situated left of Galaxy Buttress. It is cut by a left-to-right fault named *Easy Gully* in the 1954 'Ben Nevis' guidebook. This route takes a direct line up the face, crossing *Easy Gully* at one-third height.
1. 40m Start 50m right of *Easy Gully* and climb a stepped ramp into a depression at one-third height. Step left into *Easy Gully* and climb up to a stance directly under twin chimneys above.
2. 40m Climb the vegetated wall then move right to the left-hand chimney. Climb this on steep turf and belay on a small tree where the angle eases.
3. 60m Continue up and right on a vegetated ramp passing a smooth steep groove near the top to emerge on the rounded crest of the spur. Descend by continuing easily up the spur and contouring round to a grass slope that descends under the cliff.

Easy Gully 150m   II. Will Rowland. 30 Jan 2021.
Climb the gully over several short steps.

MÀM NA GUALAINN (MAMORES), North Face:
Kinlochfossen 300m   V,5 ***. James Laing, Aidan Robinson. 12 Feb 2021.
A superb adventure up the deep chasm (NN 118 629) on the north side of Màm na Gualainn following the watercourse of the Allt Teangaidh na h-Earba. Similar in character to *Rapunzel* on Beinn Fhionnlaidh, and climbed after two weeks of

sub-zero temperatures. Approach via the West Highland Way from Kinlochleven. Just as the chasm comes into view, turn left onto a path signposted 'Loch Leven & North Ballachulish' and cross the Allt na Lairige Mòire. Strike uphill left of the watercourse until flat ground is reached and the chasm can be entered at the point where it deepens. Walk to below the first chimney. (Another easier-looking gully branches off right from here.)

1. 30m Climb the chimney, moving right where it widens at its top. Continue along the river bed to belay at an ice pillar on the left.

2. 60m Walk up to the continuation groove, and climb this via an awkward entry. Easy ground leads to a huge boulder in the middle of the gully. Easy snow now leads up and right for 90m into a bay below a steep icefall with an overhanging right wall. An easier left-hand finish straight up the wide gully awaits.

3. 40m Climb the superb icefall to a snow funnel. Move up this to belay on the right wall (ice hooks useful here in the hairline cracks). A straightforward shallow gully now leads to easy ground and the top in 80m. (Topo provided.)

MULLACH NAN COIREAN, Coire Dearg:

Positive Education 85m III,4. Nathan Adam, Cameron McIlvar. 28 Dec 2020.
This climbs the wide gully just right of the left edge of the crag before it changes direction into the left-hand descent route. Perhaps easier and worth a star with consolidated snow and some ice.

1. 45m Easily up the gully to the first chockstone; surmount this and continue up another steepening to a spike belay on the right.

2. 40m Follow the continuation of the gully to easy ground and the top. (Topo provided.)

Bondage 105m III *. Steve Kennedy, Andy MacDonald. 20 Jan 2021.
To the left of the slabby buttress containing Kick Start and Turf Factory is a deep gully. Left again is a buttress with a left-slanting ramp system, the line of this route.

1. 50m Start near the foot of the gully and climb leftwards to reach the ramp. Follow the upper ramp line until below a wall. Traverse left below the wall to a break, and continue up leftwards to a belay.

2. 55m Straightforward mixed ground leads to a saddle at the top of a gully coming in from the right (possible descent) and the end of the difficulties.

Kick Start 95m IV,5 *. Steve Kennedy, Andy MacDonald. 2 Jan 2021.
The slabby buttress left of *Turf Factory*. Climbed early in the season in thin, icy conditions. Likely to be easier with more ice on the second pitch. A ledge system cuts across the lower part of the buttress.

1. 40m Access to the ledge was gained from the right, starting at a pointed block. Traverse left along the ledge for approx. 25m (passing a thin section) to the base of a small icefall flowing down slabs from the central snowfield.

2. 55m Climb the icefall (crux on thin ice) to reach the snowfield, then head up and right via a rock crevasse to join the finish of *Turf Factory*.

Triple G 80m III *. Nathan Adam. 1 Jan 2021.
The shallow curving gully just left of centre of the crag gives a good turfy route. Start 5m left of *Captain Caveman* below a small shallow chimney. Climb the chimney (tricky but may bank out) and then continue on snow and turf over some steeper steps to the top.

SGÙRR A' MHÀIM, Lag Gorm (NN 159 673):

Bottle Imp Rib 100m II. Simon Richardson. 10 Apr 2021.
The narrow buttress bordering the left side of the easy gully cutting through the right side of the small hanging corrie on the north flank of Sgùrr a' Mhàim. Climb the crest over a series of short steps and walls. (Topo provided.)

AN GARBHANACH, West Face:

Curling Rib 200m III. Simon Richardson. 9 Apr 2021.
The buttress bordering the right side of the broad square-shaped gully starting at NN 186 666. Climb easy ground right of the crest for 30m then take the second ramp cutting left. Break up right 5m before gaining the crest and move up to easier ground. Follow the crest to where it narrows to a sharp ridge. Gain a col and continue up the steepening ridge in an excellent position to the top. (Topo provided.)

West Ridge 80m III. Will Rowland, Jim Cooper. 20 Jan 2021.
This west-facing ridge lies 100m around from the bealach and joins the main scrambly ridge of An Garbhanach.
1. 50m Climb the crest with interest and belay below leftward slanting cracks.
2. 30m Climb the cracks to a huge block. Easy ground leads to the ridge. (Topo provided.)

AN GEARANACH, North Spur:

Above the path from Steall, short north-facing turfy crags are visible. The leftmost of these is most prominent and hidden from view during approach. (Topo provided.)
Hand Me the Drift 70m V,5. Will Rowland, Jim Cooper. 20 Jan 2021.
Right of the toe of the buttress a steep turfy break cuts a way through the steep wall. Start to the left of an easy gully.
1. 30m Climb a steep snowy bay surmounting a rock step. Move right to belay below the steep turfy break.
2. 40m Step on to the wall and climb a grove until it is possible to pull around left to join another turfy groove. Climb straight up and join a blunt turfy arête, continuing airily up to easier ground.

Plan B 70m IV,4. Will Rowland. 23 Jan 2021.
Start up and left of the toe of the buttress. Climb the diagonal shelf trending right and then climb steep turfy steps directly up to belay below a small roof. Move left to join the gully, pass the overlap to reach easier ground leading to the top.

An Cearcallach (NN 191 684):

Straightjacket Gully 140m II. Robin Clothier, Simon Richardson. 4 Feb 2021.
The third gully from the right when approaching from Steall, starting at NN 19139 68385. A well-defined line up a narrow defile, giving straightforward climbing with a few moderate steps. (Topo provided.)

AONACH MÒR, West Face:

Corkscrew Gully 500m I. Mike Dunn, Andrew Moore. 20 Mar 2018.
Many tens of metres left of *Downhill Gully* lies a steeper icefall to the left. The route is named from the twisting entry section. The best finish is the steeper line to right as shown in the topo (provided). Possibly climbed before.

Sgùrr Finnisg-aig:

Simon Powell notes that the first ascent details of *Smoking The White Owl* in 'Ben Nevis Rock and Ice Climbs' are incorrect. 'The first ascent that I am aware of was by Robert and Fiona Kincaid, probably in early winter 1986. But as Alan Kimber´s Cicerone guidebook says, there were quite possibly other ascents before that by staff from Loch Eil and Tulloch not to mention other local climbers. But we can´t be certain of that. According to my diary I first climbed the route solo, alongside Loch Eil staff on a training day, on 24 Feb 1986. I am aware that some other climbers came in later, I think maybe even post-1986, and claimed the route and gave it the owl name. So, Alan's title of *Sgurr Finnisg-aig: Allt na h-Aire Cascade* is probably the most accurate name. Some locals refer to the route as *Finnisgaig Falls*.'

AONACH BEAG, West Face, Teanga Buttress:

The right end of the Lower West Face blends in with the south-west spur of Aonach Beag. These are the first crags seen from Coire Giubhsachan when approaching from Steall. Routes are described from right to left. Broken ground on the right forms a bay but soon gives way to Teanga Buttress, some 40m high. (Topo provided.)

Job and Knock 140m IV,4. Will Rowland. 23 Dec 2020.
This route is on the right side of Teanga Buttress, left of the snow bay and left of the prominent slabby corner.
1. 30m A turfy ramp leads to a series of shallow grooves leading to a 'V' at the top of the buttress.
2. 90m Easy ground is followed up the rib until it is possible to move left below a tower with an obvious chimney. Climb the chimney and chockstone near its top.
3. 10m Climb the chimney to finish.

Crack Fox 155m V,5. Will Rowland, Jim Cooper. 19 Jan 2021.
Left of Teanga Buttress is a steep bay. On the right side of the bay, a steep icy gully leads to a ramp and steep headwall.
1. 40m Climb the gully, pass the chockstone and follow the ramp to the right until it is possible to climb a steep diagonal break to the left.
2. 55m Climb easy ground left then straight up to below a steep gully.
3. 60m Climb the steep gully directly then follow easier ground above to a series of groves on the right side of the tower.

Zig Zag 150m II. Will Rowland. 18 Jan 2021.
At the left end of the bay there are two short ramps leading left.
1. 70m Climb the right-hand ramp which soon zigzags right, steepens and leads to easy ground.
2. 60m Avoid the gully of *Crack Fox* and break out left on pleasant ice and turf to below an arête.
3. 20m Climb the break left of the arête.

GLEN GLOY, Coire Ceirsle Hill:

Desperado 200m II/III 200m. Will Rowland. 4 Feb 2021.
The first falls seen above the road and the most western of the cascades on the hillside.

LOCH TARFF AREA, Allt Sputach (NH 452 094):

Mind the Drop Falls 90m II/III. Will Rowland, Mike Bauermeister. 1 Feb 2021.
Climb the falls to a tree belay 60m. Follow the easy ramp up left for 30m. Descend steeply through trees.

CREAG MEAGAIDH, Moy Corrie, Hidden Buttress (NN 4138 8650):

The narrow section of cliff on the east flank of Creag Meagaidh's south ridge overlooking Moy Corrie. Lying in a depression, it is hidden from many viewpoints and the cornice can be large. Approach via the forest track as for the *East Ridge* of Sgùrr a' Charoachain then climb the west flank of the Creag Meagaidh's south ridge to the crest. Access the crag by descending 50m from NN 4108 8598 and contouring 600m NNE.

Butterfly Rib 250m II. Simon Richardson, Mark Robson. 15 Mar 2021.
Climb the skyline rib starting from NN 4149 8656 in five pitches. Straightforward go-as-you-please climbing up turfy grooves and snow patches. The top section is disappointingly easy. The cornice was passed on the right.

Backstroke Gully 150m III,4. Simon Richardson, Mark Robson. 15 Mar 2021.
The prominent gully defining the left edge of the buttress was climbed in three pitches. The third pitch over a chockstone is the crux the difficulty depending on the amount of ice present on the left wall. The easy ridge above leads to the cornice.

CÀRN LIATH, Coire Dubh:

Skyrush 60m II. Simon Richardson. 6 Mar 2021
The first buttress left of the prominent central rib of *Stormrunner*. Start up easy mixed ground, climb a right-facing ramp and finish up steep mixed ground and snow right of the crest to the top. (Topo provided.)

Lightning Racer 70m II. Simon Richardson. 6 Mar 2021
The first buttress right of the prominent central rib of *Stormrunner*. Climb the surprisingly easy turfy depression running up the front face. (Topo provided.)

Coire a' Bhèin (NN 504 925):

The following two routes are situated to the right of the wide central gully starting at NN 5038 9251. (Topo provided.)

Batwing 80m III. Simon Richardson. 6 Mar 2021
The buttress on the right flank of the wide central gully. Start at NN 5035 9248 and climb easy mixed ground to the gain the narrow gully cutting through the upper tier. Climb this with interest to the top. Low in the grade.

Batflyer 70m II. Simon Richardson. 6 Mar 2021
The buttress 80m right of *Batwing* starting from a flat platform at NN 5027 9257. Move up to a right-facing ramp and zigzag to the top.

GLEN COE

BUACHAILLE ETIVE MÒR, SE Face, Central Blackmount Buttress:
Froth Corner 55m VI,7 **. Alistair Docherty, Matt Rowbottom. 9 Jan 2021.
Immediately right of the 'undercut cave' on *The Chasm to Crowberry Traverse* is a snow bay with a steep buttress on the left cut by a prominent right-facing corner.
1. 20m Climb the right-facing corner. This is sustained and well protected with good hooks and turf. Large gear is useful for the top section.
2. 35m Climb the shattered continuation groove for 10m to where it is possible to traverse right on a ledge. From the right end of the ledge go up a corner and groove with lots of turf and shattered rock. Belay on a large terrace from a massive spike. Note: Sling stuck in thread near top of pitch is incorrectly threaded and should not be clipped. Abseil descent. (Topo provided.)

Lockdown X 50m IV,6. Alistair Docherty, Matt Rowbottom. 4 Jan 2021.
The gully 10m right of *Froth Corner*.
1. 20m Climb the snow gully to an underhung chockstone. Step right around it and belay 5m further up on the left.
2. 30m Move right up the main gully line passing another chockstone to enter a bay. Exit the bay up a steep 5m-high cracked wall on the left (crux). Spike belay 10m above this. From here, either abseil off or continue up *Lady's Gully Left Fork* in three pitches to the top. (Topo provided.)

Central Buttress, North Face:
Appauling 90m VI,7 *. Jamie Skelton, Nicky Brierley. 3 Jan 2021.
Follow the line of the summer route. Unlike summer, the turfy nature of the climb made it a rather good winter route.

AONACH DUBH, East Face, Terrace Face:
Alarming Ineptitude 45m H.Severe 4a *. Dom Scott, Danny Carden. 31 May 2021.
1. 25m. Start left of *Terrace Arête*, midway between the toe of the buttress and the arête itself. Trend slightly leftwards over bold, gentle ground to reach the right end of the slanting mid-height ledge. Belay at a jammed flake.
2. 20m. 4a. Enter the black crack above from the right, with limited gear initially, then climb it directly up the middle of the steep headwall. Possibly climbed before.

East Face, Far Eastern Buttress:
Broken Gully 80m III *. A.Spink, M.Evans. 8 Apr 2018.
The gully bounding the left side of the crag. The difficulty and length vary with build-up. It is graded for cold, lean conditions but may be 50m of Grade I/II with deep well-consolidated snow. Climb a snow ramp to the base of the corner-gully. Climb the corner over icy bulges to a block belay and finish more easily above.

North Face, Upper Face:
Kev Howett notes that 'Glen Coe Rock and Ice Climbs' attributes the first ascent of *Repossessed* to Martin Crocker in 1995. It was actually climbed by Kev Howett and Mark Charlton in May 1984. They never wrote it up as it is simply a slightly alternative pitch 2 to *Eldorado*, but it is the more obvious line and apparently gives better climbing.

Midnight Express   70m   VI,6. Will Rowland, Peter Staves. 30 Jan 2021.
Climb *Midnight Special* for three pitches. Continue up pitch 4 of *Midnight Special* until it is possible to break out on to the left wall following turfy ramps and corners trending left. Rejoin *Midnight Special* for the final steepening. (Topo provided.)

West Face, No.2 Gully Buttress:
Rose Innominate   60m   IX,9. Dave Macleod, Helen Rennard, Andy Nelson. 2 Jan 2021.
Follow the summer line.

West Face, No.3 Gully Buttress:
R2D2   140m   V,6 **. Mike Pescod, Tommy Kelly. 1 Feb 2018.
Climb the chimney on the left side of the buttress to a terrace, then the steep chimney above and step right to an excellent belay ledge (30m). Climb the short corner at the right end of the ledge, move up and right into a narrowing groove and climb this to the top of the lower tier (30m). Walk back to the upper buttress (10m). In the centre of the upper tier, gain a left-sloping ramp, and climb the steep groove straight up to a belay ledge (20m). Follow the groove directly above to the top (50m). (Topo provided.)

C3PO   140m   V,6 **. Mike Pescod, Ali Rose. 29 Dec 2020.
Start just right of the toe of the buttress and climb the right-hand groove to gain a small bay (35m). Climb up and left to the groove on the left-hand skyline, then make steep moves to an awkward pull up and right (25m). Walk back to the upper buttress and finish up *R2D2*. (Topo provided.)

H5N8   45m   IV,5 *. Mike Mason, Huw Scott. 25 Jan 2021.
The deep straight chimney near the right end of the crag. Either finish up the top pitches of *R2D2/C3P0* or descend from the middle ledge on the left. (Topo provided.)

STOB COIRE NAM BEITH:
Tarbh Uisge   65m   IX,8. Dave MacLeod, Helen Rennard. 29 Dec 2020.
Follow the summer line.

Church Door Buttress:
Kev Howett notes that the first (crux) pitch of *Temple of Doom* was climbed by himself and Mark Charlton on sight in May 1984. They failed to complete the route, which was climbed by Hamilton, Anderson and Livingstone later that July.

New Age Raiders   70m   IX,9 *. Greg Boswell, Callum Johnson. 22 Dec 2020.
Climbs steep ground to the right of *The Ninety-Five Theses* and before the easing in angle of the crag. The route aims for a line of corners and grooves to a roof at 20m and then follows the continuation groove.
1. 25m Start down and left of the roof. Climb the overhanging wall to gain a small niche on the left, make committing steep pulls up the rib to gain a sloping ramp then ledge on the left, step rightwards to another sloping ledge, then right again to gain a right facing corner. Climb steeply to gain the small ledge below the roof.
2. 45m Step right off the belay and pull round the roof into the continuation groove. Follow the groove for 15m before climbing icy ground to where the angle eases and so to the top.

False Penance 105m IX,10. Greg Boswell, Graham McGrath, Hamish Frost.
28 Dec 2020.
Takes the overhanging triangular niche on the right side of the steep and imposing
left wall of the *Un Poco Loco* buttress area.
1. 30m Start at the foot of the steep slabby wall to the left of the offwidth corner,
directly below the hanging steep niche. Climb up right then back left on the slab
to gain a small ledge at the base of the corner-niche. Climb this with increasing
difficulty to eventually pull right to gain another corner. Continue for a few more
metres to gain a semi-hanging belay position in a niche.
2. 35m Step hard right off the belay around the arête and then continue up a dirty
corner to gain a position under the roof. Make hard moves right to gain the ledge
and continue directly to the top of the great arch.
3. 40m Finish as for *Un Poco Loco* up the small corner-chimney to easier ground.

GLEN COE MINOR CRAGS, The Bendy:
Roaring Silence, Direct Start 6m E4 5c. Andy Nelson. 7 Jul 2020.
A more logical direct start to the existing route. From the big boulder move up to
the left end of the lowest ledge. Climb bouldery moves passing a small crack
(micro cam) to mantel onto the ledge at 6m. Continue up the existing route (E4
6a).

Sportline 18m 7b **. Andy Nelson, Brian Bathurst. 22 Jul 2020.
A direct sport route utilising the slender prow between *Roaring Silence* and
Quietly Burning. From the glue-in just above the pool, climb directly (first bolt
requires stick clip – placed high to lessen corrosion from spray) up to the 6-metre
ledge. Crimpy balance moves lead to the steeper prow. Side-pulls on the right and
crimpy holds on the left allow a long reach to better holds including a suspect
spike on the right. Shake out before the easier but pumpy headwall.

CREAG BHÀN, East Face:
South Gully 300m II. Andrew Moore, Tony Westcott, Paul McWhinney. 24 Feb
2018.
The upper east face of Creag Bhàn is characterised by an area of broken buttresses,
on both sides of which there are gullies. This route takes the left-hand of these to
finish on the summit. (Topo provided.)

SGÙRR NA H-ULAIDH, North Face:
Ghost Walk 450m I/II. Andrew Moore. 24 Feb 2018.
Climb slopes left of *West Gully* to gain the obvious traversing line. As the line
becomes less obvious, climb a distinct, parallel-sided gully (as shown in the topo)
or continue up mixed ground on the left to gain the summer slopes. (Topo
provided.)

SGÒRR A' CHOISE, Science Crag (NN 071 545):
This cliff lies at an altitude of 360m on the north-west flank of Sgòrr a' Choise
and is 75 minutes' walk from Ballachulish. Routes are 18 to 20m long. Belays are
situated well back so 50m ropes are recommended. Nine routes have been climbed
from VS to E4 by Brian Bathurst, Cecile Limousin and Al Docherty. No individual
descriptions were provided but a topo was supplied.

KENTALLEN, Allt Dhonnachaidh Mhic Roib:

Robs Falls 70m IV,4. Andy Spink. 1 Mar 2018.
Park on the A828 north-east of Kentallen at NH 01570 58550. Follow the NW-facing burn via short falls to steep 40m-high cascade (Grade IV) at NH 01807 58121. Continue up the burn to a second fall or steep ice slab (30m III) at NH 01852 58022.

GLEN ETIVE, Stob Coir' an Albannaich, Glen Ceitlein Slabs:

The Magical Mystery Whore 300m III,4. Andy Spink, Scott Kirkhope; Simon Verspeak, Stevie Boyle. 4 Mar 2018.
Walk past *The Whores Apron* to a large obvious deep gully. Follow this via a series of snow gullies, ice slabs and steep short ice pitches of lengths between 20m and 50m. Approx nine pitches. Entertainment and exploration at its best. The two teams climbed side by side on the first ascent.

GARBH BHEINN, Bealach Buttress:

Unnamed 95m IV,4. Will Rowland, Jim Cooper. 3 Jan 2021.
1. 50m Left of *Ordinary Route* easy snow leads to a ledge breaking out right below a steep wall. At the end of the ledge step up to join a turfy fault which leads to a belay below a notch.
2. 45m. Climb a turfy corner straight up to the arête. (Topo provided.)

South Wall, Upper Tier:

Bayonet 35m V,6 *. Jamie Skelton, Nicky Brierley. 31 Dec 2020.
As for summer route.
Sala 40m VII/VIII,9 **. Jamie Skelton, Nicky Brierley. 31 Dec 2020.
Climbed in one pitch by using the shallow left-facing corner to gain the top of the pinnacle below the route proper.

The Peeler 45m VII,8 **. Jamie Skelton, Helen Rennard. 15 Jan 2021.
Climb *Sgian Dubh* to reach the top of the pinnacle below the main pitch. This can be skipped by shorter alternatives further left.

Menghini 45m VII 8 ***. Tim Miller, Jamie Skelton. 27 Dec 2020.
Start at the shallow left-facing corner at the far left end of the top tier. Climb the corner to a big ledge. Climb the crack-line directly above in one sustained pitch to the top of the crag.

Fathomless 55m VII,7. Jamie Skelton, Matt Glenn. 3 Dec 2020.
1. 20m Climb the steep but reasonably well protected first pitch of *Excalibur*.
2. 35m Gain the long ledge above the belay, move right along the ledge and around a big block to gain a turfy groove that can be followed to the top of the crag with more ease.

Chib 60m VI,6. Jamie Skelton, Morag Eagleson. 24 Jan 2021.
Once at the top of the short corner the route becomes slabby. Make a delicate traverse left for 5m, move right around a steep wall and continue up to the belay of *Fathomless/Excalibur*. Finish up pitch 2 of *Fathomless*.

Great Ridge:

Will Rowland notes a solo ascent of the first two pitches of *Great Gully* followed by a left traverse and finish up the *Great Ridge* on 12 Feb 2021.

Pinnacle Ridge:

The Dogs of War 130m VI,7. Simon Richardson, Robin Clothier. 30 Jan 2021.
A natural winter line taking the prominent hanging ramp on the left side of the Upper Pinnacle. Good climbing and steeper than it looks.
1. 55m Start left of the toe of the buttress and climb up and right to the corner of the ramp and the retaining wall. Climb a short chimney and continue up the corner to a good ledge below a steep 5m wall.
2. 25m Gain a slanting flake-crack from a short overhanging groove on the right and pull through on to the slab above (crux). Continue up the corner to a good stance below a vertical corner.
3. 50m Step left and climb a slabby groove to regain the corner above. Continue to where the corner steepens and make an awkward step right around an edge to gain a right-facing corner that leads to easier ground. A further ropelength leads to the summit of the pinnacle. (Topo provided.)

Alastair Matthewson notes a winter ascent of *Pinnacle Ridge* with Andy Hume on 10 Apr 1994. This predates the previously recorded 2010 ascent.

North-East Buttress:

Open Secret 280m III/IV. A.Matthewson, A.Veitch. 10 Feb 2021.
A natural winter line up the right bounding corner of the slabbier section of the Second Tier (not the massive corner further right). Climb the First Tier by a short deep-cut gully on the right (70m). Climb an icy gully-groove above, avoiding a steep nose on the left (45m). Go up easier snow with a short step halfway (55m). Climb a left-facing corner-chimney, moving left at top. Harder in lean conditions (50m). Continue straight up to Second Terrace (60m). Finish up Route I to the summit of the buttress. Route length is for climbing to junction with Route I. (Topo provided.)

Hidden Agenda 280m IV,4 **. Steve Kennedy, Andy MacDonald. 10 Feb 2021.
The chimney-groove situated on the upper part of the right-hand section of the second tier, well right of the left-facing corner in the centre and not far left of the curving corner-gully (*Troll Gate*). An easy gully leads through the middle of first tier to the terrace below the second tier, almost directly below the central left-facing corner.
1. 55m. Start on the right side of the terrace, close to the lowest point of the second tier and follow a right-trending snowy ramp. Continue up icy slabs before trending back left to belay near the base of the chimney-groove.
2. 50m Make thrutchy moves up an initial groove, leading into the chimney which is climbed to a belay on the right. A fine pitch.
3. 55m Continue up the more open fault line to an apparent cul de sac below a steep wall.
4. 60m Delicate slabby moves lead out right below the wall to easier ground. Continue up to the large snow-bay below the third tier.
5. 60m Climb the open groove which breaches the third tier directly above.

Troll Gate   275m   II **. Steve Kennedy, Andy MacDonald. 6 Feb 2021.
The left-facing curving corner-gully system bounding the right side of the buttress. A fine mountaineering excursion passing through some impressive rock scenery. This is possibly the *Unnamed Gully* described in the existing guidebook, descended in July 1939 by Barber and Lomas. *Too Cave to be Brave* (*SMCJ* 2006) appears to start much further right and join this route at about mid-height.
1.60m Climb the initial gully, exiting by a through route, and follow the open gully above.
2. and 3. 105m Climb easily to a terrace and continue up the corner-groove system on the left in two pitches to a fine belay in a large cave.

STOB COIRE A' CHEARCAILL, Charcoal Buttress:
Twelve Pointer   120m   VI,6. Will Rowland, Garry Campbell. 6 Feb 2021.
1. 50m To the right of the toe of the buttress lies a steep chimney. Climb the chimney and exit left. Continue left, up corner and then back right underneath a roof. Belay at a black wall.
2. 40m Move left and climb a vague rib. Continue across easy snow to a short corner which leads to the final headwall on the crest of the buttress.
3. 30m Climb the steep obvious break, delicately traverse right then climb the edge straight to the top. (Topo provided.)

Fill In Gully   50m   I/II. Simon Richardson. 3 Jan 2021.
The gully starting at NN 018 726 that lies left of the left-hand gully mentioned in 'Glen Coe Rock and Ice Climbs'. (Topo provided.)

South-East Buttress:
East Top Buttress   80m   III. Simon Richardson. 3 Jan 2021.
Approximately 800m south-east of the main summit is a slabby buttress leading up to the 730m south-east top (NN 022 721). Climb a shallow gully in the crest of the buttress for 30m to reach a diagonal terrace. Follow this right for 20m until it is possible to cut through the wall above via a left-slanting groove. Continue up easier ground to the top. (Topo provided.)

Cheeky Bastard   100m   IV,6. Will Rowland, Connor Holdsworth. 5 Feb 2021.
To the right of East Top Buttress there are two gullies with a buttress between. Climb the buttress and belay below a steepening. Awkwardly, climb the short wall. Easy ground leads to a headwall with a corner system on the right side. Climb this, exit right and belay on the plateau. (Topo provided.)

SGÙRR GHIUBHSACHAIN, Jacobite Buttress:
The Uprising   90m   IV,5 *. Neil Adams, Kevin Hall. 29 Dec 2020.
The main corner/groove system starting near the toe of the buttress. Start just left of the lowest rocks and climb a slabby groove up right. Climb the corner, with deviations out right for gear where needed, to a belay where it meets steeper ground (35m). Climb the steep corner on the left (crux) then head straight up more broken ground. A short final groove leads to easy ground.

The Young Pretender   75m   IV,6 **. Kevin Hall, Neil Adams. 29 Dec 2020.
The wide fault-line running diagonally up the right side of the crag is trickier than it looks! Start at protruding blocks at the base of the fault. Follow easy turfy ground to pass under a huge chockstone, then exit the cul-de-sac beyond via the

right wall. Belay where the gully forks (40m). Climb the left fork (strenuous but well protected) to easier ground, then finish up the short final groove common with *The Uprising*.

White Rose 70m III,4 *. Ali Rose. 27 Jan 2021.
The obvious chockstoned gully in the steep wall up and right of *Bestial Devotion*. Climb the gully and surmount the chockstone. Continue up and right (ignoring the easy finish) to a col behind a pinnacle before continuing up the buttress above.

Flora 120m II *. Ali Rose. 27 Jan 2021.
The obvious ramp leading up and right below the steep wall. Could be a grade easier with consolidated snow.

North-North-West Face:
Chasing Wild Geese 100m III *. Neil Adams, Helen Rennard. 8 Jan 2021.
The slim gully on the NNW face of Sgùrr Ghiubhsachain. After the initial steepening, bear left at a fork up another steep section. Where this opens out above, make an awkward step up right to reach easier ground. (Topo provided.)

MAOL ODHAR, Coire nam Frithallt, Mad Man's Crag (NM 882 585):
The following routes are located on the north-east facing buttress to the north of Voodoo Buttress on the east of the north spur leading to Meall a' Bhainaiche. The buttress contains a prominent gully on the left side. Approach as for Voodoo Buttress by way of the hydro road then take an ascending line rightwards, crossing a fence before the buttress. It is possible to descend back to the foot of the buttress by a gully on the right. Routes are described left to right. (Topo provided.)

Black Sabbath 210m II *. Steve Kennedy, Andy MacDonald. 24 Jan 2021.
The ridge bounding the left side of the prominent gully on the left side of the buttress. Start near the foot of the gully and follow a ramp on the right side of the ridge leading to a steep wall and flake (25m). Traverse left onto the broad ridge and climb to a belay on the edge overlooking the gully (55m). Move up leftwards and continue up mixed ground in three pitches to finish (130m).

All the President's Men 140m V,4. Robin Clothier, Simon Richardson. 7 Feb 2021.
An attempt to find a line up the slabs on the left side of the crag. Start by climbing the gully bordering the left side of the cliff for 50m to where a sloping shelf cuts back right into the cliff.
1. 45m Move right to the end of the shelf and climb a steep turf wall for 20m to easier ground. Move left along a ramp and then back right and belay at a rock outcrop.
2. 45m Continue up and right under the smooth diamond-shaped wall to underneath the 'moustache' pitch of *Electroshock*. Climb directly up to the moustache and traverse left to its far end.
3. 50m Trend diagonally up and left up to the right side of the headwall and climb through it on good holds to the top.

Mad Men Wandering 150m III,4. Robin Clothier, Simon Richardson. 8 Jan 2021.
A natural line of weakness and the easiest route on the cliff. Start just right of the deep gully defining the left end of the crag.

1. 40m Climb grooves before trending right to belay on a ledge under a prominent overhanging wall on the left.
2. 60m Step right and climb an open gully to reach the left end of a prominent terrace rising right across the cliff. Follow this for 30m and belay below a shallow gully cutting through the rock band above.
3. 50m Climb the gully, cross a terrace and finish up a steep rocky gully on the left.

Electroshock   160m   V,5. Simon Richardson, Robin Clothier. 27 Jan 2021.
Surprisingly good climbing up the area of cliff left of centre. Start midway between *Mad Men Wandering* and the *Jaws of Doom* where a ramp cuts left across the initial wall.
1. 55m Climb the ramp (more awkward than it looks) then continue up easier ground to a steep wall.
2. 50m Move left then up the wall on well-spaced turf then trend right and up to a terrace.
3. 50m Continue up to below a smooth diamond-shaped wall and traverse right below this to where it is possible to make a 10m traverse left along a turf moustache until above the diagonal wall. Move up and right to easier ground in a wide depression.
4. 15m Continue easily up the depression to the top.

Jaws of Doom   160m   VI,6. Simon Richardson, Robin Clothier. 28 Jan 2021.
An excellent route up the central gully line. Start below a well-defined ominous-looking chimney (the 'jaws of doom') cutting through the initial steep wall.
1. 55m Climb the chimney with interest and exit steeply onto easier ground. Continue up to the next wall and climb a left-slanting groove to a good stance on the left.
2. 55m Move right and climb the steep wall on well-spaced blobs of turf and continue up easier ground to the terrace below the headwall.
3. 50m Zigzag up diagonal shelves between the gully exits of *Mad Men Wandering* and *Lobotomy Essential*. Another good pitch.

Lobotomy Essential   160m   IV,5. Simon Richardson, Robin Clothier. 25 Jan 2021.
Good climbing up the broad buttress right of centre. From the bottom of the cliff a prominent V-slot can be seen cutting the crest of the buttress.
1. 50m Start under a triangular roof and climb a steep left-slanting ramp to easier ground. Continue left then take a right-trending ramp that leads to a good belay under the V-slot.
2. 50m Step left onto a slab and climb up into a niche under the slot. Pull out right to easier ground. Continue up then right to gain a left-slanting ramp that leads to a terrace.
3. 45m Trend left to gain a prominent right-angled gully cutting through the headwall. Belay just before it narrows
4. 15m Continue over a bulge with interest to the top.

Blood Rites   160m   III,4 *. Steve Kennedy, Andy MacDonald. 30 Jan 2021.
A natural line rising diagonally left to right across the buttress from near the foot of the gully on the left. The first and third pitches correspond to the lines of *Mad Men Wandering* and *Lobotomy Essential*.

1. 45m Start just inside the gully and climb heather-filled grooves on the right wall to a notch and block belay.

2. 55m Continue rightwards following an obvious ledge system until below a small bay.

3. 60m Move up into the bay, aiming for a V-shaped groove on the skyline. A short step leads into the groove which provides a nice finish.

Wild Woman 190m IV,4. Robin Clothier, Simon Richardson. 1 Feb 2021.
The broad gully-recess line on the right side of the cliff.

1. 40m Climb up and left to the barrier wall.

2. 60m Move up left through the barrier (awkward) and continue up the square-cut gully-recess above to its top.

3. 50m Continue up easier ground to a final terrace and belay on a large tooth-like feature above.

4. 40m Zigzag up the wall above on interesting mixed ground to the top.

CREACH BHEINN, Zeppelin Face:

Kashmir 95m IV,5 **. Steve Kennedy, Andy MacDonald. 8 Jan 2021.
A fine, sustained route following the slim groove-corner line on the left side of the slab taken by *Good Times Bad Times* (immediately right of the central left-facing corner). Frozen turf essential. A ledge leads up leftwards (from the initial short left-facing corner of *Bring it on Home*) below a wall to a short, slanting corner.

1. 45m Climb the short corner and continue up the corner-groove system above to a headwall. A short right traverse below the wall leads to a block belay at the foot of a large snowy bay.

2. 50m Continue up the left side of the bay and follow a left-slanting trough in the upper wall to reach easier ground.

Good Times Bad Times 105m IV,5 **. Steve Kennedy, Andy MacDonald. 4 Jan 2021.
This route takes a line up the slab left of the prominent left-facing corner on the far right followed by *Bring it on Home*. Start at the foot of a slab forming the left wall of a short left-facing corner (the first pitch of *Bring it on Home*).

1. 35m Climb the left edge of the slab (thin), move rightwards then up a groove to reach the base of a further groove (right of a small overlap on the slab).

2. 45m Continue directly up the groove system to reach a snowy bay. A narrow hanging ramp on the right wall leads to a block belay.

3. 25m Finish up easy mixed ground.

AN T-SLAT-BHEINN, Coire Rèidh (NM 788 782):

Smooth Rider 200m III. Simon Richardson. 4 Jan 2021.
The north-east face of An t-Slat-bheinn is cut by three well-defined fault lines. This route takes the buttress between the first and second fault (from the left). Approach by descending the diagonal rake from the Sgùrr na Bà Glaise – Druim Fiaclach ridge at NM 786 781. Follow the buttress directly, mainly near the right edge, and exit up a short wide gully cutting through the final headwall. (Topo provided.)

SOUTHERN HIGHLANDS

CRUACH ARDRAIN, Meall Dhamh:
The Sicilian   90m   IV,4 **. Marco Limonci, Danny Church, Orazio Lo Tauro. 9 Feb 2021.
This route is located at the far southern end of the ridge forming Meall Dhamh and lies on its east face. At the last large boulders at the foot of the ridge, continue for a further 500m south where a large bowl will come into view with a number of lines draining into it. On the right-hand side of the bowl there is a large overhanging crag. The route climbs the centre of the bowl directly behind a small outcrop. Start at NN 39982 21676.
1. 60m Move up and right, through a small gap to the foot of a steep icefall. It is possible to go either left or right at about the same grade. Climb up the left side until it eases and reach the base of another slightly less steep icefall.
2. 20m At this point it is possible to go easily left and to the top, but more elegantly continue up the icefall until a short wall bars the way. Move left then up to finish on easy ground. (Topo provided.)

CREAG MAC RÀNAICH, Uan Dubh Slab (NN 545 250):
Approach up Glen Kendrum and at the bealach with Meall an t-Seallaidh head north-east up steep slopes to reach the Uan Dubh slab near the summit. The crag is clean, well featured and has three friendly climbs in a spectacular position with a nice grassy base. (Topo provided.)

Stone Voices   7m   MVS 4b *. Alastair MacColl, Angus MacColl. 3 Jun 2020.
The left-hand line.
No Great Mischief   7m   VS 4b *. Alastair MacColl, Angus MacColl. 3 Jun 2020.
The middle of the three routes on the slab.

Not While The Giro   7m   MVS 4b *. Alastair MacColl, Angus MacColl. 3 Jun 2020.
The third and most right-hand climb of the three on the Uan Dubh slab.

BEINN SHEASGARNAICH, Coire Sheasgarnaich:
Stuart MacFarlane and Robin Clothier repeated *King of the Jungle* on 6 Dec 2020, taking a more direct line at the start of the third pitch. Unlike the first ascent that was climbed in very snowy conditions, they found good cracks for protection and rated the climb IV,4. (Topo provided.)

MEALL NAN TÀRMACHAN, Creag an Lochain:
Frosty Peat   80m   I/II. Rosie Rothwell, Joe Barlow. 2 Jan 2021.
The route climbs the broad buttress 500m south of Arrow Buttress at NN596391. Start at the lowest point of the buttress on its northern side. Climb turfy steps and grooves to the left of a small tree to gain the broad right edge. Turn a steep wall on the right and belay at the small tree. Continue up easier ground on the right side to pass a small outcrop on the right. (Topo provided.)

MEALL A' CHOIRE LÈITH, Coire Bàn:
Hexellent   70m   II. Rosie Rothwell, Joe Barlow. 4 Jan 2020.
The gully on the far left-hand side of the crag.
1. 40m Climb the gully, passing steeper steps at the bottom. Good rock belay

possible on the left wall of the gully.
2. 30m Finish up the gully to the top. (Topo provided.)

Ban Buttress 80m III. Joe Barlow, Rosie Rothwell. 4 Jan 2020.
Start at the base of an icy turfy groove below and left of a tree 60m right of *Hexellent*.
1. 50m Climb the groove to a large ledge below a steep rock wall. Move left and climb turfy steps to ledge above. Climb up turfy steps to gain a short icefall. Climb this to belay on the right under the capping roof of the steep buttress above.
2. 30m Move right along the wide snowy ledge until under two grooves on the left. On this ascent the right-hand turfy groove was climbed, although the left-hand icy groove offers an alternative. Finish up the short gully above to a good rock belay. (Topo provided.)

MEALL GHAORDAIDH, Coire Laoghain:
Yellow Peril 275m II. Willie Jeffrey, Anne Craig. 4 Jan 2021.
Start 50m left of *The Lyons in Winter* in a straightforward shallow gully. Continue up until it veers slightly right through a small buttress where it narrows. (Topo provided.)

W.H.O.Han Whitewash 80m II. Willie Jeffrey, Paul Morris. 30 Jan 2021.
Start 15m left of *A Wee One*. Steepish start followed by easy slopes with small ice steps above. (Topo provided.)

Desmond's Dilemma 100m III. Paul Morris, Willie Jeffrey. 2 Jan 2021.
Start on the buttress at the head of the corrie which Des Rubens likened to the Great Tower on *Tower Ridge* (*SMCJ* 2013). A shallow groove leads to an open slope and belay. Follow the ever steepening mossy corner to a crux at the top.

Willie Jeffrey notes that *A Wee One* is 80m long not 60m as described in *SMCJ* 2013.

CREAG AN TULABHAIN, North Face:
The following two routes provided good climbing with multiple short ice sections, though in heavier snow conditions they could bank out and become Grade I. It is uncertain how they relate to the unnamed Grade I gully previously recorded in the corrie. (Topo provided.)

V Gully East 200m II *. Freddie Crowley, Jamie Grant. 1 Feb 2021.
The eastern gully of the pair that start in the same place. This one is not as straight but is deeper cut and has more interest.
1. 50m Straightforward climbing through a choice of narrows to belay on the right-hand side of the gully.
2. 60m Overcome the short ice and turf section and continue up to belay on the left-hand side of the gully below the crux steepening.
3. 50m Climb the ice direct and onto easier ground.
4. 40mb Cut up and right from near the top of the gully over two more short ice and turf sections to belay at the top of the crag.

V Gully West 170m II *. Freddie Crowley, Zoe Thornton. 24 Jan 2021.
The obvious dead straight gully – the western of two that start from the same place.

1. 50m Climb past two steep icy steps (could be banked out in heavy conditions) and up easy ground to belay at a small tree on the right wall.
2. 60m Easy ground to another icy steepening. Belay 10m past this, again on the right.
3. 60m Continue on to the top. If corniced, it should be passable on the right.

STÙC AN LOCHAIN, Coire an Lochain:

Cat Gully 200m I. Craig Gudmundsson, Jim McFarlane. 31 Jan 2021.
The obvious left-leaning diagonal gully behind the lochan.

Vaccinator 90m IV,4 **. Duncan Helm, Alex Urquhart-Taylor. 30 Jan 2021.
Ascend *Cat Gully* for about 50m until you come to an icefall on the right-hand side of the gully. Climb the icefall in three pitches with ice belays. (Topo provided.)

The Cat's Tale 180m III. Duncan Helm, Alex Urquhart-Taylor. 4 Jan 2021.
Start at the icefall about 40m right of *Cat Gully*. Climb up, either following the icefall, or the turfy ground left of the icefall. At about 100m, follow the ice up and left up a small gully, then continue up avoiding any rock walls on the left. Very limited protection with most belays being in turf or ice. 60m ropes useful. Climbed in early season conditions. Later in the season the icefall may improve, making gear more straightforward to arrange.

BEINN EACH, Bealach nan Cabar Crags (NN 602 164):

The following two routes are located on the right-hand of three small buttresses at Bealach nan Cabar on the ridge between Beinn Each and Stùc a Chroin. (Topo provided.)

Obh! Obh! 15m Severe 4a *. Alastair MacColl, Dominic Acland. 17 Aug 2020.
Climb directly up the obvious twin cracks in the centre of the buttress.

Slender Loris 15m VS 4c. Dominic Acland, Alastair MacColl. 17 Aug 2020.
Start up the small slab to the left of the obvious twin cracks of *Obh! Obh!* and trend left, following a small crack to finish over the obvious bulge to the left.

BEN VORLICH, South Face:

End Of The Rope 240m III,4 *. Sebastian Wolfrum, Douglas Fransson Lee. 25 Jan 2021.
The route climbs the left rib on the south face of Ben Vorlich, well left of *Door Step Route* (a winter version of *Central Rib*).
1. 60m Start at the right end of the lowest point of the rib. Climb a left-slanting gully-groove on turf, which steepens towards the top, and over a short vertical step to easier ground. Trend up and further left to a sling belay on a large block.
2. 60m Climb mostly easier ground following grooves and short steps to a good belay on a large block.
3. 60m Continue upwards, trending right, towards the high point of the rib through steeper grooves. In front of a broad broken wall turn right and climb a steep corner on the right of this wall. Continue to a belay at another wall directly above.
4 60m Climb an overhanging chimney up and right from the belay (crux) and continue via grooves towards the top. Climb a final rock wall and belay on a rock

spike above. From here, 80m of easy-angled snow leads directly to the summit of Ben Vorlich. (Topo provided.)

I Can See My House From Here 150m IV,4. James Seaman, Andreas Höhn. 23 Feb 2020.
A full description of the winter ascent of *South Face, Right-Hand Rib* (see p. 361 of 'Highland Scrambles South') that was reported in *SMCJ* 2020 follows below. The route takes the easiest way up the rib using the obvious weak points of the rib, predominantly systems of snowed-up rocky corners, turf and frozen cracks. Approach from the Loch Earn car park using the walkers' path. Continue over the summit and the connecting ridge, to the south-east summit. Descend on grassy and bouldery slopes down and right to the bottom of a rib, which in the summer marks the start of the *Right-Hand Rib* scramble. The bottom has a clearly identifiable flat ledge at an altitude of 850m.
1. 25m Climb a system of steepening corners to a small sheltered ledge.
2. 45m From the ledge go up a short steps onto a narrowed arête, then trend right up to a block belay under a steep overhanging wall.
3. 25m From the belay head left, up the corner with delicate feet but good hooks (crux, but well protected) then traverse right on a small inclined ledge and upwards on the right side of the steepening ridge. Anchor on a small, sheltered plateau with big boulders.
4. 40m The start of pitch 4 is 10m left of the previous belay on a big and flat ledge. From the belay go straight up the central rocky corner then left on a ledge towards a gully and up the exposed block and turf steps to a last belay on the narrowing, but flattening rib. Finish up open slopes to gain the summit ridge.

BEN CHONZIE, Càrn Chòis:
Nippy Sweetie (*SMCJ* 2016) was climbed in 2001 and named *Summit Gully*. A revised description follows:

Summit Gully 120m II. Angus Armstrong, Kevin Howett. 20 Jan 2001.
Climb the deep slot gully in the centre of the crag that slants right to left. It is not visible on the approach until directly below. Easy climbing leads into a V-gully and a chockstone. Pass it on the left and finish up easy slopes to the top. (Topo provided.)

Sieging the Battlements (*SMCJ* 2002) takes the full height of the buttress to the right of *Summit Gully*. A revised description follows:

Sieging the Battlements 120m IV,5. Angus Armstrong, Kevin Howett. 20 Jan 2001.
At the base of *Summit Gully* is an obvious icefall in the right wall, finishing on a ledge system below the upper rocks. Climb lower easy ice to a belay below the icefall. Climb the steep ice to small ice ledges at half-height. The vertical upper wall is split by a body-sized icicle leading to easier ground and a belay in a small outcrop. Continue up the line of least resistance more easily to the top. (Topo provided.)

Creag na Gaoith (NN 781 315):
At the head of the Glen 1.5km past Loch Turret lies the small Lochan Uaine. The track from the east side of the dam ends at the lochan and a faint boggy path heads

up to a small col. This is the easiest route to the summit of Ben Chonzie from the glen. Just to the left of the small col lies Creag na Gaoith. It is characterised by a central section of steep walls interspersed with heather ledges, a recess at its right end containing a waterfall and a big icicle, and three small gullies at the left-hand side containing ice most winters. Routes are described from left to right. (Topos provided.)

Unnamed 20m II. A.Todd. 6 Jan 2002.
An icefall left of the three gullies on the left side of the face. Short but steep.

Bored Witless 60m III. K.Howett, A.Armstrong, A.Todd, Roy A.N.Other. 6 Jan 2002.
The leftmost of the three ice gullies on the left side of the face. Climb easily up the lower ice to belay below a steep section running up left of the main gully line. This upper fall gives a continues pitch of steepish ice.

Unnamed, Right Branch 60m II. A.Todd (solo), Roy A.N.Other, Kevin Howett, Angus Armstrong. 6 Jan 2002.
The central of the three gullies. From below the main icefall, take the appealing slim ramp-corner cutting out rightwards, to finish up a hidden gully cutting back left.

An Angus Adventure 60m IV,5. K.Howett, A.Armstrong. 3 Jan 2002.
The furthest right and most prominent of the three gullies at the left side of the wall.
1. 30m Climb the easy lower slabby fall to underneath the vertical pillar. Climb this directly into the bay above and a large block belay.
2. 30m Climb the upper fall by its left edge.

Lockdown Grooves 100m III,4 *. Craig Gudmundsson, Stuart McKeggie. 30 Jan 2021.
Start just left of the toe of the buttress (NN 780 314). Climb the obvious turfy groove to crest of buttress, then follow this easily to block belay on left. Climb short awkward corner above to easier ground.

Unnamed 2 60m IV,4. Roy A.N. Other, K.Howett, A.Armstrong, A.Todd. 6 Jan 2002.
The slim icefall in the bay on the right of the crag containing the vertical ice pillar.
1. 30m Climb easy ice to under the fall.
2. 30m Follow the fall with a near-vertical section at the top.

Unnamed 3 25m VI,5. A.Todd, K.Howett. 17 Jan 2010.
The ice pillar direct.

Essential Fun 20m III,4 *. Stuart McKeggie, Craig Gudmundsson. 30 Jan 2021.
Approach as for *Unnamed 3*. At the belay stance gain the icefall on the left and head towards the furthest corner. Make an awkward move to the right to gain mixed ground and easier terrain.

Biorach a' Mheannain (NN 784 316):
To the right of the small col mentioned in the approach to Creag na Gaoith are the large broken buttresses of this outlier hill sitting above the Mòine Bheag. There

are two distinctive gullies here, both of which have been climbed at Grade I/II (Neville Holmes, winter 2000).

MEALL DUBH, Coire Cruinn:

First Ice 60m III/IV. Duncan Helm, Alex Urquhart-Taylor. 23 Jan 2021.
The prominent icefall on the short wall left of the previous routes. (Topo provided.)

BEN LOMOND, Coire a' Bhàthaich, Pioneers' A Buttress:

Break Dance 40m IV,5 *. Sam Wainwright, Sebastian Wolfrum. 5 Dec 2020.
This route lies on the rightmost buttress in the corrie, which was originally named A Buttress (see *SMCJ* January 1901). Subsequent routes climbed in the corrie have confused the location of A Buttress, hence the Pioneers' A Buttress nomenclature above. Start on the left side of the buttress just right of a small cave. Climb the open turfy groove to a short crack in the left wall, then continue trending left towards a tower, which is climbed steeply on the right, after which short walls lead to the top. (Topo provided.)

THE BRACK, Upper Tier:

End Of The Line 155m V,7. Ole Kemi, Stuart McFarlane. 4 Jan 2021.
1. 30m Climb *Elephant Gully* and belay above the first chockstone.
2. 20m Step down and follow a large ledge until it ends.
3. 20m From the turf ledge above the belay, pull up into a steep crack in the wall (crux, good hooks), then follow the crack up the slab.
4. 30m Continue up the crack, then step left to reach a good belay in the corner.
5. 55m Climb the short corner, cross a ledge (in situ Bulldog), whence short walls lead into a groove. Continue up the groove and icy walls to the top and a thread belay.

LOWLAND OUTCROPS & GALLOWAY HILLS

CAMPSIE FELLS, Slackdhu:

The following routes are all in the vicinity or to the right of *Jenny's Lum*. (Topo provided.)

Phased Return 7m Moderate. J.Seaman, Kevin Woods. 8 Jun 2020.
The short, stepped buttress with a broad crack running up the centre. It lies at the far left of Jenny's Lum Buttress.

The Writings on the Wall 10m E1 5b *. D.Macmorris. 24 Oct 2012.
A route strongly based on *Tendons*: good climbing and taking the clean face to the left. Start up a line of good holds for 6m, place gear and move left to climb thin crimps on the face. An obvious flat jug on the right allows the crack to be accessed again. Divert left and straight up on good crimps, easing toward the top.

Stone 12m E2 5b *. Kevin Woods, J.Seaman. 8 Jun 2020.
Takes a line across the centre of the buttress, with spaced gear and brittle rock. Start up the steep groove immediately right of *Tendons*. Pull over the bulge to gear. Trend up and right across the vague scoop in the centre of the face to a couple of long moves to finish.

From the waterfall a vegetated face runs rightward, eventually breaking into two ribs. The next routes take one rib each.

Easing Out of Lockdown   10m   Severe. J.Seaman, Kevin Woods. 29 May 2020.
The stepped rib.

Catgroove   12m   VS 4c. Kevin Woods, J.Seaman, 29 May 2020.
The next rib along has a broken groove on the right-hand side that climbs better than it looks. Climb to a small niche and pull over (crux) at two-thirds height.

Carleatheran:
Standmilane Gully   150m   I/II *. Jacob Davies. 13 Feb 2021.
The deep gully at the eastern end of the crag (NS 67582 92090) has a short ice step at half-height. (Topo provided.)

CRAIGMORE:
Inverlussa Crack   15m   E2 5c. Pete Roy (First ascent date not known)
Climb the crack in the bulging wall behind the Terror boulder. A steep start leads to a slabby finish.

Autobahn, Schumacher Finish   12m   E4 5c **. Tristam Fox, 6 Oct 2017.
This takes the arête above and right of *Autobahn*. Climb *Autobahn* to an incut jug at half-height. Move up then right to the arête, finishing insecurely up the nose.

Schumacher Direct   12m   E4 5c **. Kevin Woods. 30 Aug 2020.
A direct wall start to *Autobahn, Schumacher Finish*. Start by the crack on the lower right wall. Traverse left across the wall via a broad diagonal pinch, into flakes then the *Autobahn* jug. Finish up *Schumacher Finish*.

AUCHINSTARRY QUARRY, Car Park Area:
Final Cut   15m   E5 6b. Nicholas Wylie. 11 Oct 2020.
A composite route linking the crux sections of *Blade Runner* and *Promontory Runner*.

Plumline Arête   7m   E3 6a. Brendan Croft. 11 Jul 2011.
Climb *Plumline Crack* to the big flat hold. Place gear, move left to the arête and climb it, avoiding adjacent cracks.

Amphitheatre Left:
Five Miles Out   12m   H.Severe 4a *. Andi Höhn, Kevin Woods. 8 Aug 2020.
Twin shallow grooves climb the face left of *The Seven Year Plan*. Climb the left-hand groove, finishing on good holds up a short, steep corner. Small wires are useful.

Forty Six & 2   12m   VS 4c *. Kevin Woods, Andi Höhn. 8 Aug 2020.
The right-hand groove up parallel cracks, immediately left of *The Seven Year Plan*.

Shield Bay:
Shield Bay is a short crag high on the quarry's back wall, distinctive from the car park with a chiselled corner and tapering pinnacle in its centre. The crag is best

accessed by abseil from trees far back. Access from the base of the quarry is also possible by a steep, loose scramble on blocks. A steep scrambling route to the top of the quarry is located at the left end of the crag. This is a short steep corner on mostly good holds, though it is not most practical in descent and prone to overgrowing.

Lomond Corner 10m VS 4c **. Chris Miles. 1 Aug 2018.
10 metres right of Model T. The obvious corner left of a pointed pinnacle has a tricky move at mid-height.

Honda Crack 10m Severe 4a **. Thomas Wren, Steven Johnson. 25 Jun 2020.
Between *Lomond Corner* and an obvious overhang is a vertical crack. Climb the crack onto a shelf at mid-height, finishing up the shallow corner.

Sector Commander John 10m H.Severe 4b. Flo Silver. 5 Aug 2020. Start in the corner to the right of the obvious arête. Climb onto the top of the arête and then finish up the corner above, finishing on a huge block. A harder variation starts under the curving overhang left of the arête. Climb out to ascend the edge of the arête and re-join the route.

Lockdown Rules 15m MVS 4b/c *. Guy Howard, Ron Lake. 20 Aug 2020.
About 3m right of *Sector Commander John* is an obvious crack and shallow groove up a slab. Gain the bottom of the crack and follow this up to a small overlap. Follow the groove round to the right and finish up the slab. Low in the grade but protection is small wires.

Cracking Lockdown 15m Severe. Ron Lake, Guy Howard. 20 Aug 2020.
Immediately right is a deep groove and wide crack. Follow this to the top; take care with loose rock.

Covert Shielding 8m HVS 5a *. Guy Howard, Ron Lake. 24 Aug 2020.
Three metres right and up on a small ledge, is a steep wall with twin cracks. Start in the small recess beneath the cracks, move through the small overhang and finish direct.

Cautious Easing 8m H.Severe. Guy Howard, Ron Lake. 28 Aug 2020.
Just right is another recess below a small overhang and arête. Climb the recess, go over the overhang and finish direct. Loose and dirty.

The Bristol Baldy 10m E1 5b **. Guy Howard, Ron Lake. 28 Aug 2020.
Right of the broken corner is a well-defined left-leaning groove with a boulder at the base and a good belay platform. Climb directly over the boulder and follow the groove using holds on the wall and sloping ledges. Avoid the gorse by stepping right at the very top. Very limited protection until after the crux.

Blackberry Groove 10m VS 4c. Chris Miles, Jonny Martin. 12 Aug 2020.
The well-protected leftward-slanting crack in a narrow groove.

Trundle Slab:
Fool's Gold 25m E3 5b *. Brendan Croft. 27 Sept 2013.
Climb directly up the slab between *Trundle* and *Walk on the Wild Side* past thin

cracks at 5m (micro wires). Reach right and place wires in the twin cracks of *WOTWS*. Gain a prominent hold in the centre of the slab and climb on to this. A long move (crux) to a left-facing flake gains the midway ledge.

Deep Throat Walls:
Ich Siede Im Eigenen Saft   25m   HVS 5a. Kevin Woods, Andi Höhn. 8 Aug 2020.
A line parallel to and right of *Kein Trink Wasser*. Climb the stepped wall right of the groove to large ledges at 10 metres. Traverse slightly left to the base of the upper groove, then go up and right diagonally across the wall, aiming for a block on the arête underneath the top. Continue to finish by large ledges and a vegetatious top-out.

Balance of Power   20m   E4 6a **. Kevin Woods, John Milloy. 11 Jul 2020.
Takes the clean-cut arête left of *Glass*. Climb to a prominent ledge at half-height and finish directly on improving edges. Extensively cleaned (and trundled of loose rock). Likely climbed previously, before Council work destroyed sections of this buttress perhaps 20 years ago.

Forresthill Quarry:
Three routes on the high face right of *Injuns*:

Monkey See Monkey Do   9m   Font 6a. David Macmorris. 29 Aug 2020.
Takes a line up the centre. Climb to the first horizontal break. Use a sidepull on the wall to gain the second break. Finish along *Grapeshot*.

Grapeshot   10m   Font 5. Kevin Woods. 29 Aug 2020.
Climb *Rimshot* almost to the top, traverse the obvious high break left.

Rimshot   9m   Font 4. David Macmorris. 29 Aug 2020.
The right-hand side of the wall, easier than it appears.

Neilston Quarry:
Dafty Route X   8m   S.C.Watts, S.Gibson. 25 Jun 2020.
Climb the face behind the tree to easier ground then step right on to the slab and over the overhanging block using the obvious rib.

Addendum   12m   E1 5b. Stevie Weir. 24 Sep 2014.
An eliminate just right of *Punk Rock*. Start at the base of a black slab with a red streak. Climb up on small crimps through the two overhangs, ignoring the cracks to left and right (except for vital cam placement next to the engineering nut). Head for the apex of *Curving Crack* and finish right.

The Fin   3m   Font 4. Stevie Weir. 20 Sep 2014.
The rocks above and right of the main crag have three short arêtes. Climb the middle of these to the top, using the arête for hands.

CRAIGDEWS (GALLOWAY), Kid's Buttress:
Adam Russell suggests an upgrade for his route *Al Dente* to E6 6b. The route has a dynamic, reachy and unprotected Brit tech 6b crux where a fall would land you on pointy granite boulders. High in the grade.

HORSBURGH QUARRY (BORDERS, NT 284 391):

This largely south-facing quarry lies to the south of the ruins of Horsburgh Castle a couple of kilometres to the east of Peebles. It contains a number of wooden huts and other facilities used for outdoor activities and training. The slate-like rock varies in quality and parts of the quarry face are vegetated. A grassy track leads into the quarry from just north of the junction of the Peebles to Innerleithen cycle path and the offshoot that runs north towards the A72 and the Glentress Hotel.

West Flank Slab:

This slabby, south-east-facing section, footed by an open-fronted shelter, holds four lines, described from left to right. Care is required near the top of all of them as, although the angle eases, the rock quality deteriorates. There are metal stakes and concrete fence-posts to belay on at the top.

Virus Slab 9m V.Diff. Graham Little. 1 Jun 2020.
The slabby face directly in front of the shelter, bypassing the bulge on the left.

Lockdown Corner 10m Severe. Graham Little. 2 Jun 2020.
Start below the short, slim, blocky corner. Climb the slab, then the corner and broken ground above.

Elm Slab Left 11m Diff. Graham Little. 2 Jun 2020.
Climb an open groove and slab above, bypassing the dwarf elm tree to the left.

Elm Slab Right 12m V.Diff. Graham Little. 1 Jun 2020.
Start just to the right of the previous route. Climb the short rib and slab above, bypassing the dwarf elm tree to the right. Move left to finish.

Back Bay:

The back of the quarry (the north flank) is partly vegetated but there is a distinctive area of clean, slabby rock on the right side in a slight bay.

Foxglove Slab 10m Severe 4b. Graham Little. 9 Jun 2020.
Scramble up to a vegetated ledge at the foot of the clean slab. A couple of tricky moves give access to the slab, which is climbed to a vegetated exit and tree belay.

Traprain Law, Overhang Wall:

Woblet 20m VS 4c *. Bob Licznerski, Rab Anderson. 29 Sep 2020.
Start as for *Piglet* and *Wobble Direct*, surmount the overhang direct to gain a small ledge, and continue up the slab. At its top continue right under an overlap and at a black feature and cracks pull over (crux) onto the upper slab, finishing directly up a steep wall (left and separate of *Piglet*'s exit).

GALLOWAY SEA-CLIFFS, MEIKLE ROSS, Little Zawn:

Ross Hall 20m VS 4c *. Roger Everett, Dairena Gaffney. 2 Apr 2021.
Nice and surprisingly independent climbing taking the arête between *Orange Chimney* and *Green Wall*. Start below *Orange Chimney*, head up right for 3m to below a tiny overlap, then continue straight up the wall until touching *Green Wall*. Trend left to the arête, then continue straight up keeping just right of the arête and take the headwall direct.

LIMEKILNS, The Gellet Block, The South Face:

Adam Russell notes that his route *Blackout* is Tech 6b through the roof, with the first gear at 6m or 7m if you don't place side-runners in *Through the Motions*. It is a bit harsh at E4, and an upgrade to hard E5 mid 6b for the on sight is suggested.

BENARTY HILL:

Escaping the Queen   40m   III. Craig Gudmundsson, Alex Urquhart-Taylor. 10 Feb 2021.
Climb the groove on the right-hand side of the gully at NT 156 982 located at the east end of the cliff. A turfy route climbed in the dark on a very cold night.

BERWICKSHIRE COAST, Hilton Buttress (NT 969 592):

This is an impressive sandstone crag in a splendid situation. Although close to both the main A1 road and the East Coast rail line, this section of coast feels quite adventurous and you are unlikely to see other climbers on your visit. The atmosphere is enhanced by the tidal nature of the crag and also the nearby 'Smuggler's Bothy' which was built by the famous smuggler John Robertson around 1760. The downside is the rock quality. Whilst the lower section of the crag can be reasonably sound, the sandstone deteriorates further up, and extreme care is needed with copious loose rock in the upper section.

Approach: Leave the A1 at the signpost for Lamberton and park on a short stretch of tar just north of this junction. Head down the track and over the railway bridge to join the coastal path and follow this northwards for just over 1km. Follow grassy slopes down to Smuggler's Bothy then scramble down rocks at low tide to approach the buttress from the east. (Topos provided.)

The area with the best rock. This is the shorter left-hand wall when facing the main buttress. Routes are described from left to right, seaward to landward.

Pick Pocket   6m   Severe 4a. Michael Haywood, David Battle. Jun 2019.
Climb the wall left of a black hole on pockets, pinches and breaks.

Black Hole   6m   Severe 4a. Michael Haywood, David Battle. Jun 2019.
The cave and flaked cracks. Climb over the cave, mainly using the right wall to the obvious collection of flakes, and finish on good holds.

Black Magic   8m   HS 4b *. Michael Haywood, David Battle. Jun 2019. A good route. Follow the thin dog-legged crack through breaks before moving left to top out on good holds.

Double Bluff   15m   V.Diff. Michael Haywood, David Battle. Jun 2019.
Start on the large boulder at the left end of the main buttress. Climb easily on juggy pockets to a large ledge. Climb out of the corner and onto a large platform. Move to the back and climb awkwardly over the bulge.

Smugglers' Wall   43m   Severe 4a. Michael Haywood, G.Smyth. May 2019.
A good route taking a meandering line up the main face.
1. 35m 4a Start at a deep crack in the centre of the buttress. Climb the crack to the bulge. Traverse right under the bulge past a good undercling before continuing up rightwards for 4 metres. Head back left across a small exposed ledge into a niche of dark rock. Go up diagonally rightwards from the niche until it is possible

to escape onto the grassy ledge. Nut belay in the second corner crack at the right end of the ledge.
2. 8m 4a Climb the corner crack, going left at the top. Take care with extremely loose blocks and ensure the belayer is positioned away from any stonefall.

The Straight up Smuggler 43m Severe. Michael Haywood, David Battle. Jun 2019.
1. 30m Start close to the right corner of the buttress and climb diagonally leftwards onto a pocketed wall. Go directly up from here past two or three diagonal breaks onto the grassy ledge. Belay in the third corner.
2. 8m Delicately climb the corner above on very poor rock.

The Desperate Smuggler 45m Scottish VS. Michael Haywood, David Battle. Jun 2019.
An impressive-looking natural line marred by loose rock – not recommended.
1. 20m Start up a deep crack 5m right of the corner of the buttress. Continue up the shallow crack above, trending slightly right (or up the wall to the left of the crack) to reach a grass terrace and belay on a ledge at the base of next crack system.
2. 25m Traverse 2m along the ledge then climb steeply into the crack (crux). Carefully work your way to the top on appalling rock.

MISCELLANEOUS NOTES

THE W.H. MURRAY LITERARY PRIZE

As a tribute to the late Bill Murray, whose mountain and environment writings have been an inspiration to many a budding mountaineer, the SMC have set up a modest writing prize, to be run through the pages of the Journal. The basic rules are set out below, and will be reprinted each year. The prize is run with **a deadline of midnight on the last day of April each year**.

The Rules:

1. There shall be a competition for the best entry on Scottish Mountaineering published in the *Scottish Mountaineering Club Journal*. The competition shall be called the 'W.H. Murray Literary Prize', hereafter called the 'Prize'.
2. The judging panel shall consist of, in the first instance, the following: The current Editor of the *SMC Journal*; The current President of the SMC; and two or three lay members, who may be drawn from the membership of the SMC. The lay members of the panel will sit for three years after which they will be replaced.
3. If, in the view of the panel, there is in any year no entry suitable for the Prize, then there shall be no award that year.
4. Entries shall be writing on the general theme of 'Scottish Mountaineering', and may be prose articles of up to approximately 3000 words in length, or shorter verse. Entries may be fictional.
5. Panel members may not enter for the competition during the period of their membership.
6. Entries must be of original, previously unpublished material. Entries should be submitted to the Editor of the *SMC Journal* by the end of April for consideration that year. Electronic contributions are preferred and should be submitted via e-mail, although double-spaced typewritten hard copies will also be accepted by post. (See Office Bearers page at end of this Journal for address etc.) Any contributor to the *SMC Journal* is entitled to exclude their material from consideration for the Prize and should so notify the Editor of this wish in advance.
7. The Prize will be a cheque for the amount £250.
8. Contributors may make different submissions in different years.
9. The decision of the panel is final.
10. Any winning entry will be announced in the *SMC Journal*, and will be published in the *SMC Journal* and on the SMC Website. Thereafter, authors retain copyright.

THE WH MURRAY LITERARY PRIZE 2021

LIMITED THIS YEAR IN THEIR FREEDOM to visit the hills, our judges found consolation in a wealth of interesting and readable contributions to the *Journal*.

The Prize for 2021 is awarded to a new contributor, Olly Stephenson, who in 'Crack Addict' gives us an enthralling account of his personal struggle not only with an urban climbing challenge but with illness too. The judges found this 'very fresh and topical (touching on Covid) … a contemporary and taut piece of writing. It maintains a tension throughout, relaying the angst of the situation without recourse to literary ploys, or overplaying the narrative, or attempting to add humour. The drive to achieve the route is realistic and the satisfaction is shared.' The observation was also made that '… the narrative is a personal journey and deploys good imagery as well as several interesting turns of phrase.'

Another writer who eloquently describes a personal journey is George Allan, whose submission 'The Boxer' was recognised as '… very personal – perhaps initially a little morbid – and a controversial way of telling the tale.' More than one of the judges also admired 'One of Those Days' by our established contributor Mike Dixon, who successfully combines a fine description of his winter day on Seana Bhràigh with a miscellany of memories down the years. Equally adroit at mixing narrative and nostalgia is Greg Strange in 'Way Back Far East', which recalls his pioneering climbs on Beinn Eighe with the late Brian Sprunt.

Readers who enjoyed his sardonic humour last year in 'Travels with a Gun' will relish another wordly-wise piece by Tim Pettifer, 'Almost Drowning', in this year's *Journal*. Alas the conformity of this article to our Prize rubric – 'Scottish mountaineering' – was reckoned too tenuous to include it in the competition.

Several of our judges singled out 'The Naming of Routes' by Sophie-Grace Chappell as an accomplished piece of writing, while another of the Club's *literati*, Ian Crofton, won high praise for his poem 'Far from Here', composed wistfully in lockdown: 'I know it's poetry but we've all been on Buachaille Etive Mòr, and it's just so easy to visualise his clear enjoyment of that mountain. His words and phrases remain in your mind.'

It has also been gratifying to receive contributions – scarce but varied – from a few of our younger adventurers. One can only marvel at Finlay Wild's attempt to ski the gruelling 'Ramsay Round' and Callum Johnson's first ascent of an extreme line on the Shelterstone Crag, or warm to Richard Ive's youthful enthusiasm for our sea stacks.

As usual, one or two of the entries arrived after the 30 April deadline, while at least one article – Robin Campbell's masterly account of Raeburn's overseas exploits – exceeded the 3000-word nominal limit. The judges paid tribute to Robin's contribution as '… an awesome piece of research, useful to future historians.' Such historians will also be grateful to Mike Cocker for his monograph on our rather more sinister member, Aleister Crowley, of which the second and final instalment is published in this year's *Journal*.

Contributions must reach the Editor by 30 April to be considered for the Prize.

– HON. ED.

SCOTTISH WINTER NOTES 2020–21

THE 2021 WINTER can be divided into three distinct phases. The early-season phase was slow to start, but December was excellent for mixed climbing and many of the most technical ascents of the winter were made during this period. The second phase began on 5 January when Scotland entered lockdown. Those living in the city areas of Glasgow, Edinburgh, Dundee and Aberdeen were unable to visit the mountains, but elsewhere climbers were free to travel within their local authority area. For those based in Highland Region this meant almost unlimited access to the major climbing areas, although most elected to climb locally. Climbers in other regions were more creative, and there was considerable activity in the Southern Highlands. The weather was cold from December through February, although ever-increasing snow restricted activity to lower-lying cliffs. Temperatures gradually rose through March, and lockdown restrictions finally eased on 19 April, which led to the third phase of late-season activity on the Ben.

Early Season

Normally by the second half of November winter climbing is in full swing, but temperatures were significantly higher than usual and winter climbing opportunities were rare. Routes were climbed on the morning of 4 November in the Northern Corries and Braeriach, and overnight snow brought snowed-up rock routes in the Northern Corries into condition on 19 November when early-season favourites such as *Savage Slit*, *Fallout Corner*, *Hidden Chimney*, *The Message* and *Pot of Gold* all saw ascents.

Cooler weather brought out more climbers at the end of November. In the snowier west, *Gargoyle Wall* on Ben Nevis and *Golden Oldy* on Aonach Mòr saw ascents, but those looking for sport in the Northern Corries were generally frustrated by bare wind-blown crags, although teams climbing on east-facing Creagan Cha-no had better luck finding precious snow.

Greg Boswell, Callum Johnson and Hamish Frost pulled off a notable repeat on 25 November when they made the second ascent of *Curly's Arête* on Number Three Gully Buttress on Ben Nevis. This steep VIII,8 follows the right edge of the *Knuckleduster* corner and had first been climbed by Ian Parnell and Sean Isaac from Canada during the 2007 International Winter Meet.

The first significant new route of the season fell to Johnson and Tim Miller on 3 December when they climbed *The Flying Fox* (VIII,8) on the right side of the Hayfork Gully Wall on An Teallach. The following day, they climbed another new route on the Eastern Ramparts of Beinn Eighe. *Never Never Land* was graded VIII,8, which made it two new Grade VIIIs on consecutive days for the dynamic young duo.

Three days later, Iain Small and Dave MacLeod made an outstanding new addition to Ben Nevis with *Nevermore* (VIII,8), the soaring overhanging corner on the right side of Number Five Gully Buttress. This had been eyed up by several teams, but its unrelenting steepness had deterred any attempts. The buttress faces south-east which means it is very much a mid-winter venue, best climbed before the sun rises too high in the sky.

Jamie Skelton and Matt Glenn continued last season's winter interest in Garbh Bheinn by making the first ascent of *Fathomless* (VII,7) on 3 December. The route starts up the summer HVS *Excalibur* before moving right. *Fathomless* was only the second winter route to be climbed on the Upper Tier of the South Wall and

*Callum Johnson on FA of Flying Fox (VIII,8), Hayfork Gully Wall, An Teallach.
Photo: Marc Langley.*

*Callum Johnson on FA of
Never Never Land (VIII,8),
Beinn Eighe.
Photo: Tim Miller.*

Iain Small on FA of Nevermore (VIII,8), No 5 Gully Buttress, Ben Nevis.
Photo: Dave MacLeod.

follows Neil Adams and Alasdair Fulton's winter ascent of *Sgian Dubh* (V,6) back in January 2009.

The pace stepped up a gear the following week when Tim Miller and Jamie Skelton notched up the first new Grade IX of the season with the first complete ascent of the summer line of *Metamorphosis* (IX,10) on Ben Nevis. This sustained summer E2 was first climbed in winter in 2009 by Iain Small and Gareth Hughes, who had started up the deep crack of *Cranium* (an E1 alternative start to *Heidbanger*) before moving right to join the summer line of *Metamorphosis* for its third pitch. A couple of weeks later, Greg Boswell and Callum Johnson added *New Age Raiders* (IX,9) to Church Door Buttress in Glen Coe. This superb addition climbs very steep ground to the right of *The Ninety-Five Theses* just before the angle of the crag eases to the right.

An extended spell of cold and snowy weather over Christmas and New Year led to a high level of activity across the Highlands. Callum Johnson and Andy MacKinnon visited Barrel Buttress on Quinag on 28 December and came away with the first winter ascent of the summer E2 *Beefheart*. This excellent VII,7 was described as 'well protected, steep with a real out-there feeling.' Further south that day, Tim Miller, Jamie Skelton made the first winter ascent of *Groovin' High* (VII,8) on the Far East Wall on Beinn Eighe. Excellent cracks and good hooks meant the climbing was enjoyable as it is in summer.

On 24 December the Cairngorm ski road was closed owing to Covid restrictions, which limited activity in the northern Cairngorms for the rest of the season. Undeterred, Erick Baillot and Dave Kerr approached Lurcher's Crag on skis, where they made an ascent of *Shapeshifter* (VIII,8). They reported it to be an excellent climb, but possibly a little over-graded and accessible to more climbers than the rating suggests. A month earlier they visited the same area of crag and repeated *Rottweiler* (VI,7), adding the *Mongrel Mutation Finish* (V,6).

The high volume of snow meant climbing on Ben Nevis was hard work and the

Dave MacLeod on FA of Rose Innominate (IX,9) West Face of Aonach Dubh.
Photo: Helen Rennard.

Douglas Boulder area was the most popular venue. Huw Scott and Nathan Adam added *The Final Fowl* (IV,6) on the cracked wall right of Douglas Gap West Gully. The low freezing level and snowy conditions were better suited to technical snowed-up rock routes in Glen Coe, and on 28 December, Greg Boswell, Graham McGrath and Hamish Frost added *False Penance* (IX,10), the overhanging groove left of *Un Poco Loco* on Church Door Buttress. The following day, Dave MacLeod and Helen Rennard visited Stob Coire nam Beith and made the first winter ascent of *Tarbh Uisge* (IX,8). Three days later they visited the west face of Aonach Dubh with Andy Nelson and made the first winter ascent of *Rose Innominate* which resulted in a bold and technical IX,9.

The ever-tightening travel restrictions prompted many climbers to look for winter venues closer to home, which resulted in some interesting ascents in the Southern Highlands. On 2 January, Rosie Rothwell and Joe Barlow climbed *Frosty Peat* (I/II), the broad buttress 500m south of Arrow Buttress on Meall nan Tàrmachan. Two days later, the same pair added *Hexellent* (II) and *Ba Buttress* (III) to the left side of Coire Bàn on Meall a' Choire Lèith. On Ben Lomond, Sam Wainwright and Sebastian Wolfrum found *Break Dance* (IV,5) on the rightmost buttress in the corrie. Finally, on The Upper Tier of The Brack, Ole Kemi and Stuart McFarlane made a fine discovery with *End of The Line* (V,7), which takes the wall right of *Elephant Gully*.

Lockdown

Big news from Skye was the first winter ascent of *Mongoose Direct* (VIII,8) on Sgùrr MhicChoinnich by Jamie Skelton and Tim Miller. Their ascent was based on the summer line and took advantage of useful ice that had formed on the first pitch. Nearby on Blàbheinn, Ian Hall and Katharina Lenz climbed *Vaccination* (IV,4), the good-looking corner in the buttress above *Escape from Colditz*.

Back on the mainland on the Bonaidh Dhonn, Rob Giddy, Tim Miller, Callum Johnson climbed *South by South-East* (V,6), a winter-only line taking the obvious corner on the left side of the crag between *Netsky* and *North by North-West*. On Creag Ruadh's north-east face, John Mackenzie and Ian Douglas had a good late-season discovery with *Triple Decker Buttress* (III,4), on the face right of *Creag Ruadh Corner*. Further west, on Beinn Alligin, Adrian Gaughan and John Higham added *Salt n Pepper* (III), a companion route to *Saltire Gully Right to Left*.

In the Cairngorms, Cameron Richardson and Will Attridge made a couple of additions to Lochnagar. *Cac Spout* (IV,4) takes an icy mixed line on the left wall of The Black Spout. This is thought to be right of the icefall of *The White Spout* but the lines may partly coincide. On the The Stuic they were joined by Jamie Greig for *Deesider* (II/III), the gully left of *Stegosaurus Rib*.

Robin Clothier and Simon Richardson made several first ascents on Ben Nevis whilst checking routes for the new winter guidebook. *Mavericks* (V,5) takes a counter-diagonal to *Raeburn's Arête*, and *Badlands* (VI,5) climbs the line of icy grooves between *Italian Right-Hand* and *Bydand*. They also found *That Untravelled World* (IV,4) right of *The Chute*, the icefall of *Shangri La* (V,5) left of *Poseidon Groove*, and *The Last Ridge* (IV,4), the well-defined right edge of the gully of *La Petite*. Richardson later teamed up with Mark Robson for *Into the Wild* (V,5), a companion route to *That Untravelled World*, Richard Bentley for *Lost Horizon* (III,4) to the left of *Shangri La*, and Helen Rennard for *Midnight Blue* (V,5), a direct line up the front face of the steep buttress left of *Red Gully*.

There was considerable interest in some of the less frequented corries on the Ben. Will Rowland continued his exploration of Coire Eoghainn with *Strike While the Iron Is Hot* (IV,4) with James Cooper. Helen Rennard and Simon Richardson also visited the corrie and added a fine IV,4 left of *The German Night Prowler*. In early April, Richardson and Robson visited Coire Ghaimhnean, coming away with the excellent *Paradox Buttress* (III,4), which lies right of the *Five Finger Gully, Right Fork*. The same pair also added the first routes in Sloc nan Uan, the shallow corrie on the east flank of the mountain.

In the Mamores, James Laing and Aidan Robinson made an interesting discovery with *Kinlochfossen* (V,5), a superb adventure up the deep chasm on the north side of Màm na Gualainn. The route was thought to be similar in character to *Rapunzel* on Beinn Fhionnlaidh. In Coire Dearg on Mullach nan Coirean, Steve

Robin Clothier on FA of Shangri La (V,5), Ben Nevis. Photo: Simon Richardson.

Kennedy and Andy MacDonald climbed *Bondage* (III), the gully left of the slabby buttress containing *Kick Start*, and on the west face of An Garbhanach Will Rowland and Jim Cooper climbed the steep *West Ridge* (III). Earlier that day they had visited the North Spur of An Gearanach where they added *Hand Me the Drift* (V,5). Rowland later returned to climb *Plan B* (IV,4) to the left.

The most impressive achievement in Glen Coe took place on 12 March when Jamie Skelton and Tim Miller climbed the three classic Grade VIIs on each of Bidean nam Bian's big cliffs in a day: *Neanderthal*, *Un Poco Loco* and *Central Grooves*. They took 15hrs 30mins car to car.

On Buachaille Etive Mòr's Blackmount Wall, Alistair Docherty and Matt Rowbottom found the excellent *Froth Corner* (VI,7), which lies immediately right of the 'undercut cave' on the Chasm-to-Crowberry Traverse. They also added

Lockdown X (IV,6), the gully just to the left. On Central Buttress, Jamie Skelton and Nicky Brierley made the first winter ascent of *Appauling* (VI,7). Unlike summer, the turfy nature of the climb made it a rather good winter route.

Across on the west face of Aonach Dubh, Mike Mason and Huw Scott climbed *H5N8* (IV,5), the deep straight gully near the right side of Number Three Gully Buttress. This route makes a fine companion to two Mike Pescod Routes – *C3PO* (V,6) climbed with Ali Rose in December and *R2D2* (V,6), the chimney at the left side of the buttress first climbed in February 2018. Also on Aonach Dubh, Will Rowland and Peter Staves found *Midnight Express* (VI,6), a direct version of *Midnight Cowboy*.

Jamie Skelton on FA of The Peeler (VII,8), Garbh Bheinn. Photo: Helen Rennard.

There was considerable activity in Ardgour. On the South Wall of Garbh Bheinn, *Bayonet* (V,6), *Sala* (VIII,9), *The Peeler* (VII,8), *Menghini* (VII,8) and *Chib* (VI,6) saw their first winter ascents courtesy of Jamie Skelton partnered variously by Nick Brierly, Helen Rennard, Tim Miller and Morag Eagleson. Robin Clothier and Simon Richardson found the excellent *Dogs of War* (VI,7) on Pinnacle Buttress, and on North-East Buttress Al Matthewson and A. Veitch succeeded on *Open Secret* (III/IV), the right bounding corner of the slabby section on the Second Tier. Further right, Steve Kennedy and Andy MacDonald added *Hidden Agenda* (IV,4) and *Troll Gate* (II). Nearby on Stob Coire a' Chearcaill, Will Rowland and Garry Campbell climbed *Twelve Pointer* (VI,6), a direct version of *Charcoal Buttress*.

Neil Adams explored Jacobite Buttress on Sgùrr Ghiubhsachain with Kevin Hall and came away with *The Uprising* (IV,5) and *The Young Pretender* (IV,6). Ali Rose visited a month later and added *White Rose* (III) and *Flora* (II). Adams also climbed *Chasing Wild Geese* (III), the slim gully on the NNW face of the mountain, with Helen Rennard.

Heavy snow throughout January prompted the development of the low-lying Mad Man's Crag in Coire nan Frithallt on Maol Odhar. Robin Clothier and Simon Richardson were first on the scene, climbing six 150m-long routes: *All The President's Men* (V,4), *Mad Men Wandering* (III,4), *Electroshock* (V,5), *Jaws of Doom* (VI,6), *Lobotomy Essential* (IV,5) and *Wild Woman* (IV,4). Steve Kennedy and Andy MacDonald added *Black Sabbath* (II), the ridge bounding the left side of the cliff and *Blood Rites* (III,4), which may coincide in part with *Mad Men Wandering*. Kennedy and MacDonald continued their development of the Zeppelin Face on the nearby Creach Bheinn with two good routes. *Good Times Bad Times* (IV,5) takes the slab left of *Bring it on Home*, and *Kashmir* (IV,5) follows the slim corner to the left.

Lockdown restrictions resulted in continued enthusiastic exploration of the Southern Highlands. On Cruach Ardrain, Marco Limonci, Danny Church and Orazio Lo Tauro found *The Sicilian* (IV,4), and icefall on the southern edge of Meall Dhamh, and on Ben Vorlich's south face, Sebastian Wolfrum and Douglas Fransson Lee discovered *End of The Rope* (III,4), which lies left of *Central Rib*. In Coire Cruinn on Meall Dubh, Duncan Helm and Alex Urquhart-Taylor found *First Ice* (III/IV), the prominent icefall on the short wall left of the previous routes.

Glen Lyon was popular. In Coire Laoghain on Meall Ghaordaidh, Willie Jeffrey and Anne Craig climbed *Yellow Peril* (II), the gully left of *The Lyons in Winter*. Jeffrey also teamed up with Paul Morris to add *W.H.O. Han Whitewash* (II) left of *A Wee One*, and *Desmond's Dilemma* (III) on the buttress at the head of the corrie. Nearby on the north face of Creag an Tulabhain, Freddie Crawley ascended *V Gully East* (II) and *V Gully West* (II) in the company of Jamie Grant and Zoe Thornton. On Stùc an Lochan, Craig Gudmundsson and Jim MacFarlane climbed the prominent left-leaning *Cat Gully* (I), and Duncan Helm and Alex Urquhart-Taylor found *Vaccinator* (IV,4), the icefall on the gully's right wall. The same pair also climbed *The Cat's Rake* (III) the icefall 40m to the right. Gudmondsson also added two new routes to Creag na Gaoith on Ben Chonzie with Stuart McKeggie – *Lockdown Grooves* (III,4) and *Essential Fun* (III,4).

Late Season

The spring was unseasonably cold, which gave plenty of opportunities for those limited by lockdown to enjoy some late-season winter climbing in late April and

May. April was dry, which meant there were few opportunities for mixed climbing, but the gullies in the high north-facing cliffs were well filled with snow.

The classic gully lines in the Northern Corries saw many ascents, but as usual it was Ben Nevis that provided most of the late-season sport. Consistently cold mid-winter weather with no significant thaws meant that little ice had formed on the high cliffs of Gardyloo Buttress or Indicator Wall, but the natural drainage lines were lined with beautiful plastic ice. *Point Five Gully* was climbed as late as mid-May, and even at the end of the month there was still ice in Comb and Green gullies and winter was only just starting to lose its grip. Despite the late start, it had been a six-month long season. A considerable number of excellent new routes were climbed, but one can only wonder what might have been if Coronavirus had not intervened.

Simon Richardson

100 YEARS AGO – THE CLUB IN 1921

(*Italics* indicate either a route-name or a quotation from the *Journal* or other named source.)

I HOPE THAT BY THE TIME you read this the worst of the Covid-19 pandemic will be behind us. It has been bad but nothing like that of a century ago, *which resulted in more deaths than any other medical event in human history; the most recent scholarship puts the death toll worldwide at 100 million. Scotland suffered a proportionate loss of life but it was little reported at the time ... the Great War had been such a traumatic experience that the authorities, and the general public, could take no more tragic news and the result was an uncanny silence. The nation was weary of fatalities* ...[Journal of the Royal College of Physicians, Edinburgh, 2007]. The disease caused an extra 70,000 deaths in Scotland at a pre-NHS time when there was a generally poor standard of health with high infant mortality. In Edinburgh, for example, 90 babies in every 1,000 died in their first year. By 2001, the figure was down to 5.

In 1921 there was a national census which reveals that the total population of Scotland was slightly less than 5 million. This would be reduced still further as 400,000 people emigrated during the early 1920s, most of the adult males being skilled workers or from the professional and commercial classes. They had little alternative than to seek new lives overseas, largely owing to the decline of the Clyde shipyards and the loss of thousands of well-paid engineering jobs. It was a time of financial depression in Scotland despite the economic growth and prosperity elsewhere, especially in the US and the 'Jazz Age' of the 1920s. Somewhat surprisingly, the population of Scotland at the last census in 2011 was only just over 5 million.

In the past I have contrived to include a nautical reference or two, and this year is no different. During March 1921 the largest conventional civilian sailing ship ever built in the British Isles was launched at Leith by Ramage & Ferguson, having been commissioned in 1913. It was the 131m (430ft) sail-training vessel *København*, and some idea of its size can be imagined as its five masts stood nearly 20 stories high. In a mystery that rivals the disappearance of flight MH370 in 2014, the ship left Buenos Aires in December, 1928, bound for Australia with 75 people aboard. About a week later, the ship exchanged radio messages with a Norwegian steamer indicating that they were about 900 miles from Tristan da Cunha and that all was well. The *København* was never heard from again.

It is no mystery that Club members migrated to the North British Station Hotel, Edinburgh for the 32nd AGM which was held on Friday 3 December with the new President, W. Ling, in the chair. Hon. Sec. Sang reported that *the most important work undertaken ... during the year was the publication of the first number of the 'guide-books'*. An advertisement for this guide-book, appearing on the back cover of the Journal, is reproduced on p. 258.

Mr. Eric Buchanan, the new Hon. Editor, proposed that the inclusion of commercial advertisements would help to counteract the rising costs of publication and that the price of the *Journal* would rise to 2s 6d (12½p). So, for the first time, several full-page advertisements were added to the traditional contents of the *Journal*. The meeting was followed by the Annual Dinner, with the traditional toasts and speeches, attended by 73 members and guests. No mention ever seems to be made of the standard of the food.

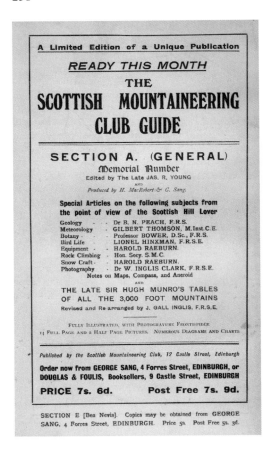

The Journal

The April edition followed the familiar format with general articles, reports, etc. Tribute was paid to the retiring Editor, Frank Goggs, who *laboured for us with a heart as full of the Scottish hills as any ... under what difficulties he did his work we shall never know*. A century later, exactly the same could be said about our recently retired Editor, Peter Biggar. J.H. Bell wrote about an arduous day from Sligachan, which included the Dubhs and Sgùrr Alasdair by way of Loch Coruisk and a stumbling trek from Glen Brittle over the Bealach a Mhàim by *Alpine candle lantern*. Walter Smith described 'A June Night in the Mountains' which, although he didn't identify it, was an ascent of Sgòr Gaoith above Glen Einich in the Cairngorms. George Sang objected to the *limit of the liberty* of the people *under a mass of oppressive legislation*. He was referring to the proposals for hydro-electric schemes, in particular the Tummel works, the loss of rights-of-way and the despoliation of *our Highland hills*. His protests would all be in vain; driven by the need to power aluminium smelting plants, within another fifty years 54 main power stations and 78 dams had been built. And are still being built, albeit as smaller-scale projects. Fortunately for him, Sang did not witness the arrival of wind turbines on the hills.

An obituary for George Gilbert Ramsay, one of the Club's founding members, reveals a cultured man who became a professor at Glasgow University at age 24. A member of the Alpine Club, he was the SMC's first President. A long letter from Percy Unna attempted a scientific explanation for *the disadvantageous effect of wearing heavy boots* and an item by E.W. Steeple recorded several new routes on Skye. Contrast that with the 2020 *Journal*, which has 60 pages of New Routes.

There was a note about the forthcoming *Mount Everest Expedition*, which was *to proceed to India this year for reconnaissance purposes*. The team included two highly experienced SMC members, Alexander Kellas and Harold Raeburn. Kellas (with Henry Morshead) had recently reached a height of 23,600ft on Kamet (25,447ft), and Raeburn, *with his wonderful capacity as a climber and his outstanding qualities of leadership, courage and endurance*, was selected to lead the mountaineers in the mixed group. The *Journal* also included a loose insert appealing for financial donations to the expedition, which was a joint venture between the Royal Geographical Society and the Alpine Club.

The October edition had an account of the first complete ascent of *The Chasm* (Buachaille) in April 1920 by Noel Odell, Mrs Odell and R.F. Stobart, although the direct finish from the Devil's Cauldron was avoided. This was an excellent achievement given the wet and chilly conditions with patches of snow on some of the pitches – a long and tiring day. A similarly lengthy climb was described by D. Menzies – an ascent of *Collie's Route*, the 2000ft SE ridge of Sgùrr a' Ghreadaidh on Skye. A leisurely start from Glen Brittle, which included stops for swimming and sunbathing, was followed by a dawning realisation about the uncertainty of the route and the mixed quality of the rock. They eventually arrived at the summit to witness a half moon rising over Blàbheinn. Negotiating *the knife edge of the summit ridge in the dim light of the midnight hour* they descended by An Dorus (referred to, at that time, as the Eag Dubh – see *SMCJ*, 42/203 (2012), p. 136) into Coire a' Ghreadaidh and were back at their farmhouse base in time for breakfast.

George Sang wrote an amusing account of the ghastly early-hour Alpine start. *Do you know that 3.45 a.m. feeling and how you hate all men ... depression fills your heart and with your whole soul you loathe mountaineering*. Finally, in 'Three Weeks in the Highlands', Howard Somervell describes an extensive climbing tour in a three-wheeled Morgan car. The full texts may be accessed online at <www.smc.org.uk/journal/downloads>.

Club Meets and members' excursions

The New Year Meet was held at Killin and Fortingal and *seldom have the mountains showed a less wintry aspect*. Nevertheless, there were plenty of hill-walking outings and *the Secretary and Raeburn took four members of the Ladies' Club up some rocks above Lochan na Lairige and then on to Meall nan Tàrmachan*. In March, members gathered at various locations in the Glencoe District for the Easter Meet, most of them staying at either the Kingshouse or the Ballachulish Hotel. The poor weather meant that *it was not a Meet suitable either for satisfactory snow or rock work but it did not prevent the usual range of hill-walking excursions. The Everest expedition was the chief subject discussed around the fire after dinner. All were glad that Raeburn had accepted the position for which he is, of all men, so well fitted, and hopes were freely entertained that our President would join him, and that these two would give Everest the same treatment they have dealt to many other difficult summits.*

These words were written by G.T. Glover, and he was referring to the news that

George Finch had been excluded from the expedition, at the final hour, on rather spurious medical grounds and William Ling had been offered the place. Ling declined the invitation, citing the short notice and his business commitments and expressing his regret. His decision seems rather out-of-character but the 48-year-old Ling may have been aware that George Mallory had been infuriated at the proposal to include another older climber in the team. Ling had written: *I am sorry that Finch has been found unfit but hope you will be able to get some other young mountaineer to take his place.* In the event, 30-year-old Guy Bullock accepted the replacement position.

Although the Everest expedition was successful in terms of reconnaissance,[1] it was a disaster for the Scottish members. Kellas suffered so badly from severe diarrhoea on the approach march that he had to be carried on a stretcher. In this weakened state his death was probably caused by heart failure. Raeburn, too, was badly affected by 'food poisoning' and was forced to return to a lower altitude to recover, thus missing any active participation in the work of the expedition. For him, the trip was a personal disaster. [See 'Harold Raeburn – The Final Journey' in *SMCJ*, 40/199 (2008), pp 41–51 for details.]

During the summer months, W.W. Naismith *spent ten days of perfect weather among the Western Pyrenees* and several members visited the Alps. G. Sang and President Ling climbed the Bietschhorn by the SW arête and later, with H.C. Bowen, were thwarted by conditions on the Grandes Jorasses. Sang noted that the glaciers everywhere *required great caution…and snow bridges had sometimes to be swum over*. Ling's diary (Book 14) reveals that he was as active as ever. Amongst other outings, in September he climbed *Needle Ridge* (Great Gable) and on his descent met Walter Parry Haskett Smith, often referred to as 'the father of British rock-climbing' after his famous ascent of Napes Needle in 1886. Ling accompanied the great man to Seathwaite *where we had tea*. Later that month, Ling climbed Bowfell Buttress (Langdale) and was active in the Lakes throughout the autumn and, in December, on Arran.

Mike Jacob

---

[1] Although not strictly relevant, members who are as fascinated as I am by the early British attempts on Everest from the northern (Tibetan) side, may view and zoom-in on Everest as never before. Photographer Renan Ozturk used specially modified drones, operated from the North Col, to capture images from previously impossible angles. See <www.nationalgeographic.com/magazine/graphics/see-what-the-summit-of-mount-everest-looks-like-in-360-degrees-feature> retrieved 6 September 2021.

200 YEARS AGO

ALTHOUGH IT IS NOT SO today, in the nineteenth century the connection between botanising and climbing was strong. Late in that century, before the formation of the Cairngorm Club or our Club, there was a Scottish Alpine Botanical Club,[1] associated with the Royal Botanic Garden, and a mountain section of the Perthshire Society for Natural Science[2]: both of these visited the summits in spring and summer in search of the rare flora found there. This tradition goes back at least as far as James Robertson, and the Reverends John Lightfoot and John Stuart, who were pioneers of this sort of expedition in the 1770s.[3] In the years between, the driving force was William Jackson Hooker (1785–1865), a Norfolk botanist who was granted the Regius Chair of Botany at Glasgow by George III in 1820, on the advice of Sir Joseph Banks, and rapidly provided a new *Flora Scotica* for his eager students in 1821. He vacated the Chair in 1841 to become Director of Kew.[4]

John Sell Cotman: 'William Jackson Hooker'. 1812. Pencil, 9.4×7in. © Victoria & Albert Museum, London.

---

[1] 'The Scottish Alpine Botanical Club', *SMCJ*, 2/2 (1892), 90–91.

[2] See my 'Salix Herbacea Floreat!', *Millennium Journal* (Perth Mountaineering Club, 2000), pp 19–23.

[3] See Ian R. Mitchell, *Scotland's Mountains before the Mountaineers* (Luath Press, 1988 & 2013).

[4] I am indebted to Joseph Dalton Hooker's 'A Sketch of the Life and Labours of Sir William Jackson Hooker', *Annals of Botany*, 16/64 (Dec 1902), pp ix–ccxx for information about his father. This 210-page *Sketch* was preceded by a much shorter and less accurate account, in a *Speech* to the University marking the opening of the New Botany Department in 1901 – *Annals of Botany*, 15/59 (Sep 1901), 551–8.

Before his appointment to the Glasgow Chair, Hooker made two botanical excursions to Scotland. He had become associated with the Yarmouth banker-botanist Dawson Turner (1775–1858) through various botanical ventures, and spent the early part of 1807 in Turner's home, recovering from a severe adder bite. Eventually Turner and his wife Mary set off with Hooker to tour Scotland. Their route was 'Melrose, Edinburgh, the Falls of Clyde, Glasgow, Dumbarton, Luss, Ben Lomond – ascended in cloud and rain, guided by the Rev. Dr. [John] Stuart, of Luss. Thence they proceeded to Inverary, Loch Awe, Oban, Mull, Ulva, Staffa, Fort William (ascending Ben Nevis in terrible weather), Fort Augustus and Elgin, visiting Mr Brodie of Brodie, F.R.S., the discoverer of *Moneses* and other rare plants in Scotland. Thence to Loch Tay (ascending Ben Lawers twice), Killin (ascending Ben Cruachan), Craighalliach and Ben More (See Hooker's *Sketch*, p. xiii, in which 'Craighalliach' must be Creag na Caillich, above Killin.)

In 1808, Hooker made a more extensive botanical tour, this time accompanied by William Borrer (1781–1862) of Henfield, Sussex. Borrer went on to become as important to British Botany as Hooker. According to Hooker's *Sketch*, p. xiii, the pair 'ascended Ben Lawers, Ben Lomond, Ben Cruachan, and Ben Nevis, and for the first time Shichallion, Ben Hope, and Ben Loyal. After visiting Mr. Brodie of Brodie, they went to Caithness and the Orkneys, returning to Sutherland'. In Sutherland they were frequently taken for French spies or – even worse – sheep-farmers, and had a difficult time as a result. Crossing Sutherland they proceeded to Skye, where they visited 'the cave of Slock Altramins', identified by Noel Williams as the Spar Cave. The northern portion of their mainland tour was accomplished 'mainly on horses or ponies, and the difficulties met with were such as can now be experienced only in the out-of-the-way parts of the globe. My father made copious pencil sketches and kept a journal, which he was vainly urged by his friends to publish. I have no idea what became of it.' (*Sketch*, p. xiv.)

On taking up his post at Glasgow, Hooker began with a clean slate, having no previous experience of lecturing, and disdaining the prior practice of botany teaching, which treated it merely as practical Materia Medica. However, Glasgow had an excellent Botanic Garden, situated in the triangle where Sauchiehall Street and Dumbarton Road meet, and Hooker lectured at the garden, including a session of studying plants from the garden at the end of each lecture, and adding weekend excursions to the Campsies, and a week-long excursion usually to Breadalbane at the end of the course. In his 1901 *Speech* (p. 554) about his father, Joseph Dalton Hooker gave some details of these longer expeditions: 'On one of my father's first excursions to some mountains beyond the head of Loch Lomond he provided a marquee holding thirty persons, which was transported in a Dutch wagon by a Highland pony; and for supplies the party depended upon the flocks and fowls of the cottagers.' Evidently an army on the march – occasionally a long march – from the ferry terminus at Inverarnan to Killin.

On the artistic front, I will end with a happy coincidence. William Hooker married Maria Turner, daughter of Dawson Turner, in 1815. By this time, Turner had turned his attention from botany to the recording of antiquities, and the great Norwich artist John Sell Cotman had been engaged by him since 1812 to teach his children to draw and etch, and to assist him in his recording of antiquities, in Norfolk and in Normandy. We do not have a date for it, but around 1821 Cotman produced what is the second known surviving drawing of Ben Nevis, which was taken from the Corpach Basin. Besides being a most beautiful drawing, this is an artistic mystery, because Cotman almost certainly never visited Scotland. Perhaps

John Sell Cotman: 'On the Caledonian Canal'. c.1821. 17× 11in. © Sotheby's.

he based it on a drawing made by Hooker or by Turner's wife or one of his daughters, but this would be a clutch at a very thin straw.[5]

Robin N. Campbell

---

[5] See my 'The Mystery of John Sell Cotman and Ben Nevis', *Scot. Soc. for Art History Newsletter*, 65, 3–5.

TIMING

It requires a reasonable amount of perseverance and skill to get good crag and action photographs for a new guidebook. The basic requirement is not only good weather but also good timing as this little tale makes clear.

One autumn, back in pre-digital days, I arranged to meet Iain Thow with the intention of getting some images of *Lurgainn Edge* on Cùl Beag in Assynt. I left Fort William quite early and despite a fairly long journey managed to arrive at the agreed time. It was a lovely day and Iain was waiting for me. I got out of the car, put my boots on and packed my rucksack. We both glanced up at *Lurgainn Edge* and saw that it was in deep shadow. We immediately realised that it was the wrong time of day to photograph that particular route.

Iain quickly suggested an alternative plan on the opposite side of the glen. We hopped in our cars and drove a little over a mile back up the road. As soon as I opened my car boot I realised that I'd left my rucksack at our previous stop. I turned round right away and drove back to where I'd been just a few minutes earlier. To my astonishment my rucksack was gone along with my cag, camera, wallet, cards, cash and lunch. I drove back to tell Iain of my misfortune. The only vehicle either of us could remember passing was a red postvan. We decided it wasn't worth chasing the postie around Achiltibuie on such a fine day. Instead we headed off towards Sgùrr an Fhìdhleir and Beinn an Eòin. It was fortunate that the weather was so good, because I was certainly travelling light.

We had a very enjoyable outing on Sgòrr Deas and Sgòrr Tuath. I managed to scrounge some food from Iain and he managed to get some photos, though with a mediocre camera. When we got back to our cars we thought about then doing *Lurgainn Edge*, but the loss of my wallet and camera was of more concern.

A pinnacle on Sgòrr Tuath.
Photo: Iain Thow.

We had no joy at the main Post Office in Ullapool – the postie was still on his round and we were told that in any case it was unlikely that he would have rescued my rucksack. We then tried the Police Station in Argyle Street, but it was closed until 4.30 p.m. They can't have a lot of crime in Ullapool. When a solitary policeman eventually appeared he reported that no rucksack had been handed in.

Although I had no cash, I fortunately had enough fuel, so I said cheerio to Iain and headed home. My wife was away, but back at the house there was a message on the answering machine. A retired GP on holiday with his son had picked up my rucksack and found my address and phone number in my wallet. He had tried to hand it in at the Police Station in Ullapool but it was closed so he'd left it next door in the Tourist Office. I must have been very close to it without realising.

Next day I had to borrow some money from a neighbour to fill up with fuel before driving back north. I discovered that the folk in the Tourist Office no longer had my rucksack. They'd handed it in to the Police Station next door. I then had to wait for several hours before the Police Station opened up again. I ate the previous day's packed lunch on my journey home.

Noel Williams

THE LAGANGARBH PAINTING: IN SEARCH OF THE ARTIST

As revealed in last year's SMCJ, the painting that hangs in Lagangarbh was bequeathed to the Scottish Mountaineering Club by Mr Stuart A. Booth, MBE, who had been a resident of the Falkland Islands and a mountaineer.

The Scottish Mountaineering Club has numerous antique objects amassed over our 132 years of existence. Here I refer not to the Committee (as some wag suggested), nor to my own unique selection of climbing equipment which has been described as a relic, rather unkindly, by many of my climbing partners! The Club antiques are mountaineering memorabilia: diaries, logbooks and heirlooms bequeathed or donated by members, their families and others. The ice-axe said to be Raeburn's, and compass said to be Munro's, are two items seen regularly at our Annual Dinners, as they are solemnly passed from the recent incumbent to the newly inaugurated President. Other treasures are less well known, but observant visitors may have noticed a fine oil painting in the sitting-room of our Club hut, Lagangarbh, in Glen Coe. As I wrote in the 2020 *Journal*, it was in December 2016 that I first saw the painting, featuring the iconic Scottish mountain, Buachaille Etive Mòr as viewed from north-east of The Kingshouse Hotel.

Publication of my article in the *SMC Journal* felt like a notable achievement, something I encourage all members to pursue; but the satisfaction felt on publication was hugely surpassed by clear evidence that someone has actually taken the time to read it. Shortly after that year's edition of our *Journal* had dropped through the letterbox I received an e-mail from the SMC Archivist, Robin Campbell, who told me he had found 'a couple of auction listings for Scottish landscapes by a 'D. McLaren'.' He continued: 'The Artists' Papers Register has an entry for correspondence between a D. McLaren and the curator at Perth Art

Gallery in the years between 1930 and 1937. This could well be your man, or perhaps woman.'

The Bell Library in Perth holds the archives of the Perthshire Art Association, the subject of McLaren's correspondence with Perth Art Gallery. Despite the Covid-19 travel restrictions, I provisionally arranged to visit the Library once the Cities of Edinburgh and Perth had achieved equilibrium in the same lockdown tier. But the novel corona virus was having none of it. I must, however, acknowledge the virtual help of Amy Fairley at the Bell Library, who furnished me with photographs of the correspondence.

Then, a few days later, I received an e-mail from the then Journal Editor, Peter Biggar, asking that I 'phone John Hay; he has interesting information about that painting.' Discussion with that erudite SMC member, always enlightening, took place that evening. Quoting from the *Dictionary of Scottish Art & Architecture* (author Peter J. M. McEwan, published by the Antique Collectors Club), John thought he had found details of the artist who had created the Lagangarbh painting, D. McLaren.

Initial elation at this news was quickly tempered by the discovery that the artist listed in the dictionary was Duncan *MacLaren*; the signature on the painting was clearly *D. McLaren*. Nevertheless, it was gratifying to receive such help, and John posted me a photocopy of the details, as he does not do e-mail (an enviable position!).

The archived correspondence provided by Amy Fairley was between the artist Duncan McLaren, based at Cashlie in Glen Lyon, and John Ritchie, the director of Perth Art Gallery, who asked McLaren to submit paintings for an exhibition planned for November 1937. In a second letter dated 29 October 1937, arrangements were made for two of his paintings to be transported by a visiting grocery van from his home in Glen Lyon, sitting between the two Munros Stùc an Lochain and Meall Ghaordaidh, to Aberfeldy, from where they would be taken by carrier or van to Dunn's Art Stores at 35 Scott Street in Perth for framing. In the 2020 article we reported that a Dunn's label was found on the back of the Lagangarbh painting when it was examined. McLaren wrote that he had had to make two large sporting paintings for Mr Wills, the tobacco baron and owner of the estate, by way of explanation for his delay in replying.

The Perth Museum & Art Gallery exhibition list for December 1937 to March 1938 featured Perthshire and Perthshire artists, and 174 items were on display. They included 'Item 75, Coruisk (pastel) by Duncan McLaren, lent by the artist', and 'Item 129, Coolins and Loch Scavaig (pastel) by Duncan McLaren, lent by the artist'. The entry in *The Dictionary of Scottish Art & Architecture* stated:

> MacLaren [sic], Duncan, 1884–1963. Born Glen Etive, Argyllshire. Part-time Landscape painter in oil, watercolour and pastel. Spent his life as a gamekeeper and deer-stalker in Argyll and Perthshire – mainly on the Wills family estate of Meggernie, apart from two years in the Argyllshire police and four years as a piper in the Black Watch and Lovat Scots [sic] during WW1. Wounded in France, whilst in hospital met an officer who in civilian life was an art teacher. This encouraged him to paint, and after marriage to Euphemia McEwan [actually to Mary McNaughton, whom he married in 1928, Euphemia McEwan being his mother's name] in 1928 he held his first one-man show. In 1959 he began to lose his sight and had to cease painting. Although not represented in any public gallery his work remains in many private collections throughout the Scottish Highlands.

Clearly Duncan McLaren and Duncan MacLaren were the same person!

Duncan MacLaren: Buachaille Etive Mòr from Loch Gaineamhach (NN300538); oil on canvas. By courtesy of the artist's grandson, Michael MacLaren.

Our archivist Robin Campbell then found his birth certificate on-line. He was born in 'Glenketland' (Glen Ceitlein), about 3km from the sea up Glen Etive, grid reference NN147479. His father was a deer forester (a keeper or stalker) and his mother was Euphemia McEwan.

McLaren was 30 to 34 years of age during the First World War. Army records confirm he served in the Lovat Scouts and perhaps the Cameron Highlanders. The Lovat Scouts was a British Army unit first formed during the Second Boer War as a Scottish Highland yeomanry regiment, and was the first known military unit to wear a gillie suit. The first contingent of Lovat's Scouts was raised by Simon Fraser, 16th Lord Lovat and 22nd chief of clan Fraser, on 26 January 1900. At the time, the Lovat Scouts was said to be made up of gillies, stalkers, shepherds and hillmen, experienced with both guns and telescopes. This impression of the Scouts persists to this day, reflecting supposedly innate qualities of the Highlander: loyalty, stoicism and martial prowess – attributes purportedly forged amid an unspoiled, rugged Scottish landscape. In 1916, the Scouts became the British Army's first sniper unit, then known as The Sharpshooters.

His grandson reported that McLaren also worked as a stalker on the Black Corries estate before moving to Glen Lyon. This explains his fondness for Buachaille Etive Mòr as a subject for his landscape paintings, as he would have been blessed with this view from his front door every morning the weather allowed. If the second painting of the Buachaille, shown here, is compared with the photograph of the bequest in the 2020 *SMC Journal* (p. 133), there can be no doubt that both came from the same artistic hand.

McLaren lived to 79 years of age so seems to have recovered well from his military wounds. 1916 was in the pre-antibiotic era and many service people who survived initial injury during the war subsequently died of sepsis from wound contamination. McLaren served for the four years of the war, suggesting he returned to fight again after recovering. He was awarded the British War Medal and the Victory Medal from the First World War.

McLaren got married in 1928, when aged 44 years, to Mary McNaughton, who was recorded as a domestic servant aged 23 years on the marriage certificate. (She died in 1984 at the age of 80.) The couple had two sons: one son, Donald, died in infancy; the other, Andrew MacLaren, had a son, Michael, who still lives near Glen Lyon, at Killin. Mary and Duncan also had a daughter, Christina MacLaren. McLaren, his wife and their infant son are buried at Innerwick church, where his headstone bears the name Duncan MacLaren.

Stuart Booth, the mountaineering resident of the Falkland Islands who made the bequest of the Lagangarbh painting, is buried in the cemetery in Stanley next to his wife Jessie. After lengthy improvement works to drainage in the graveyard area, his headstone and tomb were installed in 2020. Although many Falklands residents of a certain age recall him as the headmaster, no further information about his climbing achievements has so far emerged.

I am grateful for help from Peter Biggar, Robin Campbell, Amy Fairley (Collections Officer, Perth & Kinross), John Hay, Rosemarie King, Michael MacLaren, Ann MacDonald and Major Hugh Young. Jimmy Gauld, a former owner of the Killin Art Gallery, kindly put us in touch with the artist's grandson.

Colwyn M. Jones

DON'T MISS THE CHANCE

When I was first admitted into the SMC I didn't really appreciate one of the great opportunities I'd been given. The opportunities that I did take were to make use of the huts or attend a few informal meets at the CIC, and I never missed a Dinner. I appreciated getting the *Journal* as part of my membership and managed to get to many of the Eastern District talks during the winter months. However, I very much failed to strike up any kind of conversation with the groups of older members of the Club. My first Dinner was in 1985, at a time when the front row of the AGM was almost a *Who's Who* of Scottish and Himalayan exploration from the 1930s onwards: Murray, Mackenzie, Scott, Weir – I almost don't want to list the names for fear of missing the most prominent. When it came to Dinner weekends, I was rarely off the hill in time for the afternoon talk and was also, I am afraid to say, a rare attender at the AGM if the weather was semi-reasonable. In those days putting your name on the Dinner seating plan was a scrum, and there was every chance you'd later find your name crossed off the flip chart without you even noticing, by an older member deciding that he (and it was only *he* then) wanted your place. So much of that group's exploits are documented in the classic books, and their photographs are perpetuated even in the most recent publications. However, it would have been so interesting to chat over a drink about all the other events never written down and now maybe forgotten. What about the numerous weekends when they didn't manage a climb, the time the map and compass never came out and they found themselves descending into completely the wrong glen? As well as the hill adventures, what about all the balancing of home life and work life, the funding of such trips, and even the effort to travel to the Highlands, the Alps and the Himalayas?

Well now, just this year [2020] I was given the chance to meet a member of the Lomond Club who had quite a climbing tale to tell. John Turnbull is now resident in a care home in Lochaber, but within his small bedroom is a large painting of the Matterhorn along with some characteristically grainy black & white photos of young climbers on the top of a peak with an Alpine background. The reason for the prized painting is that in 1948 John, along with five other members of the Lomond Club, climbed the Matterhorn by the Hörnli ridge. Nowadays ascents of the ridge are counted in the hundreds per week, but when I first heard about John's climb I did suspect that an ascent in 1948 was possibly quite rare and prized. The Matterhorn is truly iconic, and although many routes and peaks are technically harder, it is a mountain that commands recognition within the mountaineering world and beyond. It is not surprising that W.N. Ling in an article in the 1936 *Journal* highlights that Ben Nevis's ridges in winter are good training for the Matterhorn. Clearly it was an almost unspoken target for Scottish climbers. Before meeting John I made a quick review of the 'SMC Abroad' sections of the *Journal*, and could see that in the 1930s and 1940s Scottish ascents were fairly rare and quite sought after. Successes and failures were commented on in almost equal numbers.

As with so many adventures, the beginnings of a trip are often a seed of an idea being planted with the right person at the right time. In the years following the end of the Second World War, John was working in Glasgow as a draughtsman when a fellow Lomond Club member, Bob Speirs, who was still retained in the Merchant Navy after the war, sent him a telegram with the simple message 'How about the Matterhorn?' By the summer of 1948 when the trip was pulled together, the team had grown to six, all from Glasgow and all members of the Lomond Club. None had previous Alpine experience. The group now consisted of Willie Gordon, Bob Speirs, Kenny Stevenson, Andy Wynd, and of course John Turnbull. (I am afraid the name of sixth member is not now known.) It seems they kept up their fitness with weekend trips to Arrochar and occasional bus trips to Glen Coe. Four of the six journeyed to Zermatt by train, with the other two choosing to use a motorbike. Bearing in mind that this was undertaken during their annual leave of just a fortnight, there was little time for an acclimatising climb. They did, however, manage to explore the area and ascend to nearby huts as acclimatisation. The planned route was the Hörnli ridge, and four of the team decided to make use of tents and so avoid the huts. As we chatted about the trip I asked John about any other climbers he met and how they were received when camping so close to the border. This was in an era when the cash you could take abroad was limited and the International borders were well patrolled. During the post-war years there was a certain amount of contraband moving across the Swiss-Italian border, and in their reports of climbing in the region many commented on the obstructive border patrols. Nevertheless, apart from friendly visits from the gendarmerie, they didn't feel too restricted, and met very few fellow climbers.

On the day of the ascent, two of the party started from the hut itself while John and the other three started from their tents a little lower down. Quite quickly they were all together before the campers overtook the first pair. The climbing went well, was largely on dry rock, and all arrived safely on the top and enjoyed the summit photos in good weather. They had stayed roped throughout the ascent and pitched much of the ridge. I asked if they met any other parties on the climb, but John remembers they had the route completely to themselves and the weather remained good throughout the day. As he said, 'The weather was kind to us.' At this point I showed him a recent guidebook with a photo of someone near the

Matterhorn from Col d'Hérens, captured by A.E. Robertson in 1908.
Photo: SMC Image Archive.

fixed ropes. I asked for John's memory of the state of any fixed protection, but he took a quick look at my photo and replied, 'Isn't that cheating a bit?' They each carried an ice-axe, which they just used low down; after that they were entirely on rock. I did ask if John still had the ice-axe, but sadly no. Judging by the photos and John's memory, the group all had typical tweed clothing with windproof cotton tops.

With the climb over, the whole team had used their remaining holiday time, and had to start the journey back to Glasgow. He did say the Lomond Club were quite impressed that all six had completed the climb. Not long after this trip Willie Gordon and John both changed jobs and moved to Lochaber. Willie had a successful career with the White Corries Ski Centre in Glen Coe, while John rose to be Chief Draughtsman at the British Alcan smelter. A full-time job, married life and children meant John did less climbing, although he never lost his love of the hills and is still surprised that others like to hear of his Matterhorn experience. In recent years John moved to a care home and still saw Willie regularly as he also visited the same home as a day visitor. Sad to say, Willie died in 2019.

Having met John, I went back to reread more of the detail in the *SMC Journal* from the 1930s onwards and try to gauge the sense of occasion of six from the same club climbing the Hörnli ridge on the same day, without a guide and in good weather. My survey only included what was reported in the SMC Abroad section of the *SMCJ* and a selection of biographies that I have. I realised this would not be fully comprehensive and would exclude some clubs, but I mainly wanted to relate their success to what was reported by SMC and JMCS members. Not surprisingly it became clear that many SMC members maintained climbing partnerships with climbers from other clubs anyway.

At the start of the 1930s A.L. Cram and A.R. Wilson recorded climbing up and down the Hörnli ridge, although after that the early 1930s were quiet for Scottish-linked ascents. In 1934, a group comprising G.G. Macphee, F.S. Smythe and C.W. Parry were successful from the Italian side and came down the Hörnli ridge. H.W. Turnbull was however turned back by bad weather. All these climbs seemed to have been done without guides. During the 1936 season W.B. Speirs plus the guide Emil Perren had hoped for a first ascent of the season but were beaten by an Englishman and two guides the day before. I did note that in 1937 Jock Nimlin,[1] who was also a member of the Lomond Club, had climbed the Hörnli ridge. He was with two others, David Browning and Ann Sheriff. It seems that Ann was climbing with a guide but Jock and David climbed on another rope. To ensure theirs could be considered a guideless ascent, just before the top Jock and David made sure they were ahead.

In 1938 a mixed contingent of SMC, JMCS and the Cairngorm Club were in Switzerland. Ben Humble traversed the mountain with guide Emil Perren up the Swiss side and down to Italy. He comments that though it was busy on the ascent, he had expected some peace on the descent into Italy. Instead they got 'war', as they met rope after rope of unhappy Italian soldiers fully kitted out with rifles and bayonets being encouraged up the mountain. Activity obviously was nil during the war years of 1939 to 1945, although the SMC Abroad section of the *Journal* just after the war does acknowledge the mountain wanderings of A.L. Cram as he made multiple escapes from prisoner of war camps.[2]

The next Matterhorn ascent was by R. Jeffrey, who climbed the Hörnli ridge with his wife. They found the route was almost all on rock but were also accompanied by a Zermatt guide. In the same year Alex Small climbed the Matterhorn with a guide. During the 1947 season a large number of the Creagh Dhu descended on Zermatt for a club meet. Several climbed the Matterhorn, including some ascending the North Face route. It is also recorded that the local Zermatt Guides did not appreciate that none of the teams even considered hiring a guide, and things may have got out of hand in the town square one evening during some local celebrations. However, Connor[3] also recognises that the whole story may have grown arms and legs in the intervening years.

This then takes me to 1948, when the *SMC Journal* has no other records of climbs on the Matterhorn, whence it would appear that the Lomond Club's was one of the few Scottish successes. I did wonder if they were inspired by the knowledge that the Creagh Dhu had had a successful season in 1947, and decided it was their club's turn. In 1948, D.H. Haworth and G.J. Ritchie attempted the Matterhorn by the Zmutt ridge but bad weather held them back and they descended. In fact that season does seem to have had particularly unfavourable weather, and many from Scotland resorted to lower-level walks between huts.

In the year after John's climb the Alps were clearly getting busier. During 1949 the conditions were favourable, with at least four ascents by SMC and JMCS members, at least two of which were guided. In 1950, W.B. Speirs reported being back again in Zermatt with his wife. She climbed the Matterhorn with the guide mentioned a few times above, Emil Perren. Speirs comments that he did not join

[1] I.D.S. Thomson, *May the Fire Always be Lit, a biography of Jock Nimlin* (Ernest Press, 1995). Reviewed in *SMCJ*, 36/188 (1997), 450–51.

[2] D.M. Guss, *The 21 Escapes of Lt Alastair Cram* (Macmillan, 2018). Reviewed in *SMCJ*, 46/209 (2018), 283–5.

[3] J. Connor, *Creagh Dhu Climber, the Life & Times of John Cunningham* (Ernest Press, 1999). Reviewed in *SMCJ*, 37/191 (2000), 472–3.

them as he had climbed it twice before and instead took photos. In the third season after the Lomond Club climb, the *Journal* reflects increased activity, with the SMC Abroad section now covering five or more pages. There was, however, no Matterhorn success for SMC members Slesser and Bennet that year. In the following years, the number of pages of this section in the *Journal* continued to expand, with new names such as Brooker, Patey and J.R. Marshall now evident. In 1952 there was one Matterhorn ascent recorded, although also with a guide. I recognise that by the 1950s the aspiration of these new younger climbers was now new routes or repeating hard, often unrepeated routes, while not necessarily aiming for ascents of particular peaks, however iconic those might be. There was also the lure of the Himalaya for those who could take longer time off work and afford to go there.

So, according to the records I have seen, it looks as if John was among a small, lucky group who found settled weather on the Matterhorn, climbed the route as a club trip and had it to themselves. They were not the first, but it would seem that six members of the same club from Scotland, all on their first trip to the Alps and all climbing the Hörnli ridge of the Matterhorn was rare. And from my point of view I am so pleased to have had the opportunity to meet John and hear of the trip. Thank you for that privilege, and thanks to John's daughter, Aileen Kitson, for sharing the photographs.

Chris Huntley

A BITTERLY DISAPPOINTED READER OF THE JOURNAL

(The author of this interesting note, Harry Hutchinson, has been researching the life of Arthur Bagley, who was evidently a thorn in the sides of the early SMC and the Climbers' Club. His attention was caught by a previous Journal article about Bagley, by Peter Warburton.[1])

Arthur Llewellyn Bagley (author of *Walks & Scrambles in the Highlands*, etc) was born in 1863 in Coventry, where he latterly ran the family ribbon-making business. Though he had always been fond of walking, his interest in climbing mountains was kindled by an ascent of Ben Cruachan in 1896. On Cairn Toul in 1899 he happened to meet Ernest Baker (author of *The British Highlands with Rope and Rucksack*), and the two became good friends. In his review of *Walks & Scrambles* Baker gives us an idea of Bagley's character:

> I think it is the company that makes a tramp with Mr. Bagley through all these glens and over all these summits most agreeable; and whether he is grumbling at the Ordnance maps, etymologizing fallaciously on Celtic place-names, describing scenery, or philosophizing, one cannot help feeling what a strange thing it is that such a clubbable chap should pervertedly insist on always going alone.

---

[1] Peter Warburton: 'An Edwardian Scrambler' in *SMCJ*, 36/189 (1992), 532–8. Mr Hutchinson has provided an extensive bibliography about Bagley, which I will be happy to share on request. – HON. ED.

The year following his 1899 trip to the Cairngorms, Bagley travelled to Kinlochewe in June. From there he climbed Slioch, walked through Glen Tulacha, and explored Beinn Eighe and Liathach (but owing to navigation problems failed to reach any of the Munros on these last two). It was after his dismal expedition on the latter mountain that the rain-soaked Bagley was interrogated by a gamekeeper on the high road – an incident that may have coloured Bagley's opinion of the laird of the Torridon estate. The following week he moved to Skye and climbed Bruach na Frithe and Sgùrr nan Gillean from Sligachan (the latter alone in nail-less boots!). In 1900 he became a member of the Climbers' Club, and his account of his holiday of the previous year was published as an extensive article in that club's journal, and later formed the basis of seven chapters in his Scottish volume.

In 1901 Bagley was again in the Highlands. On a big day (17 June) he walked from Cannich through Glen Affric to Glen Shiel. He was then shut up in the Shiel Inn by bad weather, and his lamentations found voice in his correspondence with Baker, as Baker later recalled in 'Two Excursions to Wester Ross':

> Three seasons ago, a climbing friend of mine went to Glen Shiel with an imposing list of peaks in his pocket-book, the majority of which he purposed bagging. For a week he sent me day by day the most depressing letters imaginable on the subject of Scottish weather; he also delivered himself of divers half-hearted rhapsodies on the glories of waterfalls in spate; but when word came that he had decamped to a more blissful clime, he could not report a single authentic peak captured.

The 'more blissful clime' was Broadford on Skye, which Bagley reached on foot via Bealach Ràtagain and Kylerhea. From Broadford he climbed Beinn na Cailleach on 22 June, moving on to Soay from which he climbed Garsbheinn and Sgùrr nan Eag on 26 June, before returning home via Sligachan on 27 June.

Why are Bagley's writings not better known? Writing in the *SMC Journal* some years ago, Peter Warburton commented:

> Although the format of mostly short chapters devoted to single expeditions should commend him to anthologists, he seems to have escaped their notice. His works are not even listed in other writers' bibliographies partly, perhaps, because many of them did not consider him a suitable role model.

That final statement is undoubtedly true; for example, one reviewer in the *Sheffield Telegraph* wrote:

> Mr. Bagley is really silly at times. He had no business, for example, to start climbing C Gully on Pike Crag all alone in a hailstorm, and was very lucky indeed to get out of it alive. ... There are sound doctrines in Mr. Bagley's book, and some very bad examples. We admire his spirit, but he cannot expect us to approve of certain violently rash manifestations of it.

However, I think his absence from anthologies is more likely because of the feathers he ruffled early in his mountaineering career with an article that appeared in the *Climbers' Club Journal*.

The saga began with an article in the *SMC Journal*[2] by Duncan Darroch (5th of Gourock, 1836–1910), who had bought the Torridon estate in 1875. In 'Deer and Deer Forests' Darroch began:

> To the majority of the owners and occupiers of deer forests in Scotland it is a great pleasure to be able to allow the climbing and scientific public to share

---

[2] *SMCJ*, 6/35 (May 1901), 139–41.

Duncan Darroch, laird of Torridon.
Photo by courtesy of Mrs Claire
Darroch-Thompson.

Arthur L. Bagley scrambling on Cader Idris.
Photo: A.E. Fritche in Bagley's 'Holiday Rambles
in North Wales'.

as far as possible in the delights of climbing the hills and enjoying the scenery, but the climbing and scientific public is not always aware of the great damage that may, quite inadvertently, be done to the valuable sporting interests involved, and it may not be amiss to point out some of the aspects of the case which are perhaps not generally known.[3]

The article was accompanied by approving remarks from the President, A. Ernest Maylard.[4]

Bagley was not impressed. He wrote to the *Climbers' Club Journal,*[5] and his tirade began:

---

[3] Darroch had given hospitality to a SMC party in June 1894 before their first ascent of Liathach's Northern Pinnacles, and had his keeper guide them to the hill. When sent the next *Journal* he replied: 'Dear Mr Douglas, I am much obliged to you for the photos, with the account of your expedition up Meall Dearg. I hope your very graphic description will not tend to inundate us with emulators of your prowess in the stalking season.' (I am grateful to Robin Campbell for finding this letter.) Darroch latterly spent much of each year in Torridon, being active in the affairs of the county and well regarded by his tenants. His son sold the estate in 1912. – Hon. Ed.

[4] *Ibid.*, pp 142–4. The pieces by Darroch and Maylard were followed by a series of detailed questions about deer management, with responses from the keepers on the Ben Alder and Benula estates. The Editor, William Douglas, had included this questionnaire at Maylard's instigation. – Hon. Ed.

[5] *Climbers' Club Journal*, 4/13 (September 1901), 13–22.

Two articles have appeared in the May number of the Scottish Mountaineering Club Journal on the above subject; one of them by Duncan Darroch of Torridon, the other by A. E. Maylard. The subject, to climbers and mountaineers, is obviously of supremest importance. I, a humble member of the mountaineering brotherhood, had awaited these articles with eagerness, and opened my new number of the SMCJ the other day in anxious expectation. I am bitterly disappointed. I hardly expected to find much comfort in Mr. Duncan Darroch's paper, but I am equally disappointed in Mr. Maylard's.

The aftermath is described by Harold Drasdo[6] in the *Climbers' Club Journal*, in the course of reviewing Marion Shoard's book, *A Right to Roam*:

An early issue of this Journal, just 100 years ago, included a combative essay by A. L. Bagley on gaining access to those of Scotland's mountains enclosed within deer forests. In the following issue the Journal Editor found himself obliged to apologise to the many members who'd been distressed by Bagley's sentiments and in the next again, to publish a statement from the Committee distancing itself from Bagley's views.

The affair rumbled on, and in the report of the SMC's Annual Dinner[7] of 1901 we read:

Another popular toast was that of the President. Mr Solly, in speaking to this, referred in condemnatory terms to an article on Deer Forests, which has recently appeared in the journal of an English club. The loud applause which greeted his remarks showed how much the members of the SMC dissociated themselves from the sentiments expressed in this paper, and their resentment of the tone in which the author referred to Mr Darroch and to their President.

Bagley never married (in fact his disdain for women, sometimes bordering on outright misogyny, is often apparent in his writings) and retired to Bangor in North Wales, before moving to Penmaenmawr where he died on 23 February 1936.

Harry Hutchinson

---

[6] *Climbers' Club Journal*, 23/118 (1999–2000), 162–3.
[7] Proceedings of the Club in *SMCJ*, 7/37 (January 1902), 37–8.

ANDREW LESLIE HAY[1]

The Covid-19 lockdown has been a disaster for many of our members, but it did stir me into doing something I should have done many years ago.

Our President (when Honorary Secretary) asked me to write an obituary for my father, who had been a member for 70 years (1929–1999). As an encouragement he sent me a copy of the obituary that had appeared in the *Cairngorm Club Journal* from the pen of Dr Brodie Lewis, a fellow Himalayan trekker. To my shame I never did so. But recent rummaging through old family papers has pricked my conscience into make amends – a glimpse into a life long passed.

Leslie Hay's life-long love of the Cairngorms and Donside (for forty years he was Clerk and Treasurer to Alford District Council till abolished by local government reorganisation) started when as a young teenager he holidayed at the Luib, Corgarff. From this base by foot and bike he could explore the Avon and Cairn Gorm, Ben Avon, Ben Macdui and other hills.

When he started at the University of Aberdeen as a 17-year-old, he cycled each day from his home in Peterhead to classes – a 70-mile round trip. This kept him fit, notwithstanding that a doctor thought he wasn't and had prescribed him to drink stout. (Would a doctor do this now?)

His application in 1929 for SMC membership was proposed by two notable Aberdeen climbers, 'Rocky' Garden[2] and J.A. Parker[3], both later presidents of both the SMC and the Cairngorm Club. That was a time when there was a great deal of joint membership and interaction between the two senior Scottish clubs.

---

[1] Over two decades having elapsed since Leslie Hay's death, and with all his contemporaries long deceased, it was felt more appropriate to place this biographical note here rather than the In Memoriam section of the *Journal*. – HON. ED.

[2] William 'Rocky' Garden, an Aberdeen advocate, climbed all over the world, from an early attempt on Douglas-Gibson Gully on Lochnagar with Raeburn to the Alps, Norway and the Rockies – hence his nickname. He was a member of the Alpine Club and (for 54 years) of both the SMC and the Cairngorm Club till his death in 1950. He served on the SMC Committee 1904–7 & 1929–32), and as Vice-President (1915–19) and President (1934–36). In the Cairngorm Club he also served on the committee twice (1911–21 and 1928–30) and was president 1925–27 but is best remembered as its secretary (1932–49). This was in succession to my father, Leslie Hay. He was a close friend of James A Parker and collaborated with him over many mountain issues – guidebooks, indicators etc. In 1902, after a serious avalanche on the Weisshorn when two of his companions were killed, he promised his father he would not undertake any serious or difficult mountaineering again, but he continued to walk the Scottish mountains that he loved.

[3] In many ways James A. Parker's climbing career was similar to Garden's. He was an early SMC member (1893–1946). He also climbed all over the world – Alps, Pyrenees, Japanese Alps, Rockies – but especially in the Scottish mountains. He was a very early Munro compleater.

A talented engineer of quite exceptional accuracy, nowadays he is probably best remembered for his surveying and construction of the indicators on Lochnagar and Ben Macdui and the Cairngorm Club footbridge over the Allt na Beinne at the north end of the Lairig Ghru path. But his quite exceptional knowledge of the Scottish hills gave rise to many articles in the *SMC* and *CC Journals*, and to the excellent guidebook to the Western Highlands. He indexed the first ten volumes of the *SMC Journal* and catalogued all the CC Library. He was our President in 1924–26, Cairngorm Club president in 1928–30 and its honorary president in 1945 in succession to Prof. J. Norman Collie. The footbridge over the Luibeg burn at the other end of the Lairig Ghru is known as the Parker Memorial Bridge – a fitting memorial to an exceptional man.

A.L. Hay, a member of the SMC for 70 years.
Photo by courtesy of the Society of Advocates in Aberdeen.

Present-day aspirants might be bemused by the qualifications listed in his application: 31 Munros and four winter ascents, the latter being the Black and Red Spouts of Lochnagar. Of the summer ascents, 16 were in the Affric and Strathfarrar area during what turned out to be a life-changing week-long expedition. On being settled in for an overnight stay with the Henderson family at Allt Beithe (now the Youth Hostel far up Glen Affric), Leslie Hay and his climbing companion Roy Symmers had to forgo their beds for the night with the arrival of two young ladies from the Grampian Club embarked on a similar trip. But being relegated to the barn, the men missed the nightly Bible reading that Mr Henderson did for the benefit of his young wife and children and anyone else who happened to be staying in the house. However, this preferential treatment for the ladies did not deter the men from chivalrously accompanying them as far as Loch Hourn.

It was while waiting by the shore for the boat which had been summoned by much arm-waving to take them to Arnisdale that they were met by a long column of dark figures coming down the path from Kinloch Hourn. This was a funeral procession carrying the coffin to the ancient burial site where they were patiently waiting. No question of a hearse in those days.

That was, however, only a temporary parting between the young Aberdeen lawyer and Mina Yeaman, the Dundee teacher. On researching Cairngorm Club Journals from that period, it is clear that my parents had many memorable days and demanding ascents together. My mother kept in touch with the young Henderson family with Christmas presents for the children and a piece of her wedding cake. Much later, when I used to explore Knoydart, my father would tell me about a stalker he stayed with who would make a big pot of porridge on a Saturday night, pour it into the top drawer of the dresser, and then for the next seven days cut himself a good piece to keep going. I am not sure, but this may have been the 'Mr Macdonald, Carnoch, Kinlochnevis' who also got a piece of the wedding cake. I hope he enjoyed the change of diet. Maybe a postie would jib at that delivery now.

It has proved very difficult to find out much about what my father did in the mountains in those days. He certainly climbed with Roy Symmers (Parker's assistant as engineer to the Great North of Scotland Railway Co, and probably the leading North-East climber of that period). Almost certainly he climbed Raeburn's Gully on Lochnagar – the Aberdeen test-piece of the time. However, the 1929 copy of *Munro's Tables* annotated by my mother shows that she climbed no fewer than 77 Munros between 1928 and 1931. Some of these would have been with her Dundee friends, Lizzie Morton and Polly Clarke, but undoubtedly some others were with Leslie. What a lot of mountain talent our Club forsook for over a century until the Rules were changed in 1990!

During the war my father served in the RAF as a Flying Officer at Skeabrae, Orkney, a Spitfire airfield near Scapa Flow. On being de-mobbed, he resumed his regular attendance at Cairngorm Club meets. These did not always satisfy him, as I recall after a long day in the hills he would set off for a walk around Aberdeen in the evening.

Walking was his daily exercise and later also swimming, which he learned to do when well on in years. During the thirty years he was a part-time lecturer at Aberdeen University, I do not ever recall him using a car for the journey from home to office or the midday hike over to King's and back. Some people thought he did not possess a car and would stop to offer him a lift – always politely declined. This emphasis on keeping fit and healthy even extended to his lectures, first Procedure and Evidence (1945–1964), and then Taxation Law (1961–1975), when he set up the first course in that subject in any Scottish university. The first lecture session was devoted to the subject *mens sana in corpore sano*. Although Latin was then a compulsory subject for most would-be lawyers, some may have thought they had strayed into a medical class. My father always said a sick lawyer was of no good to his client.

Mina introduced Leslie to the Alps, and over many years they visited many other mountainous areas – Afghanistan, Ethiopia, Nepal, the Silk Road etc. At the age of 60, on the centenary of Whymper's ascent of the Matterhorn, Leslie also made the ascent by the Hörnli Ridge. After that he made many treks in the

Himalaya. On his first trek to Everest he was badly affected by dysentery; but ever afterwards he proved that by careful attention to diet one could remain completely fit, and his second trek to Everest, at the age of 70, was a great success. It included the ascent of Yum Cho (16,650ft) and Kala Patthar (18,192ft). But that was not the end of his Himalayan treks. He subsequently crossed the difficult snow pass from Rolwaling to Khumbu, the Tesi Lapcha (18,881ft) so well described by Tom Weir in his book *East of Katmandu*. One such trek he was keen to do conflicted with his university work but the University kindly agreed to grant this long-serving member of staff leave of absence provided he could find a suitable replacement. By reading up the taxation law textbook every night, the present writer endeavoured to keep one step ahead of the class, but it was a close-run race and probably some of the students thought they had won.

For seventy-two years Leslie Hay was a member of the Cairngorm Club. Twice he served on its committee (1928–31 and 1949–52), twice as a vice-president (1934–38 and 1952–55), and as secretary and treasurer in 1932. He was their president from 1955–58 and honorary president 1980–84. He was the first honorary president to step down, saying that after four years the honour should be passed to someone else, a tradition which that club continues to this day.

He passed away at home nine days after his 94th birthday, survived by Mina and two of his three children.

J.Y.L. Hay

LOCKDOWN LOG

IN THIRTEEN DECADES the Club and the *Journal* have felt the impact of two World Wars, many epidemics, and numerous cycles of economic boom and recession. But it is now only our oldest readers – those who lived through the Second World War – who will be able to recall restrictions resembling those of the Covid-19 lockdowns in 2020 and 2021. As we go to press the pandemic still looms large, and a proper perspective will doubtless come with time; but here we set down a few of our members' experiences while they are still fresh in memory.

In last year's *Journal* we recorded the miracle by which the Scottish International Winter Meet was successfully concluded, just as the lights were being switched off around the world. In 'The Last Meet' Stan Pearson recalled a final visit to the CIC Hut soon afterwards, in March 2020, at which 'gradually news drifted in of coronavirus,' and presciently '… some wag suggested conditions and weather were bound to get good just as access to the hills was prohibited.' Within a day or two came the message: 'Do not go to the hills. Do not go out. Only essential travel is permitted.' And finally an apocalyptic e-mail: 'There will be no Club meets for the foreseeable future.'

Even those fortunate enough to remain healthy had now to endure a year and more of restricted movement, with only a temporary relaxation during the summer of 2020. How did we cope? Some members turned to alternative forms of exercise, as Stan recalls.

> The initial enthusiasm to take advantage of enforced time at home by tackling projects like finally scanning slides into the PC quickly waned as the diary cleared, and with it motivation and planning. Putting up a pull-up bar but not using it was typical of my enthusiasm. Without projects and objectives to aim for within any timeframe, training – a struggle at the best of times – had little appeal. A daily walk and other pursuits took over from climbing in the months at home with restricted social contact. Home bread-making improved no end, and with it perhaps the waistline grew a little.

For Alison Coull, life and work in Edinburgh suddenly changed.

> Then with one stroke of a Ministerial pen we were working from home and locked down, not allowed to see anyone else even outside. The streets of Edinburgh fell silent almost instantly. Cycling became the main activity. Glorious weather, streets with no traffic. Edinburgh as you would never experience it again.

In his frustration another Edinburgh resident, Olly Stephenson, took to hanging bat-like from the underside of canal bridges, as recounted in 'Crack Addict' earlier in this *Journal*, while others including Alison explored the minor protuberances that grace our capital city.

> I am ashamed to say that despite living in Edinburgh for over 30 years I had never been up Calton Hill, Corstorphine Hill or Craiglockhart. I didn't know the Pentlands that well. Always too busy rushing away to the Highlands, week after week, packing, unpacking. A new life began. Bouldering at Salisbury crags, cycling across the bridge. The lockdown cliché of wild swimming at a little beach 20 minutes from my house that I didn't even know existed before lockdown.

Over in the west, Billy Hood rediscovered the Renfrewshire Heights.

> Coming from Ayrshire, and having lived in Renfrewshire and now in Inverclyde, the Clyde Muirsheil Regional Park (to name it formally) has hardly

ever been out of sight, never mind very far away. Lingering snow on Misty Law has always been one sign of a good winter. Way back in December 1981 Paul Brian and I waded up the Garnock Valley to climb a frozen Garnock Spout, Ayrshire's highest waterfall. Since then, occasional bouldering at Craig Minnan and family walks to 'Windy Hill' from the visitor centre were the only visits. Now, during Covid-19, the fondly renamed 'Muirsheil Alps' have become the sanctuary, the saviour, the go-to outdoor arena.

Initially, when restrictions were tightest and with confusion about what was and wasn't allowable, the long track from Lochwinnoch to the summit of Misty Law (510m) started the new relationship: a four-hour round trip at a leisurely pace. Larks, pipits, stonechats and hen harriers, spring and summer. On one winter ascent another Paul, wearing snow-shoes, kept disappearing into the mist as the rest of us floundered in waist-deep drifts and massive sastrugi. Five and a half hours that time!

The most satisfying walk, because it felt like a day in the 'real hills', was what became known as the 'Queenside Loop'. The track from the visitor centre following the Calder Burn up to the old barytes mine had been upgraded recently to help with the removal of old electricity pylons. This meant comfortable progress and dry feet for the first 4km. Muirsheil has long had a reputation for tussocks and bogs, not least amongst the hardy 'Mountain Marathon' folk (2001 & 2019 events). Finding a dry route from 'the mines' up to Hill of Stake (522m), high point of our 'massif', took a lot of trial and error. No paths! The broad ridge to East Girt Hill and then the crossing of the Raith glen to Queenside Hill were all hags and heather, but enjoyable because feeling remote.

The views across Glasgow and beyond from Queenside Hill were impressive. Always a little gloat here to see the Campsies, the Old Kilpatricks, the Glenniffer Braes and even the Whitelees Wind Farm. On a fine day the city haemorrhages people, but for some reason not to the 'Alps'.

In summer 2020 came a loosening of the restrictions on movement; but, as Alison recalls, conditions in the Highlands were far from normal.

After 3 months we were released, but for day trips only. 'Covid No Access' signs had proliferated. Eating a snack bar beside a loch I was told, 'You are not allowed to have a picnic.' The first big hills of freedom were Ben Alder and Beinn Bheoil, only to be faced with the shocking sight of the summit having been used as a toilet. I had never seen such a mess on a Munro. I cleared it all up, not able to leave the top in that state. What was the thought process that this was an acceptable way to treat a wild place?

The usual type of spontaneous last-minute accommodation was not available, with campsites and bunkhouses unable to open under Covid restrictions. Wild camping, bivvying for the first time in over 20 years. Glorious days! Grab a cottage share – it's Scrabster, not the first place I would think of going, but anywhere but Edinburgh. Climbing walls finally opened again – masked and sanitised. It felt great though to see all the familiar faces and recover a sense of normality. Some people had managed a remarkable amount of climbing outside. Still we were only able to meet with one other household indoors.

Then another lockdown loomed. As quickly as we were released we were back where we started. But worse: a travel ban under the law – not guidance this time – well and truly confining us to the city of Edinburgh boundary from October to April. The snow came. There were truly wonderful days in the Pentlands. Snow-shoeing, or crampons needed. Often these were sunrise or sunset walks because of congestion and parking. It felt as if we were back in the bigger hills, even Alpine-like.

A rescue helicopter lights up the Orion Face, 30 January 2021. The transgressors were eventually rescued from Minus Two Gully. Photo: Noel Williams.

During winter 2020–21 the restrictions on travel and on activities like mountaineering were prescriptive. For exercise one was allowed to meet one other person, and an activity had to start and finish at the same place, no more than five miles from the boundary of a person's local authority area. In January two Glasgow climbers who flouted the rules by travelling to Fort William and attempting Minus Two Gully had to be rescued by the Lochaber MRT with helicopter support, an event that Noel Williams captured spectacularly by telephoto lens from his home at Torlundy. The two climbers were fined.

Billy Hood made the most of his second spell of confinement in Inverclyde.

> Enduring a second lockdown and watching another winter slip away was hard to bear, especially as the weather and snow conditions were so good across the Highlands for long spells.
>
> This is when the most amazing gift of all gifts arrived on our doorstep, and conditions for ski-touring turned extraordinary: blue skies, no wind, powder snow on a solid full cover, even the biggest tussocks hidden – for two days! As on small hills all over Scotland, it was ski-anywhere time. The Muirshiel Alps had turned into the Harda

Members living in the Highlands were of course to be envied, prompting Sarah Atkinson on Speyside to quote Tom Hodgkinson: 'Guilt is also a way for us to express to others that we are a person of good conscience.' She writes as follows of her winter experiences.

> Living in the shadow of the Northern Cairngorms I was privileged to have the most wonderful playground at my disposal during the lockdown of winter 2020–21. I did feel guilty. I did think of my friends and fellow SMC members

Not Norway but Renfrewshire; above a frozen Queenside Loch. Photo: Billy Hood.

Skiing from the Mòine Mhòr to Sgòr an Lochain Uaine. Photo: Sarah Atkinson.

whose homes were not so geographically advantageous – but not sufficiently to stop me.

It was a winter of extraordinary snowfall. The track to our house is a mile long; our cars were parked at the bottom of the track on Christmas Eve and did not make it up to the house again until 21 February. Each day's adventure started with a one-mile ski-run down the track, payback for this joy being the one-mile skin back up at the end of day, often laden with heavy rucksacks of gear and shopping.

The snow-gates at Glenmore were shut as lockdown began, so each visit to the Cairngorms started from the Hayfield. The snowfall was so generous it was possible to skin all the way up to the Coire Cas car park. It was a world of white – trees bent low with the weight of snow, and heather buried deeply. A tracery of mountain hare footprints adorned the surface, with occasional holes where they had dug for food. It was a hard winter for wildlife. The mountains were under such depths the buttresses were completely clothed in deep white. Snow-shoes or skis were the only way to travel, for on foot one would sink to the knee or thigh and in drifts to the waist. Having reached the summit of Cairn Gorm we would enjoy two or three runs down to Coire Raibeirt then back up to Cairn Gorm and all the way down to the Hayfield. When the 'green run' from the Cas formed a firm glassy surface, three miles of gripping snowplough would leave my thighs screaming.

Fearful that the snow cover might suddenly disappear as happens most winters, when the tours we aspire to melt into the River Spey, we ventured over to Glen Feshie with the road just passable on packed snow. As dawn broke, we skinned up Càrn Bàn Mòr. With the glen below shrouded in thick mist, we emerged into a pale blue-white world. There was no sign of the many peat hags and burns of the Mòine Mhòr, just an undulating carpet of deep snow making our journey over to Sgòr an Lochain Uaine very easy. But it is a long way for an early January day, and the shortness of daylight and the bitter cold encouraged us to keep the pace up. Even so, on our return we skied off the summit of Càrn Bàn Mòr just as the sun was setting. A starlit white world negated the need for torches in the woods and finally along the road, the sting in the tail after this most memorable day being the final skin up the track home.

But the thaw did not come; snow on snow, it just kept falling. The lower hills now became the centre of attraction. There is a healthy population of enthusiastic skiers and snow-boarders residing in Strathspey and they all seemed to congregate on Creagan Gorm (732m), the west top of Meall a' Bhuachaille, on the same day. Social media had it that the 'pow was awesome!' And it was, with excellent skiing among the half-buried pine trees to the forest edge. As one local put it, 'Aye, the wee Gorms gettin' a fair hammering the day.' Indeed, they were.

Being so close to our home, perhaps the most prized location for skiing was the Hills of Cromdale. We focused our attention on these fine wee hills (fine in winter, when the unrelenting bog is frozen!) exploring almost every ridge and gully line on the Spey side. Most days we rarely saw anyone else, except for the keepers racing about on skidoos shooting mountain hare with rifles (presumably shooting as many as possible before the ban on unlicensed culling came into force at the start of March this year). We also ventured to Geal-chàrn Mòr and Geal-chàrn Beag west of Aviemore and to Càrn an Fhreiceadain north of Kingussie, where again we witnessed keepers in pursuit of mountain hare.

Eventually play came to a stop as high winds persisted for quite some time, accompanied by temperature fluctuations the snowpack began to change. And not for the better from a skier's perspective. The winds dropped, the sun came out, the snow was sparkling! A ski tour to Ben Macdui beckoned. Abandoning skinning up to the plateau and donning crampons instead hinted at things to come. The firm snow glistened and gleamed as far as the eye could see, there would be no soft stuff today! Our skis rattled and chattered over the rock-hard surface to the summit, round the Corries and down Lurcher's Gully. Although it made for swift travel, it was quite some time before the juddering sensation left my legs. Lesson learnt. Time to put the skis aside, dig out the axes and bash up some gullies! The snow having retreated to the higher levels, our approach to the Cas was by bike rather than ski, the long slog up with a heavy pack being repaid with a swift, chilly, freewheel back down. It did not escape my notice the increase in electric bikes swiftly ascending the ski road. Observing the sometimes highly inventive ways of securing skis, climbing gear and packs to bikes was like watching a curious circus act. On one occasion an 'E-biker' was towing his companion on a standard bike – not with the climbing rope, I hope! Was this an act of kindness or of determination to ensure his companion reached the start of the route at the same time?

In April 2021, with new cases of Covid-19 in the UK still numbering a couple of thousand per day but fatalities fewer than 20, day-trips to the Highlands were again permitted. A year after his last visit, Stan Pearson returned to Ben Nevis.

I was out of touch with conditions and out of shape but quickly fell into old habits as we discussed route options, gear, weather prospects and a start-time that brought us to the foot of the Ben after an overnight frost.

Views on a fine day and conversation with a real person outside my own household eased the walk-in after many months of social isolation. There was no popping into the CIC for a brew and to see who was in: Covid restrictions meant all huts were still closed as they had been since last March.

There were plenty of routes in condition and no feared crowds. It had been a difficult year for many professions including guides and instructors, with no access to the hills or clients. It was typical late April on the Ben; the unusual thing was for this to be the first route of the season rather than the last. We decided for various reasons on the easier option of Tower Ridge and were soon at the Douglas gap. The last time I had been here was the previous March on the last Club meet before the pandemic, as we descended in rain and sleet after a route on the Douglas boulder. In the intervening year so much had changed. In keeping with the substantive difference, the weather too was different from the usual wind, spindrift and approaching gloom; it was fine bright, with good views over the mountain.

Alistair had done this route 21 times already. I had last done it in spring when the CIC extension was being built, so between us we felt we knew the way. Crampons, tools and ropes felt less familiar. The first pitch rekindled memories: moving together, short pitches, short-roping, a bonus little ice-pitch, and a variety of conditions on rock, ice and névé as the mountain unfolded before us. Though there were folk on Hadrian's Wall, Indicator Wall, Point Five Gully and Ledge Route, the other familiar routes had no parties and we heard none of the shouting so common earlier in the season in most years. There was a lovely stillness broken only by the tinkle of hoar frost falling down Point Five as the sun melted the upper slopes. Further afield, endless hills sparkled with a dusting of white in the sunshine. It was great to be out. There was a big grin on Alistair's face as he donned sunglasses. Before we knew it we were at the Eastern Traverse and then heading up the steepening rock to the little arête before Tower Gap.

Here a party emerged from Glover's Chimney and kindly waved us on. Alistair made short work of the Gap, leaving me to lead up the final snow to the plateau.

There were only six of us on the summit: the Indicator Wall party belayed to the trig point, the Point Five party and us two – and a few friendly snow buntings. What a magnificent hill, with views of the immediate mountain and in every direction, and what a tonic after months in the city! It was good to be back in the mountains.

As Thoreau wrote, 'If we will be quiet and ready enough, we shall find compensation in every disappointment.' Earlier in this *Journal* you will have heard Ian Crofton yearning for the Buachaille in his poem 'written in lockdown in London'. Donald Orr also found solace in poetry, composing the two sonnets that follow. 'It keeps me sane, relatively, during this long wait,' he said.

ROCKFACE

Crabbing across a sloping ledge,
like a jingling lobster pinching
its way somewhere from a wedge
of creviced verticality, wincing
in tiredness and fear towards
an easier-angled ramp of schist,
mica splattered and leading upwards
through greyness enhanced by mist.
No way to gauge on that rough face
how long my power would endure
as hold by hold I tried to trace
one line of comfort in the future.
The future perfect revealed itself,
a solid hold, a rising move, a broader shelf.

FOGWIND

What was this white and whistling gauze
that hid the route and hung about,
that had no substance, no reasonable cause
but only cold movement throughout
its empty passage around the face?
A breath of old air following its own way,
murmuring a half-whispered trace
of quiet sound to the lateness of the day.
What was the note fading in the hiss
of white wind that set the mind to recall
a distant rhythm, a forgotten sequence
moving the air to keep it cool?
Do I breathe this whiteness in
if this whiteness is all being?

THE SCOTTISH MOUNTAINEERING TRUST – 2020

Scottish Charity Number SC 009117

The Trustees met by Zoom on 3 April, 3 July and 16 October 2020. During the course of these meetings, support was given to the following: A. Armstrong – Advanced Avalanche Course; Mountaineering Scotland – Student SMART weekend; Munro Society – Exhibition; Moffat Mountain Rescue Team – Book; Mountaineering Scotland – Winter Climbing for Students; Jonathan Conville Memorial Trust – Scottish Winter 2021; Scottish Mountaineering Club – Journal Digitisation; Zero Impact – Greenland; Apex 6 – Bolivia; Outdoor Access Trust (D. Baird) – Glas Allt path & bridge, Lochnagar, and Coire na Ciste path, Cairn Gorm; Dundee Mountain Film Festival (R. Crawford); and Scottish Mountaineering Club – Raeburn Hut.

The present Trustees are S.M. Richardson (Chairman) – (*ex officio* immediate Past President of the SMC), D.N. Williams – (*ex officio* Convenor of the Publications Sub-Committee), G.D. Morrison – (*ex officio* Editor of the SMC Journal), J.R.R. Fowler – *ex officio* President of the SMC, R. Aitken, D.J. Broadhead, R.D.M. Chalmers, J.R.G. Mackenzie, E. Riley and I.M. Young. D. Small is the Trust Treasurer, and J.D. Hotchkis is the Trust Secretary. J.A.P. Hutchinson provides support to the Trust on developing marketing strategy.

The Trustees during the year have developed a marketing strategy and an initiative in respect of a Diamond Grant Award. The Diamond Grant is to commemorate the 60th anniversary of the Trust, which was founded in 1962. All the Trustees have been involved in the foregoing, and in particular Iain Young has kindly chaired a sub-group for the Diamond Grant Award Initiative and John Hutchinson has carried out valuable work on marketing strategy.

The following grants have been committed by the Trustees during 2020:

A. Armstrong – Advanced Avalanche Course	£100
Mountaineering Scotland – Student SMART weekend	£2253
Munro Society – Exhibition	£2500
Moffat Mountain Rescue Team – Book	£600
Mountaineering Scotland – winter climbing for students	£2100
Jonathan Conville Memorial Trust – Scottish Winter 2021, (now deferred to Scottish Winter 2022)	£1500
Scottish Mountaineering Club – Journal Digitisation Phase 5	£975
Zero Impact – Greenland	£250
Apex 6 – Bolivia (now deferred to 2022)	£500
Outdoor Access Trust (D. Baird) – Glas Allt path & bridge, Lochnagar; Coire na Ciste path, Cairn Gorm	£20,000
Dundee Mountain Film Festival (R. Crawford)	£1000
Scottish Mountaineering Club – Raeburn Hut, (£8000 loan & £8000 grant)	£16,000

James D. Hotchkis (Hon. Sec. SMT)

MUNRO MATTERS 2020

by Alison Coull (Clerk of the List)

This report covers 1 January to 31 December 2020. The five columns below give number, name and year of Compleation of Munros, Tops & Furths as appropriate. *SMC member; **LSCC member.

6745	Andrew Rogers	2013	6795	Lauren Anderson	2020
6746	Patricia Pentrice	2019	6796	Alex Rich	2020
6747	Simon Brill	2011	6797	Michael Carr	2020
6748	Martin Perry	2019	6798	Matt Paterson	2020
6749	Kenny Robb*	1980 1981 2018	6799	Colin Vose	2020
6750	Alan Mitchell	1990	6800	Deirdre Evans	2020
6751	Gordon McDougall	2009	6801	Susan J. Gardiner	2020
6752	Peter Camm	2019	6802	Charles S. Gardiner	2020
6753	Goffredo Bondanelli	2009	6803	Daniel Lennon	2020
6754	Gwyneth Jackman	2019	6804	Margaret Jones	2020
6755	Peter G.C. Ellis	2005 2017 2015	6805	William Munro	2012
6756	Stephen P Green	2019	6806	Colin Brown	2020
6757	Sarah Hudson	2019	6807	Fi Rooney	2020
6758	Ted Reilly	2019	6808	Grant Paterson	2020
6759	Stuart Bloomfield	2018	6809	Simon Hood	2020
6760	Len Cruickshank	2019	6810	Colin Hood	2020
6761	Graeme Tosh	2008	6811	John Macgregor	2020
6762	Edward Bell	2018	6812	Allon Welsh	2020
6763	Robert B Jones	2010	6813	William R. Milne	2020
6764	Iain Cassidy	2019	6814	Jennifer Tennant	2020
6765	Nicola Hardy	2019	6815	Peter Tennant	2020
6766	James Forrest	2019	6816	David W. Croft	2020
6767	Fiona Morrison	2019	6817	Chris Brydie	2018
6768	Alex W. Mason	2019	6818	Mark G. Lloyd	2018
6769	David J. Mounsey	1993	6819	Kevin Wheeler	2020
6770	David Booth	1993	6820	Calum J.B. Dinnes	2020
6771	Keith Batchelor	2020	6821	Moira J Simpson	2020
6772	Simon Thurston	2020	6822	Lesley Price	2020
6773	Dougie Brown	2020	6823	Andy Kinder	2020
6774	Colin Prestwich	2017	6824	Katharine Dyer	2020
6775	Anne Guthrie	2020	6825	Mark Dyer	2020
6776	Brian McShane	2020	6826	David Gierlowski	2020
6777	Debbie Macdonald	2020	6827	Robert Pearson	2020
6778	Diana Macdonald	2020	6828	Andrew Pennill	2020
6779	Richard Murray	2020	6829	John Fraser Grant	2020
6780	Alison Matheson	2020	6830	David T Bennison	2020
6781	Eileen Prentice	2020	6831	Christine Blake	2020
6782	Andre McKenna	2020	6832	Julia Gow	2020
6783	Patrick McKenna	2020	6833	Keith Russell	2020
6784	Lisa O'Keefe	2020	6834	Charles Taylor	2020
6785	Anne Foster	2020	6835	Margaret Bryant	2020
6786	Cath Bateman	2020	6836	Tom Ogilvie	2020
6787	Henry Pruddon	2020	6837	Gordon Robb	2020
6788	Amanda Bond	2020	6838	Karen Ashley	2020
6789	Ian Hunter	2020	6839	Douglas Robertson	2020
6790	Tilly Smith	2019	6840	Ilona Turnbull	2020
6791	Robert Lambden	2018	6841	Paul Goulding	2020
6792	Angela Ning	2020	6842	Paul Tallett	2020
6793	Ian Ragg	2020	6843	Philip Nelson	2020
6794	Steve Limb	2020	6844	Bruce Russell	2020

6845	Elaine Martin	2020	6854	Lesley Muirden	2020
6846	Michael Weaver	1995	6855	John Dougan	2020
6847	Gordon Miller	2020	6856	Brian Fraser	2020
6848	Brian Findlay*	2020	6857	Niall Ritchie*	2020
6849	Jonathon Wood	2020	6858	Mike Wilcox	2020
6850	Liam Brotchie	2020	6859	Gordon Ballantyne	2020
6851	David Hood	2020	6860	Allen McIntosh	2020
6852	Ian Taylor	2020	6861	Gavin Mackenzie	2020
6853	Kenneth W. Ingle	2020	6862	Cathy Southworth	2020

After a very busy 2019, the contrast with 2020 could not be more stark. The coronavirus pandemic dominated most of 2020, and this year's summary of Munro registrations reflects its impact. (Famously of course Sir Hugh Munro died of Spanish flu aged 63, on 19 March 1919, during the post-war influenza pandemic.) There were 117 compleations registered, 81 of these being in 2020. The pandemic coincided almost perfectly with the Munro registration year. It was on 31 December 2019 that Chinese authorities first alerted the World Health Organisation to cases of pneumonia in Wuhan.

January to March (pre-lockdown)

Traditionally this is a quiet time for Munro registrations. Key dates were the first case of coronavirus in Scotland on 1 March 2020. WHO declared a pandemic on 11 March 2020. The first death in Scotland was on 13 March 2020. Things changed very quickly after that.

During this time, the first registration of the year was from Andrew Rogers (6745) who had compleated in 2013. Andrew started recording his Munros on 'a sheet of fine writing paper' from early digs in Fort William. On his late registration Andrew said that he was glad he had taken the time to write his letter as it had stirred many great memories and enthused him to get out on the hill more.

Munroists who register late often reflect on the reasons why they did not do so earlier. Alan Mitchell (6750), who registered a 1990 compleation, said he had formerly thought it pretentious but 30 years later decided he was being pretentious for not registering.

In March I also received a very moving letter from Nadine and Irmela Romer, who sought registration on behalf of their father and husband Goffredo Bondanelli (6753). Goffredo went missing mountaineering in Scotland in May 2016. Born in the Venetian region of Northern Italy, Goffredo was always passionate about the mountains. He discovered a love for the Scottish landscape in 1990 and compleated on Ben Lomond with his family in August 2009. The weeks in Scotland were described as a purification of his body, mind and soul. Goffredo had intended to register but never found the time. It was supposed to be a special letter. Now Nadine, as the daughter of Goffredo, wrote that special letter and asked for his last wish to be fulfilled so that the certificate could be framed and given a place of honour. Nadine also thanked the Scottish police in Fort William for their outstanding, intensive and sensitive work, and the numerous volunteers and lovely people involved in the search. It showed the family how empathetic and compassionate the Scottish people are and why her father loved to be in Scotland.

March to July – the first lockdown

The First Minister of Scotland announced on 17 March 2020 that life would change significantly for all of us. Schools closed on 20 March 2020. Significantly for hillwalkers, Mountain Rescue teams asked people to stay away from the hills.

At this stage, little was known about the virus and how rescue teams would have to adapt. A national lockdown came into effect on 23 March with a stay-at-home requirement, social distancing and 'stay local' guidance. No one was allowed to meet with another household even outdoors for exercise. Advice was given that people should only go outside once a day to exercise (relaxed on 11 May). Vaccine trials started in June and single people were also allowed to form 'bubbles' with another household at that point.

Not surprisingly there were no new Munro registrations during this period, which is normally a busy time for registrations. Pete Ellis (6755) took the opportunity to register his compleation of two rounds of the Munros, in 2005 and 2018, together with rounds of the Munro Tops, Corbetts, Grahams, Donalds and Furths – the Grahams and Donalds being completed just on the cusp of lockdown. Pete had been hoping for a celebratory compleation in August but decided it was not to be, and therefore took the chance to finish early. He has also completed the Seven Summits and 99 Ultras. Pete lives in Hertfordshire, and said that despite there being no mountains it is very easy to get away from.

Nicola Hardy (6765) and James Forrest (6766) registered their compleation from 2019 which was done over a six-month period from April 2019 to October 2019.

July to October – release

On 3 July 2020 the stay-local travel restriction was removed. Holiday accommodation opened in July and face coverings became mandatory in shops. Wild camping was allowed. Four households were allowed to meet outdoors in groups of up to 15. Two households of up to eight people could meet indoors. Some areas such as the city of Aberdeen did have local lockdowns during this period, which restricted travel.

First off the mark was Keith Batchelor (6771) from Berkshire, who compleated on Beinn Sgritheall on 10 July. He was closely followed by Simon Thurston (6772), who said he had intended to complete in 2020 at his leisure. But since permission to travel was reinstated he attacked his remaining hills with some urgency in fear of another lockdown. This meant five hill-days from 6 July to 20 July to see him over the line on Blàbheinn on a fine day in his own company.

Twin sisters Debbie (6777) and Diana Macdonald (6778) compleated together on 1 August on Ben More.

A few folk started and compleated on Munros with the same name or on different summits of the same mountain. Alex Rich (6796) started on Ben Vorlich and compleated on the other Ben Vorlich. Allon Welsh (6812) started his round on Beinn Eighe and finished on Beinn Eighe. Ian Taylor (6852) started and finished on Buachaille Etive Mòr.

The pandemic restricted compleation parties: Eileen Prentice (6781) finished in August, noting that there were no big groups owing to Covid-19.

Andre McKenna (6782) made it a family affair, compleating on the In Pinn. His son Allister (6614) had compleated last year, and his other son Patrick (6783) compleated on the Five Sisters two days after Andre. His third son hopes to compleat in 2021.

Lisa O'Keefe (6784) is a former international rugby player and only came to Munro-bagging after retirement from rugby, now having free weekends and evenings. Covid also thwarted her plans but she managed a final push in August which involved six boat trips, three tents and a chair that her friends carried up Sgùrr Mòr so that she would have 'an armchair view' across Knoydart.

Angela Ning celebrates compleation on Toll Creagach. August 2020.
Photo: Ian Ragg.

Cath Bateman (6786) and her husband Henry Pruddon (6787) compleated on 13 August. Again, this was a delayed compleation. Cath and her husband had cycled into Ben Alder in March to camp for the last six hills. Aware of rising temperatures and the general feeling at the time, they thought better of it and cycled back to their van to head south. An hour into their journey the Prime Minister's 'lockdown' speech was broadcast. They drove through the night to get back to Cornwall, 'not knowing what our fate would be if stopped the following day'. They came back in August to finish the job in excellent weather.

Tilly Smith (6790), who is responsible for the Cairngorm reindeer herd, registered her 2019 compleation. Tilly was a late convert to Munro-bagging, being in her words 'Cairngorm-centric', and searching stray reindeer never took her to the summits.

Angela Ning (6792) and her husband Ian Ragg (6793) compleated in August, with friends and family present in spirit owing to the challenges of Covid. Angela collected her certificate in person, which provided me with the opportunity for some rare human interaction. Alex Rich (6796) who compleated in August on Ben Vorlich at Loch Lomond turned out to live a few doors down from me, providing another welcome opportunity for interaction on the doorstep with a certificate drop-off.

Flt Lt Matt Paterson (6798) completed in September – again a delayed compleation. Matt recounted many adventures, most notably one when he had forgotten his packed lunch and, though his wife sent him several texts advising him to abort immediately, he had carried on. Suddenly one of the SAR helicopters appeared and did a few circuits round him. Matt was initially concerned that his wife might have called Mountain Rescue. Eventually the crewman approached looking for somebody who had triggered a locator beacon. Matt took his chance to ask if they had any spare food. The crewman told him to stay low, and the helicopter flew past, depositing six Mars Bars.

During this period cases of coronavirus were rising, and new rules were introduced on 10 September restricting indoor and outdoor gatherings to six people from two households.

Douglas Robertson (6839) and Karen Ashley (6838) compleated on 3 October. They should have been on a trek to Everest Base Camp that was cancelled owing to Covid. They commented that possibly the limitations of the early lockdown drove them to explore and enjoy the freedom of the hills even more when lockdown was relaxed.

Ilona Turnbull (6840) completed on Ben Hope in October with a socially distanced and very small completion party 'in line with the Government guidance for Covid-19'. Ilona is an Australian citizen.

SMC member Brian Findlay (6848) compleated on Seana Bhràigh in October.

David Hood (6851) completed in October. His initial plan had been to do the last 44 hills over the spring and summer and have a completion trip with friends and family in October. The hotel had been booked two weeks before lockdown, so the plan was drastically revamped when lockdown was lifted, and David did his last 44 between 8 July and 10 October, enjoying a socially distanced toast at the top with some friends.

Kevin Wheeler compleating on the Inaccessible Pinnacle, September 2020. Photo: M. Airey.

Cathy Southworth (6862) compleated on Ladhar Bheinn. To celebrate, her missing friends from the Jacobites Mountaineering Club organised a 'final Munro' in Edinburgh, where they took in enough height and distance (1020m and 32km) on hills within the Edinburgh boundary to mark the occasion.

November to December – local levels and second lockdown

The four-month period of relative freedom came to an abrupt end in early November when a new five-tier system of local lockdowns was put in place. Most areas in Scotland were put in Level 3. Initially travel was permitted within a relevant Health Board area, which provided reasonable scope for hillwalkers. On 17 November, however, it became an offence to travel outside a Level 3 or 4 area except for an essential purpose. The travel ban had the effect that access to the hills depended on the local authority area you were living in, some areas having rather more hills on our lists than others! Those living in a Level 2 local authority were able to travel to another Level 2 area. Mike Wilcox (6858) from the Borders took advantage of this to compleat on Beinn na Lap in November. SMC member Niall Ritchie (6857) compleated in November as well.

There were no more compleations registered as Scotland moved to another full lockdown at the end of December. On a more positive note the new SMC guidebook for the Munros was published at the end of the year and has attracted very positive feedback. As Clerk of the List I am particularly pleased that it shows all of the Munro tops. No excuses now.

Comparing this year's data with last year (in parenthesis): New Munroists 117 (279); females 28% (20%); resident in Scotland 63% (64%); couples 8% (5%); average age 55 (55); average compleation time 25 years (26); Golden Munroists 5 (14).

This year's Golden Munroists were Len Cruickshank (6760, taking 61 years), Alex Mason (6768, 51), David Croft (6816, 52), Kevin Wheeler (6819, 50) and Brian Findlay (6848, 58).

In normal times the SMC can expect to register a number of foreign Munroists as the pastime of Munro-bagging stretches worldwide. This year I do not think there were any foreign registrations, which reflects the considerable constraints on international travel over the course of the year.

The most popular finishing Munros were Ben More on Mull (9), followed by Ben Lomond, Ladhar Beinn and Meall nan Tàrmachan (5). Beinn na Lap did not feature strongly this year perhaps because it is often chosen on account of the train journey and the possibility of a group celebration. Ben Nevis and Ben Lomond were again by far the most popular first Munros.

AMENDMENTS

No	Name	M	T	F	C	G	D
6722	Stewart Walker	2019	2019				
2106	Bob Taylor	1999	2009		2008	2020	2020
		2009					
		2019					
5482	Janet Drye	2014		2015			
5483	Roger Drye	2014		2015			
NYC	Ian George Park						2019
2343	Hayden Kingston	2000					
		2020					

720	Stewart Love	1989	1989				
3762	Robin Stevenson	2004			2019		
3044	Brian McWilliam	2003			2014	2018	2019
		2011					
2709	David Rutherford	2002			2015		
1397	Douglas R. Macleod	1995	1997	1998	2007		2019
		2000	2002	2003			
2097	Alan Duval	1999	2001	1988			
4653	Arthur Greenwood	2010		2018	2017		2020
6755	Peter G.C. Ellis	2005	2017	2015	2018	2020	2020
		2018					
5792	Kevin Woods	2013					
		2015					
		2019					
		2020					
4014	Pam Foord	2014			2019		
4015	Colin Foord	2014			2019		
359	Alf Barnard	1984	1985	1998	2019		
		2004	2004				
959	Mike Dixon*	1991	2008	2000	1996	2002	2005
		2009		2011			
		2020					
514	David H. Purser	1986	1987				
		1991					
		1995					
1798	Colin P. Watts	1997	2020	2003	2007	2012	2018
2579	Isabel M.G. Watts	2001	2020	2004	2007	2012	2018
4081	Fiona Reid*	2008	2018		2013		2020
		2018					
4082	Michael Watson*	2008	2018		2013		2020
		2018					
2345	Graham Phillips	2000	2000	2001	2013	2019	2020
NYC	Christopher Watson						2020
NYC	Robert Gemmell						2018
4120	Frank Johnstone	2003	2019	2016	2011	2020	2019
		2013					
5088	Chris Knowles	2012	2020				
280	Chris Andrews	1982			2000	2010	
6115	Paul Prior	2017					
		2020					
4320	Andy Barnett	2009			2015	2020	
2390	Colin Scott	2000	2020	2010			
		2008					
		2018					
5614	John B. Smith	2014	2020				
4169	Victoria Fuller	2008					
		2014					
		2020					
4862	Alan Puckrin	2011	2020		2018		
		2018					

1533	Graeme Morrison	1995			2009	2016	
		2009					
		2014					
		2015					
		2016					
		2020					
1534	Steven Morrison	1995					
		2020					
3355	Richard J.W. Tibbetts	2005		1999	2012	2015	2019
5670	Graham Haley	2014	2020				2019
751	Gerry Bowes	1990	1990	1987			2020
3964	Brian Fraser	2007	2020	2011			
1219	Valerie Moffat	1994	1994	1993	2004	2018	
1220	Andrew Moffat	1993	1994	1993	2004	2018	
4959	Allison Mackay	2009			2020		
4960	James Mackay	2009			2020		
3119	David Brown	2001			2009	2016	2020
2734	Elizabeth Swain	2002			2020		
6275	Sunny He Huang	2017					
		2020					
6627	David Thompson	2019	2020				
259	Derek Bearhop*	1981	1988		1991		2020
		1988			2015		
		1994					
		2007					
		2020					
6356	Mick Bradley	2018		2020			
4429	John Walker	2009					
		2020					
6329	John D. Armistead	2018	2018	2020			
4904	Michael D. McAnenay	2011			2020		
629	Kay Simpson	1988			2020		
2477	Jenny Mason	2000			2018		
5823	Jennifer May Cardno	2015					
		2020					
2712	Philip Brown	2001	2020				
455	A. Laurence Rudkin	1986	1991	1989	1995	2005	2020
		1996					
		2006					
		2013					
2158	Chris Philips	1999			2011		
3126	Keith Miller	2003	2003	2004			
2132	Steve Bell	1999			2012	2017	2017
3112	Bert Barnett	2001	2002	2002	1998	2000	2012
		2001	2009	2007	2007	2009	2013
		2009	2015	2015	2013	2018	2017
		2012			2019		
		2016					

(Entries marked 'NYC' are individuals who have not yet registered a Munro Compleation so do not have a Munroist number.)

In 2020 I heard from 63 (113) Munroists requesting amendments to entries on our Lists as follows (with last year's figures in parenthesis): New Munro Rounds 15 (33); Tops 10 (19); Furths 5 (21); Corbetts 13 (43); Grahams 8 (24); Donalds 16 (19); and Full House 7 (8).

Haydn Kingston (2343) was the first amendment of 2020, finishing a second round of Munros on Dreish in February despite Storm Dennis.

Kevin Woods (5792) compleated a non-stop winter round of the Munros finishing on Ben Lomond just as lockdown was hitting, so celebration of his achievement was somewhat constrained. Kevin experienced some epic winter storms and finished with a world looking very different from the one that existed when he started. [See his account on pages 95–8 in this *Journal*. – HON. ED.]

The Donalds are increasingly popular. Ian Park compleated in 2019 aged 23 and wondered how his age compared with other Donald compleators. Possibly quite low! His interest in the Donalds had come about when searching for a hobby when starting at university in Dumfries. Ian made the rather rash statement that he did not intend to begin another list. Now how many times have I heard that before?

Arthur Greenwood (4653) compleated the Donalds 'just before we were ordered to stay at home' and said he had enjoyed climbing in these quiet hills with the excellent SMC guidebook.

Laurence Rudkin (4553) compleated his Donald round on Windy Gyle for a Full House, suggesting it might be the longest time to compleat as he had started in June 1967. During the intervening years he was preoccupied with other hills. He commented that the Donalds are often underrated and whilst they certainly weren't his first priority they had provided some excellent days out.

On the subject of the Donalds, one or two people have been disappointed to find that Donald compleation should include all Hills and Tops – 140 summits in total (see *SMCJ*, 47/211 (2019), 252–3). Donald-baggers should also now note that Dugland NS602009 (Windy Standard), a Donald Top that was removed from Donald's List of 2000ft Hills in 1997 for lack of stature, has recently returned to the List as a Donald Top. Recent surveys and updated mapping by the OS have shown its height to be 612m and therefore over 610m (2000ft). The Keeper of the Tables has confirmed its elevated status and re-admission to Donald's List.

Val and Andy Moffat (1219 & 1220) finished their Grahams on Croit Bheinn (a notoriously tough Graham day) and confirmed that Glen Moidart is still a swamp.

SMC members also registered various amendments to the list. Mike Dixon (959) completed a second round of Munros on A' Ghlas Bheinn. Derek Bearhop (259) finished a fifth round of Munros on Ben Hope. He had set himself the target of finishing that round in his 50s as he had previously finished a fourth round in his 40s, a third in his 30s and a second in his 20s. (He missed a perfect set because on the first round he had just slipped past his twentieth birthday.) At 59, lockdown gave him some anxious moments so he had an intense flurry over the summer to climb his final 59 summits, coinciding with excellent weather. Derek also reported some previous rounds: a first round of the Corbetts (a triple Corbett compleation day), a second round of the Corbetts, and a first round of the Donalds. Derek says he had been studiously avoiding the Grahams, but the glossy SMC guidebook was finally tempting him. Kenny Robb (6749) registered his Munro compleation of 1981 along with compleations of all remaining lists over the years since then. Mike Watson (4082) and Fiona Reid (4081) registered a Donald compleation at the end of July. Their first Donald was in 2007 and they quietly chipped away at them until post-lockdown a desire to roam quiet, pathless hills drew them back to the last few Donalds. Mike did add that it was fair to say that there were many hills in the list they were unlikely to re-visit but at the same time they discovered parts of the Southern Uplands they would happily return to.

David Thompson (6627) of Edinburgh Mountaineering Club and SMC website sign-language fame compleated his Munro tops in October on Càrn Dearg of Ben Nevis. David's achievements as a deaf hillwalker have featured in several media outlets, including a short film about his experience on British Sign Language Zone from the British Sign Language Broadcasting Trust.

Sunny He Huang (6275) had a Chinese–Scottish twist on her second Munro compleation on Mount Keen, with a piper and both Scottish and Chinese flags at the summit, while mentioning that she registered in memory of her friends Steve Perry (3114) and Andy Nisbet (107).

Steven Morrison (1534) compleated a second round of Munros on Mullach Clach a' Bhlàir with his father Graeme (1533), who compleated a sixth round.

Jennifer May Cardno (5823) registered a second round of Munros aged 30.

Full Housers this year were Kenny Robb (6749), Isabel and Colin Watts (2579 & 1798, Munro Tops), Graham Phillips (2345, Donalds), Pete G.C. Ellis (6755, Grahams & Donalds) and Frank Johnstone (4120, Munro Tops & Donalds). The total number of SMC Full Housers is now 70.

Bert Barnett's (3112) multiple compleations are shown again in the hope that it is 'third time lucky' for an error-free entry.

So, in summary, a unique and unforgettable year for all the wrong reasons. Many of us have been unable to get to the hills for long periods, something we had always taken for granted and never imagined that laws would prevent or guidance advise against. Accommodation has been difficult to get, especially of an ad hoc nature. Many campsites did not open for tents. Communal dormitory accommodation that is frequently used by hillwalkers was difficult or impossible to operate in the face of an infectious and dangerous virus. Backpacking or bivvying was often the only option for getting away. Infrastructure and honeypot areas suffered with the influx of people on staycations. Perhaps it made the experiences we have had all the stronger. Certainly a number of compleationists seemed to feel a greater urgency to get out on the hills during the periods when restrictions were eased. 2021 has unfortunately started in a similar way, though with light at the end of the tunnel with the success of the vaccine programme.

Many thanks to the webmaster Martin McKenna for helping sort out different bits and pieces. The interface changed this year and it took a little while for this to be Alison-proofed. It remains a long-term objective to move to online registration. Also thanks to Mike Watson, who is responsible for uploading compleation photographs, and to Chris Hunter, Keeper of Regalia. Robin Campbell is always on hand for any historical queries, and the previous Clerk, Dave Broadhead, continues to assist, with possibly fewer questions than last year.

Registration to our six Lists is done by writing to me, Alison Coull, 258/1 Ferry Road, EDINBURGH, EH5 3AN or emailing SMCmunroclerk@smc.org.uk. For a Munro or Corbett compleation certificate please enclose an A4 s.a.e. (with correct postage – large letter). Check <www.smc.org.uk> for further details and to view the picture galleries of compleatonists celebrating their final summit.

Enjoy your hills.

Alison Coull (Clerk of the List)

SCOTTISH MOUNTAIN ACCIDENTS 2020

Mountain Rescue in Scotland is coordinated by Police Scotland. Police Scotland receive the initial callout through the 999 system and, if appropriate, contact the local Mountain Rescue Team (MRT). Each MRT is an independent organisation that submits its reports to the Statistician of Scottish Mountain Rescue (SMR), the representative body for the majority of MRTs in Scotland. There are 28 voluntary civilian Mountain Rescue Teams in Scotland, of which 24 are members of Scottish Mountain Rescue. The annual SMR Statistical Report for 2020 collates the information received from the 24 civilian teams and three Police Scotland teams that are members of Scottish Mountain Rescue, and it covers the calendar year from 1 January to 31 December 2020. Owing to space constraints the customary tables of data from this report have been omitted from this year's *SMCJ*. However, the full report can be accessed using the following link <www.scottishmountainrescue.org/wp-content/uploads/2021/05/SMR_Statistics_Report_2020_v5-pages.pdf>.

Because of the Covid-19 epidemic, 2020 was an abnormal year for Scottish mountain accidents. The SMR Statistician, Tom Adams, offers the following observations.

> 2020 was an unusual year in many respects, and mountain rescue was no exception. Teams were forced to introduce a wide range of protocols in order to effectively manage callouts, risk to team members and the public, and in order to maintain an effective response. Incident patterns were very different from most years. Despite an extended period of fantastic weather in late spring 2020, callouts were at an all-time low, Q2 being the quietest quarter on record. The weekend immediately before lockdown began was, however, one of the busiest on record. When lockdown was released in July there was a surge of activity in the hills, with a correspondingly high number of callouts in Q3 (the busiest quarter on record for SMR teams).

It should be borne in mind that three important mountain rescue teams – Cairngorm, Glencoe and Lochaber – are not members of SMR. Accident Reports from Cairngorm MRT appear later.

Moffat MRT Accident Reports for 2020
I am grateful to Chris Huntley of Moffat MRT for these reports. – HON. ED.

04 Jan   A young boy twisted his knee at the summit cairn of Tinto Hill. Assistance requested from the team but casualty's family and friends evacuated him almost to the road with small number of team in attendance.

14 Mar   Two walkers hopelessly disorientated in cloud high on the hills above Durisdeer. Using the intimate knowledge of the area of some team members, a vehicle was taken within 20 minutes of the walkers, who were assisted off the hill.

23 Mar   All of the UK went into a lockdown owing to Covid-19. Expectation was that call-outs should be almost nil as nobody was venturing far from home. In fact, Moffat MRT had no callouts until mid-May 2020.

14 May   Assistance requested to evacuate a casualty from Crichope Linn near Thornhill. Team were stood down en route as the ambulance crew and

the attending police officers were able to walk the casualty out to the waiting ambulance.

08 Jul The team were called out to evacuate a 68-year-old female with an ankle injury on Criffel. Team members attended the casualty and assisted the coastguard helicopter crew loading her into a stretcher to be winched. Team members then accompanied the casualty's husband off the hill.

24 Jul A young male had swum out to an islet on Loch Skeen but could not return. Multi-agency response but from practical view only MMRT and helicopter could help. Casualty lifted off island by coastguard helicopter, and team helped to transfer to ambulance.

29 Jul Male slipped on Criffel and suffered suspected broken ankle. Team carried casualty off hill.

13 Aug A 67-year-old female with a suspected broken ankle on Gallow Hill, Moffat. The team were stood down after the ambulance service managed to complete the evacuation.

22 Aug The team were called to assist in locating a missing male who could not be traced following a car accident on outskirts of Lockerbie. Police had searched the immediate area around the crash site with help from coastguard helicopter. The team re-searched the immediate area around the vehicle and then extended the search to the surrounding woodland. Sadly, during this search, the team found the casualty deceased.

02 Sep Search for a 23-year-old male who could not be located after a car accident at the Collin bypass earlier in the evening. The missing person was believed to be injured and disorientated. The police managed to trace his whereabouts as the team were being deployed to search.

05 Sep A female with suspected spinal injury at the Crawick Multiverse near Sanquhar. With the assistance of the team the casualty was airlifted to hospital by coastguard helicopter.

06 Sep A female casualty with a suspected broken ankle on Tinto. The casualty was airlifted to hospital by coastguard helicopter with assistance of the team.

22 Sep A female had fallen down an embankment in rural location and suffered an ankle injury. The team evacuated the casualty back to the awaiting ambulance.

27 Sep The team were called out to assist Tweed Valley MRT in overnight search for a missing female on the Southern Upland Way south of Traquair. Tweed Valley had been out searching since early evening and Moffat MRT were called out at 22:30. The casualty was found by Tweed Valley MRT at 09:15, cold but medically fit.

04 Oct Female walker who had fallen and injured her leg on Criffel. Casualty carried off the hill by stretcher to the awaiting ambulance.

11 Oct 60-year-old male with a suspected broken leg at the Crawick Multiverse near Sanquhar. The casualty was evacuated by Fire and Rescue and the SAS before the team arrived.

11 Oct 20-year-old female with a leg injury on hills near Wanlockhead. The team stretchered the casualty off the hill to the waiting ambulance.

11 Oct In third call of the day a male at Ae Forest mountain bike trail had sustained a pelvic injury. The ambulance crew had managed with the help of some other mountain bikers to evacuate the casualty as the team arrived.

28 Nov   A male mountain biker had injured his ankle in Mabie Forest. The
         ambulance crew managed to extract the casualty as MRT arrived on
         scene

29 Nov   A female with lower leg break requested help near the summit of Culter
         Fell. Casualty was transported by an ambulance service all-terrain
         vehicle, assisted by team to the roadside. Team also walked the rest of
         party off the hill in darkness.

21 Dec   Police requested assistance with search of hillsides and forestry area
         east of the M74 in Greenhillstairs, Moffat. Team members helped
         throughout hours of daylight. Nothing found by team on this day.

Skye MRT Accident Reports for 2020

I am grateful to Ben Wear of Skye MRT for these reports. – HON. ED.

03 Mar   14 team members, alongside Scottish Fire & Rescue Service, Maritime
         & Coastal Agency, and Helicopter R948, searched in the Kyleakin area
         for missing male from Kyle of Lochalsh. 168 man-hours.

12 Mar   Team alerted by mobile phone for two young male French hillwalkers.
         Neither was carrying winter equipment and they had become cragfast
         on the Cuillin ridge in steep snow and icy conditions between Sgùrr
         na Bàirnich and An Caisteal as darkness fell. 48 man-hours.

22 Mar   Trotternish: Bealach Chaplain. One member of party attempting the
         Skye trail reported suffering frostbite. 4 man-hours.

23 Mar   Reported 999 call originating from Waternish. One team-member
         checked all carparks. Nothing seen. False alarm. 999 call was from
         ongoing rescue on Trotternish at the time. 2 man-hours.

11 Apr   Glenbrittle. One team-member deployed to search for a missing
         person. 2.5 man-hours.

22 Jul   Fairy Pools. Two team members deployed to rescue a dog. 7 man-
         hours.

29 Jul   Overdue walker at the Fairy Pools. 0.5 man-hours.

08 Aug   Rescue of female walker who had fallen at rocks on the far side of
         Braes beach, Portree. Suspected broken leg. 20 man-hours.

09 Aug   At 16:23 a caller requested Mountain Rescue, stating they had been
         walking up a hill today but had left their friend, of whose name he was
         unsure, at Camusunary Bay. The missing person had been feeling
         dehydrated, in poor condition, and was now missing. A young man,
         matching given description, was later found by two team-members in
         a tent close to bridge on Landrover track – worse for wear after a heavy
         night of drinking. 8 man-hours.

14 Aug   Call out to Sgùrr Dubh Mòr, following rockfall and shouts heard from
         Coir' a' Ghrunnda. After initial search, casualty was found, north of
         the Caisteal below Sgùrr Dubh Mòr, in a gully, unconscious and with
         serious life-threatening injuries. Pain relief was given, and casualty
         prepared for helicopter evacuation. 140 man-hours.

16 Aug   Older male reported to have fallen 60m on steep grass and heather
         slope at the Quiraing. Team members gave pain relief and stretchered
         casualty to helicopter for evacuation. 32 man-hours.

17 Aug   Retrieval of casualty's rucksack from unspecified location. 24 man-
         hours.

25 Aug	Trotternish Ridge. Two backpackers, attempting Skye trail, worried about pitching tent in high winds and not being able to get down in the dark, phoned police for advice and weather forecast. 1 man-hour.
06 Sep	Sgùrr Alasdair. Team investigated after reports of rockfall and shouts from the Stone Chute. Nothing found. False Alarm. 30 man-hours.
13 Sep	Hillwalker, lacking protective clothing, became lost attempting circular route at Quiraing in stormy weather. Found on Sgùrr Mòr. 60.5 man-hours.
20 Sep	Quiraing. Team members assisted a female with vertigo near 'The Table'. Required confidence roping down to main path. 7.5 man-hours.
22 Sep	Glen Sligachan. Team assisted a young, female walker stuck because of swollen rivers and near winter conditions. 60 man-hours.
22 Sep	Coruisk. Male asked for mountain rescue owing to stormy, wet conditions. Lifeboat tasked from Mallaig to pick him off. MRT on standby to assist as several team were already located at Kilmarie & Sligachan with separate ongoing rescue. 18 man-hours.
09 Oct	Injured female at Fairy Pools. Team stood down when ambulance crew managed to pick her up. 3 man-hours.
22 Oct	Old Man of Storr. Female, on path, broke her ankle. Given pain relief and prepared for lift to R948. 18 man-hours.
22 Oct	Team called out for university student, crag fast on Sgùrr Alasdair. Reported as having bivvied at Sgùmain cave, then attempted to cross over Sgùrr Alasdair and make way down Great Stone Chute. Phone-Find put him on the west face of Sgùrr Alasdair. MRT had difficulty locating his exact location because of poor visibility and exposed & loose face. R948 eventually able to do pickoff. 100 man-hours.
01 Nov	Old Man of Storr. Female with suspected fractured tib/fib in very windy conditions (60mph). Team gave her pain relief and stretchered to waiting ambulance. 45 man-hours.
06 Nov	Druim Hain. Search and rescue of two female foreign walkers. Having set off from the Fairy Pools earlier in the day they became lost, and benighted. Phone-Find located them as being on Sgùrr Hain. Evacuated by R948. 8 man-hours.
23 Nov	Fairy Pools. Two walkers and a dog became stuck at the pools owing to waist-high water at the 'stepping-stones'. 4.5 man-hours.
26 Nov	Couple with dog, using mobile phone navigating app and online walks description, became lost in cloudy conditions at the Quiraing. After their location was confirmed using Phone-Find, they were talked down to the path by a team member waiting at Quiraing carpark. 2 man-hours.

Killin MRT Accident Reports for 2020

I am grateful to Bill Rose of Killin MRT for these reports. – HON. ED.

18 Jan	Ben Vorlich. Casualty with leg injury. Recovered by helicopter. 49 man-hours.
24 Jan	Rob Roy Way. Walker sustained ankle injury on track above lochan. 22 man-hours.
19 Feb	Ben Vorlich. Assisted Tayside MRT. 36 man-hours.

29 Feb	Glen Finglas. Female tired in snow and wind, recovered from track. 18.5 man-hours.
06 Mar	Male stranded north of Ben More summit. Rescued by helicopter. NN430244. 119 man-hours.
17 Mar	Fatal accident on Ben More. Helicopter recovery. 58 man-hours.
20 Mar	Beinn a' Chleibh / Ben Lui. Two walkers stranded on hard névé. MRT and helicopter attended. NN246258. 30 man-hours.
30 May	Two persons lost on Beinn a' Chroin were guided down by team-members. 12 man-hours.
11 Jun	Callander. Vulnerable local male missing. Search of Callander Craigs etc. Traced at Duke's Pass. 42 man-hours.
13 Jun	Search of Callander Craig and Bracklinn Falls for suicidal female. 76.5 man-hours.
14 Jun	Day 2 of search for missing female. Located in town. 240 man-hours.
09 Jul	Male with ankle injury near summit of Ben A'an. Air ambulance and MRT attended. 55 man-hours.
10 Jul	Male collapsed on Ben Ledi. Airlifted by R199 Recovery. 7 man-hours.
13 Jul	Ardvorlich. Diabetic male became unwell. Team on standby. 3 man-hours.
19 Jul	Ben Oss. MRT located person lost in mist. 16 man-hours.
28 Jul	Loch Katrine. Casualty with ankle injury. Assisted Lomond MRT with boat evacuation from lower northern slopes of Ben Venue. 2 man-hours.
03 Aug	Man and dog stuck on rocks at Bracklinn Falls. 14 man-hours.
08 Aug	Person suffered fatal heart attack on Beinn a' Chroin. Evacuated by R199. 24 man-hours.
09 Aug	Cyclist injured on Route 7 cycle path near Kilmahog. 4.5 man-hours.
12 Aug	Suicide in Callander town woodland. 100 man-hours.
16 Aug	Two persons stranded on steep ground beside Inverarnan waterfall. 55 man-hours.
28 Aug	Ben A'an. Female with broken arm evacuated by Helimed. NN 503082. 22 man-hours.
05 Sep	West Highland Way near Inverarnan. On standby for overdue cyclists. 4 man-hours.
23 Sep	Loch Voil, Monachylebeag. Rescue of a sheep. 21 man-hours.
30 Sep	Injured walker and friend lost on Stùc a' Chroin 72 man-hours.
04 Oct	Ewich, West Highland Way. Casualty suffered a suspected stroke. 18 man-hours.
05 Oct	Injured walker on West Highland Way, south of Beinglas. Recovered by Loch Lomond Rescue boat. 34 man-hours.
13 Oct	Creag Mhòr. Search for missing person. NN 391361. 105 man-hours.
14 Oct	Creag Mhòr search continued. Missing person located with serious injury, by helicopter. 77 man-hours.
18 Oct	Search for three persons missing in mist on Stùc a' Chroin. 66 man-hours.
28 Oct	Assisted Tayside MRT in search for missing fell -runner. 36 man-hours.
29 Oct	Previous day's search continued. Person found deceased. 63 man-hours.
01 Nov	Tyndrum. Female with Alzheimer's disease found deceased by burn to north of village. 95 man-hours.

04 Nov   Ben Lui, Central Gully. Male with ankle injury evacuated by helicopter. 91 man-hours.
05 Nov   Five persons without torches stranded on Beinn a' Chroin as darkness fell. 68 man-hours.
29 Nov   Beinn Tuilleachan. Two walkers who had set out from Glen Falloch became lost and ended up in Inverlochlarig. 8 man-hours.
21 Dec   Ben Lui. False activation of Garmin device. Team on stand-by. 1 man-hour.
29 Dec   Glengyle, Loch Katrine. Stand-by for injured cyclist. Resolved by police. 2 man-hours.
29 Dec   Persons without ice-axes or crampons got into difficulties on Ben More summit. Helicopter attended but persons walked off. 30 man-hours.

Assynt MRT Accident Reports for 2020

I am grateful to Sue Agnew of Assynt MRT for these reports. – HON. ED.

19 Apr   Lochinver. Paddleboarders lost on return from loch. Helicopter picked them up. 2.6 man-hours.
19 Jun   Conival, Inchnadamph. Abandoned backpack near summit of Conival. Team member walked in to retrieve. 12 man-hours.
23 Jul   Ben Klibreck. Walker experienced navigational difficulties due to low cloud. Team members walked in to rescue them. 80 man-hours.
27–28 Jul Two-day search with assistance from Dundonnell MRT. 268 man-hours.
29–30 Jul Ben Loyal. Search for missing walker. 220 man-hours.
07 Aug   Ben Loyal. Search and recovery of missing walker. 160 man-hours.
10 Aug   Achfary. Search and recovery of missing walker. 34 man-hours.
04 Sep   Suilven. Walker sustained injury following a fall. Rescued with assistance of helicopter. 60 man-hours.
07 Sep   Stoer Lighthouse. Search for missing person. 112 man-hours.
16 Sep   Ben Klibreck. Walker became lost on Ben Klibreck after navigation difficulties. Self-rescued. Team on standby. 24 man-hours.
21 Sep   Ben Hope. Walkers lost on paths. Able to walk off after GR given, and with team meeting them. 6 man-hours.
10 Oct   Ben Klibreck. Walkers became lost coming off summit. Location unknown. Team found them on route out. 182 man-hours.
26 Nov   Wailing Widows Waterfall. Walker fell and needed stretchered from walk. 30 man-hours.

Cairngorm MRT Accident Reports for 2020

I am grateful to Iain Cornfoot of Cairngorm MRT for these reports. – HON. ED.

04 Jan   Kayakers or paddle-boarders got separated on Loch Ericht. Rescue 151 picked them up safe and well. 33 man-hours.
05 Jan   Mountain biker lost in Abernethy Forest. Picked up by Rescue 151 who was passing by from above rescue. 4.5 man-hours.
13 Jan   Ben Alder Cottage. Walker called 999 asking for assistance on side of Loch Ericht. CMRT team found him and his mates in the bothy safe and well. Very annoying indeed. 195 man-hours.

19 Jan	Female with broken ankle at Daviot. CMRT helped SAS carry her out to waiting ambulance. 36 man-hours.
05 Feb	Couple 'lost' on plateau. Knew where they were, poor resilience. A small team sorted it. 36 man-hours.
29 Feb	CMRT helped Lochaber MRT probe an avalanche tip for a missing male. 360 man-hours.
29 Feb	Three climbers call saying they are lost on plateau after climbing on The Message. 48 man-hours.
29 Feb	Two other climbers reported missing, at same time as above, after climbing. Located in ski area. 48 man-hours.
03 Mar	A 78-year-old male with cardiac history collapsed on Creag Bheag at Kingussie. Treated on scene then sent to Raigmore. 20 man-hours.
14 Mar	Male skier tumbled over Mirror Direct in Coire an t-Sneachda. No bones broken; he walked out. Good effort as he had been unconscious! 66 man-hours.
16 Jun	Aberarder Farm nr Croachy. Male contractor suffered fatal heart attack. Helimed2 deployed and declared life extinct. CMRT helped police to remove the casualty. 15 man-hours.
20 Jun	Mountain biker became unwell with a high pulse-rate near summit of Càrn Dubh. He phoned ambulance for assistance. SAS asked for CMRT to stand by. 8 man-hours.
27 Jun	Asked to assist ambulance service with an injured person who had fallen out of a tree. Three team-members responded; the ambulance crew walked the casualty off but did not stand down CMRT.
10 Jul	Lost walker. CMRT asked to assist Braemar MRT. R151 found casualty in Glen Derry area. 36 man-hours.
17 Jul	Two adults and two-year-old child lost in Ryvoan area. Concern for them as they had no food or water for child. Police SARLOC confirmed location. Two CMRT members drove to pick them up. 7.5 man-hours.
31 Jul	Party of two mountain bikers. Female fell off bike into ditch on main Landrover track along lochside. Laceration to forehead and other minor injuries. Three CMRT deployed. Ambulance service on scene before CMRT and dealt with casualty. 9 man-hours.
08 Aug	Two walkers became separated while ascending Long Leachas on Ben Alder; second male failed to return to Dalwhinnie. R151 located casualty cold & exhausted on path above Ben Alder Cottage. 5 man-hours.
15 Aug	Female fell, sustaining injury to lower arm, possible fracture. Four CMRT members leaving rescue base when stood down by police. Lady had walked to Landrover track and was picked up by estate worker and police. 6 man-hours.
29 Aug	Male vomiting blood. Rescue 151 went directly to the casualty location and uplifted him. 15 man-hours.
30 Aug	Party of four became lost on the way back from Ben Macdui, location on Bynack More. Five team-members went to locate them and walk them off. 18 man-hours.
01 Sep	Young male reported overdue from three-day hiking & camping trip in the Cairngorms. Returned safe and well. 5 man-hours.
07 Sep	Two females lost in cloud on their way back from Ben Macdui (SARLOC to the east of Pt 1141m). As the cloud cleared, they were

talked off until the ski area car-park was in sight. 4 man-hours.

14 Sep Father and son returning from Ben Macdui became lost, without a torch, as darkness fell. 17 man-hours.

25 Sep Female fell when walking the Speyside Way; possible lower leg fracture. 9 man-hours.

25 Oct Female, exhausted and unable to continue walking owing to illness. Stretchered off the mountain by CMRT. 121 man-hours.

I am grateful to Lisa Hutchison for collating all these MRT reports. – HON. ED.

IN MEMORIAM

JAMES W. SIMPSON j. 1960

Jimmy Simpson passed away in Hairmyres Hospital after a short illness on 22 February 2021, a few days before his 92nd birthday. Born and brought up in Kilmarnock, he studied industrial chemistry at Glasgow University in the late 1940s, followed by National Service in the RAF, serving in Burma in the 1950s.

Jim and I met first met in the late 1950s through membership of the JMCS in Glasgow, leading to climbing adventures at home and abroad and a lifelong friendship. Jim was my senior by ten years almost to the day, and was instrumental in introducing me to more adventurous mountaineering in our hills. It wasn't long before I was going on climbing meets in both summer and winter with him. For convenience our weekend visits to the hills were limited to the more popular areas close to Glasgow, as car ownership was very limited in the 1950s and 1960s.

Arran was Jim's great favourite in the earlier days, with easy access from Glasgow by train and over to Brodick by ferry followed by a walk up to Glen Rosa with its fine campsites and superb river pools for swimming. Once camp was organised it was off to the hills and crags, where Cir Mhòr was a regular

James W. Simpson. Photo: W.H. Duncan.

favourite with its many popular routes to be climbed, especially the *South Ridge*. Jim put up several new routes on the island, including *April Arête* (with William M.M. Wallace in 1959) and *The Big Slab*, which he soloed in 1960.

Jim started his career working at the British Aluminium smelter at Kinlochleven in Argyll in the early 1950s, and that became a useful base for exploring and climbing in the West Highlands. Once established at Kinlochleven Jim was able to access the company's aluminium-hulled vessel captained by a professional seaman. During the summer periods when the vessel could be booked, the captain was more than delighted to enable Jim and his friends to visit interesting places around the Inner Isles.

Kinlochleven being close to Fort William made it a short journey for Jim to reach the CIC Hut early on a Friday evening. The Glasgow contingent of the JMCS arrived much later in Fort William, and often set out for the walk on foul winter nights. Once up to the intake dam the parties' spirits rose on seeing the light Jim had placed in the Hut's window, knowing he would have a brew on once the bobbing torches drew close.

During his stay at Kinlochleven Jim began work on a new edition of the Climbers' Guide to the Cuillin of Skye, in two volumes. He dedicated many weekends to researching route information, often alone but on many occasions with fellow climbers and friends. Eventually, with time being short, he negotiated six months' leave from BA to complete his guidebook for publication, on time, in 1969.

The BMC Memorial Hut in Glen Brittle was constructed and opened in 1965 and first visited by a group of Jim's friends over the 1966 New Year. It was around this time Jim took on the responsibility as booking secretary, a role he continued in for many years including a period as voluntary warden. For many years the hut was a popular venue for New Year, with Jim being a prime mover in ensuring that space was available for SMC members and friends. It is worth recording that Jim celebrated over 45 New Years at the Glen Brittle Hut with his wife Chris and many friends.

Like many of us visiting Glen Brittle over New Year, Jim's enthusiasm could be subdued on looking out of the window into driving rain and cloud down to sea level. But given the opportunity he was up in the corries and on the ridges enjoying Skye at its best in winter. Not everyone wished to visit the wintry high tops or was capable of doing so, and he would often forgo a good day's climbing especially on New Year's day to organise a walk out to the Rhue with its ancient Viking and Pictish constructions.

Jim visited the Alps on a number of occasions, often with JMCS and SMC members, in addition to a camping and climbing holiday in the Lofoten Islands in Arctic Norway. On all three of our own trips to the Alps, Jim and I were fortunate in having good weather conditions. At the time of the first two visits I was working for British Railways and had access to concessionary rail travel both in the UK and Europe, while Jim was required to pay full fares. He showed no envy apart from maybe a raised eyebrow, and it never stopped us having many superb and happy Alpine days. Of these, I recall two occasions in particular as special to Jim's memory for his companionship and mountain skills while out in challenging situations. The first was in the Bregaglia in 1961, when from the Forno Hut we made an ascent of the East Ridge of Punta Rasica to its airy pinnacled summit: a rock-climbing gem. From the same hut a few days later we traversed the fine, airy and snow-covered ridges of Cima di Vazzeda and Cima di Rosso, a classical mountain day in superb conditions.

A special highlight of that holiday was an invitation to have dinner with Jim H.B. Bell and his wife Pat at the Maloja Pass Hotel. Having had to descend from the Forno Hut to the hotel in the late afternoon after a day's climbing, we did justice to the meal. After a very enjoyable evening, and amply wined and dined, Jim and I then had to get back up to the hut. This was easier said than done in fading light after such conviviality, and a night under a boulder was looking highly likely until we noticed a serious lightning storm advancing down the Forno Glacier. What had started as a brisk walk now turned into a race against the advancing storm to gain the safety of the hut before the storm broke about us. We made it, just, and it exploded about us on our entry to the hut, soaked in sweat.

On another occasion while camped at Zermatt in 1960, a year that saw late accumulations of snow in the high Alps, Jim and I had only a few days remaining of a two-week holiday in which to climb the Matterhorn. Swiss guides had just managed to make an ascent during that week, giving Jim and me an opportunity to go up to the Hörnli Hut with only a day in hand to make an ascent of the mountain and return to the valley. We managed the climb, overtaking a few parties on the lower slopes above the Hut, encountering wintry underfoot conditions high on the peak and spending about forty minutes on the summit before descending quickly and safely to Zermatt in time to catch the train home.

After spending a long period at the smelter in Kinlochleven, Jim moved to the central belt of Scotland to commence work on classified equipment for the mining industries. It was during a period in 1965–66 that he suffered serious health problems requiring hospitalisation for some time in Kilmarnock. On his recovery Jim was advised to lead a more relaxed life and that climbing mountains wasn't an option. Jim, determined as ever, set out slowly to regain normality. In time he recovered a level of fitness that allowed easier hill days, choosing carefully what he could do and initially informing me on the start of our walks where the car keys were located just in case of a problem. In support of his recovery Jim required a significant amount of medication, referred to as 'sweeties' and only occasionally as 'pills'. This didn't deter him, and he eventually completed his round of the Munros by summiting Ladhar Bheinn in 1970 with his sister Isabel (an LSCC member) and a number of JMCS members and friends.

In time Jim became fit enough and confident enough in his ability to venture into the Cuillin and attempt the traverse of the main ridge. So in 1968 a small group of JMCS and SMC members walked into the Coruisk Hut by Loch Scavaig on a wet evening for the attempt. In the morning John Macleod, a Skyeman from Breakish, joined Jim and me for the attempt. Leaving the hut on a dull and damp morning with just a hint of brightness and with cloud rolling across the high tops, we had some misgivings. As we left Gars-bheinn the clouds thickened, the wind picked up and it started to rain. Further doubts arose but we continued towards the top of the Dubhs ridge, where the cloud began to lower dramatically into the corries. Soon the mood of the party changed. The sun made an appearance, producing fine Brocken spectres, and the hidden peaks on the ridge now appeared above the lowering clouds. We continued on our way ever more hopeful, as the sun dried the rocks and made it a joy to climb and traverse the more technical sections of the ridge. As we traversed the ridge between Sgùrr Thormaid and over Sgùrr a' Mhadaidh our progress was hampered by the now very hot conditions, and as we approached the Bealach na Glaic Mòire Jim decided that the heat was too much for him to continue.

We were all disappointed that he had to leave us and descend into Coire a' Mhadaidh and return to Breakish, but it was a wise decision considering the health problems he had overcome. But the traverse didn't end there, because John and I went on as Jim had wished and duly arrived on the summit of Sgùrr nan Gillean, to a sunset that only the west can produce. Here we noticed a note tucked into in the cairn, announcing that two cans of beer were also located in the cairn. Needless to say, Jim had had a hand in this very welcome gesture.

Throughout his active hill days Jim continued to foster, support and actively engage with enthusiastic members of the JMCS and friends who wished to improve their basic hill skills and gain experience of the Scottish hills in winter condition. It was not unknown for Jim to give up a perfectly good day to instruct less experienced members in winter skills. In later life when Jim's knees troubled him he would continue to support hill-goers he had helped in years past to enjoy completing their final Munro whenever he could, even if it was only at the start of the climb and welcoming them back after the ascent.

In 1975 Jim and his wife Chris moved to Chapelton near Strathaven in South Lanarkshire. By this time I had also moved north to the Highlands. Although the miles between where we lived were many, it didn't prevent us from meeting up in our respective home-area hills, at SMC dinners and at the continuing New Year meets on Skye.

On settling in Chapelton, Jim made every effort to integrate with the local community and support it by becoming a founding member of the Strathaven Bowling Club. He enjoyed many years of this pastime and became a competitive and very skilful bowler, lifting the Gentlemen's Bowling Championship in the year 2000. He further supported the local community by becoming a member of the WRVS 'Meals on Wheels' organisation, busily involved in distributing meals to the local community area. After fifteen years' service he was the recipient of the long service medal awarded on behalf of the Queen. In addition, Jim received an award from South Lanarkshire Council in recognition of his services to the community through his work with the Bowling Club and Meals on Wheels service.

Jim and I maintained our friendship throughout our lives with their many changes, and one way or another we always kept in touch through the Club's annual dinners, visits and catch-up phone calls. Having arranged a trip to visit Jim and Chris last year, I was prevented by further Covid-19 restrictions, but we

Jim Simpson on the Rosetta Stone (VS,5a), Cir Mhòr. Photo: Roger Robb.

did continue our calls with one just prior to Jim going into hospital. I remember it clearly; it was still Jim, but a little older. Here's to Jim and our long friendship. Slàinte mhath!

Roger J.C. Robb

Raymond Simpson writes:
I only met Jim a handful of times, always in Skye, but feel I have known him all my climbing life through his rock-climbing guide to the Cuillin, where the route descriptions were clear, concise and inspirational. I later learned from him that he had done most of the routes solo, even some of the harder ones, while checking them for the guidebook.

As custodian, secretary and frequent resident of the BMC Hut he was always friendly, chatty and helpful, no matter who you were or when you arrived. Linda and I first met him following a very wet bivouac on the main ridge traverse, in the days before Goretex. We descended at first light to the hut to ask permission to change our soaking garments and make a brew. Jimmy suggested a hot shower, and while we were enjoying it he cooked us a full Scottish breakfast!

We met him on subsequent visits to Glen Brittle and enjoyed days on the hill with him. He must have been well into in his 70s on one dreich drizzly day when we did Collie's Route to the Cioch. We offered him a rope at the foot of the slabs, which he politely declined before scampering up the cracks (which were running with water) like the proverbial rat up a drainpipe! We finished up Eastern Gully, where he delighted in showing us the through-route under the chokestone.

On another occasion we were descending the Sgùmain stoneshoot and a boulder rolled onto Jim's leg; although in some discomfort he carried on, but slowed down on the path. I ran back to the hut and drove to the campsite to pick him up. The next day he seemed comfortable but opted to have a 'rest day' before driving home. The next year I asked him about his leg, and he casually replied: 'Its fine now. I drove home to Strathaven but it wasn't getting better so the next week I went to A&E and they told me it was broken.'

He was a fund of stories, having spent many summers as warden at the hut. One of his favourites was the occasion when he got a lift in a chauffeured limousine conveying a Miss Dorothy E. Pilley to Glen Brittle for a last look at her route, Cioch West. Over the years he had developed a great friendship with Mrs Isabella MacRae of Glenbrittle Farm, who carried the traditional lore of the glen.

I will always associate Jim with the Cuillin, and remember his sheer exuberance and enthusiasm for the climbing there.

HAMISH MACINNES j. 1970

The day after filming of *The Eiger Sanction* had started, in August 1974, a rockfall high on the Nordwand injured one of the cameramen, Mike Hoover, and killed the British climber David Knowles. Work was immediately halted, and Clint Eastwood considered abandoning the whole project. On the advice of the other cameraman, John Cleare, Eastwood urgently had Hamish MacInnes flown out from the UK as Safety Officer. As Cleare recalls: 'At once he took charge, he gave the orders, no questions, no arguments. If the forecast wasn't good enough, if the freezing level was too high, if the team was too tired, then the mountain was out of bounds and no film was shot. Everything was prepared properly, gear was continually checked, he planned and supervised every camera position, every foot of climbing, ensuring all was cool calm and collected.' His technical mastery, presence of mind and quiet authority would bring MacInnes many further filming assignments, and augment his reputation as climber, mountain-rescue pioneer, inventor and author.

Although brought up in Kirkcudbrightshire, Hamish MacInnes (spelled 'McInnes' at his birth in 1930) was of Highland extraction, his mother hailing from Skye and father from Lochaber, and the soft cadence of his speech owed little to the Greenock shipyards of his later teenage years. His father Duncan had been in the Shanghai police before serving in the British and Canadian armies in the First World War, and was to Hamish (the youngest of five children) an authoritarian presence.

It was at Arrochar that MacInnes first tied on to a climbing rope, under the tutelage of his neighbour, Bill Hargreaves; and when only 18 he hitchhiked to Zermatt and soloed the Hörnli Ridge of the Matterhorn. National service in Austria gave access to the limestone declivities and icefields of the Eastern Alps, and acquainted him with the pegs and crampons of Continental practice. Back in Scotland and returning to the Cobbler, MacInnes began to make his name in 1951 with the first ascents of *Gladiator's Groove* and *Whither Wether*, both done with Bill Smith of the Creagh Dhu MC. The following year he put up *Wappenshaw Wall* and *Peasant's Passage* on the Rannoch Wall and accomplished the first winter ascent of *Clachaig Gully*. Other winter first ascents around this time included *Agag's Groove* (now graded VII,6) and *Raven's Gully*, climbed with Chris Bonington with whom he also made what was perhaps the first true winter ascent of *Crowberry Ridge Direct*, leading the crux in ex-WD socks.

The self-styled Creagh Dhu Himalayan Expedition of 1953 had elements of farce as well as high adventure. Beaten by John Hunt's men to their bold objective of Mount Everest, MacInnes and his sole companion John Cunningham instead mounted a post-monsoon attempt on Pumori (7161m). They attained an altitude of 6700m before avalanches and worsening weather defeated them, their consolation prize being the pinnacle of Pingero above Phalong Karpo, climbed efficiently on 'a bar of chocolate, two turnips and a tin of *pâté de foie gras* which we purchased at Thyangboche'. The expedition's equipment had cost £17, together with £12 each for expenses in Nepal.

In 1957 came the first winter ascent of *Zero Gully* (at MacInnes's sixth or seventh attempt) in combination with the Aberdonians Patey and Nicol. While Nicol favoured tricounis and Patey had 10-point crampons, MacInnes with his 12-pointers anticipated the ice-climbing revolution by 15 years. As Bill Murray wrote: 'I had often reconnoitred Point Five and Zero before the war. ... I never thought Zero would go. The big, green ice overhangs looked too savage. This seemed to me confirmed when good English parties fell out of both gullies in the early Fifties. The ascent by Patey, MacInnes and Nicol in only five hours was a truly great achievement in the history of ice-climbing.'

MacInnes was now instructing for the SYHA and the Mountaineering Association, including courses on Skye run jointly with Ian Clough, with whom he presently formed a redoubtable climbing partnership. John Temple recalled that one of the pair was '... tall and lean, hard-eyed, unsmiling, his face as sparse as his words but conveying all the information you needed to know. His companion was smaller, chubbier and, but for the Woodbine in his mouth, would

Hamish MacInnes. Photo: Tom Weir (SMC Image Archive).

have flashed a grin.' Joining them in 1958 for the first ascent of *Vulcan Wall* on Sròn na Cìche, Temple was taken aback by their liberal pegging of the climb, for aid as well as protection. It was a propensity that would earn MacInnes the 'MacPiton' epithet, his heavy hammer being 'The Message'. On the same cliff MacInnes and Clough also put up *Creag Dhu Grooves* (again with aid) and *Strappado*, together with a score of routes elsewhere on Skye.

In 1959 MacInnes was in the Alps with Don Whillans and Paul Ross, completing an ascent of the *Bonatti Pillar* on the Petit Dru despite a rockfall that fractured his skull. Deranged by the injury (or perhaps just alarmed at medical and rescue bills) he tried to abscond from hospital in Chamonix, thus prefiguring an escape from the Belford Hospital towards the end of his long life. The following summer he was back in the western Alps with Whillans, making the second British ascent of the *Walker Spur*.

It used to tickle Bill Murray (who had a warm regard for the man, and a fund of MacInnes anecdotes) to recall the dejection with which the *wunderkind* now found himself turning thirty. In truth this enterprising and single-minded man was just finding his feet. Moving to Glen Coe in 1959, MacInnes established himself at Allt na Reigh, the cottage sited just across the river from Beinn Fhada and Geàrr Aonach. Here throughout the 1960s he ran his Glencoe School of Mountaineering (originally under the SYHA but latterly independently), enlisting as instructors not only Clough but also Ian Nicholson, Jim McArtney, Allen Fyffe, Davie Crabb, Kenny Spence and Dave Knowles. Climbing with pupils or instructors, he recorded numerous new winter lines on the surrounding hills, and with Crabb, Patey and Robertson (again after half-a-dozen attempts) achieved the first winter traverse of the main Cuillin ridge in 1965. Mountain rescue soon became a preoccupation: besides his leadership (1961–94) of the Glencoe MRT and participation in the rescues themselves, which he chronicled in his book *Call-Out*, MacInnes deployed his considerable engineering talent in developing a folding stretcher that remains in use around the world. Later would come his *International Mountain Rescue Handbook*, which ran to four editions, and the award of a BEM and OBE for his voluntary services in this field.

In 1960 MacInnes married Catherine MacLeod, a GP whom he had met in the Alps. They put up several new routes together on Fuar Tholl, the Cuillin and elsewhere, and in 1965, having witnessed the effectiveness of avalanche dogs in the Alps, they jointly founded the Search and Rescue Dog Association (SARDA). Their marriage was dissolved in 1970 and Catherine died in 2019.

When staked in snow as a belay, the wooden shaft of a conventional ice-axe was sometimes snapped by a leader-fall. Motivated perhaps by such a calamity in *Zero Gully*, MacInnes designed and marketed an axe with a tubular aluminium alloy shaft in the early 1960s. Although final assembly was done in the barn at Allt na Reigh, manufacture of the steel head was subcontracted to the Manchester forgemaster B&S Massey and the finished axe sold for £4-6s under the slogan, 'Double your safety with MacInnes-Massey.' This had its pick set at an unadventurous angle, and it would be a further decade before MacInnes hit upon the steeply inclined pick and much shortened shaft of his 'Terrordactyl' axe and complementary hammer. In combination with 12-point crampons, these revolutionary drop-pick implements transformed Scottish ice-climbing technique from slow step-cutting to fast front-pointing. By way of demonstration, in March 1971 Fyffe, MacInnes and Spence made the first winter ascent of *Astronomy* on the Orion face of Ben Nevis, with Robin Chalmers's subsequent BBC film of the climb capturing the swift progress of Fyffe and his twin 'Terrors'.

Older climbers who were active at that time will recall the two-volume *Scottish Climbs* guidebook that Constable commissioned MacInnes to write. Despite its quirky adoption of UIAA grades, and more than a few inaccuracies, the 1971 first edition won praise for its wide coverage and for the photo-diagrams supplanting conventional sketches. The route descriptions owed much to previous SMC publications, including Marshall's 1969 Nevis guidebook, and although MacInnes did acknowledge 'generous help' in a preface, his election to honorary SMC membership around this time was controversial. Be that as it may, when Gerry Peet could persuade no members to help him with a gas-lift, it was MacInnes who drove at once to the dam with slings and tackle, and spent the day single-handedly marshalling payloads at the CIC Hut.

His genuine enthusiasm for mountains was always alloyed with commercial acumen and a streak of showmanship. Whether searching for yetis in later years, or climbing to Conan Doyle's 'Lost World', MacInnes deftly courted the public eye and accustomed the media to his 'old fox' image, so nicely conveyed in a 1970s TV interview with the doe-eyed Mary Marquis. In 1975 he returned to Everest, as deputy leader of Bonington's successful attempt on the SW face, and in later decades undertook a succession of challenging and profitable film-making assignments. He was also active, together with our late member Eric Langmuir, in establishing the Scottish Avalanche Information Service, and spoke out against obtrusive windfarms. He received several honorary doctorates.

MacInnes's death at the age of 90, just a fortnight before Doug Scott's, has removed one of the great men of post-war British climbing.

GDM

*MacInnes with Chris
Bonington at Glencoe in
2020. They first climbed
together in 1953.
Photo: Loreto Bonington.*

Chris Bonington writes:
Hamish has had a profound influence on my life dating right the way back to the
early 1950s when I was still at school. I had hitchhiked up to Glencoe, bumped
into Hamish who was in his early twenties and already an experienced climber,
and because there was no one else to climb with we ended up having an amazing
week's climbing that culminated in the first winter ascent of *Raven's Gully*.

I kept in touch with him and when stationed in Germany, by this time a regular
officer in the army, I sent him a postcard suggesting that we met in the Alps for
what would be my first visit. I got an immediate reply suggesting (typical Hamish)
we should meet in Grindelwald to attempt what would be the first British ascent
of the north wall of the Eiger. Conditions and the weather were particularly bad
and so we ended up hitchhiking to Chamonix with the aim of climbing the north
wall of the Grandes Jorasses. The weather was still unsettled and we ended up
making the first ascent of a very small peak above the Leschaux Glacier.

On my first attempt on the SW Face of Everest he was an important member of
the team, designing all our special lightweight box tents and being in charge of
choosing the best oxygen equipment available at that time. In 1975 on our
successful ascent he was deputy leader of the expedition. Over the years I
continued to call in to see him whenever visiting Glencoe and I am very glad that
on our visit late last summer [2020] my wife Loreto and I called in and had one
last chat and took him out to dinner. We also attended his funeral, and it was a
huge privilege to walk through Glencoe village behind the hearse carrying his
coffin with his neighbours and members of the Glencoe Rescue Team clapping
us on our way.

He was one of the great personalities not just of Scottish but also world
mountaineering and one of my dearest friends.

Davie Crabb writes:
My friend Dougie Lang and I were invited to join the Rannoch Mountaineering
Club, having met one of the club's members when climbing on Skye. The club's
base, known as 'Downie's Doss', was in an outbuilding of Hamish's house, Allt
na Reigh, and this is where I was introduced to Hamish in 1961. My first
impression of him was a tall, gaunt person. I soon got to know him better and
discovered his wry sense of humour.

At that time the Glencoe Mountain Rescue team comprised shepherds, keepers and other locals under the leadership of Hamish. The Rannoch Club were often asked to assist with rescues at weekends.

Hamish had a fertile mind for inventing equipment. When halogen bulbs first came on the market he made a searchlight and a floodlight, both hand-held, which he powered by rechargeable ex- Blue-Streak guided missile batteries. These lights were very useful on rescues, where previously only torches had been available.

He also designed his famous stretcher, which he assembled in his workshop. It was a great improvement on its predecessor, the Thomas Stretcher, as it was considerably lighter and easier to transport. I assisted Hamish to assemble the first stretcher using my index finger to hold the final knot in place while he tied it. This stretcher had only a single 26-inch bicycle wheel and a brake. The next version had a pair of smaller wheels. which aided its stability. There have been various modifications over the years since then.

Before he designed his all-metal ice-axe we did some tests with wooden-shafted ice-axes using different belaying techniques. The shafts of all these axes broke! Furthermore these older-style axes such as the Aschenbrenner had straight picks that didn't stick into the ice when pulled upon. Hamish made a prototype ice-hammer that had an angled pick (of about 30°) and asked me to try it out in the winter of 1964 when climbing *Tower Ridge* and *Observatory Ridge* on Ben Nevis. I found it to be an amazing piece of equipment – it had a very secure grip in the ice, far superior to anything I had used before. The angled pick was a major innovation. From this prototype he went on to design other axes. The first metal-shafted axe was the MacInnes-Massey axe, which had a Hiduminium shaft and 11° pick. The head was made from tool steel (EN90). This was followed by the MacInnes-Peck axe which also had an 11° pick, and the Terrordactyl with a steeper angled pick.

In the autumn of 1964 Hamish asked if I would like to help him as an instructor on the SYHA's winter mountaineering courses, of which he was the chief instructor. I willingly accepted this, although it meant I had to leave my job in Dundee. The first day of the course, participants were taught knotwork and avalanche awareness. Then we were out on the hills for the remainder. Hamish was a good person to work with and we had a lot of fun and a few epics with the courses. He had a great sense of fun. He loved 'arssading' down the snow, and one year he ordered orange fishermen's waterproofs for the instructors. This enabled us to make faster descents of snow-slopes, towing the participants behind us; no health & safety regulations then!

At that time he also invited me to join him in an attempt on the Cuillin ridge in winter. We met up with Tom Patey and Brian Robertson at Sligachan, where we spent the night sleeping in a garage belonging to the hotel. In the morning we climbed to the Sgùrr nan Gillean – Am Basteir col, climbed Sgùrr nan Gillean by the West Ridge and returned to the col. From there we progressed along the ridge. The story of our traverse has been well documented elsewhere, so I shall just include a few anecdotes. On Sgùrr a' Mhadaidh Hamish and I stopped for a cup of tea, as there was a little cave with a spring. Hamish didn't know about the spring, but I did. Soon after that one of my crampons broke on an icy slab. I managed to separate the heel-piece from the front section and attach it to my boot; that had to suffice for the remainder of the route. Hamish decided we should rope up for my safety. I was OK going downhill, but needed help to climb up icy rock. We caught up with the other two for a bivouac on Sgùrr na Banachdaich. Tom asked, 'What kept you?' I lifted my foot and showed him. We had a lovely meal of freeze-dried pork and potatoes. This was followed by what Hamish claimed to be his favourite drink – a cup of peppermint tea, made with Kendal mint cake dissolved in boiling water. Hamish thought it was lovely, but I didn't agree. Next morning when we woke up the cloud was down and it was snowing. We proceeded to the In Pin. Tom climbed the long side and top-roped the rest of us up the short side. From there the route to the summit of Sgùrr Mhic Choinnich was straightforward, and we abseiled down *King's Chimney*.

At the Theàrlaich-Dubh gap, Hamish expertly managed to lasso a large boulder on the other side and invited Tom to use the rope to climb out of the gap. I was pulled up, because of my crampon problem, and that was the last of the difficulties. We all had a tremendous thirst and were drinking meltwater out of every pocket in the rock that we could find. Three of us were sooking the water out of the pockets and Hamish, being wily, had a plastic tube to use as a straw. We continued easily over Sgùrr nan Eag and from the summit of Gars-bheinn witnessed one of the finest sunsets I have ever seen. From there it was a long glissade off the mountain and a long march through the darkness to Cuillin Cottage in Glen Brittle, where we met Catherine MacInnes and had an excellent meal provided by Mrs Campbell, the owner of the cottage.

John Cleare writes:
We first met in person in the late 1950s when Hamish had been invited down to lecture in the south. He turned up in a Morris 1000 Countryman – essentially the Traveller version of the Morris Minor, but with a half-timbered body. But the suspension had been dropped and the engine 'worked on' and Hamish claimed it was the fastest Morris 1000 in the country – it probably was too, for he was a brilliant engineer and enjoyed fast cars, subsequently running a series of E-Type Jaguars. On empty Highland roads he used them to good effect, once telling me there was always plenty of road-kill venison in his deep-freeze.

Some years later, it was the evening of the centenary day of the first ascent of the Matterhorn – the 'Year of the Alps', no less – and all Zermatt was in festive mood. Hamish and I with our small camera-crews (assistants Davie Crabb and Rusty Baillie, and among the several sherpas Eric Beard and Mary Stewart) had just directed and shot the first live TV broadcast of the ascent of the Matterhorn. For several days we'd been tenting on the Hörnli Ridge, for the hut was full of TV executives, but tonight they'd run a late cable car for us, so here we were wandering down the main street in Zermatt, very tired, very scruffy, very hungry – and very high. But something had gone wrong, somehow the BBC had forgotten us and we had nowhere to go. And Hamish was in a revolutionary mood.

Suddenly Chris Brasher appeared round the corner. He'd been doing the commentary and was shocked to find us 'stateless'. He promptly marched us into the best restaurant in town – boots, rucksacks and all. The orchestra stopped playing and conversation ceased. Chris made straight for the *maître d'hôtel*. It only took a few minutes but then the *maître* addressed the diners, telling them that we had just come straight from the Matterhorn summit, where we had put Zermatt on worldwide television. The room burst into applause, and there followed a sumptuous meal before the floor was cleared and dancing started. I was by now replete, and like most of us quite sleepy, but Hamish, especially well lubricated, had let his hair down and had no compunction about taking the floor, at first with Mary but then with several of the younger female diners, who seemed unfazed to be squired by this tall, bearded Scotsman. Despite his heavy alpine

MacInnes equipped with proprietary axe and flat cap. Photo © John Cleare.

boots he was remarkably agile. It was well past midnight when we made our way to the secluded cave behind the station and slept it off.

Not surprisingly, Hamish was especially sensitive about head injuries. In the late 1950s, before dedicated climbing helmets were available, he recommended a particular brand of keeper's thick tweed flat-hat, which he reinforced inside with thick industrial nylon wadding. We followed his advice, and the system saved my ropemate from a rockfall injury in the Alps. Years later, when we were filming on an Alpine north face, one notorious for stonefall, Hamish wore a motor-cycle crash helmet and did so again on the one occasion I joined him on an all-night technical rescue. He was always a very practical fellow.

Ken Crocket writes:
The first time I encountered MacInnes was in September 1969. For a so-called rescue we were press-ganged in the usual way and ended up on the West Face of Aonach Dubh. It was a retrieval party, doing the grunt work of stretchering down two bodies. They had been on the north face of B Buttress, overlooking Dinner-Time Buttress, which the current guide describes as having loose rock in places, requiring care. The two climbers were presumably out of luck or skill that day, and two mangled bodies lay at the foot of the rock.

A lanky figure was stooping over one of the bodies like some hungry crow, and saying in a surprised tone that one foot belonging to the late chap was almost completely detached from the rest of the corpse. Hamish, for it was he, also recognised the victim, for the unfortunate had recently been on one of his own climbing courses. My eyebrows twitched, but for once I was too careful to come out with some smart remark.

What I did do, though, was scan the face they had fallen off, looking for any evidence. The face was too broken, however, to show any obvious lines, and was not in any case very attractive. I considered myself, even at that early stage in my climbing, to be a careful and thoughtful climber, if lacking valuable experience, but that day made me even more determined to keep my wits about me at each and every step. The retrieval continued with a manic breakneck descent of Dinner-Time Buttress, holding on to one of the stretcher ropes for dear life as Willie X picked out a route. (There are several amusingly dangerous and dodgy characters called Willie on the climbing scene, and it's best to minimise any potential legal costs by forgetting which one seemed to be in charge that day.)

As I had never been one to initiate a conversation with strangers, I never joined in the frenzied grabbing of the free beer cans often made available once back at the road. In any case I stood in awe of MacInnes even then.

In later years I visited MacInnes a few times, to pick his brain for books I was researching. He even reciprocated once and asked me to supply him with any research on the dreaded midge, in order to make his life in the Glen that bit more bearable. To my surprise and disappointment, I could find very little.

Finally I visited him in August 2016, not long after he had left hospital with his mysterious illness. He was still a bit wobbly but good enough to allow me to meet him. His home in Glen Coe, which he had built, was very impressive. The structural woodwork alone was on a grand scale and would surely have withstood a serious earthquake. The actual site was of course to die for. But he would still have to endure the midges. Not even MacInnes could get round that one.

JAMES WILKIE j. 1983

In the fast-receding days when newsprint was a primary source of current information, the Letters pages of the Scotsman over decades featured frequent strong missives that intriguingly emanated from the distinctive address of Pressgasse, Vienna, above the signature of Dr James Wilkie. More often than not these eclectic epistles issued firm guidance on how we Scots should more effectively run the political life of our country and conserve our environment in its widest sense – the built heritage of our towns and villages, the Maid of the Loch, the roads around Stronachlachar, our wild landscapes, our distinctive culture. Jim Wilkie, editor, broadcaster, teacher, lobbyist, polemicist, was a passionate expatriate, Scots nationalist and internationalist. And a lifelong enthusiast for the Scottish hills, a committed if mostly remote member of the SMC.

Jim was born in Glasgow in 1933 and brought up in Clydebank, Helensburgh, Garelochhead and Clynder. After working in local government for a time, variously in libraries, youth and community and probation work, he put himself through Strathclyde University and Jordanhill to become a teacher. From the 1950s on he did a huge amount of hill-walking and climbing of the classic routes, very often with W.L. Wood but also with Ian M.M. McPhail and other Dumbarton friends. Much of that activity involved leading parties from the Garelochhead Outdoor Centre and the Loch Morlich YH, as well as a decade managing the expedition elements of the Duke of Edinburgh's Award and the Boys' Brigade. The Arrochar Alps and Glencoe were their happy hunting grounds, but Jim ranged far and wide at all seasons and in whatever conditions he might encounter – his application to the Club claims 258 Munros by 1983, and around ten winter traverses of the Aonach Eagach. The lively spirit of that time is well captured in Jim's warm obituary for Bill Wood in the 2003 *Journal* (*SMCJ*, 38/194, 464–5).

In 1968 family connections in Austria led Jim to take up an offer to pursue a PhD in constitutional history in Vienna. He seized the opportunities that provided for assiduous exploration of the Austrian and Swiss Alps – he accounted for a good selection of the big Zermatt peaks with the Vienna University Club – and to establish a wide range of friendships and influential contacts. Although he returned to Scotland to resume teaching for a while, in 1977 he was lured back to Vienna to begin a richly varied new career that evolved from broadcasting, teaching, journalism and editing, into advisory work on international liaison and policy. Dr Wilkie came to occupy a highly regarded position in the corridors of Austrian government and diplomacy, his work recognised by awards rarely given to foreign nationals. He even became a close friend of the Habsburg family to the extent that his son Alexander, now an academic in Prague, is godfather to the Habsburg heir, Archduke Valentin.

On frequent visits to Scotland Jim took every opportunity to rejoin old friends for climbing, particularly with Bill Wood in the Cuillin, and to add progressively to his tally of Munros. As holiday crew on a fishing boat he got as far as St. Kilda and other remote islands. In 1983 he was proposed for SMC membership by Malcolm Slesser, a frequent companion on these visits. His application form records a notable outing with Malcolm in 1981, a 25-mile cross-country stravaig from Loch Lubnaig over Stùc a' Chroin and the moors under Uamh Bheag to the then Slesser home at Nether Glastry above Doune; it's intriguing to imagine the discussions along the way between these two fervent Nationalists of highly independent mind. In his *With Friends in High Places* Malcolm records that Jim regularly supplied another Austrian friend, Andreas Heckmair – the last survivor of the heroic team of the 1938 Eigerwand climb – with his favourite malt whisky. It was in Vienna, which he had made his home for more than forty years, that Jim died in November 2019.

Robert Aitken

JOHN PARK j. 2017

Born on 19 December 1962 in Glasgow, the son of Eileen Taggart and Iain Park, John and his sister Lindsay spent their early years on the west coast of Scotland. As a child he enjoyed life outdoors, becoming a Boy Scout and working on a neighbouring farm in his spare time. He might have become a farmer, and chose to study ecology with a later focus on forestry, at the University of Edinburgh. He was also a rock climber while at university.

Soon after graduation in 1985 John became father to Alasdair and then a year later to his second son, Gavin. The family, with two small sons, lived in the west of Scotland, where he became an Area Manager with Scottish Woodlands. While living in Argyll he became an active member of the Glasgow Section of the Junior Mountaineering Club of Scotland between 1992 and 1995. In winter John was often partnered with Donald Ballance or me on Ben Nevis.

John left Scotland in 1995 shortly after the fall of the Iron Curtain and went to work in Russian forests for five years. A brief professional episode for Shell Forestry in the Republic of Congo ended prematurely when a civil war broke out. Moving back to Russia he met Susanne Quandel. In 2000 John and Susanne married, moved to Heidelberg and became the parents of their daughter Katerina, all in the same year. Their apartment in Heidelberg was increasingly crowded when Anton was born a year later. They then moved to the French-German border area, the Palatinate, and soon had their third child, their younger daughter Sophie Luise, who was born in 2003.

John did not take a relaxed approach to life, and he was soon benefiting from help offered by the Neuchâtel Economic Development Agency to establish Wallenberg SA together with his business partner. In building the company's international trade in paper products, it helped that he spoke Russian, French and German. The family moved and set up home in the beautiful town of Erlach in Switzerland in 2008, and his office window in the old post office in Neuchâtel had views of the Eiger and the Mönch.

By this stage Susanne had taught him to ski, and living adjacent to the Jura mountains they also took up Nordic skiing. Having established a foothold in the Neuchâtel Section of the Swiss Alpine Club (SAC), his interest in mountaineering was rekindled during this time and he trained as an SAC Level 2 winter and summer tour leader, also organising trips back to Scotland between 2014 and 2018. Living in Switzerland he climbed extensively and had climbed the Eiger, the Matterhorn (via the North Face Schmid route) and a significant number of European 4000-metre peaks. He climbed the Frendo Spur in 2019 and had previously trekked in Patagonia, from Almaty (Kazakhstan) to Lake Issyk-Kul (Kyrgyzstan), and in the Altai mountains. John was also involved in the Neuchâtel SAC's family programmes for several years, thus combining his deep love for his family and for the mountains.

Up in the mountains and in the company of climbers, he showed what kind of person he truly was: determined and powerful, but also prudent and empathetic;

John Park. Photo: Alasdair Park..

convinced of his views on life, yet full of humour and interest in other people. John was a tough athlete, an adventurous man and yet dependable – two contradictory qualities that exist only in exceptional people.

John joined the SMC in 2017, making trips to climb on Ben Nevis in winter and with Susanne attending the February 2019 ski mountaineering meet held at the Steall Hut.

On Thursday 17 December 2020, at around 12.45 p.m., John was one of two enthusiastic early-season ski-tourers on the descent from Eggenmanndli (2448m) in the Urner Alps, heading towards Brüsti. As was typical of John his party had been first to reach the summit. On the descent, John triggered and was buried by a slab avalanche. His companion immediately alerted Swiss Air-Rescue (REGA) and searched for him with the help of their avalanche transceivers; she received support from three other people who were nearby. REGA recovered his body below the avalanche slope. John died two days before his 58th birthday.

John's passion was his family, but he was also passionate about mountains. He was a very active and also very experienced alpine climber and skier, fortunate to have been raised in Scotland and later to have lived in Switzerland. John is survived by his wife Susanne, his five children and two grandchildren.

Colwyn Jones

HUGH SIMPSON

Hugh Simpson was one of the SMC's cadre of bold polar explorers. Born a son of the manse in Ceres in 1931, he took to the Scottish mountains during his medical training at the University of Edinburgh. In the EUMC he climbed with

Hugh Simpson, polar explorer & mountaineer.

fellow medics Arthur Bennet and Dennis Moore, both later to join the Club. But Hugh's particular passion was for arduous long hill expeditions, expressed in a one-day round of all the Fannichs, various circuits of the High Tops of the Cairngorms, and ultimately in 1955 the full traverse with Bill Wallace of all the 4000ers in a 44-hour marathon from Achintee to Glenmore.[1] Not surprisingly the high-energy diet selected for that epic, 10 tins of irradiated milk and 6lbs of glucose, 'caused a certain amount of alimentary disturbance towards the end'.

In his first house post after qualifying, Hugh saw that a Medical Officer was needed for four years on the research vessel John Biscoe that serviced the UK Antarctic bases. This gave scope to explore and travel with dog teams, and led to his long love of the polar regions. On his return home he was awarded the Polar Medal.

On the way back from his Antarctic tour he rendezvoused with Bill Wallace and Myrtle Emslie for some venturesome routes in the Peruvian Andes. Back in Scotland, Hugh and Myrtle married; Hugh secured an academic post in the Department of Pathology at Glasgow University, eventually becoming the Professor there.

His Antarctic stay had fostered his interest in circadian rhythms, in which the body's hormones are influenced by the length of the day. He would follow this up when with Myrtle and a newly arrived baby he spent six weeks in the Bruce Hut in Spitsbergen, experimenting with the influence of 'days' of different lengths. This research interest was developed in different places and climatic conditions. Hugh published his work in scientific journals; Myrtle wrote the various books on their escapades.

Their life of adventurous parenthood continued with undiminished enthusiasm, sometimes with a dash of perhaps unjustified risk: for example, the family once camped on the ski plateau at Glen Coe, and at night in winter blizzard conditions they had to abandon their collapsing tent. With the youngest in a rucksack they fled for shelter, only to find the rucksack empty. On retracing their flight-path they saw by the light of a torch a tiny gloved mitt poking from the snow. All was well that ended well.

In 1965 Hugh, Myrtle, Bill Wallace and Roger Tufft sledged 400 miles from the east Greenland coast to the distant west coast in the steps of Nansen.[2] A high

[1] See 'Two Long Hill Traverses', *SMCJ*, 26/147 (1956), 95–6.

[2] See 'Grønland Langrenn', *SMCJ*, 28/157 (1966), 174–81.

point was when, struggling to negotiate complex terrain on the descent to the coast, they came across a dump of myriad cans of beer dropped in an aborted supply mission to the DEW line station which they had incongruously 'discovered' on their traverse.

In 1969, in response to a newspaper offer to fund an unusual expedition, they decided to try to reach the North Pole. Hugh, Myrtle and Roger made a creditable but doomed attempt, turning back at 84° north. Hugh's exploratory trips then became summer family events using double kayaks at home or in the fjords of south-west Greenland, and navigating down the rivers of Lapland. One of the Greenland trips became a BBC documentary feature, the film unit being managed by the SMC's Robin Chalmers.[3]

With a base on Speyside, and latterly living there permanently, the Simpsons had easy access to the ski slopes at Cairn Gorm, and gave their support to its development and the boosting of winter tourism.

In the early 1980s the proposal to extend the skiing on Cairn Gorm westwards across the Northern Corries into Lurcher's Gully raised a storm of objections including from the SMC. The application was turned down after a major public inquiry. Hugh on principle took the view that the attitude of the Club, which he had joined in 1961, was unjustified and he subsequently resigned.

Phil Gribbon & Robert Aitken

RICK ALLEN j. 1994

Although Rick was a quiet, modest man, he made friends easily wherever he went. I was lucky enough to know him soon after he'd started climbing seriously in Scotland back in the late 1970s. He had developed his interest in climbing when a student of Chemical Engineering at Birmingham University. Our first meeting in June 1977 was not auspicious. I was about to depart from Falcon Crag in the Lakes when a figure fell off *The Niche* directly above me as I walked by. My companion immediately recognised 'Arthur' as a fellow member of the Midland Association of Mountaineers and he called up to enquire about his health. (All Rick's early climbing friends knew him as Arthur. The story was that someone thought he looked remarkably like the legendary Arthur Dolphin.)

As Arthur spun on the rope he related how he'd just got a job with Babcock in Glasgow. My friend politely introduced me to him, and he explained that I lived in Fort William. Arthur's eyes lit up and he asked if he could look me up when he moved up to Scotland. Such introductions don't often bear fruit, but sure enough Arthur got in touch the following winter.

Our first route together was *Smith's Route* on Gardyloo Buttress.[4] On the approach we stopped for a rest outside the CIC Hut – neither of us was in the SMC at that time. When we got to the foot of the route, I discovered that I'd stupidly left my coiled rope at the hut. There was no guarantee that it would still be there by the time I went back for it, so without more ado we swung leads using Arthur's single 9mm. We next had a superb day on *Orion Face Direct*, but only after Arthur had been insistent about doing the correct start.

[3] This film can be viewed at <www.bbc.co.uk/programmes/p03yfgzt>. Retrieved 8/9/2021.

[4] Rick described our outing in 'Gardyloo Buttress', *MAMJ*, 6/1 (1979–80), 54–6.

The following year we set off to do *Route Major* in the 'Gorms, but in poor visibility our route finding wasn't the best, and we later discovered we'd actually done *False Scorpion*. At the top 'we so far forgot ourselves' as to shake hands vigorously in the gathering gloom.

Our best route together was *Tir na Og* on Ladhar Bheinn. On the upper part of the route the weather deteriorated significantly and we battled our way to the top through constant spindrift avalanches. Con Higgins and Mike Geddes were in our party at the bothy, but they made a more leisurely start and the encroaching storm caused them to bail out before they had even reached their route. Many years later I mentioned to Arthur that snatching that route was probably my best ever winter day. It was gratifying to learn that it was also one of his best ever routes in Scotland, second only to *Silver Tear* which he'd done with Con Higgins.

Arthur and I did some memorable rock routes together as well. It's strange, considering what he later went on to do, but Arthur had problems with Raynaud's in those days and I recall one cold day on *Torro* when he kept doing windmills with his arms to improve the circulation in his hands. I also had a trip to Malham with him one spring. He took a flyer attempting a route on the left wing and his only runner came out. I was seated on the ground without a belay and got dragged over the rocky ground as he tumbled down the slope below. He was badly winded and I had a very sore behind.

While Arthur was based in Glasgow he was a fairly frequent visitor to Fort William, and he admitted that after epic weekends his employers rarely got their money's worth from him on a Monday. He was around when the An Gearanach Mountaineering Club was set up in Fort William by Moira Watts and Helen Woods – as a mixed alternative to the male-only Lochaber JMCS. Arthur was at the inaugural Christmas dinner in 1978 when we all lugged our best bib and tucker to the wardenless Youth Hostel in Glen Affric. In subsequent years Arthur would always try to attend these dinners if he was in the country.

He moved away from Glasgow all too soon, and he eventually relocated to Aberdeen when he started working for Texaco – later to become Chevron. Arthur didn't do a lot of pioneering in Scotland, but in 1984 he teamed up with Brian Sprunt to make the first winter ascent of *Raven's Edge*, a plum route on the Buachaille. In June the same year he joined a big party of friends on a boat trip to Coruisk. The weather was superb and four of us traversed the Cuillin Ridge together. Although we weren't deliberately hurrying it was my fastest ever traverse. We even soloed *Naismith's Route* with ease, something that I haven't done since. We finished on Sgùrr nan Gillean at 3.30 p.m. I persuaded our party that the shortest way to get back to base was by descending Lota Corrie and crossing over the Druim nan Ràmh ridge. The descent on the far side proved to be a bit more harrowing than I expected after what we'd just done, and I was completely knackered by the time we got back to our tents. So I was hugely impressed the next day when Arthur teamed up with Geoff Cohen to do *King Cobra*. I was only too happy to take things easy on the Sunday, and marvelled at Arthur's resilience.

Arthur started hill running around this time to improve his fitness, and over the years he took part in nine Ben Nevis races. I never managed to beat him, though being eight years his senior I was sometimes able to tease him by claiming superiority on age-adjusted time. Although he was 30 when he did his first Ben Nevis Race, he kept astonishingly fit and actually achieved his best ever time of just under two hours in 1999 at the age of 44. He was delighted to identify himself in a central position on the cover photo of *The Ben Race*, a book about the Ben

Rick Allen, about to set off on Tir na Og, Spider Buttress, Ladhar Bheinn, 24 March 1979.
Photo: Noel Williams.

Nevis Race published in 1994. In it he is wearing the number one – a consequence
of his alphabetical position as Allen from Aberdeen.

It was on a five-week trekking holiday to the Annapurna Sanctuary with a
sherpa, Pemba Norbu, in 1980 that Arthur was first smitten by the Himalaya. He

realised immediately that this was where his main mountaineering interest was going to lie. On his first proper climbing trip there in 1982, on the grandly named Scottish Garhwal Himalaya Expedition, Arthur was the most impressive participant. After a very uncomfortable solo bivouac spent near a col below the summit, he managed to make the first ascent of Kirti Stambh (6270 m) at 9.20 a.m. the next day. He was the only one of the party to summit.[5]

Two years later he made the first ascent of the South Face of Ganesh II (7118m) with Nick Kekus. They were twelve days away from base, and endured some unpleasant bivouacs as well as running low on food and fuel. In 1985 he joined the Pilkington Expedition to the North-East Ridge of Everest organised by Mal Duff. He again made the highest push of the expedition solo, reaching 8150m before he retreated. Unless my memory is defective he mentioned to me on his return that he'd discovered the body of Peter Boardman in a snow cave, as well as mitts belonging to Dick Renshaw. I don't think this was ever mentioned in the press, so I hope I'm not imagining this.

We didn't see so much of Arthur on the hill after that. Although he kept in touch and remained a dear friend, we began to realise that only the Himalaya could offer the level of challenge he was looking for. His truly exceptional determination in high mountains started to become more apparent as the 1980s wore on.

Arthur had a very strong Christian faith and it was through his church in Aberdeen that he met Alison Grigor. We were delighted to attend their wedding in 1988. I don't suppose Alison could possibly have imagined what she was letting herself in for. Neither of them was allowed to forget the 1990 AGMC Christmas Dinner which was held at the Raeburn Hut. As usual we were all allotted jobs for the dinner and Arthur was tasked with buying the booze for everyone. However, the pair of them had an epic on Creag Meagaidh with all the drink still locked securely in their car boot. We had an alcohol-free dinner, and they only managed to join us well after midnight.

It was truly tragic when Alison died of cancer in 1999.

Arthur moved abroad with his work after that, first to Central Asia. He married Zukhra Zuptarova in 2006 and assisted her in the operation of a travel company in Tajikistan. They seemed to run into scary problems with the Russian Mafia, and Arthur was relieved to eventually move on to western Australia in 2009. It was six months later before Zukhra and his two step-children, Nazira and Farrukh, managed to get visas and join him. Unfortunately he and Zukhra divorced after he retired from Chevron in 2015.

I leave his good friend Sandy Allan to say more about Arthur's Himalayan exploits. A casual observer of his record, however, will realise that on occasions he pushed the boat out to the nth degree. He had a very close call on Makalu in 1988, when he was a member of a team led by Doug Scott. He was making a semi-alpine-style summit bid with Alan Hinkes on the left side of the west face, when he was hit by an avalanche at 8100m, struck his head on a boulder, lost consciousness, plunged over a cliff and fell 400 metres. He was lucky to survive and acquired a sizeable scar on his scalp as a memento.

He remained as thin as a whippet and how he functioned for days without food on some of his trips is a mystery, though he often looked quite haggard in the aftermath. As we gradually became more portly over time he put us all to shame by always looking trim and immaculate in a dinner jacket at AGMC Dinners. He was always low-key with us about his Himalayan adventures, and after he

---

[5] Rick Allen, 'Garhwal Himalaya', *MAMJ*, 6/3 (1983–84), 10–12.

Rick at an AGMC Dinner, 12 December 2009.

summited Everest in 2000,[6] he took it in good humour when we dubbed him 'Arthur of Everest'.

I treasure the numerous postcards that Arthur sent from his various expeditions, as well as his Christmas letters. When our daughter came along he was thoughtful enough to address them to her as well. Most of the postcards were sent from base camp before he got committed to the mountain and it was only later that we learned the full details of his epics. In more recent times the postcards were regrettably replaced by more ephemeral e-mails, and by then news also travelled much more quickly.

Arthur missed the last pre-Covid AGMC Dinner because he was studying in Hertfordshire at the All Nations Christian College. He had recently moved near to Nethy Bridge and planned on becoming a church minister. Unfortunately that was not to be. There was phenomenal coverage in the media when he died on K2. He was 66, not 68 as was widely reported. All his friends will miss him dearly. We salute his amazing achievements, but just wish he hadn't been quite so fiercely driven. He certainly lived life as a tiger, the only way he knew how.

DNW

---

[6] Rick Allen, 'Selling Out', *SMCJ*, 37/19 (2001), 792–5.

Rick Allen on the summit of Nanga Parbat after doing the Mazeno Ridge, 15 July 2012.
Photo: Sandy Allan.

Sandy Allan writes:
I share Noel Williams's sentiments and echo his praise of Rick. He had an interesting and impressive Himalayan record, including Tharpu Chuli (Tent Peak) in 1981; the first ascent of Kirti Stambh in 1982; the SSW face of Ganesh II; the S face of Pumori in Nepal in 1986, with Sandy Allan; and the N face of Dhaulagiri (8167m) in 1993, with a Russian expedition.[7] He also made attempts on the unclimbed NE ridge of Mount Everest from Tibet, in 1985 (as described above) and 1987, before guiding a party to the summit by the ordinary route in 2000, on an expedition led by Henry Todd.

In the Tien Shan range, Rick made an ascent of Khan Tengri (7439m) in 1991. On Nanga Parbat he climbed the Diamir face in 2009 and made two attempts on the Mazeno Ridge, completing the first traverse with Sandy Allan on 15 July 2012.[8]

Rick died in an avalanche in July 2021 on K2, while attempting a new route. He was climbing with two others, Jordi Tosas and Stephan Keck, who fortunately survived. Rick's body once retrieved was laid to rest at K2 Base Camp, and a memorial service was held in August in Aberdeen.[9]

We will miss him very much.

---

[7] Rick Allen, 'A Different Way on Dhaulagiri', *American Alpine Journal*, 36/68 (1994), 30–34.

[8] Sandy Allan, *In Some Lost Place* (Vertebrate, 2015); also *SMCJ*, 42/204 (2013), 339–49.

[9] <https://www.youtube.com/watch?v=mG7-ORGv8FE> retrieved 7 Sep 2021.

PROCEEDINGS OF THE CLUB

At the Committee meeting in October 2020 the following were admitted to the Club:

MARK CHAMBERS (31), Fort William
STEVEN ANDREWS (40), Kiltarlity, Beauly
LUCA CELANO (33), Uckfield
TIM GOMERSALL (27) Inverness
BRIAN POLLOCK (32), Glasgow

And at the April 2021 meeting:

INNES DEANS (48), Leeds
MATTHEW DENT (44), Tain
STEPHEN VENABLES (66), Edinburgh
PAUL GILLES (70), Giffnock
DAVID KERR (45), Inverness
RYAN MCHENRY (30), Glasgow.

We warmly welcome these new members.

The One-Hundred-and-Thirty-Second AGM and Dinner
5 December 2020

For the last 132 years no world events have stopped the SMC holding our Annual Dinner. Unfortunately, during 2020 nowhere was beyond the reach of the Covid-19 virus and despite a reduction in cases during the summer months, the Club's office bearers concluded that we were better to make a decision during September, and cancel the event, rather than wait many more weeks and leave too much uncertainty for the members, the guests and the hotel. In fact, by December the situation with Covid-19 restrictions meant it would have been impossible to hold the Dinner and so this decision was clearly the correct option.

The Club did, however, hold the AGM as an online 'Zoom' meeting. As is always the case now, the Office Bearers' Reports had been emailed or posted out and the content had given the members a full account of the year. The format of Zoom does not match the traditional face-to-face meeting but it did allow questions to be raised and answers to be given.

So much of the tradition of the Club has been on hold since March 2020. The Easter Meet had to be cancelled and use of Club huts reduced to nil. The AGM did include a vote to keep all the Club officials who were due to retire from office, in position for another year. The sentiment behind this change was that it is in the interest of the club that there be minimal change in the committee composition from 2020 through 2021. The amendment was passed. However, one significant change was passed in that there will be a new Editor of the *Journal*, namely Graeme Morrison.

The meeting closed with a rendition of the club song, *My Old Hobnailers*, led by Curly Ross. This worked well, provided that all participants except Curly left themselves on 'mute' and we avoided the inevitable audio time lag.

Here's to the 2021 Dinner in more familiar surroundings! I look forward to it.

Chris Huntley

Sea Kayak Meet, Gairloch

21–23 May 2021

For some of us this was the first escape following Covid lockdown, and it was the SMC's first kayak meet, based at the Sands Campsite by Gairloch.

Despite varying degrees of wind two excellent days of paddling were had. Taking advantage of the wind on the Saturday we made a circuit of Loch Gairloch, going with the wind to Badachro in the morning and managing mostly to avoid it on return leg, hugging the coast and passing Charleston and Gairloch on the way back. On Sunday the weather was better but not good enough for our planned route, so the team headed north from Aultbea on Loch Ewe, which provided a superb paddle.

The meet was organised and led by Christine Watkins, to whom thanks are due.

The team L to R: Stan Pearson, David Myatt, Grant Urquhart, Christine Watkins, Ian Stevens, Anthony Walker, Richard Bott and Chris Ravey. Photos: Grahame Nicoll.

Members present: Richard Bott, David Myatt, Stan Pearson, Chris Ravey, Ian Stevens, Grant Urquhart, Anthony Walker, and Christine Watkins.

Skye Spring Meet at Allt Dearg Cottage

5–12 June 2021

It was a much depleted group that attended this year because we were restricted by Covid to just three households. The weather was mixed, being rather cold and windy for most of the week, so at least midges were not a problem. Sunday was quite pleasant and a party ventured out to Rubha an Dùnain to examine the various archaeological features there. One member cycled on the vehicular track which now extends as far as the wall at the north end of Slochd Dubh. It was pleasantly sunny at times, though the Cuillin remained largely in cloud. Another party bagged Arnaval at Talisker.

On Monday one team explored Coire na Seilg on the north side of Garbh-bheinn. After completing an existing scramble the party headed for an unnamed buttress spotted on a previous visit to the west of Bealach na Beiste. Despite carrying full climbing gear this proved to be a surprisingly straightforward scramble on good rock. Meanwhile another team visited Waternish and bagged Ben Geary.

The Old Man of Storr has become a major honeypot (along with the Fairy Pools, the Quiraing, and Neist Point). To cater for the hordes there is now a huge Pay & Display carpark with toilet block on the main road at the start of the walk up to the Old Man. However, on Tuesday it was somewhat quieter at Brother's Point and some dinosaur tracks were eventually located there with the aid of an academic paper. Meanwhile another team bagged Ben Lee from the cottage and discovered an interesting mini-gorge en route to the summit.

Wednesday was unpleasantly wet, but Thursday was merely showery and some exploring was done on the Trotternish peninsula. On Friday a lone soul traversed Marsco and Beinn Dearg Mheadhonach, while another two found much more to interest them in Trotternish, including an unusually long belemnite fossil.

Belemnites are extremely common fossils in Jurassic rocks, but this particular species is unusually long. The original squid-like creature would have been three times this length. Photo: Noel Williams.

One party managed a scramble on the quartzite slabs of Sleat before leaving on the Saturday.

Earlier in the week there had been reports of unstable blocks in the T-D Gap, but the weather discouraged an investigation.

Members present: Simon Fraser, Lisa Hutchison and Noel Williams.
Guests: Anne Craig and Willie Jeffrey.

DNW

Easter Meet, Inchnadamph Hotel

29 July – 1 August 2021

Members of the SMC, heading north to Inchnadamph from the sunny Lowlands and other airts, may have felt they were travelling to a very special meet – a long journey in many ways. A small group of people converging, who had neither seen nor talked to each other face to face owing to the Covid restrictions for two years; apprehensive of a hotel setting however safe, packing masks just in case, and arriving in a cooler, darker North-West with mist down on the mountains and smirrs of rain. But from the very first, apprehension fled in the warmth of meeting all one's good friends and hearing familiar voices discussing where we might spend the next few days on the hills. Seen from the hotel window, Quinag was enrobed in mist but holding much promise. Perversely, the lower the cold mist fell the higher our spirits rose!

The first evening was enlivened by Noel Williams displaying a fossil found on the coast of Trotternish during the Skye Spring Meet. (See previous page.) This was part of the internal skeleton or rostrum of a belemnite. The staggering knowledge that one was holding a part of this sea creature that lived 180 million years ago was almost too difficult to comprehend. It was quickly put away before the scampi supper appeared.

The weather forecast was not too favourable, with cloud thick and very low, but everyone got out on both days. There was no climbing but some scrambling was achieved on the Stack of Glencoul. Many other diverse Munros, Corbetts, Grahams, Marilyns and Hughs were ascended, among them Ben Strome, Ben Klibreck, Breabag, Spidean Còinich of Quinag, Cnoc an Droighinn, Ben Dreavie, Ben Hutig, Feinne-bheinn Mhòr and Beinn Rèidh. And of course the 'bone caves' were visited.

A fine 3lb trout was pulled from Loch Beannach by Bob Reid's party, while John Hay kept a benevolent eye on us by binocular from various viewpoints. Two dogs in the party were also putting in the miles and displaying sleepy smiles in the evenings. The tradition of toasting the Club courtesy of the Slesser–Smart award was maintained.

A very pleasant and rewarding meet and we all thank the President, John Fowler, who was the driving force for staying fast then going ahead with the meet in the face of uncertainty. We hope to return to Kinlochewe at Easter 2022.

Members present: John R.R. Fowler (President), Alison J. Coull, Helen G.S. Forde, J.Y.L. Hay, S. Fraser, P.F. Macdonald, J.R.G. Mackenzie, W.S. McKerrow, R.T. Prentice, R. Reid, K. Robb, D. Stone and D.N. Williams.
Guests: Eve MacKenzie and Gerrie Fellows.

Helen G.S. Forde

Easter Meet 2021 : Inchnadamph

L to R: Peter Macdonald, John Hay, Tom Prentice, Simon Fraser, Alison Coull, Noel Williams, John Fowler (President), John Mackenzie, Eve Mackenzie (guest), Kenny Robb, Helen Forde, David Stone, Bill McKerrow. Not in photo: Bob Reid, Gerrie Fellows (guest). Photo: D. Stone.

JMCS REPORTS

Edinburgh Section. Lockdown has curtailed the club's activities significantly over the last year. Social distancing and the limitation upon individuals from different 'bubbles' meeting meant that club members who are also couples had a significant advantage over the members who follow the 'married with 2.4 children' formula: while the former were able to go climbing together, the latter group had to stay indoors and home-school their offspring!

Most club activities came to a standstill. Our last weekend meet took place early in March 2020 at the Cabin, all subsequent meets having to be cancelled. Our Wednesday evening meets at local crags would have been great in the fantastic summer weather we had last year, but they also could not go ahead.

After we got better at organising committee meetings virtually, by Zoom, we also had to hold our AGM in the same way. This meant that what is usually a weekend-long event was over and done with in just over 45 minutes, which was not quite the same. Let us hope we will be able to return to the Cairngorm Hotel in November 2021 and can meet up in person, have a lot of craic and also enjoy a drink or two.

At one point there was also talk of cancelling the annual newsletter this year, but I'm glad we didn't. Our members contributed seven articles, with all but one featuring adventures in the Scottish Highlands: descriptions of Classic Rock and Hard Rock adventures, kayaking and bivvies in the hills. I have to say, there were some serious 'lockdown haircuts' in the photographs, but it was good to see members able to make use of good conditions in the short period between July and October when the restrictions were eased. Maybe this is what we can take with us from the year of Covid and living with restrictions that have not been so stringent since the Second World War. Let's not forget what great hills we have on our doorstep. But having said that, I can imagine that a lot of our club members have been perusing guidebooks of the Alps or further afield, and are very keen to travel to warmer and more exotic climes. And reading an article by the one member who was able to travel to Spain last year was also very inspiring.

The 2020–21 winter season was a complete write-off, at least for the members who live in the Central Belt and followed the government rule of only essential travel. There were reports of good winter conditions on social media in the Pentlands and Holyrood Park (i.e. Cat Nick) in January and early February, but I'm not aware whether any members were able to take advantage of these.

Let's hope we are through the worst of this pandemic and soon we'll be able to take up our regular club activities again. These include regular meets at Alien Rock and Ratho (Monday and Wednesday evenings), and during the summer months Wednesday evening meets at local and not-so-local crags. In addition, we hold regular weekend meets. (See our website <edinburghjmcs.org.uk> for details). Once we have reopened them, our huts will also be available for booking by kindred clubs by contacting the custodians, whose names are below.

Honorary President: John Fowler; President: Thomas Beutenmuller; Vice-President & Smiddy custodian: Helen Forde (helen.forde1@btinternet.com); Treasurer: Bryan Rynne; Cabin Custodian: Ali Borthwick (01383 732 232, before 9 p.m.); Membership Secretary: Nils Krichel; Committee Member: Catrin Thomas. The Secretary's post is vacant at the moment.

Thomas Beutenmuller

Lochaber Section. No report was received, owing to limited activity in 2020.

Secretary: Iain Macleod, ia.macleod@btinternet.com.

London Section. What a year! Only five meets were possible – two before the pandemic and three between the first and second lockdowns. Individual as well as Section activity was severely curtailed, and I do not recall anything particularly noteworthy being achieved in the hills in a year that is best forgotten!

The world seemed so different during our Scottish winter meet in Glen Clova: we were blithely unaware of the catastrophe ahead. Plans for the rest of the year included a now regular sojourn in Spain to enjoy some climbing in winter sunshine. But this was not to be. Instead it was 'hunker down' until the restrictions lifted slightly in the summer. Meets followed in Derbyshire, Borrowdale and the Wye Valley. The sense of freedom that comes from a good weekend away was all the greater. That pint on the Friday evening tasted even better when you had been cooped up for months. Moreover, the weather was good in both Derbyshire and the Wye Valley, where we enjoyed excellent climbing and mountain biking. The Lake District meet was a bit of a washout, but it still felt good getting into the hills for a couple of days even if it took a while to dry all the gear.

The annual club dinner in November had to be cancelled, but we had a lively get-together online thanks to Zoom. Indeed, as many people as usual attended the AGM, including some who would not have been able to do so if we had been meeting in person.

Our hut in Bethesda was closed for most of the year. Being shut from March to August resulted in damp-related damage, and some redecoration was necessary. It was frustrating that no sooner had the hut reopened than we had to close it again because of the second lockdown. However, the one positive from the pandemic is that our Section's finances are much stronger thanks to Covid-19 related grants from the Welsh authorities. This money will be invested in our hut, to make it more comfortable to stay in and easy to use.

Inevitably in a Section with an ageing membership, there was sad news. On Christmas Eve we lost John Turner, a member since the 1960s. A club stalwart, John was already an experienced alpinist when he joined and was instrumental in what might be described as the second phase of rebuilding our club hut: making and fitting the kitchen work-surfaces, and installing the cash safe and the first shower unit. We also lost John (Jeff) Howes from our Nottingham contingent. A glass or two will be raised to both when Covid restrictions lift and our programme resumes.

President: Trevor Burrows; Secretary: John Firmin
(john.firmin3@btinternet.com); Treasurer: Gordon Burgess Parker;
Hut Custodian: David L Hughes (davidlewishughes@hotmail.com).

John Firmin

Perth Section. The constraints of various lockdowns have required the Perth Mountaineering Club to be rather more resourceful in its efforts to find legitimate venues for our activities, particularly as we were confined to our council areas for much of the winter. Frequent meets were possible nevertheless, either informally in small groups or sometimes overnight, and we made the most of these opportunities. We were also particularly pleased to see our membership rise slightly to above 80 this year. The recent influx of enthusiastic younger members also means that meets continue to be well attended.

Thanks to some helpful local knowledge, courtesy of Grahame Nicoll and Craig Gudmundsson, less-frequented winter climbing venues within Perthshire were explored between December and March. Particular attention centred on the Ben Lawers area and Coire Cruinn, which both received repeated visits. There were also enterprising attempts at winter routes more locally, including around Benarty Hill in Fife. The club was able to venture further afield in the spring with visits to the Ben and Glen Coe. Other activities were also pursued in smaller groups, from bouldering and local crags in February through to winter climbing and skiing in May, following the logic of Scottish weather. The club remained a source of social activities throughout the lockdown, organising a Zoom social evening and making use of our WhatsApp group for chat and organisation of meets.

With huts remaining largely out of bounds or impractical, our meets secretary endeavoured to keep us busy over the summer. This has resulted in highly successful camping meets at Ullapool and on Skye (including a drowned-out ridge traverse attempt) and an excellent long wild camping expedition to Kinlochewe. More camping meets are planned for Arran and Glen Coe into the autumn and it is pleasing to see these being convened by newer members of the club. We continue to actively recruit and have a healthy list of prospective members whom we are keen to sign up.

On a final note, the club learned of the death of a long-standing member, Jessie Ann Dick 'Nan' Rae, aged 93. Several club members remember climbing Munros with her and her husband Ron, and recall her fond memories of the Perth JMCS. Nan Rae surprised us by leaving the club a very generous bequest of £5000, for which we are most grateful. Whilst we do not have immediate plans for the funds, our intention, with the centenary of the club occurring not so far in the future, is to do something that both celebrates our history and invests in the future.

President: Catherine Johnson; Secretary: Tim Storer (secretary@perthmountaineering-club.co.uk); Treasurer: Pam Dutton; Meets Secretary: Craig Gudmundsson.

Tim Storer

Glasgow Section. Like everyone else, our section enjoyed a markedly different year during 2020. Owing to the SARS-CoV-2 pandemic, face-to-face club events were suspended in February 2020, and at the time of writing, 14 months later, that constraint remains. The 2020 Presidential dinner, typically a most pleasant and convivial event, was cancelled. Despite the restrictions the club continues to welcome new members and guests to join the virtual events currently running, and to attend club meets once they restart.

As a club, we have ventured further into the unknown (for us) by fully embracing cyberspace. We now socialise and conduct business via Zoom,

WhatsApp, e-mail and the like. Meetings, competitions, quizzes, banter and 'Where am I' keep us linked virtually when we cannot be together otherwise. On the weekend of 3–5 April 2020, the club held the first virtual meet, seemingly at Taigh na Cnott, the Shoogly Peg Mountaineering Club Hut in Glen Banter (five miles North of Brigadoon). Alternative rooms were available in the nearby Grand Hotel, in the Hilbert's Wing, which apparently always has space! Two members ran half-marathons, virtually competing against each other via Strava and GPS, one running in Glasgow Parks and the other in London. One member, using more traditional running techniques successfully completed the Bob Graham round in mid-September well inside the 24-hour target time, a major achievement.

In November 2020 the virtual AGM was held using the Zoom software. It was reported that there were 85 current section members in total, comprising 41 ordinary members and 44 life members. Unsurprisingly the club had no new members recorded as joining in 2020. There were two new life members, David Eaton and Mark Evans, awarded after 25 years of continuous membership.

The section organised a full schedule of more than 20 weekend meets throughout 2020 including all of the five SMC huts. Four of these meets were successfully held before the SARS-CoV-2 restrictions were applied. Meets were planned every two weeks throughout most of the year, with a single meet in August. The meet venues vary each year, covering the whole of Scotland and occasionally beyond. In the late spring and summer there are normally midweek evening meets to various central belt rock-climbing venues, together with midweek indoor climbing meets in The Glasgow Climbing Centre at Ibrox throughout the year. When the restrictions are lifted the plan is to reinstate these events as soon as possible.

One of the more popular meets with Glasgow JMCS members is the late May bank holiday maintenance meet to the club hut at Coruisk. The spectacular boat trip from Elgol (free to work-meet participants) perhaps contributes to that popularity. The hut itself is usually busy at weekends, with overseas clubs now making regular bookings. To book please contact the hut custodian directly: coruisk@glasgowjmcs.org.uk
or via the Glasgow JMCS website: <www.glasgowjmcs.org.uk>
or by Facebook at <www.facebook.com/CoruiskMemorialHut/>

The Glasgow JMCS Newsletter remains an entertaining read and continues to thrive under the editorship of Dr Ole Kemi. Four issues are published per year and it can be downloaded from the Glasgow JMCS website. The newsletter publishes contributions from all authors, not just JMCS members, and we welcome material for future issues.

The winter season 2020 was disrupted everywhere by the travel restrictions. Winter climbing before lockdown included routes by our president on Buachaille Etive Mòr, Stob Coire nan Lochan, Ben Nevis and the Aonach Eagach. On the day before the March lockdown the Glasgow JMCS stand-out climb was *Minus One Gully* on Ben Nevis, reportedly on stellar ice. Contrary to all expectations no Glasgow JMCS member has admitted to being fined for breaking the lockdown restrictions.

Overseas in March while ski-mountaineering in the canton of Valais, two retired Glasgow JMCS past presidents climbed a number of peaks, the most significant being the Wildstrubel (3244m) on the 8 March and the Wildhorn (3428m) on 14 March as training peaks. Later that month all further activity was stopped by the Swiss pandemic restrictions.

One member adopted a personal challenge to break the monotony of not being

JMCS activity on Ben Nevis: Mark Gorin leads Strident Edge. Photo: Jeremy Morris.

able to access any significant hills by ascending his local peak (Caldron Hill, 332m) on the night of the full moon for a year. He has achieved seven visits to date, with his challenge now extending into 2021.

A Friday night in early July would usually be spent speeding north towards dry mountain or coastal rock, but one such evening found two members at Auchinstarry Quarry. It was raining lightly, the rock was sandy and the cracks choked with weeds from months of neglect, but it was reported to be great to be out climbing again! When restrictions eased, members were rock-climbing on The Souter sea-stack, Scafell and even on Ben Nevis following the SMC CIC work-meet in August. The same month, two members enjoyed a day traversing the Cuillin ridge, and this was followed two days later by our president on a two-day not-so-fast solo traverse. He had a good weather forecast and wanted the full experience, so chose to carry bivouac kit. Unfortunately, he found that a good forecast does not necessarily mean good weather, and so of course half of the traverse was in the wet. He reports that wet Skye rock feels quite slippery, confirmed the following day on the Clach Glas and Blàbheinn traverse.

Two retired presidents had an extended summer trip through a partly restricted Switzerland, walking and scrambling a total of 44 peaks in 54 days, with their sole 4000m peak being the Breithorn (4164m) on 13 September. The final 14 days of the jaunt were spent in Germany, thereby avoiding the need to quarantine on return to the UK. The summit of The Brocken (1141m) was also ticked, but sadly no spectres were seen.

Honorary President: Neil Wilkie; President: Ole Kemi; Vice-President: John Fenemore; Secretary: Phil Smith; Treasurer: Justine Carter; New Members' Secretary: Dave Payne

Colwyn Jones

JMCS (1925–2025) Centenary Anthology. Finally, an appeal to the readers of the *SMC Journal*. In 2025 the Junior Mountaineering Club of Scotland will be 100 years old, and the publication of an anthology of 100 articles is planned to mark the centenary. We are seeking historic material from all JMCS sections that has previously appeared in JMCS newsletters or journals or in the SMCJ, as well as new material that brings the JMCS story up to the present. The publication will form a history of the club viewed through character sketches, accounts of significant events, climbing or expedition articles, meet reports, route descriptions, activities, log-books, the club huts, photographs, and so on. If space permits, material relating to non-climbing activities such as sailing or kayaking may also be included if relevant to the club. If you have any suggestions for suitable material, either existing or original, we will be pleased to hear from you. Please contact Niel Craig by e-mail, niel_craig@yahoo.co.uk.

Colwyn Jones

SMC ABROAD

PENNINE ALPS, BERNESE OBERLAND & BREGAGLIA

As soon as the Foreign Office lifted the injunction against 'non-essential travel' in early July 2020, I escaped Scotland just as lockdown was beginning to lift, and drove to Switzerland to meet Ellen Bruce (AC/SAC) at Saas-Grund. Ellen had been climbing since April, being based in Switzerland; I had not touched rock for months. Being in a relatively 'normal' country after months of lockdown was quite a shock.

We hiked up to the Almageller Hütte, and climbed for two days on Dri Horlini, a sunny crag of golden orange gneiss with generous flake holds. A delightful place with long routes of medium difficulty – just right, given my lack of climbing fitness. Although I was hardly acclimatised, Ellen then suggested the North Ridge of the Weissmies (AD), a 2km-long rock and snow ridge finishing at 4000m. I couldn't resist. It was indeed an excellent route, mostly perfect rock that ran to handrails and foot-ledges along a knife-edge ridge, with a few technical pitches thrown in. Needless to say I was much slower than Ellen. This was to be a feature of the rest of our trip.

Encouraged by this expedition, we next tackled the Rotgrat (AD) on the 4206m Alphubel. Thick cloud, poor visibility, a bitingly cold wind and snow on the rocks of the upper buttress turned this into a truly Scottish epic. We had a good old battle for 17 hours, and I have to admit I was quite in my element leading the snow-covered rocks. The hut guardian at the Täschhütte seemed impressed when we returned, but we were both actually a bit worn out by this affair.

We decamped to the Grimsel area, and went up to the Bächlitalhütte, located in a hanging valley with two former glacial lake beds. The main attraction here was the Grosser Diamantstock (3162m) by its East Ridge (4c), a much-photographed climb that is in all the selective guidebooks and consequently very popular. Not surprisingly, the start of the climb was more like Stanage on a Sunday afternoon, but the queues were compensated for by perfect rock, interesting technical pitches and very photogenic situations. We had fitted in a couple of long lower-level rock climbs before this peak, and I was already feeling quite weary by this point.

We moved round to the Furkapass, and went up to the Sidelenhütte, from which we climbed the SE Ridge (5c) of the Gross Bielenhorn (3210m). Like the previous climbs, this was an excellent route suggestion by Ellen, with seven fine technical pitches on superb granite, followed by easier ground to the summit. I then said goodbye to Ellen, and drove down to Italy to meet Keith Anderson (SMC). Keith was particularly keen to climb the Via Cassin on the Badile, though I was by now sorely in need of a good rest. We headed to the Val Bregaglia and, having missed the last lift, walked up to the Albigna refuge.

The next day we climbed the Via Steiger (5c) on the Punta Albigna: 20 pitches of excellent granite, mostly at quite a low grade, with two of the best balance pitches I'd ever encountered. A real gem, highly recommended. We squeezed in the Via Felice (6a) on Spazzacaldera next morning. This was surprisingly good considering it was a mere 'crag' climb compared with our other routes. Back in the valley, the forecast was good for two more days, and we decided to go for it. The ascent to the Sasc Fura refuge, by the newly constructed path that avoids the Cengalo fall-out zone, was an unpleasant struggle, six hours of circuitous up and down. I lost the path at one point, and wasted much-needed energy bushwhacking in jungle. Not much hope for me on the Badile if I couldn't even follow the hut path, I reflected.

Adam Kassyk leading the fourth pitch of the Cassin route on Piz Badile.
Photo: Keith Anderson.

The Via Cassin is so well documented nothing more needs to be said about the climb. There were however two notable features of our ascent. Firstly, we were the only climbers on the entire face: remarkable, for such a famous and sought-after climb. Secondly, we discovered that the frictional properties of Bregaglia granite are unimpaired by running water. Caught in a storm three pitches from the end of the climb, we had quite an exciting time, especially on the North Ridge to the summit. Later, Keith told me about the sparks coming from his belay anchor.

We spent the night in the cramped summit shelter, and descended on a beautiful

Adam Kassyk on the upper section of the Gervasutti route on the Punta Allievi.
Photo: Keith Anderson.

sunny morning to the Gianetti refuge. The weather was holding out, so we decided
to cross to the Bonacossa Allievi hut to finish on the Gervasutti route (5c). The
Via Roma path to the hut was surprisingly long and demanding, crossing three
passes with rather a lot of wires and chains. To be honest, for such a famous
classic, the climb seemed a bit disappointing at first. There was a lot of grass and
lichen, and scope for much variation, and finding the best line seemed to be a case
of avoiding the grass as much as possible. The lower crux was a very butch
chimney-slot and hand-jam crack, well led by Keith. Rain threatened higher up,
and we contemplated retreat, but the bad weather didn't materialise. The climb
was however redeemed by a superlative upper crux pitch – sustained, absorbing
and technical – and by some further nice climbing above. We topped out in warm
evening light, with the solace of an easy descent to hand.

All that remained was to cross the historic Passo di Zocca the following day to return to Switzerland, following apparently in the footsteps of fugitives and smugglers. They must have been desperate people, I thought, for although Keith was still relatively fresh I found the descent of the remains of the Albigna glacier hard going, stumbling through unstable boulders in an advanced state of weariness.

Our final week had involved 68 pitches, and 23 pitched climbs. I drove Keith to the airport, and then retreated to the south of France for a much-needed recovery.

Adam Kassyk

TRYING TO FIND SCOTLAND IN BAVARIA

I lived for 19 years in the UK, from 1997 until 2016. First I spent five years in Preston, then three years in Dundee where I also completed the round of the Munros and started climbing, and finally ten years in Aberdeen. In 2015 an attractive job was advertised in Munich and the Brexit debate was gathering pace. So, time to go? Should I leave behind all those winter climbs, ceilidhs, kayak trips, hill-walks, the solitude of the Highlands, and all those Scottish friends? What would I lose, what would I gain? I was offered the Munich job and in February 2016 packed up my belongings, put them in a van labelled 'UMZÜGE 83714 MIESBACH', and moved to Munich.

But Munich immediately showed what it had to offer. The Alps are just 50km from my front door, the autobahn signs display names like 'Verona', major ski resorts are just one hour away, and sunny breakfasts on the balcony start in March and end in October. In summer Simon Richardson visited and we climbed in the Karwendel and did the *Kraxengrat*, a long but easy UIAA IV- ridge on the Wilder Kaiser. In autumn Arno Alpi arrived, an Austrian climbing partner of mine who had worked in Dundee and by coincidence had also started a job in Munich. Our first outing together was the Rubihorn, a wee Nordwand, but there was not enough snow and so we just scrambled to the Nebelhorn, a 2224m peak above Oberstdorf in the Allgäu.

On 27 May 2017 Arno and I tried something proper. Just over one hour from Munich and just over the border to Austria lies the Wilder Kaiser, the second major rock-climbing venue of the Eastern Alps after the Dolomites. We had planned to climb the *Dülfer Fleischbank*, graded UIAA VI, a classic 14-pitch limestone route first climbed by Hans Dülfer and Werner Schaarschmidt in 1912. That was a time when the golden and silver ages of alpinism had ended and climbers were starting to seek technical challenges instead of summits. At the time of the first ascent, the *Fleischbank* was one of the hardest climb of the day, as a long HVS/E1. The climb now has bolted belays and bolts at the cruxes but you will need nuts, slings and friends for the rest. What a climb, and what exposure! To someone for whom the Dubh Loch and the Shelterstone were the biggest cliffs so far, the Fleischbank was a step up. The Fleischbank cliff also plays a role in modern climbing history, as it has *Des Kaisers neue Kleider*, which is part of the Alpine trilogy climbed in 2019 by Scotsman Robbie Phillips.

On 15 August 2017 Arno and I then climbed Hans Dülfer's masterpiece on the Kaiser, *Totenkirchl Westwand*, UIAA VI+ and over 20 pitches long, which Dülfer first ascended in 1913 with Willy von Redwitz – an even bigger cliff with lots of

Henning Wackerhage on the 'Nasentraverse' of the Totenkirchl Westwand, with the nose itself at the top middle of the picture. The Nasentraverse requires some balance climbing on tiny holds with lots of exposure. It can be aided though; the old bit of aid tat is just to the left of the crack at Henning's left shoulder. Photo: Arno Alpi.

hard climbing for us on a hot day. Our shared rucksack was far too heavy, and I remember having the first and only bicep cramp of my life when arriving super-dehydrated on the top of the Totenkirchl towards 8 p.m. After that came a long headtorch descent with abseils and scrambles to arrive at the Stripsenjoch at 10 p.m. for the best Radler (shandy) of my life. One of the most memorable climbs and, yes, that was a proper adventure!

The years 2018 and 2019 followed, with good but less memorable Kaiser climbs, kayak and Munro-bagging trips in Scotland, mountain bike tours, a traverse of the Watzmann, many ski tours, Nordic skiing trips and even a three-day weekend in Scotland with two first ascents including an icy Grade-III gully, *Midas Touch*, in my beloved Glen Clova with Simon Richardson.

And then came 2020. Just before Covid-19 became a thing, on 19 January 2020, Arno and I drove to Scheffau to try a big, long ridge on the Kopfkraxen in winter. We hardly got to the bottom of the route, however, as the snow was waist-deep and we decided that this was for another day, perhaps at the beginning or end of the season. In June we were able to climb a Grade V, on the Geiselstein, a 1882m limestone spire in the Allgäu, another Grade V+, *König der Löwen* on the Kaiser, and in August a Grade V in Orpierre with Paul, who had emigrated from Scotland to France; and then in September the *Guffert Südgrat*, a fantastic V+ in the Rofan mountains, and finally the *Kampenwand Traverse* on a sunny, short-sleeve November day. Arno and I always climbed together and kept our distance from others, so despite Covid-19 we were able to do routes.

But one thing that was missing was a Bavarian mixed climb. I had bought a book about easy climbs in the Bavarian Alps, and we decided just to look for vegetated, simple routes and to try to climb them in winter. On 22 November, with the coming of the first snow, we drove to near Berchtesgaden and tried the *Neuer Schmidkunzweg*, which we renamed *Hacke-Strammweg* (a joke that only works in German), a UIAA III+ route up the Riedberger Horn (a 1787m limestone spire). What a great outing! The turf wasn't as juicy as in Scotland and there was no ice, but it gave plenty of good, adventurous climbing which surely is much better in winter than in summer.

On 30 December we climbed the *Berchtesgadener Rinne*, a short Grade III that had little snow so was more of a dry-tooling exercise. Here it does not matter, however, as there are no 'it's-not-in-condition' police as in Scotland.

Finally, on 14 February 2021, Arno and I took our skis plus climbing gear and skinned up to the Ruchenköpfe to try the *Westgrat*, a UIAA IV graded ridge. We found a ski depot and then walked up to the ridge which was in the sunshine and on the Western side all the snow has melted. This is typical for the lower hills of the Eastern Alps in winter, with hardly any snow on the south face in contrast to the snowy north face. The ridge involved scrambling to a polished chimney on the final head-wall that we climbed without crampons. After that came a bum-slide (some Scottish techniques work well in the Alps too) to the ski depot, and a ski descent on bumpy hard snow followed by some ski-carrying.

So whilst I miss the Highlands, the sea, the solitude and our Scottish friends, let me say that Munich, the Bavarian Alps and the Wilder Kaiser have a lot to offer Scottish mountaineers, from the 1800m-tall Watzmann Ostwand in Berchtesgaden to the very hard multi-pitch routes of the Alpine trilogy. Public transport is very good, so you can stay in Munich and then take the BOB (Bayerische Oberlandbahn) and a bus to reach your walk or climb.

Henning Wackerhage

A CHRISTMAS CARD FROM LADAKH

In recent years a number of SMC members have been involved in expeditions to the Indian Himalaya, supported by a local agent, Rimo Expeditions. As 2020 drew to a close I received an e-mail with Christmas and New Year greetings from Rimo, who are based in Ladakh. As well as the usual marketing material there was also some interesting local news:

> With no travel & tourism this year, new road building and repair of existing infrastructure happened at a faster pace. The new Rohtang Tunnel between Manali and Lahaul was inaugurated in October and has cut the Manali-Leh travel time by over three hours. The road across the Shingo La pass connecting Zanskar with Lahaul is also complete, along with the road from Linshet to Leh.

Having made this journey mostly on foot some 41 years ago, I looked out my slides and trip diary for some nostalgic reflection on what is clearly seen as progress. Back in the 1970s when I started taking an interest in the Indian Himalaya, Zanskar and Ladakh were considered remote and inaccessible. With their distinctive Tibetan Buddhist culture and climate, they form part of the predominantly Muslim state of Jammu & Kashmir, uncomfortably tucked away in a corner bordered by hostile neighbours Pakistan and China. By the middle of the decade the Indian military had begun to loosen their tight grip on frontier security and allow some access to tourists, so when I flew to Delhi in July 1979 with a return ticket valid for twelve months, my first objective was to see something of Ladakh. Nowadays there are scheduled flights all year round from Delhi to Leh, capital of Ladakh, and in summer regular buses run from Manali. Access back then was by military road from the idyllic tourist honeypot of Srinagar. When I arrived in the beautiful Vale of Kashmir, after a two-stage journey that started with an overnight sleeper train from Delhi to Jammu, followed by a tortuous bus journey through the verdant Himalayan foothills, I found there was a two-week waiting list for a seat on a bus making the two-day journey across the Zoji La (3529m) pass to Leh. Rather than hanging about, after a few pleasant days sightseeing I decided to walk across the mountains into the Suru valley and continue to Leh from there.

This journey took me eight days and turned into an adventure in itself. Leaving the road at the village of Pahalgam where thousands of Hindu pilgrims were gathering for the annual Amarnath Yatra, I branched off their route at Sheshnag lake and crossed the Gulol Gali (4406m) and Lonvilad Gali /Bhot Kol (4860m) passes. Leaving the green and wooded valleys of Kashmir behind and skirting the snowy Nun Kun massif I finally dropped into the arid Suru valley on the edge of Ladakh. At Panikar village I joined a very dusty dirt road and continued in the back of an open truck down to Kargil, and next day in the comfort of the cab of a bigger truck I finally reached Leh. Encouraged by this first experience of a serious solo trek I had learned a lot and now had the confidence to do more. Physically it had been very tough. Even with a minimum of food, fuel and equipment, my rucksack had felt very heavy, but now I was fit and acclimatised. Although I only had some very rudimentary maps, before the advent of the ubiquitous *Lonely Planet* guidebooks, I managed to find some basic route itineraries with plenty of place names. Whenever I met anyone on the trail, after a friendly greeting of *'salaam alaikum'* I would immediately announce where I was hoping to go and carefully watch the response. If you are on the wrong route, you soon find out.

Fellow travellers at the Lonvilad Gali, Kashmir.   Photo: Dave Broadhead.

Even with my few words of Hindi this proved a successful strategy, which I have used many times since. Each summer, semi-nomadic Gujar and Bakarwal shepherds move up from the plains to graze their large flocks of sheep and goats in these higher valleys, and I invariably found them to be friendly and hospitable in our many encounters.

My next plan was to trek down through Zanskar and into Lahaul and eventually reach Manali, a walk of some 170 miles. During my short stay in Leh I met an Austrian couple, Simon and Renate, who intended to follow the first part of my route, so we agreed to team up. First, we had to back-track by truck along the main highway to the striking monastery (gompa) at Lamayuru (3440m). Constructed from mud-plastered bricks, with a flat roof giving extra storage, most buildings in Ladakh looked functional and blended in well with their surroundings, with forts and monasteries usually dramatically situated on prominent hills or rocky outcrops, for obvious reasons. We stayed overnight in the gompa guesthouse and were relying on the lamas to arrange a pack animal for us. For a party of three it was sensible to share the cost and have our luggage carried along with a local to lead the way. Unfortunately, arrangements did not run smoothly and we left next morning with a poor donkey struggling under the weight of two rucksacks and a reluctant donkey-man weighed down with the third. A thirsty plod took us across the Prinkiti La (3810m) and down to the village of Wanla and another new experience, familiar from extensive reading about Tibet. My diary noted:

> Into a house to see about a horse. No horse but treated to chang & tsampa – a bit bewildered as to how to mix & eat it, but we got by.

The former is barley fermented into a refreshing and mildly alcoholic beverage, and the latter barley roasted and ground into a versatile and nutritious dietary staple that would help keep me going for the next few weeks.

Later that afternoon we struck gold in the person of Tzeran Rinzing who agreed to guide us to Padam with his pony, over nine days, at Rs60 or about £3.30 per day. (Over the course of my year travelling around the Indian sub-continent my total expenditure averaged about £3 per day.) Of indeterminate age, with a weather-beaten face beneath a woollen balaclava type cap that would not have looked out of place on a Scottish hill, he was permanently clad in a long, thick, homespun, wrap-around woollen coat, while we walked in T-shirts. Clearly well-known in the villages along our route, he was cheerful and unflappable in a crisis, and despite our limited common language he turned out to be a great travelling companion.

In the arid trans-Himalayan rain shadow, the scenery of this part of Ladakh is particularly dramatic, with the feeling of being surrounded by geology in action. Distant snow-capped peaks fed the occasional streams and rivers, while their lower slopes of sedimentary rocks were eroded into a fantastic variety of forms and shapes, leaving cliffs and screes coloured with a wide pallet of muted greys and browns. With little vegetation and only the occasional glimpse of wildlife, at best the path was a passable mule trail that sometimes almost disappeared. Walking south we were gradually climbing upstream, and occasionally the main valley narrowed into tight steep-sided gorges requiring some precarious river crossings before widening again into open plains. A few tall, thin poplar-like trees would mark the location of a small village surrounded by carefully cultivated green fields of peas and barley gradually ripening into gold. The greeting here was 'Jullay', and thanks to Tzeran we enjoyed plenty of local hospitality, usually involving chang, and soon experienced our first taste of butter tea.

An old wifie got out the wooden tea churn – knob of butter, pot of tea, a good squoosh, then back in the pot – just what I have always wanted to try – not as bad as I had thought – butter a bit rancid.

Often we were invited into the kitchen or courtyard of a house, but on one occasion we heard

…the sound of drumming and singing, went along to investigate – men & youths sitting around in a circle around a bucket of chang. Given an enamel mug between us, constantly topped up. Half a dozen or so guys started dancing – shuffle with a definite step, gentle arm waving, cocking wrists. After more chang they were very keen for us to give a show, so I executed a few *pas-de-basque*, awkward in boots, while R & S managed a sort of hopping waltz. Much applause – more chang.

Over the next nine days we crossed six more passes, including our highest point, the Singi La (5060m), before dropping to the village of Linshed, dramatically situated 'in a huge bowl full of green fields backed by steep cliffs'. This village was important enough to have its own gompa, and after pitching camp we paid a visit, noting –

… a fine *mani* wall above, some nice picture carvings, a few carpenters at work. Unusual request for a pencil rather than the familiar 'Give me one pen.' Outside main prayer hall sat down & given tea. Couple of lamas busy making candle-sized long thin offerings from *tsampa* dough – given an old one to eat. Nimble fingers very fast. Tea horn blown and up came more lamas – some into prayer hall, some sitting outside. Boots off, we went inside where the chanting, drumming and cymbal-clashing had begun. Tea served and drunk as the ritual went on for half an hour or so. An interesting experience but we all had sore bums and glad when it came to an end – could not face any more buttered tea or *tsampa*.

Our route eventually dropped down into the Zanskar valley, where the landscape became more open and we started to notice the wind sweeping across in the afternoons. Each day we woke early: *tsampa* porridge for breakfast, rucksacks packed and horse loaded, then on our way. Wearing their traditional clothing and busy with their fields and flocks most locals tended not to travel in summer, preferring winter when the rivers were frozen over and used as thoroughfares. We did meet a few fellow travellers on the trail, usually older men sporting distinctive headgear and leading a loaded horse or donkey or yak, and occasionally other westerners.

About mid-day Tzeran mentioned cha, picked up a few bits of brushwood & some dried dung, selected three suitable rocks and soon had a pot of tea on the go. Sack of *tsampa* produced and a small loaf of rather solid bread – fine if you soak it in your tea.

The dung fire was a revelation and I was delighted to be able finally to get rid of my leaky paraffin container. Hard to imagine now, but at that time plastic bottles with a good seal were very hard to come by. Relying on my faithful little primus stove, my original paraffin container did not survive the flight out and its replacement was soon punctured and had to be carefully carried. Fortunately, I was able to swap it for a little aluminium bowl, perfect for mixing *tsampa* with my tea and still used for keeping paperclips etc on my study table.

On our ninth and final day together, we arrived at Karsha, another large village with a distinctive *gompa* and more surprisingly a truck. This was about to head north-west to Ringdom Gompa, the route Simon and Renate planned to follow.

Crossing the Singi La, Ladakh. Photo: Dave Broadhead.

Tzeran was keen to start heading back home to Wanla so we quickly settled up with him and said our farewells, and I continued to Padam/Spadum, suddenly alone again. My destination for the day was not far away, on the other side of the Zanskar River, a considerable tributary of the Indus. Rather than make a long detour to the nearest bridge at Tungri, I made a rather alarming direct crossing of the torrent in a large inflatable dingy paddled furiously by two enterprising lamas wearing their traditional dark red robes. Camping overnight in Padam (3530m), the administrative centre of Zanskar, I was entertained by a group comprising

> the bank manager, police officer, radio operator and school headmaster. Kashmiris of course hating every minute of their exile in the wilderness.

The latter kindly prepared a very welcome dinner for me:

> …rice and cabbage. Ate three helpings then staggered off to tent, headtorch kaput, feeling bloated.

My solo walk continued south for the next six days, gradually climbing towards my final pass, the Shingo La. The trail initially followed the Tsarap Lingti river upstream with no route-finding problems, and I found myself meeting more French and German trekkers. Gradually I got the knack of making dung fires:

> Collected wood & dung – quite a search – started my fire with difficulty. A guy I had met during the day appeared, heading back. Not too impressed with my fire – threw away my three rocks + got three much bigger ones. That's the secret – boiled eggs (purchased earlier in the day) one of them bad & chicken soup.

At Kargyak (4000m), the last village before the pass, I fell foul of some local hospitality and suffered a sleepless night with terrible indigestion. Fortunately, I made a quick recovery and continued in high spirits next morning, planning a high camp before the pass. Although the landscape was more open and the scenery much starker, I noted:

The valley very beautiful – quite a bit of green, especially near the river. Sitting down for a rest, sense of peace and solitude – birds singing, river murmuring – few light brown squeaky marmots and saw a dusty brown fox.

I crossed the glaciated Shingo La (5100m) next morning, along with a group of Manali men leading 8 horses who had been delivering sacks of atta (wheat chapatti flour).

Rocks still covered in frost – very slippery. 09.15 top of pass – highest yet – fine view – four corries with short glaciers – snow-capped peaks to south.

Now it felt like downhill all the way, and my main interest had become the tasty goodies I was given by various trekking groups I met. Their local staff were always very kind. The following day I finally reached the police check-post at Darcha (3300m), fifteen days after leaving Lamayuru. Located beside a bridge over the Bhaga River at the end of the motorable dirt road leading up from Lahaul, a luxurious looking bus was parked waiting for the French group who had kindly fed me the night before. Fortunately, they did not take much persuading to allow me to join them on the four-day drive back to Delhi. After a night camped in the garden of the Tourist Rest House in the district capital Kyelang, we crossed the Rohtang Pass (4955m) to reach Manali.

Amazing drive. Lots of bends up to pass. On top, green meadow and houses. Hard to believe altitude. Other side lots of clouds & trees. Amazing descent. Five lammergeiers (more likely Griffon vultures) circling. So many trees.

With the inexorable spread of roads throughout the Himalaya, change has been inevitable. I was back in Lahaul a few years later and already Darcha had changed beyond recognition into a thriving if rather jerry-built village. As our friends at Rimo proudly point out:

Once the proposed Shingo La tunnel is ready, Ladakh will be connected year-round by road to Manali – a big boon to the locals who will now be able to get emergency medical care and fresh food supplies during the long and harsh winter months.

While I can only be pleased that the residents of Ladakh, Zanskar and Lahaul will now be able to share more of the benefits of modern life, I look back with a feeling of gratitude that I was able to briefly rub shoulders with these friendly and hospitable people while they were still living their traditional way of life which no longer exists.

Dave Broadhead

REVIEWS

First on the Rope: Roger Frison-Roche (reissued by Vertebrate Publishing, 2019, paperback, 256 pp, ISBN 978-1-911342-45-8, £8.99).

I'd long heard of this classic climbing novel, first published in French in 1942 as *Premier de Cordée* and translated into English in 1949 by Janet Adam Smith. But I hadn't laid my hands on a copy until Vertebrate Publishing recently reissued it. I must thank them for that, as *First on the Rope* is one of the finest pieces of mountain literature I have come across.

Frison-Roche is a vivid, precise, unpretentious writer, generally well-served by his translator – although the odd dated idiom ('Old fellow', 'You chaps', and so on) occasionally jars. Frison-Roche is focused on the world in front of his eyes and under his boots, and does not allow himself to float off into abstractions and spiritual wishful thinking in the way that, for example, his English contemporary Frank Smythe is sometimes guilty of – as was Wordsworth before him. (I am currently reading Smythe's *The Spirit of the Hills*, and, although there is much to relish, there are some horribly pious and intellectually rickety passages, for example: 'The love of hills … is a part of the spiritual development taking place in the world today, by which man is raising himself from material slime to a firm footing on the peaks of his faith.' Similarly Wordsworth, after giving a wonderful description of climbing over the Simplon Pass in bad weather in *The Prelude*, groundlessly asserts that the sights he sees are 'Characters of the great Apocalypse, / The types and symbols of Eternity, / Of first and last, and midst, and without end.') It is ironic that many Anglophone philosophers these days condemn modern French thinkers for their puffed-up waffle.

Frison-Roche, in contrast, is a master of the concrete. This is how he describes the arrival of an old guide and his apprentice at a mountain inn, as they return from Courmayeur to Chamonix over the top of the range (these were the days before either téléphérique or tunnel):

> They sat down at the common table, content to rest. The proprietress knew their habits and without waiting for an order set down before them two steaming bowls of soup, a great hunk of Gruyère, fresh from the mountains of Catogne, and half a round of bread. Placidly, the two sliced the bread and cheese into the soup …

If that is 'material slime', I'll have two bowlfuls please.

Roger Frison-Roche was born in Paris, of Savoyard parents, but as a young man moved to Chamonix, took a job in the tourist office, and began to train as a mountain guide. In 1930 he became the first member of the Compagnie des Guides de Chamonix (established in 1821) who was not a native of the valley. Chamonix, its guides and its surrounding mountains form the milieu in which *First on the Rope* is set, around 1925. Although the novel follows the lives of certain key characters, it is more concerned with the camaraderie among the guides, and their relation to the mountains, than the fate of any one individual. Frison-Roche clearly became accepted by the Chamoniards, as he is deeply in sympathy with them, while noting that it is very much a world of 'us and them'. However wealthy or successful a Chamoniard might become, whether as a hotelier or as a guide, they are, in Frison-Roch's depiction, an egalitarian lot, for whom there are only two kinds of person: a native, or a tourist. If you are a native, then, whatever you do, you're as good as the next man (or woman, although the male and female realms are largely separate in this novel). But if you're a tourist, well …

Frison-Roche's characters have no romantic delusions. The mountains are a means of making a living, and when they kill they have no beauty about them. They are not murderous, however. They are assigned no agency. That belongs alone to the men who climb them. And those men see the mountains in different lights, according to mood and circumstance. At one point the heights are 'white and mysterious', but when tragedy strikes on the Dru, the mountain becomes 'a sort of hump-backed monster with two horns, evil and absurd.' The only sound to be heard is 'the solemn voice of the torrent, the only living note in all that stony waste.' Then there is 'the rumble of a far-off avalanche or the sharper rattle of stones …' Later, the Chief Guide has to break the news of the tragedy to the wife of the dead man. He looks across the valley. 'The Dru was more dazzling than ever under its mantle of ermine. "God's mercy," muttered the Chief Guide. "Besides mountains like that, what poor little creatures we are!" But he did not shake his fist at them; it might have been a sacrilege.'

The guides know that the mountains are deadly, but indifferent. And yet they would choose no other vocation for themselves. When one old guide insists his son should enter the hotel business, it is much to the disappointment of the son and his friends. The only honourable path for them is following the craft of the mountain guide, a path of fellowship, ever-increasing skill, growing respect for the mountains and for each other. When this young man, destined for the hotel trade, sustains a head injury during a terrible epic, and thereafter suffers crippling vertigo, the greatest tragedy is that he fears he will never climb again, and takes to drink. But his friends rally round. And so he finds himself, in the company of a friend who has lost parts of his feet to frostbite, at the foot of the icy north face of the Aiguille Verte, forcing himself to face his demons …

This is not a novel of character, or of social dynamics, or of moral exploration, although there is the discovery that 'real courage' consists of 'victory over fear'. The drama here is man versus mountain, man versus himself, not man versus man. There are analogies with soldiers at war, taking responsibility for the lives of others: '…he had become the leader, the man who commands and fights, who has other lives dependent on him.' Except, in this arena, no one sets out to kill.

Frison-Roche shows us many aspects of life in the mountains: felling trees to build a new chalet; taking the cows up to the high pastures in spring; the way the meadows of dwarf rhododendrons, gentians and arnica give way to moss and lichen, and then to rock and ice. It is up there that a man can find triumph through suffering, eyes blinded by snow glare, hands burnt by frozen, hawser-laid hemp rope, as he cuts steps up unremitting sheets of ice with nothing to protect him from stonefall bar a beret squashed on his head.

Of course, none of the guides would make a fuss about any of this. It's all part of the craft, it's all in a day's work. *Ça fait mé pi pas pi!* as they say in those parts. The phrase isn't translatable, apparently, even into standard French. Frison-Roche offers this interpretation: 'Clearly, everything's not for the best, it could be a good deal better, but as you can't do anything about it, you must just put up with it. *Ça fait mé pi pas pi!* All the mountaineer's philosophy is contained in that little phrase, and its sound conveys its meaning well enough.'

So next time you find yourself retreating off some desperate winter route as darkness falls, and the abseil rope jams, and the wind picks up and blasts you with spindrift, just remember to turn to your partner and say: *'Ça fait mé pi pas pi!'*

Ian Crofton

Irish Peaks – A Celebration of Ireland's Highest Mountains: Editors Alan and Margaret Tees (Mountaineering Ireland and Zest, 2020, hardback, 256pp, ISBN 978-0-902940-22-2, €29.95).

This is a useful book for anyone interested in Irish hills. It is produced by Mountaineering Ireland, under the editorship of Margaret and Alan Tees, with multiple contributors. The style is large-format, something like a cross between our own *The Munros* book and Richard Gilbert's *Big Walks*. The book is dedicated to Joss Lynam, who was a pillar of Irish mountaineering for many years. The initial print proved more popular than expected and, at the time of writing (February 2021) was sold out; but hopefully a reprint will be available again soon and can be ordered from <www.irishpeaks.ie>.

The first 50 pages covering the 'Irish Mountain Environment' and a crucial section on access are followed by the hill-route sections describing 71 routes. There is also a useful reference guide to commonly used Irish place names. Various lists equivalent to the Scottish Munros like the 600m list and the Vandeleur-Lynam list are included for those with a ticking bent. The routes are broadly based around the 100 highest summits in Ireland. The country is broken into the four regions: Ulster, Connacht, Munster and Leinster. A modern, readily understandable format is used, with various photos of the mountain; a brief introduction box supported by a key box detailing relevant maps; where to start; parking; the nature of terrain; and a summary of the main route showing distance, height-gain and an idea of time required. In addition there is a detailed route-map usually taken from the Irish Ordnance Survey, before a more detailed text description of the route. Sometimes alternative routes are suggested. The text style varies, given the range of contributors, while the photos are all sharp and provide a good mix of inspiration and information.

The book gives a good impression of walking options in Ireland and is a welcome addition. Some notable elevated hills and walks are not included, either because of access issues or because of departure from specific criteria required for listing, just as with the Corbetts (unlike the looser Munros definition). Ireland has few points above 1000m; to exclude such as Beenkeeragh or Caher in Macgillycuddy's Reeks is an unfortunate omission from the book. However, access is not as free in Ireland as it is in Scotland, and in certain areas it can be very contentious, with no guarantee of the ability to start or finish from the most obvious place on the map. This explains some omissions, and the whole issue of access is dealt with sensitively in the book; it will be very helpful for those new to Ireland and less aware of access restrictions. Although there are introductory maps at the start of each region giving an overview of where the mountains are, it would have been helpful for the visitor unfamiliar with Ireland to have had slightly more detail to locate the particular mountain areas. These are minor observations, however.

There is plenty here for anyone interested in a visit to the Irish mountains, both the well-known ranges like the Twelve Bens, the Maumturks, the Mourne Mountains and Macgillycuddy's Reeks and many less well-known areas like Achill Island. Outside the peak holiday period and away from Wicklow many of these mountains will offer plenty of walking without the crowds now associated with many higher peaks in the UK.

Stan Pearson

Limits of the Known: David Roberts (Norton, 2019, paperback, 336pp, ISBN 978-0-393-35659-5, £11.99).

American writer David Roberts has over 25 books to his name. With a first degree in mathematics and a PhD in English literature he is an unusual man and for my money one of the finest contemporary mountaineering authors. Having done several tremendous pioneering routes in Alaska in the 1960s and 1970s he carved out a career as an 'adventure journalist,' scoping the globe with seekers of all kinds of unusual experience. In 2015 at the age of 74 he was struck down with stage-four throat cancer; somehow he pulled through sufficiently to write this fascinating study of adventure in its many guises, combined with a memoir of his own experiences, including his battles with the disease.

The prologue poses the questions he seeks to address: 'What is the future of adventure, if any, in a world we have mapped and trodden all the way to the most remote corners of the wilderness? Why do we do it? ... Why does it matter?'

The book starts with an account of polar exploration, focusing on Nansen's amazing effort to reach 'farthest north' in 1893–96. After more than a year in their icebound ship Nansen and Johansen dragged sledges to within a couple of hundred miles of the pole; on the retreat they had to abandon the sledges for self-made kayaks and were forced to overwinter in a howff of stones and moss that they built on a remote islet in Franz Josef Land. They had been alone for 15 months before they were fortuitously picked up. Roberts contrasts this self-sufficiency with modern 'adventuring.' Nowadays travel companies offer 'last degree' expeditions to the South Pole, with clients landed by plane at 89°, guided on a 69-mile ski to the Pole and then whisked off by helicopter. So-called 'unsupported' polar adventurers now have satellite phones, regular internet connection and EPIRB gadgets that send out automated distress calls with precise coordinates. While not comparing himself with Nansen, Roberts looks back wistfully at his early Alaskan expeditions when he and his friends were alone for 52 days with no contact with the outside world; he nurses 'the memory of the blissful state that disconnectedness imbued'.

The second chapter considers Shipton's 1937 'Blank on the Map' travels in the Karakoram. While exploring thousands of square miles of unknown glaciers Shipton, Tilman, Auden and Spender were completely cut off from civilisation. Having long venerated this ethos of exploration, and with his feeling for language enhancing his appreciation of Shipton's and Tilman's writings, Roberts summarises their expedition beautifully, interleaving it with his own experiences in the untouched Revelation Range in Alaska. A nice touch is the addition of a few quotations from Angtharkay's autobiography.

Roberts moves on from what we might consider conventional exploration, to describe many other kinds of adventure. A lover of the American south-west, he has spent much time exploring canyons and cliffs where the Anasazi left petroglyphs and stored grain in inaccessible alcoves on steep sandstone walls. Puzzled by how these ancient peoples scaled their cliffs, he is even more interested in their motives for doing so. His maxim, 'Fear is the mother of beauty', leads him to ruminate not just on the technical stratagems of past cliff climbers but their aesthetics. Travels to amazing sites in Mali, Peru and Mustang in Nepal lead to the conclusion that in these past cultures 'the severity of the climbing testifies to a commitment to needs both utilitarian and spiritual'.

There follow chapters on first descents of remote rivers, by raft and canoe, first contacts in New Guinea with indigenous peoples and attempts to find the deepest caves in the world, with rival teams from the USA, France and Russia exploring down to below 7000 feet. The daunting dangers of cave diving and the passions of its most dedicated practitioners are portrayed, their daring equivalent perhaps to the free soloing of Alex Honnold that has received so much greater publicity. Noting that unlike polar travel, sailing or mountaineering caving has not been 'adulterated by the machinery of communication – cell and sat phones, radio, internet', Roberts writes: 'If any exploratory endeavour nowadays truly confronts regions of the earth that are still undiscovered, it is caving. … If I could start life over as an explorer, in 2017 rather than 1960, I think I might become a caver rather than a climber.'

It is said that when Alexander the Great was a boy and was told that his father Philip of Macedon had defeated the Greeks, he wept that there were no more worlds to conquer. Roberts himself as a young man looking back at the 'golden age' of Shipton's blank on the map felt he was born too late, yet he had unparalleled scope for adventure in Alaska in the 1960s. He recalls that when he reached his sixties he wrote an essay expressing pity for the young climbers of the day, 'the born-too-late, the feeble imitators of the heroic alpinists of a more healthy age.' Ten years later he sounds a more balanced and optimistic note – perhaps every generation looks back to a golden age but there are still visionary climbers breaking new frontiers, in ranges of barely touched lesser peaks, on 'last great challenges' such as Latok I, or even indeed in bouldering where he tells us of a Finnish climber who made 4000 attempts on his 'project,' the world's first V17!

In his summation of adventure Roberts has little time for the cliché that through exposure to danger we gain self-knowledge, just as he scorns the banal conclusion of some travellers that people the world over are much the same. It is the distinctiveness and variety of cultures that interests him. And looking back on his long career, it seems to be the companionship of his closest comrades that he values the most. Seeking to understand the motive for adventure he quotes his favourite authors and concludes that we go off on our voyages because we can't help it – as Tilman said, 'it was my vocation.' While he doubts that the seafarers of ancient times were seeking adventure, I am not so sure. After all, on his own continent it took but a thousand years for humans to migrate from the Bering Strait to Tierra del Fuego. I find it hard to comprehend that there wasn't enough living space for them somewhere in between; surely we must postulate an innate exploratory motive in the most ancient of peoples.

This is a book of breadth and depth, a remarkable survey by a man of erudition and humanity who has not only run the gamut of adventure in its myriad forms, but has the self-knowledge, curiosity and cultural appreciation to situate our activities on the broadest stage. It was the well-deserved winner of the 2018 Boardman–Tasker prize.

Geoff Cohen

Nine Lives: Robert Mads Anderson (Vertebrate Publishing, 2020, paperback, 240pp, ISBN 978-1-83981-037-4, £11.96).

If you rolled your eyes at the thought of another Everest book, you aren't alone. The idea of wading through some combination of tedium and testosterone was as appealing as another lockdown, but in the spirit of 'that which doesn't kill you…' I opened the book. The frontispiece holds glowing testimonials from pop-culture mountaineers (Bonington, Venables) plus one from a journalist and one from a professional colleague in the advertising business (eh?).

But all was not lost. The writing is quickly much more engaging than expected, with chatty storytelling of highlights or lowlights of each venture rather than an attempt at a complete chronicle. The 'Nine Lives' of the title refer to Anderson's nine attempts to climb Everest by non-standard routes or means, between 1985 and 2003: in small groups or solo; pre-monsoon, post-monsoon or in winter; from Tibet or Nepal; via the Kangshung Face, various couloirs, North Ridge or South Col.

Obsession doesn't begin to describe what drives Anderson on; the awe at being 'on Everest, on the highest mountain', especially solo, is repeated even when describing yet another near-death experience. The descriptions are generally pretty good at evoking the joys and suffering of cold, fear and altitude, and are even better if you (dear reader) have some contextual framework of your own, such as Scottish winter climbing or greater-ranges expeditions. I really like the humanity of the sudden changes between delight and suffering. For example, from one paragraph to the next:

> The first person broke trail, the rest following, swapping the lead like bid racers in a peleton…like a 'Tour de Everest' all in a line, drafting through the snow and straight up the mountain. We didn't have ropes on; we were all climbers and climbers on Everest don't fall. Besides, it was more fun, more committing, more *Everest*.
>
> Inside my down suit I was soon sweating. A step, a moved ice-axe, another step, repeat….Being second-in-line one lived in hope the step would hold, was consolidated, wouldn't punch through into the step below. With the boots buried in the snow and the crampons sucking heat out of them, my toes were perpetually cold. Varying degrees of ice cubes were attached to the front of our feet. Too hot at the core, too cold at the toes, too windy on the face, breezes rustling the skin like raw sandpaper. Was there any joy? Should there be any joy on Everest? Is it even allowed?

It is an articulate accounting by a high-altitude climber who excelled at fast-and-light, and has got away with it, so far. There is little time wasted on his life between Everest engagements, so we rarely get below 5000m while reading. Occasionally there are vestiges of phrasing that indicate the editor had their work cut out for them when the manuscript arrived, and I commend the resulting readability.

What does this book add to the genre? Largely, an encapsulated, anecdotal history of Everest mountaineering that includes the entrance of the current era of commercially guided parties, complete with carpets and cinemas. The reader gets a chance to fail to achieve an expensive and life-consuming goal multiple times: Sisyphus as mountaineer. It is entertaining; the language transports you to the laden slopes or the crevasse edges, deprives you of oxygen, gives you frostbite, and opens the vast views below you. After all those trips, the bonus track (a tenth time on the mountain) is less interesting.

As a parochial bonus, SMC member Ruaridh Finlayson gets a namecheck as a guided team member on the last expedition described in the book.

Susan Jensen

Structured Chaos: Victor Saunders (Vertebrate Publishing, 2021, hardback, 180pp, ISBN 978-1-912560-66-0, £24.00).

As a preface to this review, I should declare that I haven't read Victor's other two mountaineering books but have been on two expeditions with him: to India in 1992 and to Tibet in 1998, although only on the latter did I actually climb with him.

Structured Chaos has many of the characteristics of an autobiography, in that it covers family background, childhood, education, early career, climbing career and has an epilogue that brings us bang up to date, including a reference the coronavirus pandemic. However, it is selective in its inclusions, in part, I guess, to avoid duplication of content from earlier books and in part to exclude more personal and family related matters.

Victor's prelude opens with: 'Mountains have given structure to my adult life. I suppose that they have also given me purpose, though I still can't guess what that purpose might be.' This statement says a lot and yet it leaves a lot unsaid.

There is very little in this book about Victor's motivation for what amounts to a climbing obsession and neither is there much indication as to how this has impacted upon other aspects of his life. His wife and son are only mentioned in passing and his career as an architect is fleetingly covered. Victor does focus upon the value of friendship but, perhaps inevitably, these friendships all seem to be in a climbing context. It is clear that good climbing partnerships are built upon a shared vision and high levels of trust.

The early non-climbing chapters are very enjoyable, with the return to his roots in Malaysia being particularly affecting and his time on board a cargo ship sailing from Tokyo to Montreal, via a circuitous route, spiced with keen observations and humour.

This book, inevitably, describes a number of mountaineering tragedies and includes some interesting analysis about what went wrong. Just as being in the right place at the right time with the right partner is normally a prerequisite for pleasure and 'success', so flipping any of these 'rights' to 'wrongs' greatly increases the risk of 'failure,' injury or fatality.

In the latter part of the book, Victor covers the effects of the ageing process on acuity and physical performance. He is, however, still driven to test himself in the high mountains.

Mountaineering, especially on high peaks, is a bizarre pursuit that sometimes feels like a search for something else. It often involves great discomfort, risk and uncertainty, and much of the pleasure seems to come in retrospect. Victor's book well illustrates this reality through a series of gruelling expeditions – perhaps perfectly encapsulated in his two-man attempt on the Diamir Face of Nanga Parbat in winter. So what drives him (or us) to do it is a question I wanted Victor to ask himself and to have a shot at answering!

Victor is a fine writer, with a vivid authenticity to the narrative of his mountaineering adventures. I really enjoyed much of *Structured Chaos* but was ultimately frustrated at being no further towards understanding what makes him tick. For me, he remains an enigmatic character, in search of a purpose.

Graham Little

The Black Cuillin – The Story of Skye's Mountains: Calum Smith (Rymour Books, 2020, paperback, 352pp, ISBN 978-0-9540704-3-4, £22).

With a slightly misleading title, this is a very readable 'new and exhaustive history of climbing' in the Cuillin of Skye. These unique hills will need no introduction to readers of this Journal, though details of their climbing history may be a little vague to many. Mike Lates's excellent Climbers Guide *Skye: The Cuillin* (2011, SMC) gives a good brief summary, though I suspect this is the least perused section, a last resort on one of those bad-weather days occasionally experienced in the Cuillin. History has been described as a tapestry of stories woven together and Calum Smith has been very effective in doing exactly that. His lists of 'References' and 'Sources' at the back of the book indicate extensive and thorough research, even unearthing some of my earliest scribblings in the EUMC Journal (though attributing the wrong date). In order to make this new history even more interesting and relevant, the author also brings in a wide range of human, social and historical issues as well as describing the gradual development of our sport. His light and sometimes quirky touch reminded me of Fergus Fleming and his popular alpine history *Killing Dragons: Conquest of the Alps.*

Ian Spring, a climbing pal of the author (and co-founder of Rymour Books) contributes a short introduction which sets the scene and whets our appetites, going back to 1587 and Johann Muller's forward-looking comments about the appreciation of mountains in general. Chapter 1, 'The Lake of Terror', starts even further back with one of the earliest references to the Cuillin by Donald Monro, 'High Dean of the Isles' in 1549, followed by cartographer Timothy Pont, whose ominous note in Joan Blaeu's *Atlas* of 1654 describes 'Extreme Wilderness; many Woolfs in this country; and black flies seen souking men's blood.' Right from the start, Smith makes an effort to personalise the many and varied characters whose stories he recounts, ranging from a brief mention of their occupation to some very illuminating mini-biographies but modestly not a word about himself. One of the many fascinating threads running through the early chapters concerns 'cartographic confusion' caused by inaccurate early maps, which continued into the twentieth century. While explaining the problems this caused the pioneers, the author offers no apology for not providing the reader with any maps for reference, so you will need to supply your own (as you normally would on the hill?). As the confused cartographers gave way to the Romantic artists and writers such as J.M.W. Turner and Walter Scott, the first tourists started appearing, and once again the author does a good job putting this relatively small geographical area into a wider context. Climbing started in 1836 with the first ascent of Sgùrr nan Gillean by James David Forbes, the young professor of natural philosophy at Edinburgh University and by Chapter 2, 'The Dearest of Islands', climbing is well under way. Stories and themes continue to unfold roughly chronologically over the following chapters, each with a cleverly chosen heading. Most will recognise the classic collaboration of famous climber and local guide explored in Chapter 3, 'Norman Collie and John Mackenzie,' but I was taken aback to learn that 'in the likes of the Sligachan Inn, despite being great friends, Mackenzie could not be accepted as a social equal; he was denied access to the smoking room and had to dine in the gillies' quarters.' Gradual development of the three main climbing bases at Sligachan, Glen Brittle and Coruisk forms another interesting theme, along with changing ways of recording and publicising climbing activity that began with hand-written entries in the Sligachan Climbers' Book. The heading of Chapter 5, 'Joyous Days Upon the Mountainside (1895–1905)', may puzzle anyone who has not attended an SMC Annual Dinner, until all is revealed when the author imagines the scene in the Sligachan smoking room where 'another popular pastime was singing, raising the rafters with rousing choruses like the SMC club song.' (No doubt the gillies and guides were disappointed to miss that!)

Another fascinating thread follows developments in climbing clothing, footwear and of course hardware. Before their introduction by the Pilkington brothers in 1880, on their first ascent of the Inaccessible Pinnacle, the use of ropes was actively discouraged on Skye. 'Alpenstocks, shoulders, plaids and wooden staffs were all acceptable means of upwards assistance, but not ropes.' To hold the reader's attention the author sometimes slips his tongue into his cheek. For example, referring to Sir Hugh Munro and 'his Tables' he informs us that 'surprisingly the number of Munros and Tops is not constant but fluctuates over the years due to surveying inaccuracies, isostatic rebound and the need to keep Munro-baggers on their toes.' Some readers may find this sort of comment irritating but I enjoyed a few chuckles, and a more general reader with little knowledge of Scottish mountaineering would also find this an interesting and informative read. There are of course plenty of descriptions of climbing, usually involving the crux of the route in question, but these are easy to skip (unlike most cruxes). The involvement of women climbers is well covered, and with his recent sad passing in mind I was amused by Nea Morin's comments from the summer of 1958: 'That evening coming down Eastern Gully we heard sounds of ironmongery high above us. This was Hamish MacInnes, "Piton Hamish" or "MacPiton" trying out a new artificial route on the Cioch Upper Buttress and he and his friends were making an unconscionable row, hurling blocks of rocks about, dropping pitons and karabiners.' Finally, Chapter 12, 'The Competitive Edge', brings history up to the present, describing the astonishing rise in modern rock-climbing standards and the impressive series of record-breaking Ridge traverses in both summer and winter. Earlier in the book the author reminded us of the toughness and resilience of our predecessors. some of the early New Year and Easter SMC Meets, climbing conditions were distinctly wintery though this was invariably understated in subsequent accounts. I suspect this was partly thanks to those 'big hobnailers' celebrated in the Club song, and to round off his history the author gives an excellent review of modern winter climbing in the Cuillin, from 'the start of front-pointing in the 1970s'.

Weighing in at 663g this is a substantial and well produced paperback. Apart from two sentences where some text has disappeared into the ether, I spotted very few typos. After it had languished for several weeks on my table, I could still not decide about the front cover, featuring a painting by Fred Schley. On the back, alongside Ben Humble's famous atmospheric (but unattributed) photo of Bill Murray on the tip of the Cioch above a sea of cloud, there are glowing and well-deserved endorsements from Jim Perrin and Dennis Gray. Humble's earlier history, *The Cuillin of Skye*, appeared way back in 1952 and along with two maps used the limited black and white images available at the time very effectively. Sadly, this new book similarly relies on some 47 monochrome images crowded into two sections with many of them disappointingly small and only two showing winter conditions. We will have to wait for Stuart Pedlar's much anticipated Skye history, for which I am sure Noel Williams will have organised some superb illustrations (and hopefully a map). A short 'Postscript' recounts some recent threats to the integrity of the Cuillin, emphasising how fragile the future of this fantastic range of mountains remains. The author concludes by reminding us: 'We all have a duty to promote mountains appropriately and responsibly and help protect fragile areas like the Cuillin.' In the words of the late Tom Weir, 'We all have to do our bit, no matter how small.'

Dave Broadhead

The Goatfell Murder: Calum Smith (Rymour Books, 2020, paperback, 227pp, ISBN 978-0-9540704-8-9, £11.99).

The well-known Scottish writer, Jack House, wrote a book published in 1984 with the title *Murder Not Proven*. The same year BBC Scotland put out a three-part series based on this book, with Part 2, *Death on the Mountain*, telling the story of the death of Edwin Rose, a 32-year-old builder's clerk from London. The synopsis of Part 2 reads: 'On a busy steamer sailing to Arran in July 1889, Edwin Rose met John Laurie for the first time. A few days later the two young men walked up Goatfell, the island's highest peak, but only one came down.' John Laurie was a 25-year-old pattern maker from Coatbridge.

In the 2001 *SMC Journal*, our very own Robin Campbell wrote a detailed, 12-page article on the same incident, 'The Arran Murder of 1889'. And now we have this book, also penned by an SMC member. Not having seen the BBC series is perhaps a good thing; it may well have been an entertaining half-hour but could influence my thoughts on the book.

Several initial comments on the book should be made. The front cover, for dramatic effect on a potential purchaser, is not of Goatfell, but instead is of the more impressive south face of Cir Mhòr, with dark lighting and rolling clouds above. The back cover uses what must be a prison photograph of Laurie, with views of his front, side and hands. It's quite good, considering its origin. Inside there are eight pages of photographs. Sadly, there are no maps, which would have added considerably to the overall picture of the scene. The book would also have been improved by making the recto headings provide the chapter names, rather than the author's name.

Smith has done an impressive amount of research for this book, but this is let down by the way in which it is used. Under the heading 'Sources' is a list of books and newspapers referred to, but there are no connected references given in the main text. There is an index, albeit a short, three-page one, while weirdly Smith lists the names, addresses and any given profession of all 100 witnesses listed in the court papers, many of whom were not even called during the trial.

One good feature of the book is the picture which Smith paints of the 'doon the watter' period that was expanding at this time. The last decade of the nineteenth century saw its climax, with hordes of visitors and families taking to train and boat for the summer delights of the Firth of Clyde. As a child, I too enjoyed my first taste of the seaside holiday in the same way.

Another useful plus is the insight given to the legal process which ensued, both in the trial and in the long incarceration of Laurie following the guilty verdict. As Smith remarks in the blurb in the back cover, Laurie holds the record as the longest-serving prisoner in a Scottish jail, though this may have been aided by his behaviour while a prisoner. Bad enough being in jail for so long, but serving it in the north-east coastal town of Peterhead, with outside work as a stone-breaker in a quarry would chasten most people. The length of his incarceration was in marked contrast to the actual trial, which was a rushed, two-day affair, taking in a Friday and Saturday.

Of course, the overall, burning question that will engage any reader of this story is whether or not Laurie deliberately killed Rose. And did so on a Scottish mountain, no less. To do this would of course be an absurdly simple thing to do, at least considering the mechanism. The simple slip so well known in hillwalking deaths is easily confected into a simple push. All one has to do is wait, or craftily manoeuvre a chosen victim into a suitable position, then ...

Pushing someone over a cliff has happened more recently in Scotland, though it may have been forgotten by some. On the night of Friday 13 October 1972, a Dutchman named Ernest Dumoulin enjoyed the view from the top of the 100ft-high Salisbury Crags in Edinburgh. He was with his new bride, 18-year-old Helga Konrad. At the trial he confessed to attempting to defraud insurance companies, and lodged a special defence of self-defence, stating that Helga had tried to push him. He was found guilty and served 16 years in Saughton Prison.

In 2006, a reporter from the German newspaper *Bild* interviewed Dumoulin in a small German town. While in prison, Dumoulin stated that he had 'found God'. He certainly studied theology for five years, becoming a Protestant minister, his work following release from jail. He described the murder to the reporter. He had placed his hand on her shoulder after they had stood up to leave the cliff edge, acted as though he had tripped, and pulled her so that she fell off the cliff. 'He had not wanted her to know he was a murderer.'

Though these fatalities were some 83 years apart, Laurie and Dumoulin appeared to be equally stupid. Laurie was a chronic liar, perpetually attempting to convert his vanity into some increase in stature through wearing brighter clothing. He had an eye for the ladies, and had several brief affairs, none of which led to marriage. Following the incident, in fact, Laurie was seen wearing some of the clothing owned by Rose.

It surely would have been the easiest thing to have pushed poor Rose down the gully, then claim that it had been an accident. The gully was indeed not the best route of descent, with easier, zigzagging routes on either flank. There were two steep and potentially dangerous sections. Neither of the two men was very experienced, however, and they certainly had not done much research into the route of the day.

Alternatively, perhaps it was indeed an accident, which Laurie then decided to take advantage of. To what advantage though? As Smith lays out, Rose came from a middle-class family, contrasting with Laurie, whose background was working class and who had a desire for upward mobility.

Because this book can be read, and probably will be read, as a 'who-dunnit' or rather 'did-he-do-it' piece of entertainment, I should forgo adding any more information. I will say that I enjoyed the read, learning much about the social life of this period as well as the fate that awaited anyone guilty of a serious crime. As a reader you may end up knowing just about as much of the story as the jury did. I leave it to you to make up your own mind whether or not Laurie was a murderer.

Ken Crocket

The Last Hillwalker: John D. Burns (Vertebrate Publishing, 2019, paperback, 320pp, ISBN 978-1-912560-45-5, £9.99).

Most mountaineering careers follow a recognisable trajectory, from the incompetence of youth to the decrepitude of age, with a few memories stored up along the way, whenever work and family commitments allow. In *The Last*

Hillwalker John Burns examines this journey in a manner that those who are approaching, or indeed have arrived at, its far end can readily identify with. Like most of us, Burns began by hillwalking – in his case a comically ill-equipped and shambolic stumble along the Pennine Way. Leaving the main path to try to gain the summit of The Cheviot, he and his companion are confronted with rain, mist and knee-deep liquid peat. This is too much, even for teenage enthusiasts. They are defeated and turn back – as I did, in similar circumstances.

Burns's progress takes him from hillwalking to rock climbing and to the Scottish mountains in winter, the beginning of a long enthusiasm. Again, there are many episodes from his apprenticeship that will evoke smiles, or shivers, of recognition in his readership – the trepidation of one's first abseil in a serious situation; climbing with unreliable companions or, indeed, being an unreliable companion oneself; struggling with unfamiliar and recalcitrant gear. Bill Murray defined the beginning of a climber's maturity as the time when the rope ceases to be an opponent and becomes an ally. Burns expresses more or less the same sentiment about crampons, as he learns how and when to put them on and, perhaps even more importantly, when not to take them off.

Many of the locations Burns visits will be familiar to readers of the *Journal*. He is sufficiently old-school to climb gullies, winter ascents of Green Gully and Glover's Chimney being vividly described. Munro-bagging is disdained as artificial and prescriptive but, in late middle age, Burns takes up bagging bothies instead. His celebration of bothy culture is rather romanticised, but evocative nevertheless. Brought up in Bebington on the Wirral, Burns's employment as a social worker enabled him to move to Inverness. While in the north, he diversified, participating in performance poetry, stand-up comedy and, notably, writing and performing a one-man play based on the life and mountaineering exploits of Aleister Crowley. It is perhaps his evident disenchantment with his day job that leads Burns to characterise Alfred Wainwright as having wandered the fells 'as an antidote to the tedium of his working days'. This is a projection for which there is no evidence, either in Wainwright's own writings or in Hunter Davies's definitive biography. A conscientious, meticulous and orderly man, Wainwright never complained about his work as Kendal's Borough Treasurer. Whatever compelled him to the hills, it was not his profession of accountancy.

Burns returns, several times, to his theme that the Scottish hills provide a 'timeless' wilderness experience, particularly in winter. But, sometimes even on the same page (p116 for instance), he also acknowledges that the Highland landscape is not at all pristine but is rather the product of centuries of human interaction and exploitation. This contradiction is never resolved. Perhaps it is an ambiguity or tension that many hill-goers feel, and few of us wish to examine too closely.

The Last Hillwalker is essentially an eloquent and light-hearted meditation on ageing. Returning to the hills after his second career as a performer, Burns finds it a struggle even to walk up to Ryvoan bothy. He is wearing his 'outdated plastic boots'. Don't do this. Leather footwear, like elderly climbers, may wear gradually into dilapidation, but plastic boots can fail catastrophically and without warning. The last time I was climbing steep ice, my trusted white Koflachs, more than 30 years old, suddenly split at the heel and fell off, taking my crampons with them. Fortunately, I was only a few feet of the ground, on indoor ice at Braehead. It did, however, occur to me to wonder what might have happened had I been elsewhere. Old age and ill-health may be difficult for a mountaineer to bear but, as Burns knows well, there are worse fates.

Are there really fewer young people going on the hills than there were 40 or even 20 years ago? The author seems to think so. The title of his book refers to a chance encounter with a lone walker in the remote bothy at Maol Buidhe. Burns ponders whether he may have met one of the last of a vanishing breed, those who enjoy visiting such places. He knows he is a member of a lucky generation, benefiting from student grants at one end of his professional life, and early retirement on a generous pension at the other. He worries that increased economic and social pressures are now depriving young people of the time and opportunity to develop a love of nature. Indoor climbing is a poor substitute for real adventure. But the last time I was at Aultguish, there were plenty of vigorous, youthful men and women in the bunkhouse. Of course, being even older than Burns, I stayed in the hotel.

Malcolm Nicolson

The Munros – SMC Hillwalkers' Guide, 4th edition: Rab Anderson and Tom Prentice (Scottish Mountaineering Press 2021, hardback, 384pp, ISBN 978-1-907233-38-8, £30).

A weighty, striking, and modern inspiration – the SMC has reached new heights! I challenge anyone to open the pages of this book and not be inspired to pull on their boots, shoulder their rucksack and head into the majesty of our Scottish mountains. Arguably, this is the most attractive, clear, and informative book ever published on the Munros.

The book is a larger format than previous SMC publications, which does ample justice to the vast array of excellent and truly inspiring photography. It is extremely fitting to see included, alongside Rab and Tom's evocative work, photos by Andy Nisbet and our very own modern day 'Hugh Munro.'

As you would expect from any great guidebook to the hills, there are clear route descriptions, including not just the 'main drag' but alternatives too. Woven into the text are additional snippets of background information to some key points of interest along the way, such as the RAF Canberra wreckage found on Càrn an t-Sagairt Mòr and the Sappers' Bothy near the summit of Ben Macdui.

The book recognises the changing nature of our game, with numerous references to the use of mountain bikes to aid access into the more remote hills, a trend that has very much become the norm since the last edition was published. And how refreshing to see that the hills are not just the domain of the bearded male! Numerous photos are enhanced by the inclusion of a diverse range of people enjoying the mountain landscape. However – and this is just a tiny wee criticism here – it would appear that there is not a single photo credited to a lady. And I'm pretty certain there are plenty of our female membership who would have had some cracking shots to grace the pages.

Clear topos give a good overview at the start of each section and the new format mapping gives a much clearer impression of the actual routes – a great development from the old editions which sported heavy black lines and little usable detail. Not that I'm suggesting these maps ever take the place of an OS or Harvey Map; no-one is going to be tempted to carry this weighty book on the hill. Its place is definitely on the coffee table, to be savoured with a dram in hand, planning and dreaming of future adventures in the hills.

Oh, and for those who just love that 'Munro Baggers' Tick List', you won't be disappointed. Tucked in the back of the book is your very own space to 'tick off' the date you climbed each mountain. What's not to like?

Heather Morning

The Unremembered Places: Patrick Baker (Birlinn, 2021, paperback, 224pp, ISBN 978-1-78027-724-0, £9.99).

Scottish landscape currently seems to be the subject of a plethora of books where, as Kathleen Jamie suggests, 'Lone enraptured males boldly go …. and quell our harsh and lovely land with lyrical words', the literary equivalent of selfies embellished with an overdose of introspection and metaphysical speculation.

The Unremembered Places breaks this mould. It describes Patrick Baker's refreshingly quirky explorations on foot or kayak, often with his children, of remote and obscure locations. He recounts the wild histories of secret caves, loch islands, burial grounds, clearance villages, hermits' cells, illicit stills, clootie wells and transhumance routes.

The forgotten places are described as he found them, warts and all, together with some historical detail to provide a socio-political context for their existence or abandonment. For example the caves in the Arrochar alps where 'a counterculture redefined the sport of mountaineering and resulted in a surge in standards and technique'; or the burial grounds of 'The Children of the Dead End' who built the Blackwater Dam in a period when legions of unemployed roamed the byways of the UK looking for work and accepted the brutal and dangerous conditions of dam construction.

Farther back in time he explores transhumance via neither roads nor tracks but sketchy routes which served the most remote Highland communities and communicated and maintained their culture across vast tracts of wild land. He describes the importance of cattle and droving to the Highland economy before the lairds sold out to the 'Cheviot and the Stag'. The unruly drovers themselves were absorbed into the British army for their hardiness and martial skills and, as General Wolfe himself said, it was 'No great mischief should they fall'. The abandoned stills, which for a period before the licensing of whisky production provided employment for smugglers, gave an economic boost to the Highlands that was even associated with a brief increase in the population!

The book's sub-title, *Exploring Scotland's Wild Histories*, counters notions of 'wilding' or 'rewilding' without people. The landscape was wild although much more densely populated, the people's light footprints being part of the ecology.

The author describes the subsequent 'tyranny of land ownership and trade which starved the living out of remote communities' in fertile straths. This is witnessed by the ruins of townships and field dykes across the Highlands still unavailable for settlement but more recently proving lucrative in terms of renewables and carbon credits.

He does not confine his research and exploration to the Highlands but also includes the industrial and military archaeology of the abandoned slate isles, Atlantic walls and sea fortresses which sometimes created a 'palpable sense of disturbance.'

In the last pages Baker does speculate on the metaphysics of the places, how some disturbed him or resonated with him. He poses the final question, 'Am I feeling the people of this place or the power they have always found in it?'

Raymond Simpson

The Hunt for Mount Everest: Craig Storti (John Murray, 2021, hardback, 301pp, ISBN 978-1-529-33153-0, £20.00).

The centenary of the first Everest expedition falls this year, and in a new book, Craig Storti in his own words 'stops where the others start' and gives an account of the developments that led to that expedition, leaving aside the subsequent attempts on the mountain culminating in the 1953 ascent.

Let me first declare a personal agenda. Despite a detailed biography of Alexander Mitchell Kellas appearing a decade ago,[1] this is the first subsequent book to give due credit in all areas to that Scottish mountaineer and SMC member, who sadly died on the 1921 expedition and was the mountain's first 'martyr'. That alone leads me to recommend the book to the reader, but it has other merits.

Storti attempts to put the Hunt for Everest in the political and historical conditions of the time, the Great Game between Russia and Britain for control of Central Asia. Mountaineering and exploration were about politics as much as adventure. He illuminatingly covers this conflict, lasting the century before 1914. Emphasising that the route to Everest was opened as much by politics – indeed by military intervention – as by exploration, Storti deals in detail with the invasion of Tibet in 1903–4 led by the great Victorian 'hero' Younghusband, a prime mover till his death in the attempt to 'conquer' Everest for imperial glory. This invasion was, the author correctly states, 'one of the most shameful episodes in British imperial History' (p11), which resulted in the machine-gun massacre of thousands of pathetically armed Tibetan soldiers and unarmed civilians, and forced the Tibetans to allow British traders and explorers into the country. And then to pay reparations for being invaded! Wrongly Storti comments that these troops 'for the most part refrained from looting' (p.166). Incorrect – they looted palaces and monasteries on a grand scale.[2]

A fault of omission rather than commission: Storti explains well the origin of mountaineering in the Golden Age of the Alps, but I think the reader would have benefited from an account of the attempts – and the characters – involved in early Himalayan mountaineering, and the lessons learned. Collie, Crowley, and Eckenstein are conspicuous by their absence, as are the early attempts on Nanga Parbat, Kangchenjunga and K2 that preceded any forays towards Everest.

Coming to the 1921 expedition itself, Storti (an American) delights in recounting the combination of amateurism and incompetence that characterised early British attempts at exploration and mountaineering, such as this one. The Mount Everest Committee was rent by squabbling between its Alpine Club and Royal Geographical Society components as to whether this was to be a reconnaissance or an exploration. The leader was Howard-Bury, a man of independent means who suggested his own participation and indicated that he would pay his own expenses and contribute to other costs. This counted: his mountaineering experience Storti politely describes as 'slight'. 'Non-existent' would be better. Then there was the doctor, Wollaston, who had 'no interest in medicine – in the one hospital job he accepted he lasted all of two days' (p.184). The catalogue goes on but reaches its climax in the choice of the mountaineering party, excellently described as follows:

...the only two climbers with Himalayan high altitude climbing experience were

[1] Ian R. Mitchell & George Rodway, *Prelude to Everest – Alexander Kellas, Himalayan Mountaineer* (Luath Press, 2011).

[2] Michael Carrington, 'Officers, Gentlemen and Thieves – the Looting of Monasteries during the 1903–4 Younghusband Mission to Tibet' in *Modern Asian Studies,* 1 (2003), 81–109.

by their own admission too old to climb higher than 24,000 feet...and the two climbers who were fit enough to climb that high had never climbed anything more than half the height of Everest.

Mallory was one of the fit duo, and for his climbing companion he said, 'I wanted to have Finch because we would not be strong enough without him' (p.186). George Finch did not 'fit in' with the chaps, he was slightly bohemian – he had lived in France b'god! – and worse, he was *Australian*. In a medical that may or may not have been rigged, Wollaston – our doctor– declared him unfit. (On the expedition itself Wollaston proved his worth when he failed to insist on Kellas returning to India when grievously ill. 'For this,' Mallory wrote, 'I am afraid some folk at home may be inclined to criticise him.' And only the day after Kellas's death did Wollaston insist that the equally ill Raeburn return, thus saving his life.)

Among the other climbers apart from Mallory there was Harold Raeburn, at 56 far too old for the rigours of the expedition. After being invalided out he never recovered his health. Storti is too kind in suggesting that Raeburn was chosen 'on the basis of his Himalayan experience'. This was slim – a reconnaissance around Kangchenjunga in 1905, when he had reached 20,000 feet. He was chosen more for his abilities on rock and ice, superbly demonstrated in the Alps and the Caucasus – though some years previously. And everyone hated the arrogant, grumpy, pig-headed Raeburn. Indeed, this was an expedition where everyone, as Storti shows, actively hated almost everybody else.

But they all loved Kellas! Storti calls him 'the most popular of all the British members of the 1921 Everest expedition'. And Mallory said of Kellas: 'Kellas I love already. He is beyond description Scotch and uncouth in his speech .... He is an absolutely devoted and disinterested person.' Storti gives a résumé of Kellas's achievements before coming on the 1921 expedition: the most experienced Himalayan mountaineer of his day in Sikkim, the Garhwal and elsewhere; a man who had been above 20,000 ft for longer, much longer, than anyone alive or dead, and had conquered more virgin Himalayan peaks than any rival, and who (unbeknown to himself, and to others for 100 years) held the world summit altitude record with his ascent of Pauhunri in 1911. Enough? No! He was also undoubtedly the person who knew more about the effects of altitude on the body from a scientific as well as a personal perspective than did any rival. He had published seminal texts on the subject, carried out acclimatisation experiments on Kamet in 1920, and was on the 1921 Everest expedition mainly to conduct further such oxygen-related work. Storti wonders how Alexander Mitchell Kellas can have remained so little unknown? Kind, modest, unassuming Aberdonians don't get far in this wicked world, I would suggest.

Read through Storti's well-written account of the comedy, nay tragedy, of errors in this expedition and wonder how it got so far. After all, it found the way to the foot of the mountain through much unmapped territory, *incognita* to white men, and Mallory with two others got to the North Col, the key to later attempts on Everest. Also reflect: was Mallory's death in 1924 the greatest blow to a successful ascent of Everest before 1953? Or instead was the lonesome death of Alexander Kellas on the bleak Tibetan plateau in 1921 the greatest setback? Not only did he not carry out his intended experiments on altitude and its effects, but neither did the British inter-war expeditions which followed that of 1921.

When Kellas died he was internationally known and respected, but he later fell into an obscurity from which he has only recently been lifted. Raeburn, interesting codicil, never fully recovered from 1921 and was later hospitalised, becoming convinced that he had killed Kellas! He did not; and now – thanks to Craig Storti's book, written for the general reader as much as the mountaineering specialist, and sure to have a wide circulation – Kellas lives.

Ian R. Mitchell

The Great Sea Cliffs of Scotland: Guy Robertson (Scottish Mountaineering Press, 2020, hardback, 256 pp, ISBN 978-1-907233-37-1, £35).

We present two reviews of this important new publication, from the perspectives of different generations.

What a stunner! It's an epic browse through the greatest sea cliffs and sea climbs and climbers of Scotland. The visual impact of the book is immediate, and for an armchair has-been it was a glory to browse and to read. Every page has its magnificent picture. It takes you through the Northern Isles out to Shetland then along the east coast of the Highlands, the Outer then Inner Hebrides – Lewis, Mingulay, Pabbay, St Kilda, then Skye – and finally loops back north up the western mainland coast to Cape Wrath. Blair Fyffe's overview of the Hebrides notes 'these great cliffs will give you an experience to be treasured forever'. Well, this book refreshed my own experiences in truly great colour as well as treating me to some very great adventures.

It's a book to savour at home, weighty and of quarto size, a delight to handle and almost suitable for casual display on your coffee table except that trivialises its impact. If the core of the book is its pictures, the writing too can be breathtaking to the lesser mortal: it's rare to find, as here, an entire page devoted to the abseil approach to a route, including the memorable phrase 'the theory at least was sound' –an improvement I suppose on 'It works in practice but will it work in theory?' And excavating cam placements into 'Weetabix-like' stale bread sounds like something definitely not to be trifled with. When it moves into territory familiar to the lesser human the book evokes with an immediacy the lived experience of these borderlands between rock and sea: the suck of the waves, the cry of the birds, the remote position – even the search for the 'obvious clump of thrift' marking the abseil. Largely it dwells in the world of the modern mid-extreme climber; there are but a handful of references below Extreme, even a Severe. The virtuoso displays of commitment fall mostly at the very top end, pace the first ascent of Am Buachaille. The whole of the book is however an irresistible display of the offerings of Scotland's sea-cliffs.

The photography makes the book. Full-page spreads in gorgeous evening light, action shots of many a first ascent, sensitive landscapes of spring flowers, foaming tides blocking our sea-stackers' retreat. Pictures of Pabbay's Great Arch gave a sense of scale when my search for the figures said to be climbing brought back memories of children's searches for the red-hatted boy: 'Where's Wally?' The figures now found, my gaze turned to other pictures of *Prophecy of Drowning*. A shame, I thought, that such a tremendous and popular route had not merited its own text.

The structure is familiar, and works to good effect. An initial overview, foreword, ecological notes, then a series of geographical blocks with introduction by separate authors, followed by individual cliff sections in the first person, again with various authors. The usual geological section is omitted in favour of putting geology into the text itself. Navigation is easy, helped by an overarching location map and page footers individually labelled to each section. The brief guidebook list, on the overview map, is limited to SMC guides except for Shetland. There is no index.

Each geographical block is headed by a poem to evoke the approach, the commitment, the history, the satisfaction at the end of the day. They are also a nice pointer to some of the less obvious route-name references. In my rather plain-spoken approach to the written word I can often tend to irritation at overblown bombast and exceptionalism or at a blow-by-blow account of upwards struggle. To be sure, the writing here is full of glory, beauty and upwards tension. But it passes my testy scrutiny with flying colours not only because it is so nicely larded with dry humour but because it evokes so well my own admittedly lesser experiences. Some individual sections lower themselves perhaps a bit from the best, but by and large the texts wonderfully paint what it means to be in these special worlds.

Jules Lines's foreword ruminates on 'why we need books like this one', and answers that such books give reflection on the explorers of previous years, insights into the minds of those in modern exploits, and inspiration and ambition to those still active and upcoming. It fulfils all those objectives. For those like me now somewhat restricted to glory in their memories, it also serves to bring those memories truly back to wonderful life. As Jason Currie writes, 'a catalyst that initiated a recursion of half forgotten memories, ... re-awakening a deep-seated desire to return'.

The work is a monument to its community of authors, climbers, photographers, and compiler. It is, I think, all the more remarkable for having been substantially produced in the dry times of the Covid-19 lockdowns. I have, of course, to find minor fault. Not, as I might so often, with the use of the passive tense to describe climbing adventures as that is very largely absent. But there is a peculiar choice of ferry from Kirkwall to Hoy that strains belief. And there is confusion whether *Atlantic Wall* on Am Buachaille is HVS or E1. Apart from two or three redundant instances of 'so' scattered through the book, that's it.

The authors make so bold as to claim on the frontispiece that the contents of the book are true in all but immaterial respects. Hats off to them!

Gordon Macnair

The Great Sea Cliffs of Scotland is a large-format coffee-table book exploring the coastline of Scotland through a climber's lens. The book's initial draw is its bold images. Inside you will find detailed gripping accounts and individual stories of first ascents, new crag discoveries and personal experiences, not only of the climbing but also of the equally daunting trip to reach these often very remote areas.

The Scottish sea-cliffs are adventurous by their very nature – bar a small, often idyllic minority – and so the book's focus is mainly on the most breath-taking cliffs throughout the country. The book is broken into selected regions covering The Northern Isles, Caithness, The Hebrides, The North-West Coast and The Aberdeenshire Coast. From this list of areas it is clear the book leans more towards the north of Scotland, and unsurprisingly, given the topography and sparser population, this is where the most adventure awaits.

Flicking through the book for the first time, the most striking elements are the large high-quality images, giving an impression of the variety of rock and climbing that the book covers (as well as some sweaty palms). Many of the images were taken specifically for the book, and have been collated from active climbers' collections, so almost all have not been published before. There is much to look over and get inspired by before being drawn into the accompanying history and audacious accounts.

Unlike a standard guidebook, the book doesn't thoroughly describe the area, instead the storytelling style of the book gives a unique personal insight into the cliffs and their centrepiece routes. The accounts vary between the storytellers, ranging from the discovery of some of the most adventurous and inspiring sea-cliffs in the UK, to more individual affairs, which build a good picture of the character and feeling of the cliffs.

There are so many amazing crags covered and stories told in this book, it's hard to select any individual one to cover, but being particularly interested in the adventure aspect of first ascents and having attempted a visit before, I was drawn to Kevin Howett's writing on the discovery of the Giant's Pipes on the south facing cliffs of Beàrnaraigh.

After one particular trip, Kevin describes convincing the boatman to take them round the island to look for any potential new crags. As they bobbed past the massive cliffs, many of which are broken and bird infested, they peered into a small geo and spied the wall that would later become the Giant's Pipes. This small glimpse was enough to whet the appetite for a return trip to look for any potential lines up the cliff.

Returning in 1997 it took them until the final day of the trip to commit to abseiling in, and once down they were shocked to find that their crack system, beautiful-looking from above, was in fact a terrifying offwidth. Faced with a decision between the offwidth, a hard arête or a good old swim (no chance!) they managed to wrestle their way up the offwidth. Above this was fantastic climbing, and on topping out they established the first route on the cliff, *Barra Head Games*, E3.

Having myself stood at the top, with a friend, looking down, I can say that Kevin does justice to the feelings of sheer dread when you are about to commit to the abseil, often the scariest bit of the day.

Of course this story is also accompanied by fantastic pictures of Kevin and Graham Little on the first ascent, courtesy of Grahame Nicoll, and also a double-page shot of the wall. These pictures, coupled with the text, are enough of a catalyst to inspire an entire trip. I think this section perfectly encapsulates all that is great about the book.

Some other highlights include Dave MacLeod's new routing excursion with Calum Muskett to Nebbifield, a crag on Foula, one of the most remote inhabited islands in Scotland. Dave describes a welcoming group of locals who helped them get set up with food and transport. The pictures accompanying this are all Dave's and Calum's, and one of the drone shots looking down the cliff, with them at the top, gives a good idea of scale. The pictures also show the rather unusual formations and texture of the rock, which they describe in very contrasting terms, depending on the pitch. This is everything from bullet-hard to 'Weetabix'. In the end they cleaned and climbed an impressive new E7 up a formidable section of the cliff. Their account of the route is excellent and will, I hope, inspire more to visit and add their own routes and tales to the cliff, which is still in its infancy for climbing.

Not all the crags covered are remote and massive and possess that big adventure aspect. Smaller and more local crags like Earnsheugh offer sea-cliff outings on a condensed scale that can't be found at an inland crag. I have not climbed on the

Aberdeen coastline much, although I've always been intrigued by it, as it is so local to a large city and so expansive; it's clearly a great resource for Aberdonian climbers to hone their craft. Grant Farquhar gives a brief introduction on the discovery of the crag by modern climbers, and the first routes that went up there, largely pioneered by Dougie Dinwoodie. Grant goes on to describe his forays at Earnsheugh, that included a number of failed attempts at a classic E6, Thugosaurus, before eventual victory and a first ascent stolen from under nose of Dinwoodie in a good-humoured way.

Of course this is merely a taster and there is too much to cover in a single review. *The Great Sea Cliffs of Scotland* is a fantastic book that is brimming with inspiration. It leaves you with a sense of wanting to explore, or alternatively, a return trip.

Martin McKenna

The Climbing Bible – Technical, Physical & Mental Training for Rock Climbing: Martin Morbraten and Stian Christophersen (Vertebrate, 2020, paperback, 352pp, ISBN 978-1-912560-70-7, £24).

The authors' aim was for this book to be a comprehensive, yet accessible and understandable book about training for rock climbing. It is organised into six chapters: the first three chapters cover the primary subjects of technique and physical and mental training for rock climbing. It then builds on these foundations with chapters on tactics, injury prevention and training plans. The book is intended to be inspirational as well as educational, and it achieves this by the liberal inclusion of scenic climbing photographs from around the world, together with inspirational quotations and stories from notable climbers.

The technique chapter is one of the more comprehensive that I have read, and it is well illustrated with sequential photos that demonstrate the various techniques, and how to experience their benefits whilst climbing. It also gives a pragmatic explanation of which techniques may be beneficial in which climbing situations. If you are at least an experienced intermediate climber, then you will likely not learn many new techniques from this chapter, but I think it is still a very worthwhile and thought-provoking summary to reflect on.

The physical training chapter is a summary of exercises and training régimes that may be used to improve grip strength, climbing endurance and contact strength, without becoming too heavy. This book does not include an in-depth discussion on how the proposed exercises relate to human physiology and different energy systems, such as can be found in Eric Horst's *Training for Climbing* book. I did, however, find this chapter to be a concise and pragmatic explanation of which exercises and régimes could be used to bring about which respective physical improvements. I think most of the proposed exercises are well known, but there is an interview with Eva Lopez on her training research, which I had not read about and appreciated before.

The first two chapters on technique and physical training are quite structured and occupy the first half of the book by volume. The following four chapters read more like a flowing smorgasbord of interesting tips, advice and anecdotes that may enhance the reader's enjoyable climbing progression. I found the section on the benefits of training periodisation to be interesting, and I can see how it could be adopted in place of a more ad hoc bouldering and climbing wall attendance, without becoming onerous. Some aspects of the section on visualisation were also new to me, although a very vivid imagination may be needed to implement some of the suggestions. I think most climbers would find helpful hints and ideas in these chapters that would have a positive impact on their enjoyment of climbing.

Despite being about training, the book recognises the importance of having an appropriate balance between specific training for climbing and just enjoying a good variety of climbing with friends. Overall, I found the tone of this book to be quite light-hearted and I enjoyed reading it.

Stuart McLeod

To Live: Fighting for Life on the Killer Mountain: Elisabeth Revol (Vertebrate, 2020, hardback, 160pp, ISBN 978-1-83981-017-6, £19.20)

To Live is an almost real-time first-person account of Elisabeth Revol's rescue from Nanga Parbat in winter, starting with her summit day and ending four days later with her dramatic rescue, which enthralled the media at the time. It is a relatively short book (154 pages, 28 of which are the appendix) and is an easy read, but in a good way as it is a gripping narrative. The book offers a different perspective from what was presented in the media and gives the reader the chance to learn her point of view.

As it was covered so widely in the media at the time, I am unlikely to be giving away the story here. In January 2018 Elisabeth and her climbing partner Tomek Mackiewicz made the second winter ascent of Nanga Parbat in pure Alpine style via a new route. On the summit, however, they realised Tomek could no longer see and he rapidly deteriorated from there. They managed to descend during the night to a crevasse at 7283m, where they bivvied and Elisabeth set in motion a rescue through her InReach (satellite communication device). Sad to say, Tomek quickly faded and Elisabeth was persuaded by friends to descend and leave him. She was rescued two days later by Denis Urubko and Adam Bielecki, members of the Polish K2 expedition who were dropped by helicopter several thousand metres below and climbed through the night to reach her. There is a very brief account from Bielecki of the rescue in the appendix.

The main content of the book is the story that was missed from the headlines: Elisabeth's descent from the summit to where she was rescued. In the news broadcasts you would think of her as a passive rescuee; but while there may be some truth in this for the final stage of her rescue, she first made it down from the summit to circa 6000m on an 8000m peak in the middle of winter. For the first 1000 or so metres of descent she was also guiding her blind and deteriorating friend down, and she survived three nights out with no food, water or shelter in winter. This is an incredible story of survival and of her determination to live; the best thing about this book is that it gets her story across.

In the book, Elisabeth shows wonderful insight into the climber's psyche: she describes how conflicted she is about her motivation for climbing and accepts that while many may think it is ultimately pointless, for a climber it is addictive. She accepts that she can never really explain to people what it is like to be on a very high peak: 'Up there, I feel at home; I live singular, magical experiences that are complex to describe and share on my return.' (p.79). There are also fleeting glimpses into the difficulties she has had since returning from Nanga Parbat, the survivor's guilt she has felt, and the criticism she has faced in the media.

The strength of this book lies in hearing Elisabeth's story directly from her, but it would perhaps benefit from additional voices telling other aspects of the story.

There is space here to have a journalist write about the events, in particular how the rescue was played out live through social media and through 24-hour rolling news. As the book is solely from Elisabeth's point of view it does not cover how one of the most remarkable rescues in Himalayan history was organised nor how it unfolded and so it feels one-sided. Perhaps that was outwith the scope of the book, but she is critical of how long the rescue took to organise and that a helicopter could not come higher to rescue Tomek. So perhaps an explanation of why it took so long and why a helicopter couldn't rescue them at 7200m would help to bring balance. It is not possible for a helicopter to get to so high an altitude, and the organisation of the rescue party was delayed in part because Elisabeth and Tomek had not paid a rescue bond to cover rescue by helicopter, and so this money had to be fund-raised. There is no permanent mountain rescue in Pakistan as there is, for example, in Chamonix, and this greatly complicates the logistics of finding people acclimatised enough to carry out the rescue and getting them to the mountain. By leaving this information out, Elisabeth also plays down the heroic efforts of those who did rescue her. In the first half of the book she seems to recognise and emphasise that climbing an 8000m peak in winter, in alpine style, and in a team of two means you may as well be on the moon in terms of rescue, but this seems to be forgotten in the second half of the book where her focus is on her criticisms of the rescue efforts.

The book feels unfinished or incomplete in some respects: there seems to be an assumption that the reader already knows the story, and perhaps it would have been better written by an observer rather than the protagonist, but then the harsh reality of her survival might be missed. Elisabeth hints at other things, such as her survivor's guilt and a feud between Tomek and Simone Moro, but never fully explores or explains them. Elisabeth's incredible survival and rescue is a story worth telling and this insight into her part of that story is well-written and fascinating. However, it only seems to cover part of the whole narrative of the events and has perhaps been written as a response to the coverage by the media. To Live is well worth a read for those who followed the media coverage of the rescue, as it provides a further dimension to the story and gives a good insight into the savage reality of high-altitude winter climbing.

Timothy Elson

WINTER 8000: Bernadette McDonald (Vertebrate, 2020, hardback, 272 pp, ISBN 978-1-912560-38-7, £19.20).

Once again Bernadette McDonald has produced in fine detail and in her unique writing style a well-researched chronicle of the first winter ascents of the world's fourteen 8000m peaks. This is an outstanding read and one cannot help but be drawn into the detailed and often very personal accounts of outstanding athleticism, hardship and determination from some of the most outstanding mountaineers in the world. It would of course be preferable (certainly to me) if all these amazing climbers wrote their own stories and made them available to us in the English language, but unfortunately this is not the case. In one fine book, however, Bernadette delivers a splendid account of all their ascents for us to enjoy. It is logically laid out and easy to read. *Winter 8000* is produced by Vertebrate Publishing, who have delivered an excellent hardback, with ample photographs and a comprehensive index.

Most members of the SMC know too well the hardship and pain encountered climbing in winter, and it is said around the world, somewhat tongue-in-cheek, that climbing in the Himalaya is good preparation for Scottish winter. But we all know that the hardship, the bitter cold and desperate winds in the high Himalayas during the winter season are almost as bad as visiting the non-existent WC in the old CIC Hut. Within the wonderfully descriptive pages there is much made of suffering and the art of suffering. We know that climbing is voluntary, however, and while I understand why climbers talk up the hellish conditions of climbing in the Himalayan winter, it's the choice of the climbers to try such peaks and I cannot help but feel that this art of suffering is perhaps overstated just a bit in the story line. Nevertheless, I stand in awe at the amazing ascents and determination of all the sherpas, climbers and other support people involved. The 'Alpine-style' ascents of these peaks in winter are truly remarkable and a joy to read about.

This is an outstanding piece of work, timely done, and the detailed interviews and conversations with the participants are incredibly interesting. I highly recommend this book to the Club's readers.

Sandy Allan

The Way of the Cuillin: Roger Hubank (Rymour Books, paperback, 210pp, ISBN 978-0-954070-49-6, £10.99).

This novel will delight and surprise. Set in 1938, *The Way of the Cuillin* opens with Stephen Marlowe, retired Professor of Greek and family patriarch, boarding a six-seater for his first ever flight. Marlowe, a reserved and thoughtful character who has been deeply affected by his painful war experiences, reflects on past memories and early pre-war trips to Skye.

The Marlowe family gather in Glen Brittle Lodge to celebrate grandfather Stephen's first ascent of *Marlowe's Variation*, a route that he and his brother-in-law put up in the years before the First World War. The plan is for three generations of the family to repeat the route during the holiday.

The little plane lands on the meadow near Glen Brittle House. The rest of the family and various friends and hangers-on are arriving in stages by boat or car. The reader is introduced to a colourful array of characters and helpfully provided with a much-needed list for reference. Stephen and his wife Millie have children and grandchildren of various ages, ranging from grandson Richard who has returned badly traumatised from fighting in the Spanish Civil War to the young twins who want to explore, have imaginary adventures and build dams in the burn.

Hubank sets the scene with a short history of the MacAskill family, who farmed in the Glen for generations as tacksmen of MacLeod of Dunvegan. They lived in a house then known as Rubh' an Dùnain. A shooting lodge was later built behind the house, and after the last MacAskill died the tack was handed on to an outsider who then rented out the Lodge to visitors. Hubank tells how Professor Collie used to rent the Lodge season after season and it became 'a home from home for mountaineers … for Collie was a generous host and held open house for his friends.' Marlowe remembers sleeping on the floor of the smoking room on one of those occasions. In the novel, some real-life local characters appear as themselves but the MacRath family who run the Lodge and host the family are fictional.

Hubank's feel for descriptive prose, which he intertwines skilfully with narrative, creates atmosphere and builds tension. The Cuillin provide a dramatic backdrop, with the tranquillity of Glen Brittle offering contrast and light relief.

This large family, freed from the strains of pre-war London and wonderfully looked after by the MacRaths, spend days enjoying walks, climbs and boat trips and exploring other parts of the Ridge and surrounding coastline. In the evenings after dinner, they huddle around a wireless set to listen to the news of Hitler's latest advances and Chamberlain's attempts to prevent war. On the first night heated political discussion over dinner threatens to erupt into a full-scale row. Marlowe attempts to defuse the tension by asking if anyone has read about Strutt's recent address to the Alpine Club on the latest developments on the Eiger Nordwand. Hubank writes: 'It was a clumsy manoeuvre but one in which his son was happy to join forces. "Yes, I did," replied Henry, setting a foot firmly on the safer shores of mountaineering.' Despite Stephen's 'clumsy manoeuvre', the discussion still veers towards the fascistic tendencies in German alpinism, the Spanish Civil War and Guernica, and it is not long before Richard leaves in disgust at a comment from his aunt. As the holiday unfolds, the sense of foreboding mounts, war seems inevitable and Stephen's son Leo, an MP, departs urgently for Parliament in Westminster. In an atmosphere that becomes increasingly threatening, dark family secrets begin to emerge.

Through his eloquent prose and compelling narrative, Hubank interlaces descriptions of stunning landscape and mountaineering exploits with historical perspective, and political uncertainties with personal struggles and family life. This is really a story of a family struggling to hold itself together while deep divisions threaten to break it apart – in many ways a family at war. Older family members are firmly rooted in the English right-wing upper-class establishment, and others, younger and passionately idealistic, have moved far away from that comfortable complacent world either into bohemian Fitzrovia or in Richard's case to fight with his communist comrades in Spain. We see them all through Stephen's eyes as they face the very real prospect of the coming catastrophe in Europe.

Initially the *Marlowe's Variation* project borders on feeling a trifle contrived – a writer's device, a mere hook to bring the extended family together – but Hubank keeps the plot moving and avoids this potential pitfall becoming much of a problem. In the end it is a vehicle for connecting the past to the present time. Stephen reflects on his own experiences in the Great War and this resonates with Richard's experiences in war-torn Spain. The enthusiasm of the younger generation to climb famous routes such as *Crack of Doom* reawakens Stephen's memories of his younger self. However, the veneer of a happy holiday is gradually stripped back to reveal deep struggles and dark tensions within the apparently comfortable upper-middle-class English family. Political turmoil and instability echo the personal experiences of three generations which are brought to life in the present.

Hubank's beautifully gripping prose and constant reference to the setting with description of landscape and local characters, hold our attention as the book moves to its conclusion.

There are cameo appearances from W.H. Murray and Professor Collie as the book evokes a previous long-lost era in mountaineering. There is fascinating historical detail on the Spanish Civil War and the twists and turns of the dying stages of Neville Chamberlain's government as he increasingly desperately tries to avert war with Germany.

Hubank makes demands on our attention initially to get to know the rather confusing array of characters, but the narrative and descriptive prose soon bring them to life in a more memorable way. This is definitely worth a read.

Jane Naismith

Lake District Climbs – A guidebook to traditional climbing in the English Lake District: Mark Glaister (Rockfax, 2019, paperback, 490pp, ISBN 978-1-873341-53-7, £34.95).

How does the Rockfax format work with a guide to trad climbs? Surprisingly well. The guide is extremely usable, with all the stuff you'd expect from Rockfax: little symbols telling you whether to expect to be pumped or scared or technically challenged, etc; when the crag gets the sun; technical notes; graded list; logistics; and so on. I was particularly impressed that it still manages to adhere to the standard Rockfax layout of route descriptions being on the same page as the relevant topo, which (given the extra detail supplied for trad climbs where there isn't a line of bolts to follow) is pretty remarkable. Flicking through and comparing random descriptions with FRCC and Wired guides, in many cases the Rockfax guide actually has significantly more detail. I confess that in places I feel there may be too much, remembering my own joy (and relief) at finding for myself the crucial little undercut on a Borrowdale classic, but that's just a personal gripe.

With almost identical dimensions to its most obvious competitor, the Wired guide, it's not for stuffing in your pocket on multi-pitch routes, though obvious options include taking a photo on your phone, or, as in the case of a friend, cutting the page out of the guide that you claim only belatedly to realise is actually your mate's.

Given lockdown I didn't expect to get to try it for real, but stretching the rules just a little, my partner in crime and I crossed the border on a beautiful midweek April day and headed for Quayfoot Buttress to test our eyesight.

It has to be said that, as a test of a guidebook, Quayfoot Buttress is not a particularly challenging venue, but it has some routes that we hadn't done (or else had forgotten – I can't always be sure these days), and the action photo of Mandrake looked appealing, as did its billing as a 'Top 50' route. (The guide notes that 'there are more than 50', an approach to Lakes rock of which your reviewer thoroughly approves.) We also took along the Wired and the comprehensive FRCC guides for comparison and can happily confirm that all three got us safely through the three minutes from the car park to the foot of an otherwise deserted crag. Incident-free ascents of *Aberration* and *Mandrake* (plus another route from the comprehensive guide, The Mound, the exclusion of which from the selective guides seemed very fair) would also appear to confirm that the topo and descriptions are fit for purpose, though we did *Mandrake* in two pitches and that did feel more logical. Certainly in most cases you would seem unlikely to get lost. I couldn't check exhaustively, but did find one error, with *Little Nose* and *The One That Got Away* on Upper Heron being mislabelled and the description of the latter referring to the wrong routes. There will be others, as there always are, but that's all I spotted.

So in practical terms a very usable and informative guide. But that's only part of the story. I think the photographs, both of crags and action shots, are exceptional and are what really set the guide apart. A guide that will surely enthuse any trad climber and cause them to be overtaken by a compelling urge to visit the Lakes, including places they have previously never even considered, is surely a worthwhile addition to an area that is already well-served by top-quality climbers' guides.

Bob Duncan

Above the Clouds: Kilian Jornet (Harper Collins 2020, paperback, 223pp; ISBN 978-0-00-8411212-8, £14.99).

Kilian Jornet is the pre-eminent mountain runner of our time. Now in his early 30s, he is a full-time professional athlete who has been at the top of his sport for over 15 years. A Spaniard, he is also a hugely talented mountaineer and international ski-mountaineer. His particular speciality is fast technical movement over all types of ground. His achievements are extraordinary; the modern era of professionalism requires these to be measured in records achieved on the mountains, usually in the form of 'fastest known times'. The internet can supply the details, and there are several documentaries available of Kilian Jornet's feats available as films. This is his third book.

Above the Clouds headlines on his remarkable feat of climbing Mount Everest without oxygen twice in the space of one week in May 2017. It also offers us tales from a clearly amazing catalogue of stories, including a rapid ascent of the north face of the Eiger with Ueli Steck, an ascent of the Colton–McIntyre route on the Grandes Jorasses with French guide Simon Barasoain; and a solo ascent of the north face of the Matterhorn; as well as anecdotes from many of his extraordinary mountain-running exploits both in races and on his own initiative. My mind remains blown by his effort in ascending – and descending – the Matterhorn by the Italian Ridge from Breuil to Cervinia in just 2 hours 52 minutes. Woven into this are musings on his motivations; some insights into what is clearly a complex, highly perceptive but introverted personality; comments on the world of professionalism and sponsorship which he inhabits somewhat uneasily; and descriptions of the lifestyle and training régime that are required to perform at the level he does.

The material is undoubtedly fascinating; but so beyond the average person are Kilian's feats that he leaves too big a gap between himself and his audience for the reader to relate to his story without much more explanation of how this is at all possible. We need to hear more about his motivations and feelings, about how he has evolved to be quite as fit and strong as he is, about his personal life, and about the impact of his pursuit of his goals on his relationships. The book is quite an easy read, and that means it is light on the detail not of his feats but on how they are achieved. We need to see that there is suffering as well as outcome, and we need to feel that pain if we are to understand.

Kilian Jornet has achieved enough to fill several lifetimes and many volumes with his endeavours, but he needed to do his mountains greater service in Above the Clouds by better informing us, whether with more comprehensive descriptions or the use of diagrams and photographs. The former are in short supply, however, and the latter are absent. The chapters are unbalanced, some giving quite full treatments of their subjects, others reading like a series of unrelated blog-posts and lacking in context. And the prose style is on a musing wavelength – if you are with it, you will enjoy the book; if you're not, you may feel frustrated to find that this fascinating individual has eluded you.

Alec Keith

The Munros in Winter: Martin Moran (2nd edition, Sandstone Press, 2020, paperback, 256pp, ISBN 978-1-913207-38-0, £11.99).

As many will know Martin Moran lost his life in the Himalayas in 2019. His book *The Munros in Winter*, first published in 1986, has now been reprinted in handy paperback format with a foreword by Martin's widow, Joy. The book recounts a continuous round of the Munros in 83 days in 1985, the first ever achieved in winter.

Continuous rounds are now fairly common in summer but to do them in winter conditions is an altogether different proposition. As recounted on pages 95–8 of this Journal, Kevin Woods completed a round in 97 days, just before lockdown in 2020; it is possible he may write a book in the future. Mike Cawthorne did a winter traverse of the 1000m Munros documented in his book *Hell of a Journey*. Steve Perry (SMC), who died in a climbing accident in 2019, completed a remarkable winter round in 1995; but because his completion was done entirely on foot his round extended into the Spring period. See <www.tgomagazine.co.uk/news/one-man-one-winter-284-munros/>. (Retrieved 9 September 2021.)

Martin's book is, however, the first and only fully documented account of a winter round. Although it is very much a personal account and not a guidebook in the true sense, anybody not familiar with the Scottish hills in winter would find it a very useful reference, as each chapter is broken down into the various Munro geographical locations. Martin and Joy used a campervan between locations, but even then some remarkable long days on the hill had to be undertaken in all weathers. The appendices give a brief account of notable rounds and record attempts. Any continuous winter round is likely to be determined by weather conditions.

Martin went on to do a traverse of the 4000m Alpine peaks in less than perfect conditions, a story that is told in *Alps 4000*, published in 2012. That book together with *The Munros in Winter* and his many guidebook contributions will remain a fitting tribute to Martin.

Kenny Robb

CORRECTIONS & CLARIFICATIONS

'A man should never be ashamed to own that he has been in the wrong, which is but saying in other words that he is wiser today than he was yesterday.'
– Alexander Pope, *Miscellanies* (1727) Vol. 2.

The following errors occurred in the 2020 *SMC Journal*:
- p. 142 'a run on loo roles' should be 'a run on loo rolls';
- p. 151 'Cladh A Bearnaig' should be 'Cladh a' Bhearnaig';
- p. 154 'Am Burgh' should be 'Am Burg';
- p. 155 'Innaccessible Pinnacle' should be 'Inaccessible Pinnacle';
- p. 171 'Sròn na Breun Leitir' should be 'Sròn na Breun-Leitire';
- p. 182 'Coire Dondhail' should be 'Coire Dhondail';
- p. 208 Photograph should be entitled 'Stob Coire nan Lochan';
- p. 253 Bert Barnett's Donalds were finished in 2012, 2013 & 2017;
- p. 298 131st AGM & Dinner were on 30 November 2019 not 2018;
- p. 350 Hon. Reporter on Accounts should be John A.P. Hutchinson.

As always, these errors have been corrected in the archived version of the *Journal*.

ORDERING THE SMC JOURNAL

Members should automatically receive a copy of the *Journal* when it is published. Members wishing to order extra copies or non-members wishing to place a regular order should contact the Distribution Manager, Dave Broadhead, by **e-mail** <journal.distribution@smc.org.uk>.

SMC JOURNAL BACK NUMBERS

Back numbers of the *Journal* may be obtained from Clifford Smith:
16 House o' Hill Gardens, Edinburgh, EH4 2AR.
e-mail: <journal.archive@smc.org.uk>
tel: 0131-332 3414   mob: 07748 703515

The following years are available: post and packaging are extra.

	Year			Year
£5.00	1972		**£12.95**	2000
	1977			2001
	1978			2002
	1979			2003
	1980			2004
	1983			
			£13.95	2005
£5.50	1985			2006
				2007
£5.70	1986			2008
	1987			
	1989		**£14.95**	2009
	1990			2010
	1991			2011
	1992			2012
				2013
£6.95	1993			2014
	1994			
	1995		**£16.95**	2016
				2017
£8.95	1996			2018
	1997			2019
	1998			2020
£11.95	1999			

SCOTTISH MOUNTAINEERING CLUB HUTS

Bookings can be made to stay at any of the five Club Huts by contacting the relevant Custodian.

CHARLES INGLIS CLARK MEMORIAL HUT, BEN NEVIS

Location: (NN 167 722) On the north side of Ben Nevis by the Allt a' Mhuilinn. This hut was erected by Dr and Mrs Inglis Clark in memory of their son Charles who was killed in action in the 1914–18 War.
Custodian: Robin Clothier.
e-mail <cic@smc.org.uk>

LAGANGARBH HUT, GLEN COE

Location: (NN 221 559) North of Buachaille Etive Mòr near the River Coupall.
Custodian: Bernard Swan, 16 Knowes View, Faifley, Clydebank, G81 5AT.
e-mail <lagangarbh@smc.org.uk>.

LING HUT, GLEN TORRIDON

Location: (NG 958 562) On the south side of Glen Torridon.
Custodian: Patrick Ingram, 119 Overton Avenue, Inverness, IV3 8RR.
e-mail <ling@smc.org.uk>.

NAISMITH HUT, ELPHIN

Location: (NC 216 118) In the community of Elphin on the east side of the A835.
Custodian: John T Orr, 8 Fleurs Place, Elgin, Morayshire, IV30 1ST.
e-mail <naismith@smc.org.uk>.

RAEBURN HUT, LAGGAN

Location: (NN 636 909) On the north side of the A889 between Dalwhinnie and Laggan.
Custodian: Gordon Lacey, 10 Alder Avenue, Lenzie, G66 4JG.
e-mail <raeburn@smc.org.uk>.

SCOTTISH MOUNTAINEERING CLUB GUIDEBOOKS
Published by SCOTTISH MOUNTAINEERING PRESS

HILLWALKERS' GUIDES
The Munros
The Corbetts and other Scottish hills
The Grahams & The Donalds
The Cairngorms
Central Highlands
Islands of Scotland including Skye
North-West Highlands
Southern Highlands

SCRAMBLERS' GUIDES
Highland Scrambles North
Highland Scrambles South
Skye Scrambles

CLIMBERS' GUIDES
Scottish Rock Climbs
Scottish Winter Climbs
Scottish Sports Climbs
Inner Hebrides & Arran
Ben Nevis
The Cairngorms
Glen Coe
Highland Outcrops South
Lowland Outcrops
North-East Outcrops
Northern Highlands North
Northern Highlands Central
Northern Highlands South
Skye The Cuillin
Skye Sea-Cliffs & Outcrops
The Outer Hebrides

OTHER PUBLICATIONS
Ben Nevis – Britain's Highest Mountain
The Cairngorms – 100 Years of Mountaineering
A Chance in a Million? – Scottish Avalanches
Hostile Habitats
The Munroist's Companion
Scottish Hill Names – Their origin and meaning
Mountaineering in Scotland: the Early Years
Mountaineering in Scotland: Years of Change

APPS
SMC guides to the Northern Corries and Polney Crag are available on the Rockfax App <https://www.rockfax.com/publications/rockfax-app/>.

E-BOOKS
Please see <https://www.smc.org.uk/publications/ebooks>

APPLYING FOR MEMBERSHIP OF
THE SCOTTISH MOUNTAINEERING CLUB

The following notes are provided outlining the principles by which climbers may be admitted to membership of the Club.

The Committee does not lay down any hard and fast rules when considering applications but considers each case on its own merits. Candidates must be over 18 and have experience of mountaineering in Scotland in both summer and winter. This experience should have extended over a period of at least four years immediately prior to application and should not be confined to just a single climbing district.

The normally expected climbing standards include:

- Experience of winter climbing including several routes of around Grade IV standard and the ability to lead climbs of this level of difficulty.

- Rock climbing experience including climbs of Very Severe (4c) standard and the ability to lead routes of this level of difficulty. In considering applications, emphasis will be placed on multi-pitch climbs in mountain locations.

- The ascent of at least 50 Munros of which at least one third should have been climbed in snow conditions.

In short, the candidate should be able to show – by producing a detailed list of climbs – that they are competent to lead a variety of outings in the mountains of Scotland in both summer and winter. The technical standards specified refer to applicants currently active and may be varied at the discretion of the Committee for older candidates provided that the applicant's routes reflect a reasonable standard for their time. Climbing in the Alps and elsewhere is taken into consideration. Candidates who do not fulfil the normal qualifications listed above but who have made special contributions to Scottish mountaineering in the fields of art, literature or science may receive special consideration.

It is essential that each candidate, before applying, should have climbed with the member proposing the application. It is also desirable that a candidate should be introduced to a member of the Committee before the application is considered. Application forms must be obtained on behalf of candidates by members of the Club who may not propose or support candidates for election during their own first two years of membership. The annual membership fee is £40.00 (£30.00 for those aged 65 and over) which includes the *SMC Journal*.

A fuller version of these notes for members wishing to propose candidates is available from the Club Secretary who is happy to advise candidates and members on any aspect of the application process. Please contact Tom Prentice, Honorary Secretary at:

e-mail: <secretary@smc.org.uk>

OFFICE BEARERS 2020–21

INSTRUCTIONS TO CONTRIBUTORS

The Editor welcomes contributions from members and non-members alike. Priority will be given to articles relating to Scottish mountaineering. Articles should be submitted **by the end of April** to be considered for inclusion in the *Journal* of the same year. Material is preferred in electronic form and should be sent by e-mail direct to the Editor. Most common file formats are acceptable.

Illustrations not relating to an article should be sent to the Photos Editor. All images should be high resolution and have explanatory captions including the source. Books for review should be sent to the Reviews Editor by the end of April.

The Editorial team reserves the right to edit any material submitted.

INDEX OF AUTHORS

INDEX OF PEOPLE

Bold numerals denote an article by the person; *italic numerals* denote an image of the person.

INDEX OF PLACES & GENERAL TOPICS

Italic numerals refer to a picture; *fn* indicates a footnote.
FA = first ascent; FWA = first winter ascent.

INDEX OF PHOTOGRAPHERS & ARTISTS

INDEX OF REVIEWS
(Reviewer in parenthesis)